# The Constitution Explained

## A GUIDE FOR EVERY AMERICAN

## DAVID L. HUDSON, JR., J.D.

# ABOUT THE AUTHOR

An attorney-author who works as First Amendment Scholar for the First Amendment Center at Vanderbilt University, **David L. Hudson Jr.** writes regularly on the Supreme Court, as a contributing editor to the American Bar Association's *Preview of U.S. Supreme Court Cases*. He also teaches several classes at the Nashville School of Law. He is the author of more than 25 books, including *The Rehnquist Court: Understanding Its Impact and Legacy* (Praeger, 2006). He is a graduate of Duke University and Vanderbilt Law School.

# The Constitution Explained

## A Guide for Every American

### David L. Hudson, Jr., J.D.

Visible Ink Press®
43311 Joy Rd., #414
Canton, MI 48187-2075

Visible Ink Press is a registered trademark of Visible Ink Press, LLC.

Most Visible Ink Press books are available at special quantity discounts when purchased in bulk by corporations, organizations, or groups. Customized printings, special imprints, messages, and excerpts can be produced to meet your needs. For more information, contact Special Markets Director, Visible Ink Press, www.visibleink.com, or 734-667-3211.

Managing Editor: Kevin S. Hile
Art Director: Cinelli Design
Cover Design: John Gouin
Typesetting: Marco Divita
Proofreaders: Larry Baker and Christa Gainor
Indexer: Shoshana Hurwitz
Cover images: Shutterstock.
Chapter art: Architect of the Capitol (aoc.gov).

ISBN: 978-1-57859-750-5 (paperback)
ISBN: 978-1-57859-772-7 (ebook)
ISBN: 978-1-57859-776-5 (hardbound)

Cataloging-in-Publication Data is on file at the Library of Congress.

Printed in the United States of America.

10 9 8 7 6 5 4 3 2 1

# OTHER VISIBLE INK BOOKS
# BY DAVID L. HUDSON JR.

*The Handy American History Answer Book*
ISBN: 978-1-57859-471-9

*The Handy Law Answer Book*
ISBN: 978-1-57859-217-3

*The Handy Presidents Answer Book*, 2nd edition
ISBN: 978-1-57859-317-0

*The Handy Supreme Court Answer Book*
ISBN: 978-1-57859-196-1

# ALSO FROM VISIBLE INK PRESS

*The African American Almanac: 400 Years of Triumph, Courage, and Excellence*
by Lean'tin Bracks, Ph.D.
ISBN: 978-1-57859-323-1

*The American Women's Almanac: 500 Years of Making History*
by Deborah G. Felder
ISBN: 978-1-57859-636-2

*The Big Book of Facts*
by Terri Schlichenmeyer
ISBN: 978-1-57859-720-8

*Disinformation and You: Identify Propaganda and Misinformation*
by Marie D. Jones
ISBN: 978-1-57859-740-6

*The Handy American Government Answer Book: How Washington, Politics and Elections Work*
by Gina Misiroglu
ISBN: 978-1-57859-639-3

*The Handy Boston Answer Book*
by Samuel Willard Crompton
ISBN: 978-1-57859-593-8

*The Handy California Answer Book*
by Kevin Hile
ISBN: 978-1-57859-591-4

*The Handy Civil War Answer Book*
by Samuel Willard Crompton
ISBN: 978-1-57859-476-4

*The Handy History Answer Book: From the Stone Age to the Digital Age*
by Stephen A Werner, Ph.D.
ISBN: 978-1-57859-680-5

*The Handy Military History Answer Book*
by Samuel Willard Crompton
ISBN: 978-1-57859-509-9

*The Handy New York Answer Book*
by Chris Barsanti
ISBN: 978-1-57859-586-0

*The Handy State-by-State Answer Book*
by Samuel Willard Crompton
ISBN: 978-1-57859-565-5

*The Handy Texas Answer Book*
by James L. Haley
ISBN: 978-1-57859-634-8

*The Handy Wisconsin Answer Book*
by Terri Schlichenmeyer and Mark Meier
ISBN: 978-1-57859-661-4

*The Latino American Almanac: From Columbus to Corporate America*
by Nicolas Kanellos
ISBN: 978-1-57859-611-9

*The Native American Almanac: More Than 50,000 Years of the Cultures and Histories of Indigenous Peoples*
by Yvonne Wakim Dennis, Arlene Hirschfelder, and Paulette F. Molin
ISBN: 978-1-57859-712-3

# DEDICATION

To my father, David L. Hudson Sr.: profound thanks for your sacrifices, guidance, and love.

# TABLE OF CONTENTS

## The Sixth Amendment ... 233

## The Eighth Amendment ... 245

## The Ninth and Tenth Amendments ... 267

## The Fourteenth Amendment: The Second Bill of Rights ... 273

## Miscellaneous Amendments ... 307

## Continuing Constitutional Controversies ... 321

# PHOTO SOURCES

Architect of the Capitol (aoc.gov): p. 39.

Arizona State Prison: p. 226.

Tom Bell: p. 78.

California Department of Corrections and Rehabilitiation: p. 252.

Collection of the Supreme Court of the United States: pp. 72, 110, 158, 191, 217, 305.

Wes Colley: p. 96.

Edmond J. Safra Center for Ethics: p. 228.

Executive Office of the President of the United States: pp. 68, 113, 115.

FDR Presidential Library & Museum: p. 319.

Gerald R. Ford Library & Museum: p. 56.

*Harper's Weekly*: p. 280.

Harris & Ewing: pp. 138, 240.

Harvard Art Museum: p. 33.

Historical Society of the District of Columbia Circuit: p. 189.

Jewish Museum of Maryland: p. 123.

John F. Kennedy Presidential Library and Museum: p. 300.

King of Hearts (Wikicommons): p. 297.

Library of Congress: pp. 7, 62, 65, 82, 103, 129, 136, 137, 162, 165, 166, 180, 193, 235, 253, 269, 278, 284, 294.

Library of Virginia: p. 121.

Metropolitan Museum of Art: p. 21 (bottom).

National Archives and Records Administration: pp. 2, 169.

National Archives at College Park: p. 111.

National Gallery of Art: p. 127.

New York Public Library: p. 50.

Office of the Vice President of the United States: p. 9.

Ourdocuments.gov: p. 25.

Joel Seidenstein: p. 173.

Shutterstock: pp. 4, 19, 31, 38, 46, 53, 77, 81, 85, 87, 90, 98, 100, 105, 108, 116, 141, 144, 147, 150, 154, 160, 163, 175, 176, 179, 182, 187, 199, 203, 204, 205, 207, 212, 214, 222, 225, 231, 238, 239, 242, 246, 249, 257, 260, 264, 271, 290, 291, 292, 295, 298, 310, 313, 323.

Tboyd5150 (Wikicommons): p. 316.

U.S. Army Signal Corps: p. 130.

U.S. Congress: pp. 44, 59.

U.S. Department of Justice: p. 73.

U.S. Government Archives: p. 133.

U.S. Navy: p. 83.

The Well News: p. 274.

The White House: pp. 27, 30.

White House Historical Association: p. 21 (top).

Wmpetro (Wikicommons): p. 14.

Yale University Art Gallery: p. 23 (bottom).

Public domain: pp. 22, 23 (top), 24, 122, 157, 198, 209, 255, 277, 302.

# ACKNOWLEDGEMENTS

I would like to thank Roger Jänecke of Visible Ink Press for giving me the opportunity and platform to write this book. My association with Visible Ink Press has given me the chance to write about many subjects I love, and certainly none is more valuable than writing about the Constitution. I would also like to thank editor Kevin Hile, who improved the text with his incisive skill.

My love for the Constitution increased during my time working with the Center for Civic Education's "We the People" program—a program designed to increase constitutional literacy in elementary, middle, and high schools across the country. Many people I have met during my decades of work with We the People—too numerous to name, but a special few deserve recognition—are Janis Kyser (who started it all), Maria Gallo, Terry Morley, Roger Desrosiers, Sue Leeson, and Joe Stewart, all of whom helped me during my journey. A special thanks to my dear friend and mentor Lindsey Draper, a man of such genuine good will that it humbles me.

I would be remiss not to thank many of my colleagues during my more than 17 years at the First Amendment Center at Vanderbilt University. Founder John Seigenthaler Sr. was a mentor who guided me toward a deeper understanding of the Constitution and much more. I miss him daily. Thanks also to R. B. Quinn, Ken Paulson, the unforgettable Jeremy Leaming, the late Corey Q. Bradley (rest in peace), Tiffany Villager, Brian Buchanan, Tam Gordon, Anjanette Eash, Jimbo Eanes, Natilee Duning, and a most caring boss, Gene Policinski, another person of genuine good will.

In my career, I got to work for two judges: former trial court judge Marietta Shipley and Tennessee Supreme Court justice Sharon G. Lee. Judge Shipley gave me my first full-time job out of law school and tolerated many mistakes. Justice Lee, a beacon of justice and a jurist who cares for the underdogs, had a work ethic second to none. I admire her passion. I'd also like to thank another jurist and close personal friend, Judge Mark J. Fishburn.

I have had the privilege of teaching at three laws schools: the Nashville School of Law, my alma mater Vanderbilt Law School, and Belmont Law School. Currently, I am a full-time professor at Belmont. I would like to thank Dean Alberto Gonzales for his leadership and support. All my colleagues at Belmont deserve mention, but I would like to single out three: Jeff Kinsler, Jeffrey Usman, and Charlie Trost. Jeff Kinsler is the founding dean of Belmont who first brought me on campus as an adjunct professor. Jeffrey Usman is a constitutional law genius but also a genuinely kind and gentle soul. Charlie Trost is a trusted friend and a person who helps others in need, including me.

I would like to thank my wife, Carla Hudson, for her unwavering love and support, and my parents, Carol and Dave Hudson, for educating me and guiding me along the way—stumbles and all. I would also like to thank scholar Ronald K. L. Collins, a true genius, for his help along the way.

And, then there are my students. No one enters teaching (or should, at least) unless they care for their students. One of the best things about teaching is that we learn from our students. I may have learned more from my students than they learned from me. Some of my students are lifelong friends. There are too many to mention, but here are a few: Bill Spaniard, Andrew David Brink, David Medalia, Elizabeth Reneiris, Jim Edwards, Bill Edwards, Tim (yes you got an "A" in con law) Horne, the brilliant Daniel Horwitz, Brian Horowitz, Maryam Saad, Braydon Tsuyuki, Alexandria Rivera, Jacob David Glenn, Ken Wilkinson, Chris Rogers, John Morris, the incomparable Christian Cahill, Andrew Lockert, and some guy named Kenny Dyer.

I care about my students—I hope they know that. Thank you for giving purpose to my life.

# INTRODUCTION

The U.S. Constitution serves as the charter of our government, the governing super-contract that binds us all together. Its Preamble provides that the Constitution's purposes are to "form a more perfect Union, establish Justice, ensure domestic Tranquility, provide for the common defense, promote the general Welfare, and secure the Blessings of Liberty."

People vigorously disagree about how well the country has lived up to the Preamble's lofty goals, but the Constitution still exists largely in the same form as it was when it was created during the hot summer of 1787 in Philadelphia, Pennsylvania. It is astonishing that there have been only 27 amendments to the document since its passage, and ten of those, our Bill of Rights, were added a mere four years later in 1791.

Some historians have extolled the Constitution as a "miracle" while critics have called it a covenant with Hell. Its original form included references to the awful institution of slavery, but the country has moved painstakingly slowly toward freedom and equal rights. Dr. Martin Luther King Jr. wrote in his *Letter from the Birmingham Jail* (1963), "History is the long and tragic story of the fact that privileged groups seldom give up their privileges voluntarily."

But the U.S. Constitution contains provisions that make allowances for social progress. Consider the First Amendment's protection of freedom of religion, speech, press, assembly, and petition. Without the freedom of assembly, women's suffragists could not have marched in the streets as so-called "rampant women" to demand the right to vote. Without the freedom of the press, newspapers could not have exposed the evils of segregation, and without the freedom of speech, protestors could not have criticized the system nearly as vigorously.

Many years after ratification, the so-called Radical Republicans of the 39th Congress passed three amendments during the period of Reconstruction that breathed a spirit of equality into the Constitution. Perhaps none stands out as much as the Equal Protection Clause of the Fourteenth Amendment, which says that "no state shall deny any person … the equal protection of the laws."

*The Constitution Explained: A Guide for Every American* seeks to demystify and unpack much of the language of this venerable document. It initially provides a brief history of how our country's leaders realized the need for a Constitution, a charter that could create a powerful, central government yet not trample on the rights of individual states. It details how the so-called "Founding Fathers" framed the government, set forth its structure and powers, and helped move toward the ideal of a "common good."

In law school curricula, constitutional law is often taught as Con Law I and then Con Law II. Con Law I examines the principles, the structure, the powers of each branch of government. Con

Law II focuses more on individual rights—chiefly Due Process, Equal Protection, and First Amendment freedoms.

This book roughly follows that pattern by examining the first three Articles of the Constitution—the parts that spell out the powers of the three branches of government: the Legislative, Executive, and Judicial branches. These articles are examined in some detail, realizing that there is no hermetic sealing off of these branches. In our constitutional government, separation of powers remains a sacrosanct concept, but the realities are much different.

The book also examines many of the 27 amendments to the Constitution. Not all are discussed, however (for the full text of the Constitution, consult the appendix at the back of this book). After all, some of these amendments are more historical than current. Take the example of the Third Amendment that says that during times of peace, no soldier shall "be quartered in any house, without the consent of the Owner, nor in time of war, but in a manner to be prescribed by law." This amendment was passed in direct response to events during the Revolutionary War.

Contrast that with the first 45 words of the Bill of Rights, the First Amendment. Controversies over the "First Freedom" only have exploded with the passage of time. Did the 45th president, Donald J. Trump, incite imminent lawless action on January 6, 2021, or did he merely engage in protected political speech? Did state governments trample on the freedom of religion by prohibiting public gatherings, even church services, during the height of the pandemic?

These and many other questions remain pressing and relevant.

*The Constitution Explained* was a labor of love, and I hope you find much to enjoy in the ensuing pages.

# Introduction to the Constitution

Though its origins arose in secrecy, the Constitution remains a great achievement in the annals of the world's politics and law. As Justice William J. Brennan Jr. (1906–1997) said in a speech in 1985 at Georgetown Law School, "[t]he Constitution is fundamentally a public text—the monumental charter of a government and a people." The Constitution has been described as a contract between the governed and the governors, between the People and the Government.

However, the U.S. Constitution begins in its Preamble with the words "We the People." Under the Constitution, popular sovereignty rests with the people.

## Preamble to the U.S. Constitution

We the People of the United States, in Order to form a more perfect Union, establish Justice, insure domestic Tranquility, provide for the common defence, promote the general Welfare, and secure the Blessings of Liberty to ourselves and our Posterity, do ordain and establish this Constitution for the United States of America.

The original U.S. Constitution is on display at the National Archives in Washington, D.C.

The U.S. Constitution has ensured that the United States is governed by the rule of law rather than by a dictator. There is no king under the Constitution. There is a chief executive—the president of the United States—but even the president is not above the law. Mechanisms exist in the Constitution even to impeach a sitting president. Indeed, four sitting U.S. presidents have felt, or nearly felt, this power.

The Constitution separates power among three branches of government—legislative, executive, and judicial. It ensures that no one branch can dominate the other two branches by distributing power between the branches through a system known as checks and balances. The Constitution sets up a federal system with dual systems of government—national and state. American citizens elect local, state, and national representatives.

Before delving deeply into the Constitution and its myriad provisions, we must discuss a few key terms that will be important for our purposes.

# Federalism

The Constitution reflects several principles that distinguish it from the rule of law in other countries. The two most important are federalism and separation of powers. Federalism refers to a system of government in which power is divided between a nation and its states. The general or federal government possesses ultimate control, but the various state governments retain many powers. The concept seems natural to Americans of the twenty-first century. But it was very difficult for many Americans to accept in 1787 and 1788. In fact, many members of the Founding Fathers' generation were gravely opposed to the idea of a strong central government. They fervently believed that too much power was given to this new government. They were known as Anti-Federalists.

At the Constitutional Convention in 1787 in Philadelphia, James Madison (1751–1836) and others had to work very hard to convince several of their colleagues that they were not infringing on the authorities of the different states. Recall that many of these state leaders fervently desired independence. Little more than a decade earlier, they had shed blood to free themselves from the rule of King George III (1738–1820) and the British redcoats. They certainly did not want to move from one tyrant to another—even if the new tyrant had a different name.

Well-known lawyer and legal scholar Archibald Cox (1912–2004) wrote: "The key idea was extraordinarily imaginative two hundred years ago. Even today those who grow up in other countries find the concept difficult to comprehend."

Disputes over the relationship of power between the federal and state governments continue to this day. Some Americans believe that the federal government plays too large a role and intrudes on the power of the states. These critics point to the sheer massive size of the federal government. Other Americans believe that the federal government should take a more active role. Regardless, the political reality is that state and federal governments affect Americans' lives.

# Separation of Powers

The Framers understood that dividing power among the different branches of government would ensure that no single branch would become too powerful. This concept is known as the separation of powers. Many of the Founding Fathers understood the importance of separating powers between the branches of government. Many of them had read French philosopher Baron de Montesquieu's (1689–1755) *De l'Esprit des lois* (The Spirit of the Laws), which talked about this principle.

In the *Federalist Papers,* Madison described Montesquieu as "the oracle who is always consulted and cited on this subject." Madison described the principle as "the accumulation of all powers, legislative, executive and judiciary, in the same hands, whether of one, a few, or many, and whether hereditary, self-appointed, or elective, may justly be pronounced the very definition of tyranny."

Separation of powers is a philosophy in which each branch has its own powers. U.S. Supreme Court justice Anthony Kennedy (1936–) explains: "Separation of powers was designed to implement a fundamental insight: Concentration of power in the hands of a single branch is a threat to liberty."

Our Constitution adheres to this principle. The powers of Congress are described in Article I, the powers of the executive branch are detailed in Article II, and the powers of the judicial branch are listed in Article III.

Sometimes one branch will encroach on territory that the other branch considers is its own power. This occurred in the 1950s when President Harry S. Truman (1884–1972) issued an executive order, seizing the country's steel mills and placing them under the control of the

There are three branches comprising the federal government: legislative (the U.S. Congress, consisting of the House of Representatives and the Senate, which make the laws of the land), judicial (the Supreme Court, which interprets the law), and executive (the president, who is charged with enforcing the law).

federal government. Truman claimed he had the authority as commander in chief to ensure that the steel mills would continue to produce products necessary for the war effort.

Several steel companies, including Youngstown Sheet & Tube Company, challenged the president's actions in federal court. These companies claimed that Truman had exceeded his authority under the commander in chief clause of the Constitution. In *Youngstown Sheet & Tube Co. v. Sawyer*, the U.S. Supreme Court ruled 6–3 in favor of the steel companies. Justice Hugo Black (1886–1971) wrote: "If the President had the authority to issue the order he did, it must be found in some provision of the Constitution." The court determined that the president violated the separation of powers principle by committing a legislative act. In other words, the high court ruled that the seizure of the steel mills was a legislative act that must be done by Congress.

Closely related to the separation of powers principle is the notion of checks and balances. The Constitution grants each branch of government the power to check certain actions by the other branches of government. For example, the president is the commander in chief of the armed forces, but Congress has the power to declare war. The Congress can pass legislation, but the president has veto power. The legislature can pass laws, but the judicial branch has the power to declare those laws unconstitutional.

# Interpreting the Constitution

A major issue in constitutional law is how to interpret the Constitution. People disagree about how to interpret the Constitution. Some argue for a literal interpretation of the words in the Constitution. This method often seeks the "Framers' intent," or what the original intent of the Founding Fathers was.

Such interpreters argue that we should strictly construe the language of the Constitution. Those who advocate this type of reading of the Constitution are called strict constructionists. They believe that it distorts the Constitution to extend it beyond its plain language. Reasonable minds disagree over how to interpret various parts of the Constitution. This is not surprising, because the Constitution is written in very general language. For example, consider the phrase "unreasonable searches and seizures." Under the Fourth Amendment of the Constitution, government officials cannot engage in unreasonable searches and seizures. When exactly is a search reasonable or unreasonable? Another famous phrase in the Constitution is the term "necessary and proper," a clause in Article I, Section 8 of the Constitution that refers to a power of Congress. Thus, Congress can pass laws that are "necessary and proper," but people can disagree over when something is "necessary and proper." There are numerous other examples of this type of language.

# Originalism

One method or school of interpreting the Constitution is called originalism—the idea that judges should consider the original intent of the Founding Fathers when interpreting the Constitution. Another definition of originalism, according to constitutional law scholar John Hart Ely in his classic work *Democracy and Distrust: A Theory of Judicial Review*, is "judges deciding constitutional issues should confine themselves to enforcing norms that are stated or clearly implicit in the written Constitution." An originalist—a person who subscribes to originalism—would view the death penalty as constitutional and not a form of "cruel and unusual punishment" that violates the Eighth Amendment, because the Constitution itself in the Fifth Amendment speaks of "capital" crimes. The originalist would realize that the original view of the Founders was that the death penalty was an acceptable form of punishment.

Originalists generally believe that the Constitution's meaning is fixed and static, that the general public's view of the Constitution's meaning doesn't change unless there is an amendment to the Constitution.

# Textualism

A related method of constitutional interpretation is textualism—that we determine the meaning of the Constitution primarily by focusing primarily on the text of the Constitution. Textualism may make more sense when it comes to interpreting different laws as opposed to the Constitution, because as already discussed, many of the key phrases in the Constitution are quite general.

Justice Antonin Scalia (1936–2016) is considered one of the premier advocates of textualism. Constitutional scholar Jonathan Siegel writes that "Scalia did an important service in recalling attention to the importance of text in statutory interpretation."

# Nonoriginalists

In stark contrast to originalists are those who believe that the Constitution and constitutional norms evolve over time as society changes. Sometimes called nonoriginalists, they believe that the Court must interpret the Constitution in recognition that the world changes. It is, as Ely stated, "the view that courts should go beyond that set of references and enforce norms that cannot be discovered within the four corners of the document."

Nonoriginalists often criticize the originalist model as too inflexible, claiming that it is a nearly impossible task to determine original intent. For example, attorney Alfred Knight (1937–2011) writes: "Original intent? Whose intent? The fact is that trying to apply the Framers' intent is like trying to breathe the atmosphere of the moon. Whether it is a good idea or a bad one is beside the point—the problem is there is nothing of substance to work with."

Nonoriginalists believe in what is called a "living Constitution." As Justice William J. Brennan once said, "It is arrogant to pretend that from our vantage we can gauge accurately the intent of the Framers on application of principle to specific, contemporary questions."

Nonoriginatlists believe that judges should consider contemporary social values in interpreting the Constitution. Brennan said that as a Supreme Court justice, it was his duty to apply the Constitution through the current day. He said: "We current Justices read the Constitution in the only way we can, as Twentieth Century Americans.... For the genius of the Constitution rests not in any static meaning it might have had in a world that is dead and gone, but in the adaptability of its great principles to cope with current problems and current needs."

There are variants of both originalism and nonoriginalism. Critics of each approach tend to overstate the positions of their opponents. For example, those who believe in a "living Constitution" tend to argue that originalists only focus on the fixed meaning of the Constitution in 1787. However, that is not the case with most who subscribe to originalism.

U.S. Supreme Court Justice William J. Brennan Jr. served on the court from 1956 to 1990.

Chief Justice William Rehnquist (1924–2005), often described as an originalist, explained that "the framers of the Constitution wisely spoke in general language and left to succeeding generations the task of applying that language to the unceasingly changing environment in which they would live."

One example where both the originalist and nonoriginalist points of view seem to have made their mark is in death penalty jurisprudence. Originalists point out that the Constitution presupposes the existence of the death penalty. After all, the Fifth Amendment to the U.S. Constitution specifically mentions "capital" crimes. Nonoriginalists have argued, however, that the Eighth Amendment, which prohibits "cruel and unusual punishment," must be interpreted according to the "evolving standards of decency." Thus, it once was perfectly acceptable for persons to be executed by the state in public hangings before literally tens of thousands of people. It was the people's gallows for sure. These events were akin to rock concerts interspersed with fiery religious sermons. Over time, executions changed so that they now occur behind closed doors with a different method of execution, primarily lethal injection.

To take another example, consider freedom of speech. The First Amendment states that "Congress shall make no law ... abridging the freedom of speech." The Founding Fathers surely interpreted that provision to prohibit the government from imprisoning a person for criticizing government officials. But that's not exactly true, because that is exactly what happened to Vermont representative Matthew Lyon (1750–1822), who was reelected to Congress from a jail cell because he had the temerity to criticize President John Adams (1735–1826). Lyons felt the full force of a federal law known as the Sedition Act of 1798. That is also what happened to famed labor organized and frequent presidential candidate Eugene Debs (1855–1926), who was imprisoned for violating the Espionage Act of 1917. His crime—criticizing World War I and the draft. He spent time in prison before President Warren G. Harding (1865–1923) commuted his sentence.

However, the Founders did generally believe that the First Amendment protected pure political speech—the core type of speech that that Amendment was designed to protect. But did the Founding Fathers believe that the First Amendment should protect commercial advertising, pornography, and even burning the flag as a form of political protest? Did the Founding Fathers ever imagine the Internet?

Fortunately, the Founding Generation understood that they were writing not just for their own time but for posterity too. Liz Wehle explains in her book *How to Read the Constitution and Why* that "the Constitution … is a relatively terse document that leaves much of its necessary terms and meaning unwritten."

What is the meaning of "abridge the freedom of speech," "the establishment of religion," "necessary and proper," and "regulate commerce"? Each of these terms ultimately has led to years and years of litigation, much of which has reached the U.S. Supreme Court. In fact, for many constitutional questions, the U.S. Supreme Court is the ultimate arbiter. The justices have determined the fate of the death penalty, affirmative action policies, abortion, and even presidential elections.

Consider that in 2000, the United States faced a potential constitutional crisis in the presidential election between Democratic candidate Al Gore (1948–) and Republican candidate George W. Bush (1946–). The election hung in the balance when it was too close to call in the deciding state of Florida. The dispute involved both major political parties, all three branches of government in the state of Florida, and the court of last resort—the U.S. Supreme Court.

The U.S. Supreme Court reversed a Florida Supreme Court ruling that had ordered a recount of the votes in the state of Florida. Five justices of the U.S. Supreme Court determined that there were not enough "procedural safeguards" to assure "uniformity" in how the votes were counted in the statewide recount. The net result of the ruling was that Bush maintained his slim lead over Gore in Florida, giving him enough electoral votes to win the presidency.

Many disagreed with the Court's decision in *Bush v. Gore*, but the country moved forward calmly. Other countries might have erupted into violence, revolution, or civil war as a result of a disputed election.

Many criticized the electoral college system because for the first time since 1876, the winner of the popular vote (Gore) lost the election. Others criticized the news media for displaying bias for Gore and projecting a winner too soon. The federal government established a special commission to examine the voting system in this country. Despite deep divisions over the election results, the country proceeded peacefully because of respect for the Constitution.

But what makes the United States of America different from many countries around the world is that its Constitution provides its citizens with a peaceful mechanism to resolve governmental issues.

Credit for the Constitution must go to the Founding Fathers. Historians Christopher Collier and James Lincoln Collier write that "the generations of Americans who have grown up under the Constitution they struggled so hard to make are eternally in their debt." Americans often praise their Founding Fathers. George Washington (1732–1799) is called the Father of the Country. James Madison is called the Father of the Constitution. Washington, Madison, and other Founding Fathers accomplished much in their distinguished careers. Historian Joseph Ellis writes that the Framers were "the greatest generation of political talent in American history."

Even though Democratic candidate Al Gore, a former vice president, won the popular vote in the 2000 presidential election, he lost the Electoral College vote after a dispute about the Florida vote count that would have sent other countries into revolution.

However, as former U.S. solicitor general Archibald Cox writes, nothing they accomplished compares to the Constitution, which "gained a majesty and authority far greater than those of any individual or body of men."

Former U.S. Supreme Court chief justice Warren Burger (1907–1995) said it best: "The Constitution was indeed a watershed in the history of governments and more important, in humanity's struggle for freedom and fulfillment. It behooves [benefits] all of us to read it, understand it, revere it, and vigorously defend it."

What follows is an effort to discuss in some detail major facets of the U.S. Constitution. The next three chapters talk about the creation of the Constitution, the Constitutional Convention of 1787 that led to the Constitution, and the eventual ratification of the Constitution.

The subsequent four chapters then discuss in detail the seven articles of the U.S. Constitution. The first three articles are discussed in much greater depth, because they are much longer. Article I deals with the powers of the legislative branch, Article

II deals with the powers of the executive branch, and Article III deals with the powers of the judicial branch. A remaining chapter handles Articles IV through VII.

The book then examines several of the most important freedoms in the Bill of Rights, the first ten amendments to the Constitution. Separate chapters examine the First, Second, Fourth, Fifth, Sixth, Eighth, Ninth, and Tenth Amendments.

The book then discusses the Fourteenth Amendment, which in many senses was a second Bill of Rights, because it ultimately extended most of the Bill of Rights to the states. The chapter focuses on two of the most important guarantees of individual freedom—equal protection and due process. A following chapter examines a miscellaneous group of amendments. Finally, the book concludes with a look at some continuing constitutional controversies.

I hope you enjoy the ride. It has been a wild one that hopefully will continue for centuries to come.

# From the Articles of Confederation to the Constitutional Convention

Oftentimes, Americans and other individuals around the globe view the United States Constitution in sacrosanct terms. Many assume that it was the country's first constitution. It was not. In large part, the U.S. Constitution was founded because the country's first Constitution—the Articles of Confederation—was an abject failure.

## The Articles of Confederation

In June 1776, representatives of the colonies met at the Second Continental Congress in Philadelphia, Pennsylvania. At this meeting, they agreed to form "a firm league of friendship." The result was the first Constitution of the United States of America—the Articles of Confederation.

In November 1777, the Continental Congress endorsed the Articles of Confederation and specified that they would go into effect when all 13 states ratified them. It took until 1781 before the last state, Maryland, ratified the Articles and they went into effect. Unfortunately, the Articles of Confederation did not provide enough power to Congress.

During and immediately after the Revolutionary War, many colonial leaders had feared a strong central government more than anything else. The excesses of

English king George III (1738–1820) and the legislative body that made the laws in England, known as Parliament, convinced many colonial leaders that power should not be concentrated in one central government. Rather, power should be spread among the states.

The basic principle under the Articles was that each state remained free and independent. Like many nations, states under the Articles were sovereign, or accountable only to themselves. Article II of the Articles provided that "each state retains its sovereignty, freedom, and independence." Article V of the document further provided that each state would have "one vote" in Congress.

Bluntly stated, the Articles of Confederation failed to create a national legislature that could rein in the states. Justice Sandra Day O'Connor (1930–) explained this in *New York v. United States* (1992) when she wrote: "Under the Articles of Confederation, Congress lacked the authority in most respects to govern the people directly. In practice, Congress could not directly tax or legislate upon individuals; it had no explicit 'legislative' or 'governmental' power to make binding 'law' enforceable as such."

|| *The basic principle under the Articles was that each state remained free and independent. Like many nations, states under the Articles were sovereign, or accountable only to themselves.* ||

From 1781 until the adoption of the U.S. Constitution, the states fought over trade and commerce issues. They fought over boundaries and whether new states should be created in the western territories. The Articles of Confederation created a weak government that was unable to raise revenue (money), raise troops, regulate commerce, settle disputes between different states, or enforce its own laws.

Under the Articles of Confederation, the Confederation Congress could not force state governments to raise monies for the federal government but had to depend on them to supply it voluntarily. The Confederation Congress could declare war but it could not raise an army. The states had to do that. New York political leader Alexander Hamilton (c. 1755–1804), the nation's future first secretary of the Treasury under President George Washington (1732–1799), wrote to colleague James Duane (1733–1797) in 1780 about the problem with the Confederation Congress, which he described: "The fundamental defect is a want of power in Congress."

Hamilton believed that Congress must have the power to form a military force. He called it "an essential cement of the union." Hamilton realized that the fledgling country was still far weaker than the world's two superpowers at that time: Great Britain and France. In fact, the nation's survival often depended upon a delicate balancing act between these two great countries. The late U.S. Supreme Court chief justice Warren Burger (1907–19954) wrote in his book *It Is So Ordered: A Constitution Unfolds* that nearly two hundred years later, the Articles "were barely more than a multinational (many nations) treaty between thirteen independent, sovereign states."

The Articles established a one-branch government composed of a unicameral Congress (one with only one chamber as opposed to the two we have today). There was no executive branch, or president, that could execute the country's basic leadership needs. There also was no judicial branch, or Supreme Court, that could interpret the nation's laws.

An even greater problem was that the Articles did not provide the Continental Congress with sufficient authority to deal with foreign nations. America's old foe, Great Britain, had closed off trade with the states. Its troops refused to leave the Great Lakes area. Meanwhile, the Spanish controlled key portions of the Mississippi River. In 1784, Spain closed New Orleans and the lower Mississippi to American navigation.

These problems caused some American leaders to recognize the need for greater central authority. In a letter in 1785 to fellow Virginia leader James Monroe (1758–1831), James Madison (1751–1836) wrote that "the defects of the federal system should be amended" or the new nation would suffer what he called "severe distress." Madison recognized that the Articles were woefully inadequate for the momentous task of nation-building. Madison worried that the country could fall apart if political change was not made.

Washington, Madison, and others became convinced that the country needed a central government that could command respect internally and externally.

# A Stronger National Government

The push for a stronger national government began shortly after the Articles of Confederation were ratified in March 1781. Congress appointed a three-member committee of James Madison of Virginia, James Duane of New York, and James M. Varnum (1748–1789) of Rhode Island to recommend changes to the Articles. The committee recommended giving Congress power over the armed forces and power to compel payments from the states to the government. In 1783, Alexander Hamilton of New York and James Wilson (1742–1798) of Pennsylvania, who were to play significant roles in the Constitutional Convention four years later, recommended that Congress amend the Articles to give Congress the power to collect a land tax.

Similarly, John Jay (1745–1829) of New York—who would later serve as the country's first chief justice of the U.S. Supreme Court—wrote to Gouverneur Morris (1752–1816) of Pennsylvania: "I am perfectly convinced that no time is to be lost in raising and maintaining a National spirit in America." In 1785, the Massachusetts legislature recommended that Congress call a grand convention to modify the Articles of Confederation.

The call for a "national spirit" gained even greater momentum when Washington and Madison—both of Virginia—pushed for a new meeting.

## Annapolis Convention

In March 1785, delegates from Virginia and Maryland met to discuss matters related to the Potomac River, which separates the two states. The delegates met at Mount Vernon, Washington's Virginia home. After the Mount Vernon Conference, Madison, one of the representatives from Virginia, told the Virginia Assembly that Congress should have the power to regulate commerce between the states.

The Mount Vernon Conference led to another meeting in September 1786 called the Annapolis Convention. Representatives from all the states were welcome. In the end, only representatives from five states—Virginia, Pennsylvania, New Jersey, Delaware, and New York—attended. Other states were too busy with their own problems and did not send delegates.

The delegates used the Annapolis Convention to promote the call for national unity. The commissioners petitioned Congress to call a meeting of all the states to be held in May 1787 at Philadelphia, Pennsylvania, to discuss how to create a better government. Drafted by Hamilton, the petition asked Congress to allow the states to propose revisions to the Articles of Confederation.

The commissioners wrote that the Articles of Confederation contained defects, which led to many "embarrassments," both foreign and domestic. Some have called the meeting in Annapolis, as Chief Justice Burger wrote, "the most successful failure in American history" because, though eight states did not send representatives, it led to another meeting in Philadelphia.

In October 1786, Virginia became the first state to approve sending delegates to an upcoming convention in Philadelphia. The Confederation Congress endorsed the movement to revise the Articles of Confederation in February 1787. However, Congress did not endorse the drafting of an entirely new Constitution.

## Shays' Rebellion

It took an armed rebellion for many Americans to wake up and realize that a new constitution was needed. Most people at this time believed that the call for a stronger national government was either unnecessary or unwise. They had just won their independence from the Parliament and king of Great Britain. As colonies, they had been unfairly taxed without having adequate representation in Parliament. Now

Shays' Rebellion was a reaction to people being taxed by their new government.

that they were a new nation, they did not want to suffer at the hands of a tyrannical or oppressive central government.

However, more and more leaders of the country came to believe that the system of government needed improvement. An uprising of farmers in Massachusetts called Shays' Rebellion strengthened this sentiment. In 1786, hundreds of farmers upset that they were taxed and in debt marched in armed rebellion toward county courthouses. They wanted the courts to cancel their debts.

Daniel Shays (1747–1825), a former Revolutionary War hero and indebted farmer, organized the uprising. Shays led his forces to an attack on the federal arsenal at Springfield, Massachusetts. Though General Benjamin Lincoln (1733–1810) and other government militia stopped the rebellion, the incident showed many leaders that they needed a stronger central government because the states were virtually powerless to stop such violence. Shays' Rebellion provided the key, final piece of evidence for the case for a new Constitution.

## A Herculean Task

The leaders realized that they needed a new central government that could command respect at home and abroad, but they also realized they faced a difficult task.

The states were nearly as different as separate countries. One Convention delegate, Pierce Butler (1744–1822) of South Carolina, wrote that the interests between the North and the South were "as different as the interests of Russia and Turkey." Much like Russia and Turkey, the states differed in many ways, including their economies, religions, attitudes, customs, and ethnicities.

For his part, George Washington saw a difficult task ahead at Philadelphia. In a letter to Madison, Washington warned that the cause may be lost and a proposal for a new Constitution might be "altogether defeated." In other words, Washington feared that even the results of the Convention may not hold the country together.

In a letter to his son, another famous Founding Father from Virginia, George Mason (1725–1792), wrote: "It is easy to foresee that there will be much Difficulty in organizing a Government upon this great scale." Mason would prove prescient.

The task of creating a new Constitution would prove most difficult.

# The Philadelphia Convention and the New Constitution

The members of the Confederation Congress did not have time to study changes to the Articles of Confederation. They were too busy with the day-to-day demands of running a government. The states elected delegates to represent them at the Philadelphia Convention. There were no specific limits on how many delegates each state could send. Some states sent only three or four delegates. Other states sent many more, such as the larger states of Virginia and Pennsylvania, which had seven and eight delegates attend respectively.

## The Plans of James Madison and His Fellow Virginians

Even though the Convention did not begin until May 25, 1787, James Madison (1751–1836) and several of his fellow delegates from Virginia arrived early. They met to discuss plans for the Constitution. They mapped out ideas and produced a scheme of government. Madison used his early arrival to his advantage.

Madison was very interested in politics. He studied governments and knew the art of political persuasion. To prepare himself for the task of helping to create a new government, he studied diligently. He had asked Thomas Jefferson (1743–

1826), then serving as ambassador to France, to send him books on political topics. The erudite "Sage of Monticello" complied with his friend's request and sent him hundreds of books.

A month before the Convention, Madison wrote a document called "Vices of the Political Systems of the United States." In it, Madison detailed various defects in the Articles of Confederation.

According to Madison, the states had too much "independent authority" that was "fatal" to the "present System" of government. Madison pointed out that the states disobeyed federal authority by making their own treaties with the Indians or with each other. Madison also said that different states had violated the country's peace treaties with other countries. If states violated treaties, then certainly other countries would as well.

Madison wrote that the states were violating the rights of the other states, often interfering with the commercial intercourse of other states, and not cooperating in matters of common interest. Madison also pointed out that the states would not even fulfill their duties during the Revolutionary War. He also noted that the state governments had ratified, or officially approved of, the Articles of Confederation. Madison criticized this, believing that the people should ratify the new government through special conventions.

As can be seen by reading his "Vices," Madison wanted to create a powerful central government that could command respect and unite the differing interests of the states. Because he was a great political thinker and experienced politician, he knew he would gain an advantage by raising the issues first.

## Rules of the Convention

The Convention did not begin until May 25 when a majority of the states, seven out of thirteen, were represented. Bad weather delayed the travel of many delegates. Travel was slow. As historian Fred Rodell notes in his book *55 Men: The Story of the Constitution,* "There were no airplanes, no railroads, no four-lane concrete highways in those days."

When a quorum of seven states was present, the delegates unanimously approved of Revolutionary War hero George Washington (1732–1799) as president of the Convention. In fact, after Pennsylvania delegate Robert Morris (1734–1806) nominated Washington, there were no other nominations. Washington originally did not want to attend the convention at all. He preferred to stay in Virginia and enjoy the outdoors, rather than listen to political arguments all day in a stuffy room. But he acceded to the demands of his fellow Virginians, particularly Madison.

Washington was the easy choice, as his leadership during the Revolutionary War was legendary. To many he was uniquely responsible for the miraculous defeat of the British. After the war, he retired from public life—or so he thought. Washington did not want to attend the Convention. In January 1787, his favorite brother, John Augustine Washington (1736–1787), had died. In March, he suffered a bad bout of rheumatism.

But other leaders recognized his value as the leading American. Madison knew that Washington was a larger-than-life figure, a hero to many for his crucial role in the Revolutionary War. Madison wrote him, pleaded with him to attend the Philadelphia Convention, and, ultimately, convinced him that his presence was necessary for the success of the Convention.

The Convention members established basic rules of procedure and etiquette. For example, the delegates agreed that each delegate should rise when speaking and should not be interrupted. This resulted in some delegates, such as Maryland's Luther Martin (1748–1826), speaking for hours at a time.

One key rule was secrecy. The Framers created the new Constitution in secret. The delegates ensured that the public would not be able to attend their sessions. The matters were simply too important for outside distractions or influences. If the sessions were made public, it was feared the public and press would emphasize the differences among the delegates.

Hero of the Revolutionary War and acknowledged leader of the newly forming nation, General George Washington was a natural choice to be president of the Convention.

The delegates also voted that their conversations must be kept secret. They adopted the following rule: "That nothing spoken in the House be printed, or otherwise published or communicated without leave."

Once, after an unnamed delegate left behind a piece of paper with his notes, Washington sternly lectured his colleagues the next morning: "I must entreat gentlemen to be more careful, lest our transactions get into the newspapers and disturb the public response by premature speculations. I know not whose paper it is, but there it is [throwing it down on the table], let him who owns it take it." No one ever dared to claim the piece of paper lest they face Washington's wrath.

During the Convention, the delegates did not move in a straight line, settling issue after issue. As historians Christopher and James Lincoln Collier note, the Convention "moved instead in swirls and loops, again and again backtracking to pick up issues previously debated."

The delegates often wanted to revisit issues. Thus, they employed a legislative procedure of deciding questions before a committee and then before the whole body. However, instead of naming a committee of a few delegates, they created a Committee of the Whole so that all delegates could participate in committee. This process enabled various politicians to test out ideas in smaller committees before presenting them to the entire body. The Convention also assigned drafting tasks to different committees through the course of the summer. Federal and state legislatures follow these same procedures today. They assign tasks to different committees who then report to the entire lawmaking body.

The Founders engaged in spirited debate, as they came from different backgrounds and possessed different political philosophies. But these delegates, or Framers as they are called, endured the hot summer of 1787 and the heated debates to draft the U.S. Constitution.

# The Framers of the Constitution

Seventy-four men were selected as delegates to the Constitution, but only 55 arrived in Philadelphia. All were white males, and the vast majority of them were Protestant. There were only two Catholics and a few Quakers. Thirty-three of the delegates were lawyers. Eight of them had signed the Declaration of Independence, and three were governors of their respective states.

The Convention was mostly made up of fairly young men. They ranged in age from the 26-year-old Jonathan Dayton (1760–1824) of New Jersey to the venerable, 81-year-old Dr. Benjamin Franklin (1706–1790). Some of the leading members of the Convention included Madison, Washington, Gouverneur Morris (1752–1816), Edmund Randolph (1753–1813), Roger Sherman (1721–1793), and James Wilson (1742–1798).

## James Madison

Described as "no bigger than half a piece of soap," James Madison was only 5' 2". But he was a giant at the Constitutional Convention. Though he spoke in a very low voice, others listened when he talked. His impact at the Convention was so large that he has been called "the Father of the Constitution."

Madison graduated from the College of New Jersey (now Princeton University). He had originally studied to be a minister but instead opted for a lifelong career in politics, which caused him to devote large amounts of time to studying governments. He had played a significant role in drafting Virginia's state constitution when he was only 25. At the time of the Convention, he was only 31.

After the Convention, Madison had an illustrious political career. He served as Thomas Jefferson's secretary of state. After Jefferson declined to run for president again, Madison ran and succeeded his friend as the fourth president of the United States. Madison served two terms, from 1809 until 1817.

Historians owe a debt of gratitude to Madison because he produced a set of detailed notes about the Convention. The Convention had an official secretary named William Jackson (1759–1828), but he did little more than record votes. New York delegate Robert Yates (1738–1801) published his notes on the debates in 1821, but they were not as comprehensive as Madison's. Yates left the Convention in early July, while Madison participated as much as any delegate until the conclusion of the Convention in September.

Madison instructed that his detailed notes of the Convention were not to be released until the last delegate at the Convention died. The last delegate turned out to be Madison, who died in 1836 at the age of 85.

James Madison

## George Washington

Washington was the undisputed leader of the Convention even though he rarely spoke. Washington achieved public fame for his leadership during the Revolutionary War. For his skill and leadership during the war, Washington has been called the "Father of our Country."

Washington was not only a larger-than-life figure, but he also was a large man, standing 6' 3". He became a surveyor and explored the Shenandoah Valley over the Blue Ridge Mountains. His familiarity with exploration landed him in the thick of the French and Indian War in the 1750s.

After serving in the French and Indian War and rising to the rank of general, Washington be-

George Washington

came a gentleman farmer for many years. He also became a leading figure in Virginia politics. He achieved his great fame when he went as a Virginia delegate to the Second Continental Congress in Philadelphia in May 1775 in his old army uniform.

When the leaders of the Continental Congress were discussing whom to select to lead the army, Washington was a natural choice. He was a veteran of the French and Indian War, had a commanding presence, and even showed up in an army uniform. He got the job.

Washington's leadership during the Revolutionary War led to his role as president of the Convention. He was so quiet that he did not speak in the debates until the last day of the Convention on September 17, 1787. But he was essential to the Convention's success. Historian Catherine Drinker Bowen writes in her book *Miracle at Philadelphia*: "His presence kept the Philadelphia Convention together, kept it going, just as his presence had kept a struggling, ill-conditioned army together throughout the terrible years of war."

## Gouverneur Morris

Another Founding Father who had a leading role at the Philadelphia Convention was Gouverneur Morris, a prodigy who had graduated from Columbia College at age 16. He was 34 years old at the time of the Convention and was considered one of the country's best lawyers. Morris had a wooden leg but did not let that stop him from playing an active role in politics. Some historians write that the Pennsylvania delegate spoke more frequently than any other delegate at the convention.

Gouverneur Morris

Morris took the lead role on the Committee of Style near the end of the Convention. This was the committee responsible for crafting the wording of the Constitution. Morris took 23 articles or resolutions and condensed them into seven articles. James Madison, who also served on the Committee of Style, credited Morris with writing the final form of the Constitution.

## Edmund Randolph

When historians think of leading politicians from Virginia, the names of Washington, Jefferson, and Madison immediately come to mind. Edmund Randolph is somewhat forgotten, but he had a significant impact at the

Convention too. Randolph was 33 at the time of the Convention. A graduate of William and Mary, he later became the country's first attorney general, the nation's leading attorney, and its second secretary of state under President Washington. At the time of the Convention, he served as the governor of Virginia. He introduced the famous Randolph Plan during the Convention, which was debated for three weeks.

Ironically, Randolph would later refuse to sign the Constitution at the end of the Convention, in part because he believed his constituents in Virginia would disapprove of the Constitution. He argued that the people in the states, through their representatives, should have the "full opportunity" to propose amendments to the Constitution. However, during the ratification battle in his home state of Virginia, Randolph fought for its adoption.

Edmund Randolph

## Roger Sherman

Some politicians have a knack for compromise. Roger Sherman was a politician from Connecticut who had that gift, and he showed it at the Convention. It is not an exaggeration to say that Sherman created a compromise that saved the Convention and the Constitution. Under the so-called Great Compromise, the states would be represented equally in the Senate and proportionally in the House of Representatives based on population.

Sherman has the distinction of signing several great American documents—the Declaration and Resolves of 1774 (a document where the colonists declared their resolve to oppose British power), the Declaration of Independence, the Articles of Confederation, and, finally, the U.S. Constitution. Like Washington, Sherman was a surveyor. From being appointed New Haven County surveyor at age 23 until his death at the age of 72, Sherman held various political offices.

Roger Sherman

James Wilson

## James Wilson

Not all the Founding Fathers were born in the United States. For example, James Wilson of Pennsylvania came to the United States from Scotland, where he was born and educated at the University of Edinburgh. Wilson signed the Declaration of Independence and argued that the leader of the executive branch should consist of one person called the president. He also passionately argued for a government that was truly democratic and placed the people in power.

At one point during the Convention, he reminded his distinguished colleagues that they were making a government for the future. "We should consider that we are providing a Constitution for future generations and not merely for the circumstances of the moment."

Historians regard Wilson as an unsung hero of the Constitution. He is also known for proposing the electoral college—the system we still use today in electing the president of the United States.

# Significant Issues Facing Framers

The Founding Fathers faced many pressing issues during the Convention. Many times, they would debate an issue and not resolve it. They then would refer the matter to the Committee of the Whole or to a separate, smaller committee. This allowed them to discuss a tough issue at a later date. Often, this would allow compromise measures to be introduced.

Among the leading issues facing the Framers were representation in the new Congress, division of power between the central government and the state governments, the president, slavery, and admission of future states in the West.

# The Plans of Government

The starting point for the discussion of the major issues began with the introduction of different basic plans of government. Several delegates introduced plans that dealt with the basic structure of the new government. In the convention, four plans of government were introduced. All were named after the person who introduced them: the (Edmund) Randolph Plan, the (Charles) Pinckney Plan, the (William) Paterson Plan, and the (Alexander) Hamilton Plan.

The Pinckney and Hamilton plans were minor compared to the influential Randolph and Paterson plans. The Randolph plan favored a stronger central government, while the Paterson plan favored a weaker central government.

# Virginia Plan/Randolph Plan

The Virginia Plan, introduced on May 29, 1787, formed the basis of the Convention and was debated word by word. The plan contained 15 resolves. It was the first plan introduced in the Convention and the one that most closely resembled the Convention's final product.

It proposed that the powers of the federal government should be expanded to accomplish three goals: "common defence, security of liberty and general welfare. Resolve number three provided for two houses of the Congress, or a bicameral legislature. Under the Virginia Plan, the people would elect the first branch. Then, the members of the first branch would elect the second branch of the "National Legislature."

Under the Virginia Plan, the U.S. Congress would possess great power. Resolve number six granted Congress the power to negate, or veto, any laws passed by state legislatures. Resolve number seven provided Congress with the power to appoint the "National Executive," or leader of the country. Thus, under this plan, Congress, not the people, would select the national leader. Resolve number nine provided for a "National Judiciary," or a set of judges that could hear cases throughout the country.

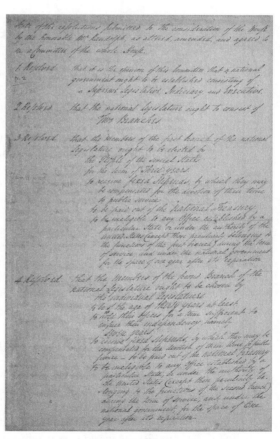

Drafted by James Madison, the Virginia Plan proposed the Constitutional Convention be held to establish a central government with a bicameral system and three branches of government.

# Pinckney Plan

Charles Pinckney (1757–1824) of South Carolina introduced a plan of government on the same day as the Virginia, or Randolph, Plan. The plan was similar in some respects to Madison's ideas. In fact, some historians suspect that Madison gave little mention to Pinckney's plans in his notes because he did not want the Pinckney Plan to receive credit.

Pinckney's plan also argued for a strong national government. The Convention as a whole never debated Pinckney's plan. However, it was referred to a later committee, the Committee of Detail, which made use of it. Christopher and James Lincoln Collier write: "Many of Pinckney's ideas, and even his language, ended up in the final Constitution of the United States."

Pinckney made many speeches during the Convention in which he argued for the delegates to think about a central government. Historian Charles Warren writes that on June 25, Pinckney made a particularly passionate speech: "Into the debates which had so largely turned on devotion to the States, Pinckney now breathed a spirit of Americanism."

## Paterson or New Jersey Plan

On June 15, William Paterson (1745–1806) from New Jersey introduced the Paterson Plan. "Can we, as representatives of independent states, annihilate the essential powers of independency?" Paterson said when introducing his proposal. He wanted a weaker central government.

The New Jersey Plan contained many features, including a single-bodied, or unicameral, legislature and a multiperson executive. Under the New Jersey Plan, Congress could only act on certain matters. Congress would elect the members of the federal executive. Congress could remove the persons of the federal executive if a majority of state leaders voted such action necessary.

Interestingly, the New Jersey Plan contained language providing that the laws of the U.S. Congress "shall be the supreme law of the respective States." This formed the basis for the supremacy clause of the U.S. Constitution. The supremacy clause provides that the laws of the national, or federal, government are the supreme law of the land and trump the laws of the various states.

## Hamilton's Plan of Union

On June 18, 1787, New York delegate Alexander Hamilton (c. 1755–1804) introduced his own plan. Hamilton, perhaps more than any other delegate at the Convention, desired a strong federal government. Hamilton greatly admired the British government. He said: "I believe the British government forms the best model the world ever produced."

The British government consisted of the monarchy, headed by a king or queen, and Parliament, a legislative body consisting of two branches—the House of Commons and the House of Lords. The House of Lords was composed of aristocrats who earned their place by heredity rather than election. Hamilton greatly admired the House of Lords. He believed a similar institution in America would be a conservative check on popular democratic passions.

He spoke for six hours when introducing his plan. Under his plan, the members of the Senate and the leader of the executive branch would serve life terms as long as they engaged in "good behaviour." Hamilton proposed that a one-person "Governor" would serve as what we now call the president.

Alexander Hamilton

## The Main Difference between the Two Major Plans

The Founders mainly discussed the Virginia and New Jersey Plans. The Virginia Plan was favored by the larger states, while the New Jersey Plan was favored by many of the smaller states. The biggest area of disagreement between the two focused on representation in Congress.

The larger states, such as Virginia, wanted representation in Congress based on the population of the state. This is called proportional representation. Proportional representation would favor the larger states because they had greater populations.

The smaller states, such as Delaware, opposed proportional representation. Many of the delegates from the smaller states feared the power of the larger states. They tried to ensure that each state would possess equal power under the new constitution. Gunning Bedford (1747–1812), a delegate from Delaware, expressed his concerns: "I do not, gentlemen, trust you. If you possess the power, the abuse of it could not be checked; and what then would prevent you from exercising it to our destruction?" Bedford went so far as to suggest that the smaller states would seek support from foreign countries to protect their interests.

They advocated the position of the New Jersey Plan—equal representation. Equal representation would favor the smaller states because they would have the same numbers of representatives as their larger neighbors. This issue nearly led to a premature ending of the Convention.

"There was an ever-present danger that the Convention might dissolve and the entire project be abandoned," writes historian Catherine Drinker Bowen. Delegate Luther Martin of Maryland admitted years later: "We were on the verge of dissolution scarce held together by the strength of a hair."

However, many delegates recognized that they must come to some agreement. If the delegates could not agree, their country might fall prey to foreign powers. Elbridge Gerry (1744–1814) of Massachusetts warned his colleagues: "If we do not come to some agreement among ourselves, some foreign sword will probably do the work for us."

# Creating a Congress

The different states were very divided over how to distribute power in the new legislature. On May 31, the Committee of the Whole voted in favor of resolve number three in the Virginia Plan: "That the national legislation ought to consist of two branches."

The problem for the delegates continued to be how to determine representation in each branch of the legislature.

Fortunately, delegate Roger Sherman of Connecticut proposed a measure that would eventually save the Constitution. Sherman played an influential role in the Convention, but he is most remembered for his compromise that saved the Convention and the Constitution. Under this so-called Great Compromise, the states would be represented equally in the Senate, and the states would be represented proportionally in the House of Representatives based on population. This proposal reflects our current system. In the House of Representatives, states have representatives based on the state's population. In the Senate, each state has two senators.

However, Sherman's proposal was voted down 6–5 when it was first introduced. The delegates continued to argue over the issue of proportional versus equal representation. On July 2, the states voted 5–5 on the question of equal representation in the Senate. The states of Connecticut, New York, New Jersey, Delaware, and Maryland favored equal representation. The states of Massachusetts, Pennsylvania, Virginia, North Carolina, and South Carolina opposed equal representation. The state of Georgia could have broken the tie, but the two Georgia delegates present—William Houstoun (1746–1813) and Abraham Baldwin (1754–1807)—split.

Four delegates from Georgia were present at the Convention. However, two of the members, William Few (1748–1828) and William Pierce (1753–1789), left the convention for New York to vote on pressing matters in Congress. Few and Pierce would have voted against equal representation.

The Convention was hanging in the balance. The small states would have lost the question of equal representation this day if it were not for the vote of Abraham Baldwin. Baldwin had lived in Connecticut virtually his whole life, having moved to

Georgia only three years before the Convention. Some historians believe that Baldwin saved the Constitution, because he split the vote in Georgia and saved the small states.

The Convention then agreed to allow a committee of one person from each of the 11 states to be formed to explore the question of how to organize the Congress. The states voted 10–1 in favor of such a committee. The committee was composed primarily of individuals who were in favor of a Senate chosen by equal representation.

On July 5, the committee read its report to the entire delegation. The report called for proportional representation in the House and equal representation in the Senate. Many of the delegates who had wanted proportional representation in both houses had conceded this issue, realizing that the delegates from the small states might leave if they did not get their way.

## The Great Compromise

On July 16, the delegates approved of the proposal introduced by Sherman a month earlier. Under it, each state would have equal representation in the Senate, and each state would have one representative in the House for every 40,000 citizens. Since it saved the Constitution from being dissolved, Sherman's proposal is justly called the Great Compromise.

The Convention adopted the Great Compromise by a vote of five to four with Massachusetts being evenly divided. Historian Charles Warren writes: "The acceptance of the compromise was not only essential to the continuance of the Convention; but it also had the important effect of converting the representatives from Connecticut, New Jersey, and Delaware into ardent supporters of the new Constitution."

Delegates from the smaller states, after they had equal representation in the Senate, now pushed hard for a stronger central government.

## The Executive Branch—A Single Person or an Executive Committee

Some delegates feared that creating a single-person executive would be dangerous and lead to a monarch, such as George III (1738–1820). George III was the king of Great Britain who taxed the colonies and battled them during the Revolutionary War. Above all else, the majority of the Framers wished to avoid creating a king. Most of the delegates assumed that George Washington would become the country's chief executive.

For this reason, James Madison wrote to Thomas Jefferson that it was "peculiarly embarrassing" to have the delegates arguing about whether they could trust

The Oval Office in the White House (shown here during Donald Trump's administration) is where the president does the daily work of the executive branch.

a single executive. It was "embarrassing" because Washington sat quietly while this discussion proceeded.

George Mason from Virginia proposed that there be a three-person executive branch. He said that one individual would come from the North, one from the South, and the other from the Middle states.

The delegates disagreed about whether to create a strong independent executive or an executive who would be far less powerful than Congress. The delegates also changed their positions on the length of the president's term. The Committee of Detail originally proposed in its August 6 report that the president would be elected by the legislature for one seven-year term.

Finally, on August 31, another committee—the so-called Committee of Eleven—considered an earlier proposal by delegate James Wilson from Pennsylvania that a group of people called electors would choose the president. Under this system, each state would have the number of electors "equal to the whole number of senators and representatives of the House of Representatives." This proposal was another compromise measure between the larger and smaller states. In a direct popular election, the votes in the larger states would dominate. In an electoral college system, the larger states would have more electors but the smaller states would still have a significant role.

On September 6, the delegates approved of the electoral college as the way to select the president. The electors would meet in the various state capitals and vote for two persons. The person with the highest number of electoral votes would be president. The person with the second highest number of votes would be vice president. The House of Representatives would select the president in case of a tie. The Founders did not foresee that the two highest vote getters might be political opposites.

# Federal vs. State Governments

Many of the Founding Fathers had a deep-seated distrust of one central power. They preferred for power to reside in their state governments. However, many others realized that one general government was needed to deal with foreign nations. Delegate John Dickinson (1732–1808) of Pennsylvania offered the following explanation of the power between a general government and various state governments: "Let our government be like that of the solar system. Let the general government be like the sun and the states the planets, repelled yet attracted, and the whole moving regularly and harmoniously in their several orbits."

On July 10, two delegates from New York, John Lansing (1754–1829) and Robert Yates, left the convention. These delegates believed that the Convention had strayed too far from its original purpose and were creating a central government that was too strong.

## Slavery

Many of the Southern delegates argued that slavery must be protected. The plantation economy of the South thrived on the labor of enslaved workers. The Northern states were not dependent on slavery, and several Northern states had already abolished the practice.

Madison had warned that the biggest obstacle to overcome at the Convention was between the Northern and Southern states. The North and the South had different economies and attitudes.

An 1856 engraving shows a slave auction being held in Richmond, Virginia. Slavery was a contentious issue, but it made its way into the Constitution.

Many of the Framers from Southern states were strong supporters of slavery. For example, Charles Pinckney of South Carolina represented the view of many Southern and other Convention delegates when he said: "If slavery be wrong, it is justified by the example of all the world.... In all ages one half of mankind had been slaves."

Unfortunately, only a few delegates spoke out against slavery. George Mason of Virginia, who himself owned slaves, was one of the few who spoke against the abominable practice, saying that it would "bring the judgment of heaven on a country."

However, the vast majority of the delegates did not want to dissolve the Union over slavery. Many members from the Southern states would leave the Convention rather than agree to the abolition of slavery.

The issue of slavery was closely tied to the question of representation in Congress. The Southern states wanted to count slaves in their population numbers because they would obtain more seats in the House of Representatives. The Northern states did not want to count slaves for purposes of legislative representation since slaves would not vote or pay taxes. The Northern states also did not want the Southern states to obtain more power.

The delegates eventually agreed to tie taxation to representation and count slaves as three-fifths of a person. Some historians contend that the Convention agreed to this compromise over slavery and representation in exchange for the exclusion of slavery in the Northwest Ordinance of 1787. The Northwest Ordinance dealt with the settlement of lands in the West north of the Ohio River.

The Northern and Southern delegates bargained over the issues of slavery and trade well into the month of August. On August 24, the Committee of Eleven issued a report that contained four provisions: (1) Congress could not prohibit the exportation of slaves until 1800; (2) Congress could tax imported slaves; (3) exports could not be taxed; and (4) Congress could pass navigation acts by simple majority. The Northern states, which depended on commerce, wanted Congress to pass laws regulating trade.

The Constitution would extend the date to allow the importation of slaves until 1808. The Constitution also contained a clause, called the Fugitive Slave Clause, that allowed Southerners to go into Northern states to recover runaway slaves. Unfortunately, the Fugitive Slave Clause enabled the capture of free blacks in northern territory by southern slaveowners.

Because the Constitution did not prohibit slavery, the famed abolitionist William Lloyd Garrison (1805–1879) said the Constitution was a "covenant with death and an agreement with hell."

But many historians have concluded that the delegates had no choice. Most states had not formally abolished slavery yet, and delegates from the Northern states recognized that their Southern counterparts at the Convention would never agree to the Constitution without slavery remaining in place. Sadly, the Northern delegates were not willing to risk the union in order to protect African Americans.

Madison spoke about the Constitution and slavery at the Virginia ratification convention. Madison said: "The southern states would not have entered into the union of America, without the temporary possession of that trade." However, Madison pointed out that under the Articles of Confederation, the slave trade could have continued forever. At least under the new Constitution, the importation of slaves would end in 20 years.

## Fear of Future States in the West

Many of the delegates were also concerned with how Congress would admit new states into the union. Many members of the Convention viewed the people on the Western frontier with suspicion.

Elbridge Gerry made a motion that the Constitution set a limit on the number of Western states that could enter the Union. He proposed that the admission of new states be limited "in such a manner that they should never be able to outnumber the Atlantic states." However, other delegates argued that it would be unfair to deny peoples in other parts of the country to apply for statehood. Roger Sherman of Connecticut pointed out: "Besides, we are providing for our posterity, for our children and grandchildren, who would be as likely to be citizens of new Western states as of the old states."

Elbridge Gerry

## Finalizing the Constitution: The Work of Committees and Compromise

In order to move things along, the delegates would appoint committees. On July 23, the Convention appointed a small committee of five members to put into place the various measures that had been voted and approved. Called the Committee of Detail, it consisted of delegates Edmund Randolph, James Wilson, Nathaniel Gorham (1738–1796), Oliver Ellsworth

(1745–1807), and John Rutledge (1739–1800). The committee made a report on August 6. This report led to debates that would culminate in the U.S. Constitution.

The rest of the Convention adjourned while the members of the Committee of Detail worked to produce their report. The Committee used much of the terminology that we recognize today. For example, the committee used the term "Congress" instead of "Legislature of the United States." The first branch became "the House of Representatives," and the second branch became "the Senate." The committee also listed the necessary qualifications for members of Congress. Many of these, such as the age and years of citizenship, were taken from similar provisions in state constitutions.

Perhaps even more significantly, the Committee of Detail decided to list or enumerate the specific powers of Congress. The committee could have simply given a general grant of power to Congress, but instead it listed 18 different powers of Congress. In its draft, the committee also inserted several limitations on Congress's powers. For example, the committee limited Congress's power to levy export taxes on the states.

From August 7 until the end of the Convention, the delegates debated the draft produced by the Committee of Detail. Much of this debate focused on the powers of Congress. On August 20, the delegates debated the necessary and proper clause. This clause provided in part that Congress should have the power "to make all laws that shall be necessary and proper for carrying into execution the foregoing powers." Opponents of this clause during the ratification debate would refer to it as the "sweeping clause" because it gave great power to Congress.

On August 22, the Convention debated the restraints on the power of Congress. That day, Representative Gerry of Massachusetts introduced a measure that would prohibit Congress from passing any bill of attainder or ex post facto law. Bills of attainder refer to laws that declare a person guilty of a crime without a trial. Ex post facto laws take conduct that was legal and make it illegal after the conduct occurs.

On August 31, the full Convention debated how they were going to ratify the new Constitution. Some delegates argued that the new Constitution must be ratified by all thirteen states. However, many delegates recognized that not all 13 states would ratify the document. For example, Rhode Island had refused even to send delegates to the Convention.

# Committee of Style and Arrangement

On September 5, five men were chosen to form a so-called Committee of Style and Arrangement. These five were William Samuel Johnson (1727–1819), Alexander Hamilton, Gouverneur Morris, James Madison, and Rufus King (1755–

1827). The duty of this committee was to "revise the style of and arrange the articles which had been agreed to by the House."

The Committee of Style had to condense 23 different articles. They eventually condensed the document into seven articles. Morris did the bulk of the work. In his notes, Madison acknowledged the accomplishments of Morris, noting that "the finish given to the style and arrangement … fairly belongs to the pen of Mr. Morris."

The delegates signed and submitted the Constitution to Congress on September 17, 1787. Near the end of their debates, the delegates had to decide whether the Constitution should be ratified by the state legislatures or at state conventions. The delegates voted 9–1 in favor of popular conventions. On September 28, 1787, Congress submitted the Constitution to the various states. This began the process of ratification.

# Ratifying the Constitution and the Bill of Rights Issue

Given the importance of the Bill of Rights in our legal system, it is perhaps surprising that the Convention contained almost no discussion about the Bill of Rights. However, at the time, the delegates had to deal with other pressing political issues. They had to decide the structure of the three branches of government, the thorny issue of representation, the ugly specter of slavery, and countless other issues. After all, the Constitutional Convention almost ended in failure.

Delegate Charles Pinckney (1757–1824) of South Carolina made the first motion for freedoms now contained in the Bill of Rights. On August 20, 1787, he proposed that three clauses be added to the Constitution. These clauses concerned the liberty of the press, the quartering of troops in private homes, and a standing army. At that time in history, newspapers were the dominant mode of communication. Today with flagging newspaper sales and the ubiquity of the Internet, many may not appreciate just how much influence newspapers had. Thus, freedom of the press was important. The second freedom Pinckney advocated for was prohibiting the quartering of troops in private homes. This concern ultimately led to the Third Amendment. The third freedom concerned a standing army. Some delegates did not want the country to have an army during times of piece.

Pinckney was not alone in calling for a Bill of Rights. On September 12, George Mason (1725–1792), the author of the Virginia Declaration of Rights, said he "wished the plan had been prefaced with a bill of rights and would second a

A signer of the Declaration of Independence, Charles Pinckney was also a governor of South Carolina and served in the House and Senate.

motion if made for the purpose." Massachusetts delegate Elbridge Gerry (1744–1814) made the motion and Mason seconded it. The delegates voted down the motion unanimously. Gerry, who later served as vice president for the first 21 months of President James Madison's (1751–1836) second term, actually refused to sign the Constitution because it failed to have a bill of rights. He specifically emphasized the protection of the right of conscience and a free press.

However, the bulk of the delegates voted against including a bill of rights. Many delegates contended that adding a Bill of Rights to the U.S. Constitution was unnecessary, because many of these freedoms—such as freedom of the press or the right of conscience—were protected in state constitutions. Even today, most state constitutions contain what are called a declaration of rights. These are state bills of rights. These delegates reasoned that since these rights were already listed in state constitutions, there was no need for them to be listed in this newly minted U.S. Constitution.

Other delegates argued that a bill of rights would not provide any greater liberty. For example, Roger Sherman (1721–1793) of Connecticut famously said: "No bill of rights ever yet bound the supreme power longer that the honeymoon of a new married couple, unless the ruler were interested in preserving the right." Finally, as historian Catherine Drinker Bowen writes in her book *Miracle at Philadelphia,* "The framers looked upon the Constitution as a bill of rights in itself; all its provisions were for a free people and a people responsible."

A few delegates opposed the Bill of Rights because they saw that it might led to the abolition of slavery. General Charles Cotesworth Pinckney (1746–1825), a delegate from South Carolina (not to be confused with the aforementioned Charles Pinckney, his cousin once-removed, also from South Carolina), bluntly stated his objection to a bill of rights: "Bill of rights generally begin with declaring that all men are by nature born free. Now, we should make that declaration with a very bad grace, when a large part of our property consists in men who are actually born slaves." Reading between the lines, Charles Cotesworth Pinckney meant that a bill of rights and its emphasis on individual freedom would provide support against slavery.

## Signing the Constitution

Thirty-nine of the 42 delegates present at the end signed the Constitution on September 17, 1787. The respected Benjamin Franklin (1706–1790) called upon his fellow delegates to show unanimity and spirit and sign their name to the Constitution even if there were parts of the Constitution with which they disagreed.

Of the 42 members present at the end of the Convention, all but three signed the document. These three were Elbridge Gerry of Massachusetts, George Mason of Virginia, and Edmund Randolph (1753–1813) of Virginia. Both Gerry and Mason opposed the Constitution in large part because it did not contain a bill of rights. A few days earlier, Mason said in colorful language: "I would sooner chop off my right hand than put it to the Constitution."

Mason honestly believed that the system of government would produce either a "monarchy or a corrupt oppressive aristocracy." He also felt that he and his colleagues had formed the Constitution "without the knowledge or idea of the people." Mason believed that the delegates had exceeded their authority by secretly creating a powerful national government that would take away the powers of the states.

Randolph also refused to sign the Constitution. This was somewhat ironic, as it was Randolph who had introduced the so-called Randolph or Virginia plan, one of the major contributions to the Convention. However, Randolph felt that states should be allowed to offer amendments at a second convention. The Convention unanimously rejected Randolph's call for a second convention.

However, the other 39 signed the document, including John Hancock (c. 1736–1793) in noticeably large print. Legend has it that Franklin wept as he signed the document. Franklin made a famous remark that when he looked at the picture of a sun on George Washington's (1732–1799) chair, he felt it was a rising, not a setting, sun and said:

> Painters have found it difficult to distinguish in their art a rising from a setting sun. I have often and often in the course of the session, and the vicissitudes [changes] of my hopes and fears as to its issue, looked at that behind the president [of the Convention] without being able to tell whether it was rising or setting. But now at length I have the happiness to know that it is a rising and not a setting sun.

## Ratification in the States

Article VII of the new Constitution provides that "[t]he ratification of the conventions of nine states shall be sufficient for the establishment of the Constitution between the states so ratifying the same." This meant that the "real fight" did not come on the convention floor. It

*Scene at the Signing of the Constitution of the United States (1940) by Howard Chandler Christy.*

came in the states over whether to ratify the Constitution. Many merchants, manufacturers, and big plantation owners in the South favored the Constitution. They knew the new Constitution would help protect their business interests.

However, many small farmers did not want to sacrifice their individual freedom and become dependent on the business people. Historian Fred Rodell wrote that these individuals "no more wanted to go ahead under such a Constitution that they wanted to go back to King George III [(1738–1820)]." The battle over ratification became a great issue of the day. It captured the headlines and great space in the newspapers. Pamphlets were printed on each side. Newspaper editors featured various pieces either praising or denigrating the new Constitution.

On September 28, the Congress directed the state legislatures to call ratification conventions to vote on the new document. Under the ratification process, the state legislatures would vote to call special conventions. Delegates, often the state legislators themselves, would vote at the conventions. The ratification process was far from easy. Political leaders were divided. Supporters of the new Constitution, with its strong central government, called themselves Federalists. Opponents of the Constitution were called Anti-Federalists. Many of them opposed the Constitution because it failed to provide for a bill of rights and gave too much power to the federal government at the expense of the state governments.

The Anti-Federalists were particularly concerned with the so-called "necessary and proper" clause of the new Constitution. Article I, Section 18 provided Congress with the power to "make all Laws which shall be necessary and proper" for executing its powers vested in the Constitution. Other Anti-Federalists were concerned with the supremacy clause in Article I. Many Anti-Federalists viewed this clause as wiping out the powers of state governments.

*Many Anti-Federalists also argued that the Constitution gave too much power to the president. Some feared that the president and the Senate would unite to become like the king of England and the House of Lords.*

Many Anti-Federalists also argued that the Constitution gave too much power to the president. Some feared that the president and the Senate would unite to become like the king of England and the upper house of the English Parliament, the House of Lords. The king of England and the House of Lords represented aristocrats, the upper class of society, and tended to ignore the interests of regular people.

In the most populous states of New York and Virginia, the Anti-Federalists fought hard. After the Philadelphia Convention, James Madison cowrote a series of articles with Alexander Hamilton (c. 1755–1804) and John Jay (1745–1829) that became known as *The Federalist Papers*. These 85 essays written under the pen name "Publius" are still considered the definitive work on the Constitution. Thomas Jefferson (1743–1826) once called them "the best commentary on the principles of government which ever was written." U.S. Supreme Court justices regularly cite *The Federalist Papers* in their opinions when dealing with complex questions of constitutional law.

These articles discussed the framework of the Constitution, including the principles of checks and balances and separation of powers among three branches of government. Hamilton, Jay, and Madison sought to persuade the readers that the newly designed government was the best course of action for the young country. Hamilton wrote that the nation faced a "crisis." He wrote that if the country voted against the new Constitution, that decision would "deserve to be considered as the general misfortune of mankind."

In *Federalist Papers,* No. 45, Madison argued that the state governments did not have much to fear from the federal government. Madison wrote: "The powers delegated by the proposed Constitution to the federal government are few and defined. Those which are to remain in the State governments are numerous and indefinite."

It was not just the Federalists who used the power of the pen. Several Anti-Federalists also wrote articles under pen names attacking various aspects of the Constitution. An Anti-Federalist who called himself the "Federal Farmer" critiqued the Constitution in a series of letters published in the *Poughkeepsie County Journal* from November 1787 to January 1788. The letters also appeared in pamphlet form. For many years, it was assumed that Richard Henry Lee (1732–1794) of Virginia was the author. Now, some historians believe the author was New York Anti-Federalist Melancton Smith (1744–1798).

The "Letters from the Federal Farmer" criticized the new Constitution and its proponents as showing a "strong tendency to aristocracy." The "Letters" argued that the Constitution concentrated too much power in the central government. The author also made some accurate predictions about the future of our government. For example, he writes: "This system promises a large field of employment to military gentlemen and gentlemen of the law."

Robert Yates (1738–1801), a New York judge who served in the Convention until he left in July, wrote a series of articles under the pen name "Brutus." Brutus was the Roman republican who helped assassinate Julius Caesar (100 B.C.E.–44 B.C.E.) to prevent Caesar from overthrowing the Roman Republic. In one of his articles, Yates criticized the powers granted to the judicial branch. He wrote: "The supreme court under this constitution would be exalted above all other power in the government, and subject to no control."

The battle between the Federalists and Anti-Federalists was intense. However, the Federalists possessed advantages. They enjoyed most of the media support. The large newspapers from Boston, New York, and Philadelphia took up the Federalist cause. They also seemed to have the best ammunition—the detailed document known as the Constitution. Though the Anti-Federalists made many arguments against provisions of the Constitution, they did not have their own document. The Anti-Federalists could only criticize the new document.

# The Lack of a Bill of Rights

However, the Anti-Federalists seized upon the lack of a bill of rights as a prime weapon in the ratification battles. Historian Robert Rutland writes: "The Federalists, failing to realize the importance of a bill of rights, miscalculated public opinion and found themselves on the defensive almost from the outset of the ratification struggle."

Delaware became the first state to ratify the Constitution, and it did so unanimously on December 7, 1787. Then, an intense battle began in Pennsylvania. James Wilson (1742–1798) took the lead in defending the Constitution in his home state. In a well-known address delivered on October 6, 1787, Wilson argued that the inclusion of a bill of rights was "superfluous and absurd." The new Congress, Wilson argued, "possesses no influence whatever upon the press." Wilson pointed out that many Anti-Federalists were criticizing the new document because it provided for a standing army. Wilson responded that a nation must appear strong and a standing army would help the new nation survive in a world dominated by superpowers overseas.

*George Washington once wrote: "If a weak State with the Indians on its back and the Spaniards on its flank does not see the necessity of a General Government, there must I think be wickedness or insanity in the way."*

The state assembly had to vote on a state convention. Many of the Anti-Federalists in the state legislature refused to attend the assembly. They did not want the assembly to have a quorum, or a sufficient number of members to take a valid vote. Allegedly, a mob of people broke into a local home and dragged two Anti-Federalists to the assembly floor in order to create a quorum. The delegates voted 45–2 in favor of a ratification convention. The state convention met for five weeks. Finally, on December 12, the delegates voted for ratification by a vote of 46–23. The vote upset some citizens with Anti-Federalist sympathies. A mob of such people attacked Wilson in Carlisle, Pennsylvania.

After Delaware ratified, Pennsylvania became the next state to ratify a few days later by a vote of 46–23. The Pennsylvania delegates also considered 15 amendments proposed by Anti-Federalist Robert Whitehill (1738–1813). These proposed amendments were similar to what would later become the U.S. Bill of Rights. The delegates voted against the amendments by the same 2–1 margin. The Anti-Federalists then issued "The Address and Reasons of Dissent of the Minority of the Convention." This document spread the push for a bill of rights.

New Jersey became the third state to ratify the Constitution, and it did so unanimously on December 18, 1787. Georgia also ratified the new Constitution on January 2, 1788. Many members of the Georgia convention supported the new Constitution because of security concerns. Georgia was bordered by Indians and Spanish territory. George Washington once wrote: "If a weak State with the Indians on its back and the Spaniards on its flank does not see the necessity of a General Government, there must I think be wickedness or insanity in the way."

Connecticut became the fifth state to ratify, and it did so overwhelmingly by a vote of 128–42. Roger Sherman, who played a large role at the Philadelphia Convention, took the lead in ensuring that his state ratified the Constitution. The crafter of "the Great Compromise" was equally if not more effective in his home state, and his popularity and persuasion helped carry the day there.

Ratification was more difficult in the populous states of Massachusetts and New York. The debate in Massachusetts was particularly intense. Massachusetts voted 187–168 in favor of the Constitution on February 6, 1788, only after the Federalists agreed to recommend amending the Constitution to include protections for individual liberties.

Massachusetts became the first state officially to recommend amendments to the Constitution during the ratification process. Though the nine proposed amendments bear little resemblance to the final U.S. Bill of Rights, their importance lies in the fact that Massachusetts started a pattern of attaching amendments. This process of attaching amendments to the Constitution led the push in what ultimately culminated in a Bill of Rights.

Maryland ratified in April 1788 by a vote of 63–11. Its convention members followed the pattern established by Massachusetts and recommended adding amendments to the Constitution. In May, South Carolina ratified by a vote of 149–46.

New Hampshire became the required ninth state on June 21, 1788, voting 57–46 in favor of the Constitution. Although the Constitution was technically in effect after New Hampshire ratified it, the support of Virginia was essential because Virginia was such a large and powerful state. When they voted, Virginian politicians did not know that New Hampshire had become the necessary ninth state.

The battle was extremely tough in Virginia, as the state featured both leading Federalists and Anti-Federalists. Consider that Virginia was the home of James Madison, George Washington, and Thomas Jefferson, all of whom supported the Constitution. However, the state was also the home of a group of well-known Anti-Federalists, including Patrick Henry (1736–1799) and George Mason.

The battle was brutal at times. Madison fell ill and was bedridden for three straight days. Some great statesmen, such as the brilliant orator from Virginia, Patrick Henry, led the Anti-Federalists. During the debate on the ratification in his state, Henry asked: "What right had they [the Constitution delegates] to say, 'We the People'?"

In arguing against the Constitution, George Mason once again seized on the fact that there was no Bill of Rights. Mason argued that "there never was a govern-

Patrick Henry, an attorney, farmer, and politician well known for his "Give me liberty, or give me death!" speech, was a leader of the Anti-Federalists.

ment over a very extensive country without destroying the liberties of the people." Delegate Edmund Pendleton (1721–1803) countered in the Virginia Ratification Convention, emphasizing that it would be impossible to have any liberty at all if there was no government: "In reviewing the history of the world, shall we find an instance where any society retained its liberty without government?"

On June 4, 1788, the first full day of debate in Virginia, Governor Edmund Randolph stood up and spoke in favor of the Constitution even though he had failed to sign it the previous September. Randolph explained that he did not sign because the document did not contain necessary amendments. However, he said that because other states had proposed amendments to be passed after ratification, he would vote in favor of ratification. He also pointed out that eight other states had already ratified. The insistent Henry charged that Randolph had been persuaded to change positions by none other than George Washington. Though this charge cannot be proven beyond a shadow of a doubt, Washington did later name Randolph his first attorney general.

James Madison managed to gather enough support for the Constitution in the Virginia state convention on June 25, 1788. The delegates narrowly approved of the Constitution. Two days later, a committee at the convention proposed a bill of rights to be added to the Constitution. Virginia voted in favor of ratification by a narrow vote of 89–79. Virginia also attached proposed amendments as well, many of which would later be contained in the Bill of Rights.

Some Anti-Federalists were very upset and wanted to resist the new Constitution. However, at a meeting in Richmond, Patrick Henry said that they must accept defeat. "As true and faithful republicans [honorable citizens] you had all better go home." Many Anti-Federalists became supporters of the new government. For example, Anti-Federalist Elbridge Gerry, who refused to sign the Convention later became James Madison's vice president.

George Washington acknowledged the contributions of the Anti-Federalists and others who opposed the Constitution. "Upon the whole, I doubt whether the opposition to the Constitution will not ultimately be productive of more good than evil; it has called forth, in its defence, abilities which would not perhaps have been otherwise exerted that have thrown new light upon the science of Government, they have given the rights of man a full and fair discussion, and explained them in so clear and forcible a manner, as cannot fail to make a lasting impression." The Federalists and the Anti-Federalists each made lasting contributions to the U.S. Constitution.

The Constitution was ratified—but the battle over the Bill of Rights continued. Here is where the genius of James Madison changed American history for the betterment of individual liberty.

# Using the Bill of Rights to Save the Constitution

James Madison, who had worked so hard at Philadelphia, did not want the Constitution altered or changed. He recognized that the lack of a bill of rights was a trouble point. Though Madison had originally not wanted a bill of rights, he recognized that the Anti-Federalists were gaining popular support for their pro–bill of rights position.

> *Madison originally subscribed to the view of his fellow* Federalist Papers *author Alexander Hamilton that the Constitution itself was a bill of rights.*

Madison originally subscribed to the view of his fellow *Federalist Papers* author Alexander Hamilton that the Constitution itself was a bill of rights. There is some support for this view, as the Constitution prohibits ex post facto laws—laws that criminalize acts retroactively or increase punishment for them after they were committed. It also prohibits so-called bills of attainder, laws targeting specific individuals. Madison also disparaged the Bill of Rights as a "paper barrier" that would not offer any real protection to the people and may even expand the power of the government.

However, Madison's mentor and fellow Virginian Thomas Jefferson—the so-called Sage of Monticello—convinced him that a bill of rights was necessary. The two engaged in a correspondence across the Atlantic Ocean because Jefferson was serving his country as the minister to France. Thus, while Madison took a leading role at the Philadelphia Convention, Jefferson could only wait to hear from overseas.

The two Virginia politicians engaged in a series of letters about a bill of rights. The correspondence began with Madison's letter of October 24, 1787, in which he informed Jefferson that the legal blueprint that came out of Philadelphia contained no bill of rights. Madison initially wrote Jefferson that he did not see the need for a bill of rights, that the structural protections in the existing Constitution would suffice.

From Paris, France, Jefferson responded to Madison's doubts in a letter dated December 20, 1787, in which he criticized the omission of a bill of rights, writing:

> Let me add that a bill of rights is what the people are entitled to against every government on earth, general or particular, and what no just government should refuse, or rest on inference.

To secure popular support for the Constitution, Thomas Jefferson (pictured) persuaded people like Madison that a Bill of Rights needed to be added.

Jefferson persuaded Madison that the inclusion of a bill of rights was necessary to secure popular support for the new Constitution. Jefferson emphasized that the Constitution begins with the words "We the People" and there must be popular support for this new document. After all, the framers were asking a lot of the people to accept a strong, new central government. Madison wrote to Jefferson in October 1788 that "My own opinion has always been in favor of a bill of rights." However, Madison also wrote in his letter that he believed a bill of rights would be a mere "parchment barrier" that could not protect citizens from an oppressive majority.

Madison believed that the real danger to individual liberty lay not in the government "but from acts in which the Government is the mere instrument of the major number of the Constituents." In other words, the real danger came not from the government but from what French observer Alexis de Tocqueville (1805–1859) called "the tyranny of the majority."

Madison ultimately accepted Jefferson's argument that a bill of rights was necessary to secure popular support for the new Constitution. He also believed that a bill of rights would not be very effective in protecting liberties against the will of the majority. In his letter to Jefferson, Madison expressed only lukewarm support for a bill of rights: "I have favored it [a bill of rights] because I have supposed it might be of use and if properly executed could not be of disservice."

During the meeting of the First Congress in 1789, some political leaders were calling for a Second Constitutional Convention to amend the Constitution. Madison feared that these calls would lead to drastic revisions of the Constitution, which would reduce the power of the federal government. He considered these calls a serious threat to the Constitution. He feared that such calls could lead to the dissolution of the new Constitution and the country.

When the First Congress met under the newly ratified Constitution, Madison introduced a measure to add a bill of rights to the Constitution. He took his proposed amendments from the various proposals discussed at the state ratifying conventions.

Madison had to act quickly because Anti-Federalists from New York and Virginia were urging for a Second Constitutional Convention to discuss amendments to the Constitution. He believed that by carefully selecting amendments dealing with individual liberty, he could redirect the popular support currently enjoyed by the

Anti-Federalists. Many amendments had been proposed by the various state ratifying conventions. Though Madison did not create these provisions, he knew which amendments to introduce and which to exclude. Madison's genius was not in creating the provisions that became the Bill of Rights. His genius was his political ability to select the proper amendments to introduce. He included provisions protecting individual liberty and left out those amendments that would have taken away power from the federal government.

Madison got most of the proposals he submitted from existing state declaration of rights in state constitutions. Many of the freedoms in the ultimate Bill of Rights came from either the Virginia or the Pennsylvania Constitution.

Madison was looking for provisions that dealt with individual liberties, such as freedom of religion, freedom of the press, and the right to be free from unreasonable searches and seizures. In fact, nearly all of Madison's proposed amendments dealt with issues of individual liberties. He avoided the demand for structural amendments to the Constitution.

> *Madison was looking for provisions that dealt with individual liberties, such as freedom of religion, freedom of the press, or the right to be free from unreasonable searches and seizures.*

On June 8, 1789, Madison delivered in the House of Representatives what historian Robert Goldwin has called "one of the most consequential political orations in American history." Madison passionately argued for the inclusion of a bill of rights, saying that it would soothe anxiety of the general public, many of whom had reservations about at least some parts of the new Constitution. He also famously stated: "You ought not to disregard their inclination, but, on principles of amity and moderation, conform to their wishes and declare the great rights of mankind secured under the Constitution."

Thus, James Madison urged his colleagues to pass what he called "the Great Rights of Mankind." Madison had much clout for this performance at the Philadelphia Convention. It is no accident that he is called "the Father of the Bill of Rights."

The House of Representatives passed the Bill of Rights by a vote of 37–14 on September 24, 1789. The Senate approved the Bill of the Rights the next day by an unknown vote. The states then ratified the Bill of Rights. When Virginia became the necessary final state, the Bill of Rights was officially added to the Constitution on December 15, 1791.

Goldwin persuasively argues that Madison used the Bill of Rights to "save the Constitution." It is hard to argue with Goldwin's persuasive argument, because that is exactly what James Madison did—he was able to use the Bill of Rights as a way to help secure more permanent and popular support of the new Constitution.

# Article I—Congress

Article I, the longest article in the Constitution, explains the legislative branch of the government. It reflects the Framers' belief that the legislature must be bicameral, consisting of two houses of Congress—the House of Representatives and the Senate. It also reflects the Framers' careful concerns with both checks and balances and separation of powers.

It contains qualifications for each House of Congress and then a detailed list of Congress's powers. However, the Framers also worried about the legislative branch becoming too powerful, so they included many limitations as well. What follows is a list of nearly every clause of Article I, followed by an explanation. Some of the explanations run much longer because there are a bevy of Supreme Court decisions involving and interpreting that particular constitutional power or provision.

## Vesting Clause

All legislative Powers herein granted shall be vested in a Congress of the United States, which shall consist of a Senate and House of Representatives.

Article I begins with the Vesting Clause, providing that all legislative powers found in Article I are found in Congress, a bicameral body with a Senate and a House of Representatives. Article I is the longest part of the Constitution. Most Framers assumed that the legislative branch would be the most powerful branch of government. It certainly has more enumerated, or listed, powers than the other branches of government.

The Founders, however, wanted to make sure that Congress did not have unlimited powers. They feared the unlimited power of the English Parliament, which passed onerous taxing laws on the colonies that led to the Revolutionary War.

Congress has the essential power to make the laws. That is the essence of the legislative branch. The members of Congress debate and vote on different bills, measures introduced into Congress. A small number of these bills actually pass the legislative process of Congress and become signed into law.

Article I later lists quite a few powers of Congress, primarily in Article I, Section 8. The basic point is that a law is only constitutional if Congress had the power to pass the law. If Congress does not have the power to pass a law, then that law is unconstitutional.

The division of power between a House and a Senate was a seminal achievement during the summer of 1787. The previous form of government only had a unicameral, or one, legislative body. Under this process, each state had the same number of votes. As we will see in a later chapter, this was a major source of disagreement at the Founding Convention between the large and small states.

Ultimately, under something known as the Great Compromise, the Framers created a Congress that tied one body of Congress—the House of Representatives—to a state's population. The Framers also created another body of Congress—the Senate—in which each state would have equal representation in the form of two senators.

The Old City Hall on New York's Wall Street was the location of the First Congress's meeting in 1789.

# The Issue of Administrative Agencies

Nowhere in the U.S. Constitution does it mention executive agencies or Congress's explicit power to create them, but the federal government today has a litany of administrative agencies. The Supreme Court has ruled that Congress under its lawmaking powers can create executive agencies if they meet the standards that other laws do, such as passing both houses (called bicameralism) and being presented to the president (presentment).

# Membership, Election Terms, and Qualifications to Vote for the House

The House of Representatives shall be composed of Members chosen every second Year by the People of the several States, and the Electors in each State shall have the Qualifications requisite for Electors of the most numerous Branch of the State Legislature.

The Framers designed the House of Representatives as the body of Congress most tied to the People. That is why members of the House are far more numerous than members of the Senate. It also explains why members of the House are subject to two-year terms rather than the six-year terms of the senators. The House of Representatives is known as "the People's House."

The Constitution does not set term limits for members of the House and Senate, unlike the president, who is now limited to two terms by the Twenty-third Amendment. This has led to some members of Congress serving for an extremely long time. John Dingell Jr. (1926–2019) of Michigan served 59 years in the U.S. House of Representatives, from 1959 until 2015.

The second part of this section provides that those who can vote for members of the House are set or established by the voting standards or requirements set by the largest branch of each state's legislature. This unfortunately meant that voting was restricted only to white males with a certain level of income. Certainly, African Americans and women were flatly excluded from voting in the country. African Americans largely were deprived of the right to vote until the passage of later constitutional amendments, such as the Fifteenth Amendment, which prohibited discrimination on the basis of race when it comes to voting, and the Twenty-fourth Amendment, which prohibited poll taxes. Similarly, it took the country an embarrassingly long time to give voting rights to women. Congress passed the Nineteenth Amendment in 1920, which gave women the right to vote.

# Qualifications Clause for the House

No Person shall be a Representative who shall not have attained to the Age of twenty-five Years, and been seven Years a Citizen of the United States, and who shall not, when elected, be an Inhabitant of that State in which he shall be chosen.

The Qualifications Clause explains who can serve in the U.S. House of Representatives. It requires that members of the House be (1) at least 25 years of age, (2) a U.S. citizen, and (3) live in the state in which they are elected.

Despite the clear constitutional language regarding the required age, William Charles Cole Claiborne (1775–1817) served as a representative beginning in 1797 when he was only 22 years old. Perhaps even more remarkably, he had served on the Tennessee Supreme Court previously when he was 21. Claiborne was elected to a second term in Congress when he was only 24. Claiborne did not seek a third term but instead was appointed by President Thomas Jefferson (1743–1826) to serve as governor of the Territory of Mississippi. He later served as governor of the Orleans Territory and governor of Louisiana.

The House of Representatives shall chuse their Speaker and other Officers....

The most important member of the U.S. House of Representatives is the Speaker of the House. The Speaker is the presiding officer of the House and controls the flow and movement of how the House proceeds in its sessions. The Speaker serves as both the political and parliamentary leader of the House.

The position of Speaker traces its origins to the British House of Commons, which had a leader as well. The House elects its Speaker at the beginning of each term of Congress. The very first Speaker of the House was Frederick Muhlenberg of Maryland, who served as Speaker during the First (1789–1791) and the Third Congresses (1793–1795). Some of the more influential Speakers in American history were Henry Clay (1777–1852) from Kentucky, Thomas Brackett Reed (1839–1902) of Maine, Joseph Cannon (1836–1926) of Illinois, and the legendary Sam Rayburn (1882–1961) of Texas. In total, 54 different individuals have served as Speaker of the House.

... the sole power of impeachment ...

The Speaker traditionally is the head of the Rules Committee and has a large role in the overall agenda of the House. The Speaker is a member of the majority party in Congress. For example, the current Speaker of the House (in 2022), Nancy Pelosi (1940–) of California, is a Democrat, and the Democratic Party has a majority in the House of Representatives.

The House has the sole power to impeach federal officials, including the president of the United States. The House considers articles of impeachment and votes. All that is needed to impeach a federal official is a majority vote. Article II, Section 4 of the Constitution further provides that "The President, Vice President and all

An illustration of the 1868 impeachment trial of President Johnson in the Senate. While the House of Representatives has the power to impeach, the actual trial is held in the Senate.

Civil Officers of the United States, shall be removed from Office on Impeachment for, and Conviction of, Treason, Bribery, or other high Crimes and Misdemeanors."

While the House has the impeachment power, the Senate actually holds the impeachment trials. Thus, the House impeaches, and the Senate either convicts or acquits. The power of impeachment is limited to removal of office, but if someone is removed from office as a result, they can never serve in that office again.

Impeachment is reserved for serious misdeeds. As Alexander Hamilton (c. 1755–1804) wrote in *Federalist Papers,* No. 65, impeachment applies to "misconduct of public men, or in other words from the abuse or violation of some public trust."

# The Senate

The Senate of the United States shall be composed of two Senators from
each State, for six years, and each Senator shall have one vote.

Article I, Section 3, examines the U.S. Senate—the smaller body of Congress.
While the House of Representatives has 435 members, the Senate only has 50—
two from each state. This was the result of "the Great Compromise" developed by
Roger Sherman (1721–1793) that saved the Constitutional Convention in 1787 from
collapsing.

The original language provided that senators were "chosen by the Legislature
thereof," meaning that a state legislature elected the senators. However, the Seventeenth Amendment to the Constitution amended the Constitution to provide for
the direct election of senators.

Senators also serve much longer terms than representatives—six years as compared to two years. Thus, senators must think more about national interests than
members of the House. The Senate is considered the more deliberative body of
the Congress. As in the House, some members of the Senate have served an extraordinarily long time. For example, Robert Byrd (1917–2010) of West Virginia
served in the U.S. Senate for more than 51 years, from 1959 until 2010. Two current
members of the Senate—Patrick Leahy (1940–) of Vermont and Chuck Grassley
(1933–) of Iowa—have both served at least 40 years in the Senate.

# Rotational Elections

Immediately after they shall be assembled in Consequence of the first
Election, they shall be divided as equally as may be into three Classes.
The Seats of the Senators of the first Class shall be vacated at the Expiration of the second Year, of the second Class at the Expiration of the
fourth Year, and of the third Class at the Expiration of the sixth Year, so
that one third may be chosen every second Year.

Article I, Section 3 also provides that elections in the Senate are spaced out
in three categories. That means every two years, there is a different set of elections
for certain Senate seats. The idea here is continuity and stability. If all sitting senators
were up for reelection in the same year, there could be a massive change in membership and a loss of necessary experience.

# Role of the Vice President

The Vice President of the United States shall be President of the Senate, but shall have no Vote, unless they be equally divided.

Article I, Section 3 also provides that the vice president shall be president of the Senate. This means that the vice president can preside over the Senate. However, if the vice president does not preside over the Senate, that duty devolves to the Senate's president pro tempore, or someone designated by the president pro tempore.

The other significant role of the vice president is that of a tie-breaking role. For example, if the Senate is tied 50–50, the vice president can cast the deciding vote. Some vice presidents have cast many tie-breaking votes in American history. John C. Calhoun (1782–1850), Andrew Jackson's (1767–1845) vice president, cast 31 different tie-breaking votes from 1825 to 1832. The very first vice president, John Adams (1735–1826), has the second highest number of tie-breaking votes with 29, from 1789 to 1797.

# President Pro Tempore

The Senate shall chuse their other Officers, and also a President pro tempore, in the Absence of the Vice President, or when he shall exercise the Office of President of the United States.

The president pro tempore, or president pro tem, presides over the Senate in the absence of the vice president. Because the vice president has many duties in the executive branch—including representing the United States in many foreign countries—the day-to-day activities often fall to the president pro tempore.

The Senate elects the president pro tempore. Traditionally, the honor often goes to the longest serving senator of the majority party. The Senate's president pro tempore is third in line for presidential succession behind the vice president and the Speaker of the House. Aside from being in the line of presidential succession, the president pro tem lacks the authority of the Senate majority and minority leaders.

# Impeachment Trials

The Senate shall have the sole Power to try all Impeachments. When sitting for that Purpose, they shall be on Oath or Affirmation. When the President of the United States is tried, the Chief Justice shall preside: And no Person shall be convicted without the Concurrence of two thirds of the Members present.

Judgment in Cases of Impeachment shall not extend further than to removal from Office, and disqualification to hold and enjoy any Office of honor, Trust or Profit under the United States: but the Party convicted shall nevertheless be liable and subject to Indictment, Trial, Judgment and Punishment, according to Law.

While the House has the sole power of impeachment, the Senate holds the impeachment trials. The Constitution requires that senators take an oath or affirmation when they preside over impeachment proceedings. This provision also provides that the chief justice of the United States presides over the Senate impeachment trials of presidents. Thus, Chief Justice Salmon P. Chase (1808–1873) presided over the impeachment trial of President Andrew Johnson (18-08–1875); Chief Justice William H. Rehnquist (1924–2005) presided over the impeachment trial of President Bill Clinton (1946–); and Chief Justice John G. Roberts Jr. (1955–) presided over the first impeachment trial of President Donald J. Trump (1946–). (President pro tems preside over impeachment trials involving nonpresidents. Since Trump was no longer president during his second impeachment trial, Senator Patrick Leahy presided over the trial.)

Although there have been several impeachment trials, no U.S. president has yet been thrown out of office by the Senate. The closest it has come to that was when President Richard M. Nixon resigned in order to avoid impeachment.

The Constitution also requires that the senators must vote by a two-thirds majority to convict a president during the impeachment trial. This has resulted in no president ever being found guilty in an impeachment trial.

If a person is convicted after impeachment, they are removed from office but not subject to further criminal penalties. However, the person removed from office may be disqualified from holding future office.

# Elections

The Times, Places and Manner of holding Elections for Senators and Representatives, shall be prescribed in each State by the Legislature thereof; but the Congress may at any time by Law make or alter such Regulations, except as to the Places of chusing Senators.

Article I, Section 4 begins with a provision that provides that each individual state establishes the time, place, and manner of elections. However, the provision also says that Congress can change the rules. The problem often becomes a matter of politics, as both political parties often seek to redraw district lines to increase their political representations in Congress. Both political parties act for partisan advantages, all to control the House and Senate.

# Meet at Least Once a Year

The Congress shall assemble at least once in every Year, and such Meeting shall be on the first Monday in December, unless they shall by Law appoint a different Day.

Article I, Section 4 also provides that the Congress shall meet at least once a year. Readers may ask about this provision, as Congress meets all the time during most of the year. The Framers included this provision, however, to avoid the problems faced by colonial legislatures, which often were not allowed to meet because of the arbitrary actions of royal governors. The Constitution provides that Congress shall convene the first Monday in December, but that changed with the Twentieth Amendment, which provided that Congress would meet beginning each year on January 3.

# Each House and Its Members

Each House shall be the Judge of the Elections, Returns and Qualifications of its own Members, and a Majority of each shall constitute a Quorum to do Business; but a smaller Number may adjourn from day to day, and may be authorized to compel the Attendance of absent Members, in such Manner, and under such Penalties as each House may provide.

Article I, Section 5 establishes the rules of each body of Congress. It begins with the language that each house of Congress can judge its elections. This means that in a razor-thin election, a losing party might petition Congress and question even the recount in their own state. Perhaps the most notorious example of this was the bitter 1984 House race in Indiana between Democratic incumbent Frank McCloskey (1939–2003) and his Republican challenger, Richard D. McIntyre (1956–2007).

McIntyre, the Republican challenger, had been declared the winner by 34 votes one day after the election and by 418 votes after a state-ordered recount. However, McCloskey petitioned the House, and the General Accounting Office deemed that McCloskey actually won the election by four votes. A three-member task force in the House recommended to the full House that McCloskey be declared the winner.

In March 1985, the full House then voted 236 to 190 in favor of the Democratic incumbent McCloskey. Many Republicans stormed out of the House in protest, accusing their Democratic colleagues of "abuse of power" and "legislative tyranny." The Republicans then vowed to institute a series of "McIntyre" reforms to ensure this did not happen again in the future.

Article I, Section 5 also speaks to the qualifications of members of Congress. However, if a person is qualified and wins election to the House, it is highly questionable whether Congress may refuse to seat that person. This occurred in the 1960s with the reelection of Adam Clayton Powell Jr. (1908–1972), a powerful congressman from New York.

Reports surfaced about improprieties with Powell's travel budget and payments to his spouse. The House refused to honor Powell's seat in Congress. Powell and 13 voters from his 18th congressional district in New York then sued the Speaker of the House for his House seat. Powell's lawsuit alleged that he was effectively expelled from the House but without the necessary two-thirds majority required by Congress to remove one of its members. While his suit was pending, Powell was reelected in the 1968 congressional elections and seated in Congress. The U.S. Supreme Court ultimately ruled in *Powell v. McCormack* (1969) that the House could not create additional qualifications for office other than those provided for in Article I.

Article I, Section 5 also speaks of the necessity of a quorum for the House and Senate to do their work. This makes sense, because without a quorum requirement, the business of Congress could be completed by a minority of legislators. The thinking is that it would not be in the country's best interest to have the people's business conducted by only a few legislators.

# Punish and Expel

Each House may determine the Rules of its Proceedings, punish its Members for disorderly Behaviour, and, with the Concurrence of two thirds, expel a Member.

Each House can determine how it operates—what rules of parliamentary proceedings that it adopts. It also means that the House controls the House, and the Senate controls the Senate. In other words, one house of Congress cannot dictate to the other house how it operates. The House Rules Committee sets the rules for its members. For example, the House sets time limits for how long its members can speak on the legislative floor.

The provision also provides that each house can punish its members for "disorderly Behaviour." This can take the form of an expulsion, but that requires a two-thirds vote—something unlikely to happen in the current two-party system. Neither political party will want to lose a member when the balance of power between the two parties is so close.

The Senate has expelled 15 senators. Most of these were for supporting the Confederacy during the time of the Civil War. Several senators have resigned when confronted with expulsion proceedings. For example, Robert W. Packwood (1932–), a Republican senator from Oregon, resigned from office in 1995 for sexual misconduct and abuse of power.

There are less drastic forms of punishment, including a censure. A censure is a significant action that does not lead to expulsion but can lead to a member losing prestigious committee positions. In Senate history, only nine senators ever have been censured. They are listed in the table on page 60.

The House also has seen its fair share of censures in its history, beginning with the 1832 censure of House member William Stanberry (1788–1873) of Ohio, who was censured for insulting Andrew Stevenson (1784–1857), the Speaker of the House. Stanberry said Stevenson's eye might be "too frequently turned from the chair you occupy toward the White House." Some of the censures

The most recent case of a senator being censured is that of David Durenberger. The Senate voted unanimously against him for ethics violations, including collecting $40,000 in travel reimbursements against the rules and taking over $100,000 in speaking fees.

appear harsh. Consider that in February 1868, Rep. Fernando Wood (1812–1881) of New York was censured for referring to a piece of legislation as "a monstrosity, a measure of the most infamous of the many infamous acts of this infamous Congress." The legendary Charles Rangel (1930–) of New York was censured for misuse of congressional letterhead for fundraising and inaccurate federal tax returns.

| Senator | Year Expelled | Reason |
| --- | --- | --- |
| Timothy Pickering | 1811 | Reading confidential documents |
| Benjamin Tappan | 1844 | Releasing a confidential vote to the press |
| Benjamin R. Tillman and John R. McLaughlin | 1902 | Fighting in the Senate |
| Hiram Bingham | 1929 | Employing a lobbyist on his staff |
| Joseph McCarthy | 1954 | Abuse of power |
| Thomas Dodd | 1967 | Using political campaign funds for personal gain |
| Herman Talmadge | 1979 | Improper financial conduct |
| David Durenberger | 1990 | Personal use of campaign money |

The House has an even lesser form of punishment known as a reprimand. It represents a less serious expression of disapproval than a censure. The first known reprimand in House history came in 1976, when the House reprimanded Robert L. F. Sikes (1906–1994) of Florida for using his office for personal gain. Sikes had failed to reveal that he had a financial interest in two companies that did business with the government. Some of the reprimands in House history are for interesting conduct. For example, Barney Frank (1940–) of Massachusetts was reprimanded for fixing parking tickets in 1990, and Joe Wilson (1947–) of South Carolina was reprimanded in 2009 for interrupting President Barack Obama's (1961–) remarks to a joint session of the House and Senate, which was found to be a "breach of decorum and degraded the proceedings of the joint session."

# Keeping a Journal

Each House shall keep a Journal of its Proceedings, and from time to time publish the same, excepting such Parts as may in their Judgment require Secrecy; and the Yeas and Nays of the Members of either House on any question shall, at the Desire of one fifth of those Present, be entered on the Journal.

The United States prides itself on open government, operating in the open rather than in shrouds of secrecy. This is somewhat ironic, as the Founding Convention of 1787 was conducted in absolute secrecy. Nevertheless, the Constitution begins with the words "We the People," and the elected representatives are supposed to serve the people. The Constitution requires both the House and Senate to keep a journal of its proceedings.

## Both Houses Working Together

Neither House, during the Session of Congress, shall, without the Consent of the other, adjourn for more than three days, nor to any other Place than that in which the two Houses shall be sitting.

The last clause in Article I, Section 5 is premised on the concept of efficiency, that Congress will be more effective if both Houses are working at the same time in the same general location. The Framers also wanted to avoid certain cagey legislators seeking an adjournment of their House to avoid voting on a measure or to engage in dilatory action merely to stall legislation. Furthermore, sometimes there needs to be some synergy between both houses of Congress in making sure that companion bills in the House and Senate are cleaned up.

## Compensation; Speech and Debate Clause

The Senators and Representatives shall receive a Compensation for their Services, to be ascertained by Law, and paid out of the Treasury of the United States. They shall in all Cases, except Treason, Felony and Breach of the Peace, be privileged from Arrest during their Attendance at the Session of their respective Houses, and in going to and returning from the same; and for any Speech or Debate in either House, they shall not be questioned in any other Place.

The first clause of Article I, Section 6 ensures that members of Congress will be paid out of the U.S. Treasury, by the federal government, instead of the individual states. This provision ensures that the representatives are federal, not state, officers. This differs from the Articles of Confederation, which had representatives paid by the respective states.

The next clause is one of the more interesting ones in the Constitution—the Speech and Debate Clause. Legislative attorney Todd Garvey explains that this

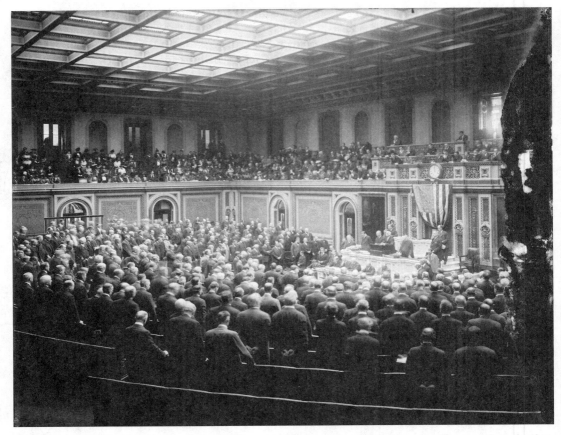

The Speech and Debate Clause in the U.S. Constitution protects congressional leaders from fear of persecution or legal action for speaking their minds during debates and speeches. It protects Congress from interference by the judicial or executive branches.

clause is a "key pillar" in the concept of separation of powers, shielding members of Congress from intrusions by the executive and judicial branches. Garvey explains: "The Clause, which derives its form from the language of the English Bill of Rights and has deep roots in the historic struggles between King and Parliament, serves chiefly to protect the independence, integrity, and effectiveness of the legislative branch by barring executive or judicial intrusions into the protected sphere of the legislative process."

This measure ensures that members of Congress have absolute immunity from prosecution or questioning for their speeches and comments in Congress. The Clause provides ample room for free debate. Legislators do not have to worry that their speech might lead to prosecution or other sorts of legal trouble. Thus, a key facet of the Speech and Debate Clause is that legislators receive both criminal and civil immunity for their legislative acts—not just their speech but their work product in Congress.

While there is no disagreement about the scope of the clause to protect legislators for prosecution for their speech in Congress, lower courts disagree about whether the Speech and Debate Clause extends beyond this to prohibit the disclosure of legislative documents during an investigation. For example, let's say that agents of the FBI raid the office of a member of Congress to look for evidence of criminal wrongdoing. Can the member assert that any legislative documents are immune from executive branch scrutiny because they are protected by the Speech and Debate Clause? The argument for the legislator would be that the legislator should have the ability, under the Speech and Debate Clause, to examine the documents to determine whether they are covered by the privileges afforded by the Speech and Debate Clause before they are examined by federal agents. Garvey explains, in a report for the Congressional Research Service, that the extent of these privileges has divided lower courts and is "ripe for Supreme Court review."

# Emoluments and Incompatibility Clauses

No Senator or Representative shall, during the Time for which he was elected, be appointed to any civil Office under the Authority of the United States, which shall have been created, or the Emoluments whereof shall have been encreased during such time; and no Person holding any Office under the United States, shall be a Member of either House during his Continuance in Office.

The last clauses in Article I, Section 6 appear to provide that a member of Congress not take a position when the salary of that position has been increased by Congress. The Framers' idea was that members of Congress should not be able to create high-paying jobs for themselves, as some members of Parliament had done. For example, in 1987, President Ronald Reagan (1911–2004) had considered the possibility of elevating Senator Orrin Hatch (1934–) to the U.S. Supreme Court. The question was whether such an appointment would violate this provision of the Constitution since the salary of Supreme Court justices had increased while Hatch was a senator. Even more recently, the issue resurfaced when President Barack Obama appointed Hillary Clinton (1947–) to be his secretary of state. The potential problem was that the salary for secretary of state had increased while Clinton was a U.S. senator. The Office of Legal Counsel for the Department of Justice had different positions on this. The department reasoned that the Hatch appointment would be unconstitutional, and that Hatch could only be appointed when his Senate term ended. However, the office reached a different conclusion with regard to the Clinton appointment.

One response to this was the so-called "Saxbe fix." This refers to when President Richard Nixon (1913–1994) wanted Senator William Saxbe (1916–2010) to be his attorney general. The problem was that the U.S. attorney general position had an increase in pay during Saxbe's congressional tenure. So Saxbe took a pay cut so that he would not violate this part of the Constitution.

The last clause provides that no member of Congress can become an officer of the United States in the executive branch. This means, for example, that a member of the House or Senate cannot become a member of the president's cabinet. Such a dual appointment would destroy the concept of separation of powers and present conflict of interest problems.

What is most interesting is that only Article I has such an Incompatibility Clause. This means that there is no similar textual limitation on members of the executive and judicial branches. There have been times, for example, when U.S. Supreme Court justices performed executive branch functions. A prime example of this is when U.S. secretary of state John Marshall (1755–1835) also held the position of chief justice of the United States. Similarly, Chief Justice John Jay (1745–1829) negotiated a significant peace treaty on behalf of President George Washington's (1732–1799) administration. Such double duty by government officials is viewed as an anachronism today, but there remains no incompatibly clauses for the executive and judicial branches.

# Origination Clause

All Bills for raising Revenue shall originate in the House of Representatives; but the Senate may propose or concur with Amendments as on other Bills.

Article I, Section 7 begins with the Origination Clause—that all revenue bills must originate in the House of Representatives rather than the Senate. The Framers took the Origination Bill from England, where revenue bills had to originate in the House of Commons rather than the House of Lords. The thinking behind the Origination Clause is that it is better to have revenue bills originate in the House of Congress, which is more responsive to the people. Note, however, that the Senate can propose amendments to revenue bills, giving the more deliberate body a say in the process.

# Presentment Clause

Every Bill which shall have passed the House of Representatives and the Senate, shall, before it become a Law, be presented to the President of the United States; If he approve he shall sign it, but if not he shall return it, with his Objections to that House in which it shall have originated, who shall enter the Objections at large on their Journal, and proceed to reconsider it. If after such Reconsideration two thirds of that House shall agree to pass the Bill, it shall be sent, together with the Objections, to the other House, by which it shall likewise be reconsidered, and if approved by two thirds of that House, it shall become a Law. But in all such Cases the Votes of both Houses shall be determined by Yeas and Nays, and the Names of the Persons voting for and against the Bill shall be entered on the Journal of each House respectively. If any Bill shall not be returned by the President within ten Days (Sundays excepted) after it shall have been presented to him, the Same shall be a Law, in like Manner as if he had signed it, unless the Congress by their Adjournment prevent its Return, in which Case it shall not be a Law.

Article I, Section 7 provides that every bill that passes Congress must be presented to the president for signature. The president can sign the bill, in which the case the bill becomes law. The president can object to the bill. This act is known as the veto. Interestingly, the term "veto" is not mentioned in the Constitution. The president must identity his objections to the bill when issuing a veto.

The president has ten days to either sign the bill or veto it. The Constitution provides, however, that Congress can override a presidential veto by reconsidering the measure and passing it by a two-thirds supermajority. When Congress passes a bill by a supermajority, the bill does not need to be presented to the president. Thus, Congress by a two-thirds majority can still pass a bill even after a presidential objection or veto.

If the president does not sign the bill or veto within the ten days, then the bill automatically becomes law unless Congress adjourns before the running of the ten days. Such a situation is known as a pocket veto. The Congressional Research Service explains:

For example, if a bill were to be presented to the President in the 116th Congress,

President Warren G. Harding is shown here signing a bill. Every bill that is passed by Congress needs to go to the president for a signature or veto.

The Constitution Explained

and the bill presentment period extended beyond January 3, 2021, an unsigned bill could not be received by the since-concluded 116th Congress. A new bill and process to pass the measure would have to begin in the 117th Congress for it to become law.

Thus, Congress cannot override a pocket veto. To avoid this situation, Congress simply has to present bills to the president and be available to meet without adjournment after the ten-day presentment period has passed.

# Presentment of Resolutions Clause

Every Order, Resolution, or Vote to which the Concurrence of the Senate and House of Representatives may be necessary (except on a question of Adjournment) shall be presented to the President of the United States; and before the Same shall take Effect, shall be approved by him, or being disapproved by him, shall be repassed by two thirds of the Senate and House of Representatives, according to the Rules and Limitations prescribed in the Case of a Bill.

The Presentment of Resolutions Clause provides that any measure requiring the affirmance of both houses of Congress must be presented to the president. In other words, Congress cannot avoid the reach of the Presentment Clause by classifying its measure as a resolution or order rather than a bill. For example, when Congress declares war, it does so in the form of a joint resolution. Such a joint resolution must be presented to the president.

The Supreme Court emphasized the importance of this clause in the case *INS v. Chadha* (1983), writing: "Presentment to the President and the Presidential veto were considered so imperative that the draftsmen took special pains to assure that these requirements could not be circumvented. During the final debate on Art. I, § 7, cl. 2, James Madison [(1751–1836)] expressed concern that it might easily be evaded by the simple expedient of calling a proposed law a 'resolution' or 'vote,' rather than a 'bill.'"

The Court in *Chadha* ruled unconstitutional a provision in an immigration law that allowed one house of Congress to veto an action by the attorney general of the United States. The Court reasoned that under the Constitution, the veto power resided with the president, not Congress.

It bears mentioning that in the *Chadha* case, those defending the immigration measure that allowed for one-house vetoes emphasized that it was much more efficient than the cumbersome method provided by the Presentment Clause of Article

I, Section 7 and the requirement of bicameralism. The Supreme Court responded with a civics lesson:

> The choices we discern as having been made in the Constitutional Convention impose burdens on governmental processes that often seem clumsy, inefficient, even unworkable, but those hard choices were consciously made by men who had lived under a form of government that permitted arbitrary governmental acts to go unchecked. There is no support in the Constitution or decisions of this Court for the proposition that the cumbersomeness and delays often encountered in complying with explicit constitutional standards may be avoided, either by the Congress or by the President. *See Youngstown Sheet & Tube Co. v. Sawyer* (1952). With all the obvious flaws of delay, untidiness, and potential for abuse, we have not yet found a better way to preserve freedom than by making the exercise of power subject to the carefully crafted restraints spelled out in the Constitution.

# Article I, Section 8

## Tax and Spend Clauses

> The Congress shall have Power to lay and collect Taxes, Duties, Imposts and Excises, to pay the Debts and provide for the common Defense and general Welfare of the United States; but all Duties, Imposts and Excises shall be uniform throughout the United States....

Article I, Section 8 may be the most important part of Article I, because it lists the powers of Congress. These powers are broad and extensive, though Article I also imposes some limitations on the powers of Congress in the next section.

Congress has the broad power of taxation. Congress later passed the Sixteenth Amendment, which gave Congress the power to impose an income tax, but the power to tax is truly an awesome power of Congress. Congress, after all, is the branch of government that has the power of the purse.

Congress's taxing power came into prominence in a hotly debated Supreme Court decision, *National Federation of Independent Business v. Sebelius* (2012), often called the ObamaCare case. The Supreme Court narrowly upheld 5–4 a provision of the healthcare law that required persons to purchase health insurance. In his opinion, Chief Justice John G. Roberts Jr. reasoned that this individual mandate (to purchase health insurance or pay a penalty) provision was a tax and fell within Congress's taxing power. Roberts explained that the individual mandate is calculated like a tax in the sense that it is based on a percentage of a person's income.

President Obama and Vice President Biden celebrate the passage of the Affordable Care Act in 2010, which was later upheld in the U.S. Supreme Court case of *National Federation of Independent Business v. Sebelius.*

Justice Antonin Scalia (1936–2016) bitterly disagreed, writing that "our cases establish a clear line between a tax and a penalty" and that the individual mandate is a penalty, not a tax.

Congress also has the power to spend money for the general welfare of the country. Generally speaking, Congress has broad power to spend money however it wants provided that it does not violate another provision of the Constitution. The Supreme Court ruled in *Steward Machine Co. v. Davis* (1937) that Congress could, under the Social Security Act, provide for unemployment compensation. The Court identified this as falling within Congress's spending clause powers.

Similarly, Congress had the authority under its Spending Clause powers to provide for an older age pension program in the Social Security Act. The Supreme Court upheld this part of the Social Security Act as yet another example of Congress's Spending Clause powers.

The reach of the Spending Clause powers extends to congressional conditions on grants to state governments. In other words, Congress has the ability to place conditions on grants to state and local governments as long as the conditions are clear, there is a relationship to the purpose of the spending programs, and they are not too coercive.

The breadth of Congress's Spending Clause powers can be seen through the Supreme Court decision in *South Dakota v. Dole* (1987). South Dakota at the time allowed persons to purchase alcohol if they were at least 19 years old. In 1984, Congress passed a federal law directing the secretary of transportation to withhold a percentage of federal highway funds from those states that allow persons under 21 years of age to purchase alcohol.

South Dakota then sued the United States, contending that the federal law violates the constitutional limitations of Congress's Spending Clause powers and violates the Twenty-first Amendment of the Constitution, which empowers states to regulate the sale of alcoholic beverages.

The U.S. Supreme Court upheld the federal law as a valid exercise of congressional authority under the Spending Clause. First, the Court determined that the law was in pursuit of the general welfare. Writing for the majority, Chief Justice William Rehnquist found that the law easily served the general welfare. He also found that the law had a clear purpose, writing that "the condition imposed by Congress is directly related to one of the main purposes for which highway funds are expended—safe interstate travel."

The majority also determined that the law was not too coercive, because it only withheld 5 percent of the available federal funds. The Court recognized that at some point financial inducements could cross the line into unconstitutional coercion—but this was not one of those situations.

Justices William Brennan (1906–1997) and Sandra Day O'Connor (1930–) both wrote dissenting opinions. Brennan wrote that the Twenty-first Amendment provides that states, not the federal government, have the power to regulate alcohol sales. For her part, Justice O'Connor wrote that "establishment of a minimum drinking age of 21 is not sufficiently related to interstate highway construction to justify so conditioning funds appropriated for that purpose."

## Borrow Money

To borrow Money on the credit of the United States

The second clause of Article I, Section 8 provides that Congress can "borrow money on the credit of the United States." Congress does this by issuing bonds, creating and adding to the country's national debt.

# Commerce Clause

To regulate Commerce with foreign Nations, and among the several states, and with the Indian Tribes.

Congress's greatest power hub is its Commerce Clause power. The Commerce Clause has been used to justify federal civil rights laws, federal criminal laws, securities laws, environmental laws, and many others. Constitution law expert Erwin Chemerinsky writes that "[f]rom the perspective of constitutional law, the commerce clause has been the focus of most of the Supreme Court decisions that have considered the scope of congressional power and federalism."

Under the Commerce Clause, Congress can regulate the channels of interstate commerce, the instrumentalities of interstate commerce, and activities that substantially affect the flow of interstate commerce. The channels of interstate commerce would include, for example, highways, waterways, and air channels—the methods by which goods move through the country. The instrumentalities of interstate commerce concern things such as ships, boats, railways, and airplanes. The third category focuses on activities—even if seemingly of a state or local nature—that have a substantial effect on interstate commerce.

Congress has construed its Commerce Clause powers to justify federal civil rights laws, such as the Civil Rights Act of 1964. The Heart of Atlanta Motel, which practiced racial segregation, contended that Congress did not have the authority to pass a law that regulated how it conducted its business. The motel had 216 rooms and was located only a few blocks from two major interstates. However, 75 percent of the guests at the motel were from outside of Georgia, a key fact the Court relied on to talk about the flow of interstate commerce.

The Court in *Heart of Atlanta Motel v. United States* (1964) recounted the extensive congressional testimony that African Americans faced much discrimination and many burdens when traveling through parts of the country that practiced segregation. The Court also noted that much testimony showed that the discrimination was across the United States, not just in the South, and that such uncertainty in obtaining suitable lodging had a real, discernible impact on many African Americans, who opted against travel to avoid such problems.

The Supreme Court explained that "the determinative test of the exercise of power by the Congress under the Commerce Clause is simply whether the activity sought to be regulated is 'commerce which concerns more States than one' and has a real and substantial relation to the national interest." The Court had little trouble in finding that segregated hotel practices had a national impact on commerce and the economy.

The Heart of Atlanta Motel argued that it was a local business that only impacted local affairs, not national matters. The Court was not persuaded; instead, it found ample evidence about the harmful impact that racial discrimination had upon the flow of interstate commerce. The motel also argued that Congress primarily seemed focused on moral wrongs, not economic ones, in passing the Civil Rights Act of 1964.

The Court also rejected this argument, saying that while Congress was concerned with moral wrongs too, Congress had established through its hearings and debates that the moral wrong of racial discrimination had very real and negative impacts on interstate commerce.

On the very same day, the Supreme Court also upheld the application of the Civil Rights Act of 1964 to a Birmingham, Alabama, restaurant, Ollie's Barbecue, which contended that it had the right to exclude African Americans from seating in its main seating area. The restaurant allowed African Americans to order food and pick it up from the back of the restaurant, but African Americans were not allowed to dine in the restaurant.

> *The Heart of Atlanta motel argued that it was a local business that only impacted local affairs, not national matters. The Court was not persuaded.*

The owners of the restaurant argued that their activities were local in nature and that Congress could not reach their local activities through the Commerce Clause. The Court noted that evidence showed that nearly half of the meat procured by the restaurant came from out of state. "The record is replete with testimony of the burdens placed on interstate commerce by racial discrimination in restaurants," Justice Tom C. Clark (1899–1977) wrote for the Court. "A comparison of per capita spending by [African Americans] in restaurants, theaters, and like establishments indicated less spending, after discounting income differences, in areas where discrimination is widely practiced." He concluded:

The power of Congress in this field is broad and sweeping; where it keeps within its sphere and violates no express constitutional limitation it has been the rule of this Court, going back almost to the founding days of the Republic, not to interfere. The Civil Rights Act of 1964, as here applied, we find to be plainly appropriate in the resolution of what the Congress found to be a national commercial problem of the first magnitude. We find it in no violation of any express limitations of the Constitution and we therefore declare it valid.

Since the New Deal era, the Supreme Court has interpreted the Commerce Clause quite broadly, giving Congress a wide berth when it came to passing laws premised on its Commerce Clause powers. In fact, from 1937 until 1995, the Supreme Court did not rule a single federal law as exceeding Congress's powers under the clause.

Justice Tom C. Clark wrote an opinion that racism in America does impact interstate commerce negatively, and Congress, therefore, could pass legislation against it under the Commerce Clause.

That finally changed in *United States v. Lopez* (1995), a case involving a 12th-grade student at Edison High School in San Antonio, Texas, who was charged with violating a federal law known as the Gun-Free School Zones Act of 1990. The law prohibited an individual from knowingly carrying a firearm within 1,000 feet of a school. Alfonso Lopez was found with a concealed .38 caliber handgun and five bullets. He said he needed the gun for self-defense.

However, federal authorities prosecuted him for violating the Gun-Free School Zones law. Lopez waived his right to a jury trial. At a bench trial, the judge found him guilty and sentenced him to six months in prison and two years of supervised release.

Lopez's attorney challenged the constitutionality of the Gun-Free School Zones Act and lost in the lower courts, but the U.S. Supreme Court reversed in a stunning victory. Writing for a five-justice majority, Chief Justice William Rehnquist identified the operative question as whether the regulated activity in this case—gun possession—substantially affects interstate commerce. Rehnquist reasoned that the law is a "criminal statute that by its terms has nothing to do with 'commerce' or any sort of economic enterprise."

Rehnquist reasoned that possession of a handgun "in a local school zone is in no sense an economic activity that might, through repetition elsewhere, substantially affect any sort of interstate commerce." He noted Lopez was a local student at a local school and there was no evidence that Lopez had traveled out of state with the gun.

Ultimately, Rehnquist reasoned that this was a matter for state or local regulation, not federal regulation. In a concurring opinion, Justice Anthony Kennedy (1936–) noted that more than 40 states already have laws on the books prohibiting the possession of guns at or near schools. Justice Clarence Thomas (1948–) would have gone even further than his colleagues in the majority. He called for the Court to "temper our Commerce Clause jurisprudence" and reject the substantial effects interstate commerce test. "My review of the case law indicates that the substantial effects test is but an innovation of the 20th century." Thomas worried most about what he called "the aggregation principle." Under the aggregation principle, a single item may not substantially affect interstate commerce, but when one considers that product in aggregation across multiple state lines and in multiple locations, it might have a substantial impact on interstate commerce.

Four justices dissented. Justice John Paul Stevens (1920–2019) wrote that "guns are articles of commerce and articles that can be used to restrain commerce." He added that the possession of guns is commercial activity. Justice David Souter (1939–) also wrote a dissent, and he emphasized the aggregation principle. He said that to consider whether the gun had a substantial impact on interstate commerce, you don't just consider the single gun possessed by Alfonso Lopez but "rather the cumulative effect of all similar instances (i.e., the effect of all guns possessed in or near schools)." Souter added that Congress could have found, "given the effect of education upon interstate and foreign commerce, that gun-related violence in and around schools is a commercial, as well as a human, problem."

The Court reached a similar result in a case styled *United States v. Morrison* (2000), examining a federal law known as the Violence Against Women Act, which provided a federal civil remedy for victims of gender-related violence. Christy Brzonkala, a student at Virginia Tech University, alleged that two members of the Virginia Tech football team, including Antonio Morrison, assaulted and raped her. She filed a complaint under the school's sexual assault policy.

Chief Justice William Rehnquist reasoned that sometimes the government was overstepping the intention of the Commerce Clause in applying it to non-economic crimes.

Morrison admitted that he had sexual contact with Brzonkala, and a school judicial committee suspended him for two semesters. Morrison indicated that he intended to challenge this process in federal court, and the school held a second hearing at which Morrison was only found to have committed the offense of "using abusive language." Virginia Tech's administration set aside Morrison's punishment, and Brzonkala dropped out of school.

She later sued Morrison, the other player, and Virginia Tech in federal court under the Violence Against Women Act of 1994. Once again, the Supreme Court found that Congress had exceeded its powers under the Commerce Clause in passing this federal law, which had no substantial impact on the economy. "We accordingly reject the argument that Congress may regulate noneconomic, violent criminal conduct based solely on that conduct's aggregate effect on interstate commerce," Chief Justice Rehnquist wrote for the majority.

Justice Thomas again wrote separately to question the Court's use of a "substantial effects" test. He warned that "[u]ntil this Court replaces its existing Commerce Clause jurisprudence with a standard more consistent with the original understanding, we will continue to see Congress appropriating state police powers under the guise of regulating commerce."

To the majority, particularly Justice Thomas, Congress had stepped into the role of the states in passing this federal civil rights law that was more appropriately addressed at the state level.

Justice Souter wrote a dissenting opinion, noting that there was a "mountain of data assembled by Congress, here showing the effects of violence against women on interstate commerce."

However, since 2005, it appears that the Supreme Court has been more deferential to Congress's broad powers under the Commerce Clause. The Court, for example, upheld the application of the federal Controlled Substances Act (CSA), which criminalizes marijuana. This federal law conflicted with a California law, called the Compassionate Use Act of 1996, which allowed for the medicinal use of marijuana. Two women, Angel Raich and Diane Monson, who needed marijuana to combat crippling physical pain filed a federal lawsuit challenging the application of the federal CSA to their in-state use and growth of a few marijuana plants.

|| *The U.S. Supreme Court upheld the federal law, noting that "Congress had a rational basis* || *for concluding that leaving home-consumed marijuana outside federal control would similarly* || *affect price and market conditions."*

The U.S. Supreme Court upheld the federal law, noting that "Congress had a rational basis for concluding that leaving home-consumed marijuana outside federal control would similarly affect price and market conditions." The Court applied the aggregation principle to find that Congress had a rational basis for passing the law and applying it even to home consumption of marijuana.

Justice Sandra Day O'Connor wrote a dissenting opinion, noting that "the Court's definition of economic activity is breathtaking." She warned that "the Government has made no showing in fact that the possession and use of homegrown marijuana for medicinal purposes, in California or elsewhere, has a substantial effect on interstate commerce." She wrote that "there is simply no evidence that home-grown medicinal marijuana users constitute, in the aggregate, a sizeable enough class to have a discernable, let alone substantial, impact on the national illicit drug market—or otherwise to threaten the CSA regime."

Once again Justice Thomas wrote separately, questioning the Court's modern Commerce Clause jurisprudence. He warned that "[i]f Congress can regulate this under the Commerce Clause, then it can regulate virtually anything—and the Federal government is no longer one of limited and enumerated powers." He also would recognize the ability of a state like California to "provide much-needed respite to the seriously ill."

## Dormant Commerce Clause

We often talk about the Commerce Clause as a positive grant of power to Congress to pass federal legislation that substantially impacts commerce. However, the Commerce Clause has another power—it limits state laws that unduly restrict the free flow of interstate commerce. This is what is known as the Dormant Commerce Clause.

The Dormant Commerce Clause prohibits states from passing laws rooted in economic protectionism that restrict the free flow of goods. Under the Dormant Commerce Clause, if a state law discriminates out-of-state actors or nonresident economic actors, then it is constitutional only if the law is narrowly drawn to serve a very important state interest.

An example of a law deemed to violate the Dormant Commerce Clause was a Tennessee law that imposed a two-year residency requirement on all individuals and businesses who sought to sell liquor. The Supreme Court viewed this as a protectionist measure that discriminated against non-Tennesseans. The Court concluded that the law violated the Dormant Commerce Clause.

## Naturalization and Bankruptcy

To establish an uniform Rule of Naturalization, and uniform Laws on the subject of Bankruptcies throughout the United States....

The Fourth Clause in Article I, Section 8 provides Congress with power over two significant areas of law: immigration and bankruptcy. The Naturalization Clause gives Congress the power to decide naturalization—the process by which a person can become a citizen of the United States. Back in 1892, the Court defined naturalization as "the act of adopting a foreigner, and clothing him with the privileges of a native citizen."

Immigration law is a massive body of law that deals not only with whether and how a person can become a citizen but also when Congress can deport a noncitizen, or alien. Similarly, bankruptcy law also is a matter of federal law. This gives Congress the power to pass various laws that regulate how and why individuals and businesses can obtain bankruptcy relief.

## Coinage Power

To coin Money, regulate the Value thereof, and of foreign Coin, and fix the Standard of Weights and Measures....

Congress has the power to coin money, and this power has been interpreted to cover the regulation of currency in virtually all facets. For example, under this power, Congress can create a national bank, regulate gold and other commodities, and engage in a variety of other revenue-related activities.

## Counterfeiting Power

To provide for the Punishment of counterfeiting the Securities and current Coin of the United States....

Congress also has the power to pass laws regulating counterfeiting and other forgery-related laws.

## Postal Power

To establish Post Offices and post Roads....

Under the postal power, Congress can create new post offices and pass a variety of laws to ensure the safe and effective delivery of the mail. This power also means that state laws that seek to regulate the postal offices or transportation of the mails is superseded by the postal power. The Supreme Court has invalidated state laws that regulate the route of mail travel. It is Congress's power to regulate such travel, not the states'.

## Copyright Clause

To promote the Progress of Science and useful Arts, by securing for limited Times to Authors and Inventors the exclusive Right to their respective Writings and Discoveries....

The Copyright Clause of Article I, Section 8 means that Congress can regulate the law of copyrights, patents, and trademarks. In other words, copyright laws are federal laws, not state laws. Another way of explaining this is that the area of intellectual property is largely governed by federal law, not state law.

The Framers intended for the Copyright Clause to be an engine of free expression, giving inventors protection for their own original creative works. However, when a copyright law restricts speech or prohibits speech from entering the public domain, some argue that such copyright laws infringe on the First Amendment.

The Constitution grants Congress the power to mint coins and print paper money.

Some inherent degree of tension exists between the First Amendment and copyright. Copyright allows creators of expressive conduct to control the flow of certain information and expression, while the First Amendment ensures the free flow of information and expression.

A primary purpose of copyright law is to provide protection for the creator of an expressive work. The main purpose of the First Amendment is to ensure public access to information. Copyright protection reduces access to some information by limiting the extent to which it can be copied by others.

Copyright creates property rights for the creators of certain works. This is why copyright, along with patent and trademark law, is labeled under the rubric of intellectual property. If a person copies another's work without permission, that person has trespassed on the creator's property, or copyrighted expression. This is called copyright infringement. If a person directly copies another's expression, that person has committed direct copyright infringement. If a person or company enables others to commit copyright infringement, they have committed contributory or vicarious infringement.

Copyright exists to increase knowledge. It does so by providing creators with an economic incentive to produce work. Copyright protects "original works of authorship fixed in any tangible medium of expression." It protects books, artwork, sculptures, paintings, musical compositions, and many other forms. The U.S. Supreme Court has written: "It should not be forgotten that the Framers intended copyright itself to be an engine of free expression."

The theory is that copyright law already has built-in free-expression principles that ensure its compatibility with the First Amendment and free expression. These are the fair use doctrine and the idea–expression dichotomy.

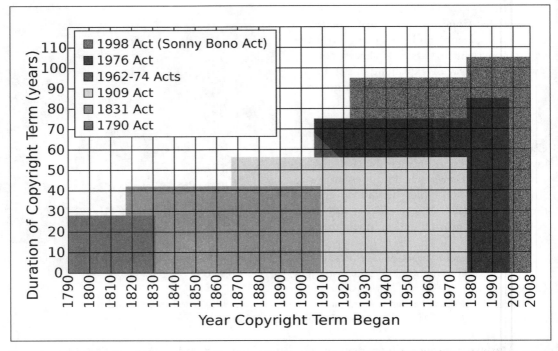

Several copyright laws have been passed over the decades, with each one adding to the length of time applied to a copyrighted work, depending on when it was created, as shown in this chart.

Fair use means that there are times when someone can use someone else's copyrighted work without it constituting infringement. Fair use became an important part of the common, or judge-made, law. The Copyright Act of 1976 incorporated, or codified, the common-law concept of fair use. Section 107 of the 1976 copyright law begins with a preamble: "The fair use of a copyrighted work ... for purposes such as criticism, comment, news reporting, teaching (including multiple copies for classroom use), scholarship, or research, is not an infringement of copyright." For example, a book reviewer could quote portions of a book in writing her review without committing copyright infringement. The book reviewer's quotations would qualify as fair use.

Copyright law lists four nonexclusive factors as especially relevant in determining fair use:

1. The purpose and character of the use, including whether such use is of a commercial nature or is for nonprofit educational purposes.

2. The nature of the copyrighted work.

3. The proportion of material that was copied.

4. The effect of the potential market for or value of the copyrighted work.

The idea–expression dictomony recognizes that if copyright law is too rigid, then there will be a dramatic reduction in the public's access to information. Copyright law attempts to resolve this dilemma to a degree by distinguishing between expression and ideas. This is called the idea–expression dichotomy.

> *Copyright law attempts to resolve this dilemma to a degree by distinguishing between expression and ideas. This is called the idea–expression dichotomy.*

The Supreme Court has been very reluctant to find copyright laws as violative of the First Amendment. The Court tends to reason that copyright law already has these built-in protections for free speech—the idea–expression dichotomy and the fair use doctrine.

The Supreme Court upheld Congress's copyright clause power to pass the Copyright Term Extension Act of 1998, a law that extended the terms of copyright protection by 20 years. The Court, in an opinion by Justice Ruth Bader Ginsburg (1933–2020), did not see the law as an incursion into free-speech principles. "Copyright law contains built-in First Amendment accommodations," she wrote, noting the fair use doctrine and the idea–expression dichotomy.

Similarly, Ginsburg wrote the court's majority opinion in *Golan v. Holder* (2012), rejecting a First Amendment challenge to a U.S. copyright law that extended copyright protection to some foreign works that had previously been in the public domain. Ginsburg viewed the law as an attempt for the United States to join international copyright law protections rather than a denial of viewpoint or a violation of other generally applicable First Amendment principles. Once again, she viewed copyright law's built-in First Amendment accommodations as sufficient.

## Creating Lower Courts Power

To constitute Tribunals inferior to the supreme Court....

The Constitution calls for one supreme court and such lower courts as Congress deems necessary. Article I, Section 8 further explains that Congress has the power to create lower courts or tribunals. The federal court system is composed of three levels: (1) the federal district court level; (2) the federal circuit court of appeals level; and (3) the U.S. Supreme Court.

The federal district courts are the trial courts in the federal system. There are 94 federal judicial districts in the United States. Some states only have one, while other states have three. A party that loses before a federal district court can then appeal to the federal circuit court of appeals. These are the intermediate appellate courts in the federal system. In 1891, Congress created the Judiciary Act, commonly known as the Evarts Act, which established nine federal circuit courts of appeals. Currently, there are 13 federal circuit courts of appeals. There are 11 numbered circuits (from the 1st Circuit to the 11th Circuit), the D.C. Circuit, and the Federal Circuit.

The power to create inferior tribunals means that Congress can create additional federal judicial district courts (trial courts) and additional federal circuit courts of appeals (intermediate appellate courts). In 1982, Congress created the 11th Circuit because the 5th Circuit was considered too large.

The current debate is whether Congress should create a 12th U.S. Circuit Court of Appeals—making the total number 14—because the 9th Circuit is too large. For several years, proposals have been introduced into Congress to break up the 9th Circuit into two circuits. In June 2021, the 9th Circuit Court of Appeals Judgeship and Reorganization Act of 2021 was introduced. Under this proposal, federal courts from Alaska, Arizona, Idaho, Montana, Nevada, Oregon, and Washington would become the 12th U.S. Circuit Court of Appeals instead of the 9th Circuit.

## Piracy Power

To define and punish Piracies and Felonies committed on the high Seas, and Offences against the Law of Nations;

When the Framers created the Constitution, the fledging nation needed to ensure that its ships were protected on the high seas and oceans. The British Navy was still the dominant force in the world, and other countries—Spain and France—had significant naval forces as well. Piracy was also a problem at that time in the world. We don't generally think of piracy as one of the grave threats facing the nation, but it was a significant problem in the late eighteenth century.

## Power to Declare War

To declare War, grant Letters of Marque and Reprisal, and make Rules concerning Captures on Land and Water;

One of Congress's most significant powers is the power to declare war. This is called the war-making power. Congress has issued formal declarations of war pursuant to this power in five different wars in American history: the War of 1812 with Great Britain, the war with Mexico in 1846, the War with Spain in 1898, the First World War, and the Second World War. In each case, the president, as commander-in-chief, had sought a formal declaration of war from Congress, and Congress ruled in favor of such a declaration.

Congress has thus far created 11 circuit courts of appeal, plus the D.C. Circuit and Federal Circuit.

Congress also has passed different joint resolutions that offer the authorization of the use of force to defend American interests. For example, Congress never formally declared war in either the Korean or the Vietnam conflict. Instead, it was the president who committed American troops to battle. However, Congress did pass a joint resolution, known as the Gulf of Tonkin resolution in 1964, that "promote[d] the maintenance of international peace and security in southeast Asia." Congress ultimately repealed the resolution in 1971 in the wake of increasing unrest and dissension over the Vietnam War.

In 1973, Congress passed the War Powers Act, which purportedly limits the president's power to declare war. Under this law, the president must give notice to Congress of military deployments and remove troops after 60 days if Congress does not authorize the use of military force. The Supreme Court has never ruled on whether the War Powers Act is constitutional.

A somewhat similar occurrence happened in response to the terrorist attacks on U.S. soil on September 11, 2001, when planes crashed into the World Trade Center towers in New York City and the Pentagon in Arlington, Virginia. President George W. Bush (1946–) consulted with leaders of Congress, which overwhelmingly passed a joint resolution sanctioning the president with the ability to take appropriate measures to deal with those responsible for the terrorist attacks. The resolution authorized President Bush:

The president cannot declare war; that is something the Congress has to do, but then the president will need to sign the declaration. President Franklin D. Roosevelt is shown here in 1941 signing the declation of war against Germany.

to use all necessary and appropriate force against those nations, organizations, or persons he determines planned, authorized, committed, or aided the terrorist attacks that occurred on September 11, 2001, or harbored such organizations or persons, in order to prevent any future acts of international terrorism against the United States by such nations, organizations or persons.

The unusual thing about this resolution was that it authorized military force not only against offending countries but also "organizations or persons." This was because the terrorist group al-Qaeda was behind the terrorist attacks, and that organization was not a nation-state. Thus began the so-called War on Terror, which ultimately led to numerous legal conflicts that led to several U.S. Supreme Court decisions.

The clause also speaks about Congress granting letters of marque and reprisal. This is another historical anachronism of sorts, as it deals with sailing ships. Such a letter would authorize private vessels to attack ships of an enemy nation.

Finally, the clause also speaks of Congress having the power to deal with "Captures on Land and Water." This means that Congress can seize the property of those in conflict with the United States. For example, the U.S. government confiscated property owned by some German corporations during World War I and World War II.

## Army and Navy Power

To raise and support Armies, but no Appropriation of Money to that Use shall be for a longer Term than two Years.

To provide and maintain a Navy;

Article I, Section 8 empowers Congress to maintain a professional military service in the form of an army and a navy. During the Revolutionary War, a standing army was of grave concern to the colonists. They feared that the standing army would consist of loyalists—those more loyal to the king of England than the individual colonies.

During the time of the framing, there was no air warfare. The Framers knew that war was fought on land and sea. Thus, there was a need for an army and a navy. However, the advent of air warfare in World War I showed the need for an Air Force. This falls under an implied power of Congress under these two provisions. There is a branch of the U.S. military called the U.S. Marine Corps. Its origins owe to the so-called Continental Marines who fought during the Revolutionary War. In 1834, Congress approved of the Marines as following under a branch of the U.S. Navy. Federal law provides three main statutory duties of the Marines, including:

- Seizure or defense of advanced naval bases and other land operations to support naval campaigns;
- Development of tactics, technique, and equipment used by amphibious landing forces in coordination with the Army and Air Force; and
- Such other duties as the President or Department of Defense may direct.

These clauses also give the Congress the power to approve of various reserve components to the armed forces, such as the U.S. Army Reserves. There are seven components to the armed reserves:

A U.S. Army Reserve sergeant major instructs a U.S. Navy midshipman during a live fire exercise.

- Army National Guard
- Army Reserve
- Navy Reserve
- Marine Corps Reserve
- Air National Guard
- Air Force Reserve
- Coast Guard Reserve

## Rulemaking for Armed Forces

To make Rules for the Government and Regulation of the land and naval forces;

Members of the military operate under a different set of rules than civilians. Members of the military are subject to the Uniform Code of Military Justice. Congress passed the modern version of what is known as the UCMJ in 1950, with President Harry S. Truman (1884–1972) signing the measure into law. The military does not possess all of the legal protections that civilians enjoy under the Bill of Rights.

## Militia Clauses

To provide for calling forth the Militia to execute the Laws of the Union, suppress Insurrections and repel Invasions;

To provide for organizing, arming, and disciplining, the Militia, and for governing such Part of them as may be employed in the Service of the United States, reserving to the States respectively, the Appointment of the Officers, and the Authority of training the Militia according to the discipline prescribed by Congress;

Congress has the power and authority over the militia, though the Constitution gives much of that control to the individual states. The U.S. Supreme Court explained this in *Houston v. Moore* (1820), writing that Congress had strong power over the militia:

being unlimited, except in the two particulars of officering and training them ... it may be exercised to any extent that may be deemed necessary by Congress.... The power of the state government to legislate on the same subjects, having existed prior to the formation of the Constitution, and not having been prohibited by that instrument, it remains with the States, subordinate nevertheless to the paramount law of the General Government.

Congress brought the militias, which had been largely under state control, under the auspices of the federal government with the National Defense Act of 1916. The law divided the militia into the National Guard and the Unorganized Militia. The Unorganized Militia refers to the reserve militia.

## D.C. and the Nation's Capital

To exercise exclusive Legislation in all Cases whatsoever, over such District (not exceeding ten Miles square) as may, by Cession of particular States, and the Acceptance of Congress, become the Seat of Government of the United States, and to exercise like Authority over all Places purchased by the Consent of the Legislature of the State in which the Same shall be, for the Erection of Forts, Magazines, Arsenals, dockYards, and other needful Buildings;

The Framers wanted the nation's capital to be located in an area—a district—free from state control. The Framers also disagreed about where the capital of the

Washington, D.C., was established as separate from the states of Virginia and Maryland with the intention of denying any one state control of the nation's capital.

United States would be. New York City was the initial capital of the United States, but only for one year. Then, the capital city became Philadelphia for ten years.

New York and Philadelphia were not long-term solutions for the capital city, as the Constitution here in Article I, Section 8, Clause 17 calls for the creation of a new federal enclave that would serve as the nation's capital. The Clause also gives Congress plenary power over the laws of this new capital—what became known as the District of Columbia.

The District of Columbia has more than 700,000 residents. There have been several proposed amendments to the Constitution that would give D.C. residents voting representation in Congress, give the District of Columbia to the State of Maryland, and even to make the District of Columbia a separate state. In June 2019, Eleanor Holmes Norton (1937–), a D.C. delegate to Congress, introduced the Washington, D.C. Admission Act, which would have granted D.C. statehood. The measure was reintroduced on January 4, 2021.

## Necessary and Proper Clause

To make all Laws which shall be necessary and proper for carrying into Execution the foregoing Powers, and all other Powers vested by this Constitution in the Government of the United States, or in any Department or Officer thereof.

The Necessary and Proper Clause is the so-called Elastic Clause or Sweeping Clause because it gives Congress many implied powers to carry out its other stated powers in Article I, Section 8. In other words, the Necessary and Proper Clause supplements Congress's other listed powers in the Constitution.

Chief Justice John Marshall gave a broad reading of the Necessary and Proper Clause in the celebrated case of *McCullough v. Maryland* (1819), which asked the fundamental question of whether Congress had the authority to create a national bank. Marshall explained:

> Is this the sense in which the word "necessary" is always used? Does it always import an absolute physical necessity so strong that one thing to which another may be termed necessary cannot exist without that other? We think it does not. We find that it frequently imports no more than that one thing that is convenient, or useful, or essential to another. To employ the means necessary to an end is generally understood as employing any means calculated to produce the end, and not as being confined to those single means, without which the end would be entirely unattainable.... A thing may be necessary, very necessary, absolutely or indispensably necessary.

# Article I, Section 9

## *habeas corpus*

> The Privilege of the Writ of habeas corpus shall not be suspended, unless when in Cases of Rebellion or Invasion the public Safety may require it.

*Habeas corpus*, known as "the Great Writ," essentially means that the government may not hold someone unconstitutionally or arbitrarily arrest someone. Prisoners often file a writ of *habeas corpus* in federal court, contending that their constitutional rights were violated somewhere along the way in their criminal proceedings, often in state criminal court proceedings.

The provision suggests that *habeas corpus* may be suspended during times of rebellion or invasion. President Abraham Lincoln (1809–1865) suspended the writ of *habeas corpus*, except that he did it without congressional approval beforehand, though Congress did ratify his actions. The Supreme Court ruled in *Ex parte Milligan* (1866) that though the suspension of the writ of *habeas corpus* was lawful, a civilian could not be tried via military tribunals. The Court noted that "there should be a power somewhere of suspending the writ of *habeas corpus*.... [The Constitution] does not say that after a writ of *habeas corpus* is denied a citizen ... shall be tried otherwise than by the course of the common law."

*Habeas corpus* says that it is against the Constitution for the government to arbitrarily arrest or imprison someone.

During the War on Terror, the Supreme Court ruled in a series of cases that even enemy combatants detained at Guantanamo Bay, Cuba, had a right to access the courts through a writ of *habeas corpus*.

## Bills of Attainders and Ex Post Facto Laws

> No Bill of Attainder or ex post facto laws shall be passed.

The Constitution prohibits both bills of attainders and ex post facto laws. Bills of attainders are laws in which a legislature targets a person or group of persons and imposes punishment without a trial. The U.S. Supreme Court defined ex post facto laws in *Calder v. Bull* (1798) as "that [which] makes an action done before the passing of the law, and which was *innocent* when done, criminal; and punishes such action," or "that *aggravates* a *crime*, or makes it *greater* than it was, when committed." Thus, an ex post facto law increases the penalty for an existing crime to the detriment of a person who already had committed the crime. Another version of an ex post facto law is a law that makes criminal what was innocent conduct when the person committed the action. Many sex offender registration and notification laws have been challenged as ex post facto laws, but the Supreme Court generally has held that they are not primarily punitive and deemed them not to be ex post facto laws.

## Taxes Must Be Proportional

No Capitation, or other direct, Tax shall be laid, unless in Proportion to the Census or enumeration herein directed before directed to be taken.

This provision requires that capitation, or direct taxes, must be applied proportionally in accordance with the population taken by the census. A direct tax is a tax levied directly on a person or property, as opposed to an indirect tax, which is levied on an activity, such as importing goods. The provision's mention of proportionality was done to try to ensure that states were taxed only to their proportional share, that rural areas with less population would not face crushing taxes.

## Limits on Congress Taxing States

No Tax or Duty shall be laid on Articles exported from any State.

No Preference shall be given by any Regulation of Commerce or Revenue to the Ports of one State over those of another; nor shall Vessels bound to, or from, one State, be obliged to enter, clear, or pay Duties in another.

These two provisions try to ensure that Congress treats states fairly and does not tax them to death like the English Crown. The first provision bans export taxes. The idea here is that it would be unfair for Congress to impose a tax on a particular crop grown mainly in one state. For example, this provision prohibited Congress from imposing export taxes on tobacco, which would hurt Virginia disproportionately, or on cotton, which might hurt Mississippi disproportionately.

The second provision tries to promote the free flow of interstate commerce and not allow a preference to be given to one state over another state when it comes to navigation and trade. In a sense, Congress agreed to not discriminate or pick favorites among states when it came to commerce.

## Appropriations Must Be Authorized

> No Money shall be drawn from the Treasury, but in Consequence of Appropriations made by Law; and a regular Statement and Account of the Receipts and Expenditures of all public Money shall be published from time to time;

It has been said that Congress has the power of the purse. Congress also has the power to make sure that other branches of government are spending money properly. This provision essentially means that Congress authorizes or approves all expenditures. Ultimately, it is the people's money, and thus, there needs to be publication of the public money.

## Titles of Nobility

> No Title of Nobility shall be granted by the United States: And no Person holding any Office of Profit or Trust under them, shall, without the Consent of the Congress, accept of any present, Emolument, Office, or Title, of any kind whatever, from any King, Prince, or foreign state.

The United States is democracy, not a monarchy. The Framers passed this provision in order to ensure that this country did not follow the path of Great Britain. Alexander Hamilton once referred to this provision as "the cornerstone of republican government." It also forbids the president and other federal officials from accepting gifts from foreign governments without congressional permission. In other words, we do not want American officials being bought or persuaded by foreign countries by money.

This provision was little talked about until the presidency of Donald J. Trump, because Trump had substantial business interests—including many hotels—in foreign countries. Some accused President Trump of violating this ban on emoluments.

# Article I, Section 10

Article I, Section 10 imposes a series of limitations not on Congress but on the individual states. It was, after all, a new federal government, and the idea was that states should not be able to thwart the national interests.

President Donald Trump, who in private life owns properties ranging from hotels and casinos to golf resorts and condominiums, has been accused of violating the emoluments clause, especially when it was found that many dignitaries from foreign countries had been patrons of his businesses.

No State shall enter into any Treaty, Alliance, or Confederation; grant Letters of Marque and Reprisal; coin Money; emit Bills of Credit; make any Thing but gold and silver Coin a Tender in Payment of Debts; pass any Bill of Attainder, ex post facto law, or law impairing the Obligation of Contracts, or grant any Title of Nobility.

The Framers wanted to make sure that individual states did not commit egregious wrongs like passing bills of attainders and ex post facto laws or granting titles of nobility. The states cannot deal with foreign governments themselves and enter into treaties; that is the job of the central, federal government.

This provision also contains the Contracts Clause. The Framers passed this largely because states were passing laws granting various debtors a significant amount of relief—often against out-of-state creditors.

No State shall, without the Consent of the Congress, lay any Imposts or Duties on Imports or Exports; except what may be absolutely necessary for executing its inspection Laws; and the net Produce of all Duties and Imposts, laid by any State on Imports or Exports, shall be for the Use of the Treasury of the United States; and all such Laws shall be subject to the Revision and Control of the Congress.

During the time of the Articles of Confederation, some states made a significant amount of money by taxing imports from other states. States engaging in personal, financial gain was part of the reason why there was a need to create a strong, central government to instill some unity and national spirit in the country. This provision gives Congress the power over trade with other states and countries. This was a necessary provision for the creation of a new country.

No State shall, without the Consent of Congress, lay any Duty of Tonnage, keep Troops, or Ships of War in time of Peace, enter into any Agreement or Compact with another State, or with a foreign Power, or engage in War, unless actually invaded, or in such imminent Danger as will not admit of delay.

This provision ensures that states know their place. They are states, not nations. No individual state can enter into war or enter into treaties with foreign countries. Only the United States of America can do these things. States also cannot keep standing armies or engage in war unless they are invaded.

# Article II—The Powers of the Presidency

## The Vesting Clause

The executive Power shall be vested in a President of the United States of America.

Article II examines the powers of the executive branch and does so in just about 1,000 words. Much of the language, as elsewhere in the Constitution, is written in very general terms. However, the first line refers to the fact that "the executive power shall be vested in a President of the United States of America." This first sentence is known as the Vesting Clause. It establishes the office of the presidency. This was no foregone conclusion, as we saw with the Articles of Confederation. Furthermore, the Framers at the Philadelphia Convention actually argued over whether the executive branch should have a single leader or a council of three or more. The most common proposals put forth were a three-person presidency and a one-person presidency. The one-person presidency obviously won out.

The vesting clause, at a minimum, establishes that there is a president. Some contend that this clause gives the president executive powers, which includes various implied powers that are not given explicitly in other provisions of Article II. Some scholars further argue that the Vesting Clause gives the executive a great deal of power. For example, law professor John Yoo writes in his book *The Powers of War and Peace* (2005) that "Article II's Vesting Clause requires that we construe any ambiguities in the allocation of power in favor of the President." This school of thought is associated with the term "unitary executive"—meaning that the president often has the sole authority to act in certain circumstances.

*The vesting clause, at a minimum, establishes that there is a president. Some contend that this clause gives the President executive powers, which includes various implied powers that are not given explicitly in other provisions of Article II.*

Arguments over the Vesting Clause matter most when the president acts in a way that does not seem consonant with the concept of separation of powers. For example, can the president terminate a treaty with a foreign nation without congressional approval? Or can the president interpret a treaty, or does that fall to another branch of government? Again, some legal scholars such as Yoo argue that the Vesting Clause gives the executive branch greater power with regard to treaties.

Those who give Article II's Vesting Clause a more expansive reading compare the language of the Vesting Clause for the executive in Article II with the Vesting Clause for the legislative branch in Article I. Recall that the Vesting Clause in Article I provides: "All legislative powers herein granted shall be vested in a Congress of the United States." Article I's Vesting Clause contains the words "herein granted" while Article II's Vesting Clause does not. To those who favor a more expansive interpretation of presidential power, the difference of these two words "herein granted" are very significant. They contend that the "herein granted" serves to limit Congress's powers to those enumerated or listed in Article I, while the omission of these words in Article II's Vesting Clause mean that the president has a host of nonenumerated powers, or powers not specifically listed.

Other scholars disagree over the significance of the words "herein granted." For example, Louis Fisher in his book *Defending Congress and the Constitution* (2011) argues that Yoo and others are making too much of the slight difference in wording. He points out that Congress, like the president, also has a host of implied powers from those listed in the Constitution and also points to the Necessary and Proper Clause in Article I.

He shall hold his Office during the Term of four Years, and, together with the Vice President, chosen for the same Term, be elected, as follows

Article II provides that the president shall hold four-year terms. The Founders wanted to avoid at all costs the creation of a king, like that found in England. A king could serve for 40 or 50 years. A president can only serve for a limited amount of time. The Constitution originally did not place a limit on the number of terms that a president could serve. Our first president, George Washington (1732–1799), served two terms. He likely could have served for a third term, as he was by far the most popular politician of that era and still considered a hero of the Revolutionary War for many Americans. Washington believed that a president should not serve too long. The Constitution did not solve this issue until the presidency of Franklin Delano Roosevelt (1882–1945), who won election to the presidency four times, passing away early in his fourth term. Roosevelt's four terms led Congress to pass the Twenty-second Amendment, which limits the president to a total of two terms (plus less than two years if the president was serving out the remainder of the previous president's term).

Periodically, a member of Congress will introduce a measure to repeal the Twenty-second Amendment. This usually occurs when a member of Congress is in the same political party of a sitting two-term president and wishes that that person could run for a third term. For example, Democratic representative Barney Frank (1940–) introduced a measure to repeal the Twenty-second Amendment in 1999, toward the end of Democratic president Bill Clinton's second term. Rep. Steny H. Hoyer (1939–), a Democrat, introduced a measure to repeal the Twenty-second Amendment in 2005 as Democratic president Barack Obama (1961–) was entering his second term. However, that is not always the case. In 1995, Republican senator Mitch McConnell (1942–) and Democratic senator Harry Reid (1939–) introduced a joint resolution calling for the repeal of the Twenty-second Amendment.

# The Electoral College

> Each State shall appoint, in such Manner as the Legislature thereof may direct, a Number of Electors, equal to the whole Number of Senators and Representatives to which the State may be entitled in the Congress: but no Senator or Representative, or Person holding an Office of Trust or Profit under the United States, shall be appointed an Elector.

Article II provides that the president shall be elected by the Electoral College. This remains one of the more controversial pieces of language in the U.S. Constitution. Several times in American history, the person who won the popular vote did not win the presidency. In the 2016 election, Democratic candidate Hillary Clinton (1947–) captured more popular votes than Republican candidate Donald J. Trump (1946–) , but Trump won the Electoral College by a vote of 304 to 227. In the 2000 election, Democratic candidate Al Gore (1948–) narrowly won the popular vote over Republican candidate George W. Bush (1946–), but Bush managed a 271–266 triumph in the Electoral College.

These recent examples are not the only times this has happened in presidential elections. It also happened in 1824, 1876, and 1888. Andrew Jackson (1767–1845) won the popular vote in 1824 but lost to John Quincy Adams (1767–1848); Samuel

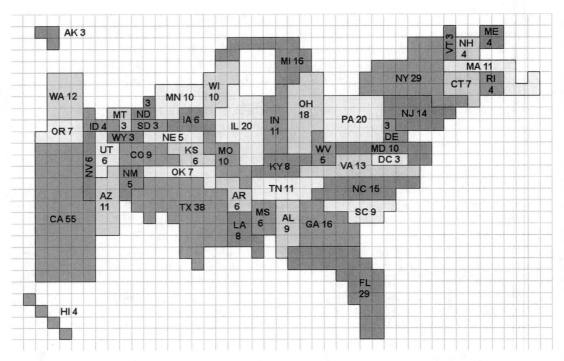

These are the electoral votes assigned to each state based on population figures from the 2010 U.S. Census.

Tilden (1814–1866) won the popular vote in 1876 but lost to Rutherford B. Hayes (1822–1893); and Grover Cleveland (1837–1908) won the popular vote in 1888 but lost to Benjamin Harrison (1833–1901). Thus, a total of five presidents—John Quincy Adams, Hayes, Harrison, Bush, and Trump—captured the presidency even though they did not win the popular vote. Interestingly, four of those five victors were from the Republican Party—all except Adams.

The Electoral College consists of 538 electors, and a candidate needs to win 270 electors to capture the presidency. States have a different number of electoral votes depending upon the population of the state. Thus, the larger states have more electoral votes. California, as the most populous state, has 55 electoral votes, while the least populous states of Alaska, Montana, North Dakota, South Dakota, Vermont, and Wyoming all have only 3 each, as does the District of Columbia. One idea behind the Electoral College is that it puts a little more emphasis on the votes of those individuals registered to vote in smaller states.

In recent years, there are certain states that almost always go blue (for the Democrat) and certain states almost always go red (for the Republican), so the presidential election is about capturing votes in certain battleground states. Similar to the Twenty-second Amendment, there have been numerous proposals introduced in Congress through the years to abolish the Electoral College. For example, Steve Cohen (1949–), a Democratic representative from Tennessee, introduced a measure in January 2021 calling for the abolition of the Electoral College. The measure begins with language that "the Founders of the Nation established the electoral college in an era of limited nationwide communication and information sharing." The measure also identifies the Electoral College as "an anachronism."

# More on the Electoral College

In every Case, after the Choice of the President, the Person having the greatest Number of Votes of the Electors shall be the Vice President. But if there should remain two or more who have equal Votes, the Senate shall chuse from them by Ballot the Vice President.

The Constitution originally provided that the person receiving the highest number of electoral votes would be president and the person receiving the second highest number of electoral votes would be vice president. This presented quite a problem in the election of 1796 when two former members of President George Washington's cabinet ran against each other—Washington's vice president, John Adams (1735–1826), ran against Washington's first secretary of state, Thomas Jefferson (1743–1826). In the election of 1796, Adams edged out Jefferson in the Electoral College 71 to 68. This produced the most unusual result that Adams of the Federalist Party was president, and his political enemy, Jefferson of the Democratic-Republican Party, was vice president.

Congress addressed this anomaly by enacting the Twelfth Amendment to the U.S. Constitution. This amendment—although quite wordy—essentially separates the president and vice president. A person runs exclusively for president or vice president. The result of the Twelfth Amendment is that a president and vice president run together for the same political party on the same ticket. It avoided the thorny problem of having a president and vice president from opposite political parties.

# Qualifications for President

No Person except a natural born Citizen, or a Citizen of the United States, at the time of the Adoption of this Constitution, shall be eligible to the Office of President; neither shall any person be eligible to that Office who shall not have attained to the Age of thirty-five Years, and been fourteen Years a Resident within the United States.

The minimum qualifications to take the oath of office of president of the United States are fairly basic: You need to have been born in a U.S. state or territory, be at least 35 years old, and have been a resident of the country for at least 14 years.

Article II, Section I, Clause 5 contains the eligibility requirements for the president. There are three requirements: (1) that the president be a natural-born citizen; (2) that the president be at least 35 years of age; and (3) that the president have been a resident of the United States 14 years.

The natural-born citizen requirement has come up at times in presidential elections. For example, some questioned whether John McCain (1936–2018), the Republican candidate for president in 2008, qualified because he was born in the Panama Canal Zone. Some charged that his Democratic opponent, Barack Obama, was ineligible, as they accused him of being born in Kenya rather than Hawaii, as his birth certificate shows.

The age requirement is higher for president than it is for the Senate (30 years) and for the House of Representatives (25). Every president so far has been at least 40 years of age. Theodore Roosevelt (1858–1919) was 42 years old, when, as vice president, he became president when President William McKinley (1843–1901) was assassinated. John F. Kennedy (1917–1963) was 43 years old when he was elected president.

The residency requirement means that someone has lived in the United States for a period of time. Residency requirements also apply for those serving in Congress, though the period for president is much longer.

# Removal of a President for a Disability

> In Case of the Removal of the President from Office, or of his Death, Resignation, or Inability to discharge the Powers and Duties of the said Office, the Same shall devolve on the Vice President, and the Congress may by Law provide for the Case of Removal, Death, Resignation or Inability, both of the President and Vice President, declaring what Officer shall then act as President, and such Officer shall act accordingly, until the Disability be removed, or a President shall be elected.

One might think there was no need to clarify this language, that it makes sense that once the president leaves office for any reason, the vice president will assume command. However, the language in "the Same shall devolve on the Vice President" is not terribly clear. This became something of a controversy when William Henry Harrison (1743–1841) died on the 32nd day of his presidency and he was succeeded by Vice President John Tyler (1790–1862). This was the first time that a sitting president had died in office and that a vice president was elevated to the position of the president. Some politicians argued that this language in the Constitution meant that the vice president acquires the *powers* of the president but does not actually *become* the president. For example, John Quincy Adams articulated the view that Tyler should be known as "the Vice-President acting as President." Tyler disagreed with this forcefully. He assumed office and took the presidential oath. Both houses of Congress passed a resolution declaring that Tyler was the president, but that did not stop critics from disparagingly referring to Tyler as "His Accidency."

The issue also raised its head in the 1950s when President Dwight D. Eisenhower (1890–1969) suffered a stroke. His vice president, Richard Nixon (1913–1994), took over presidential duties at least temporarily but was careful not to use the president's office or overstep his constitutional authority in any way. Furthermore, there were concerns about what would happen if a vice president who becomes president then suffers a disability and can no longer serve. If there is no sitting vice president, then the line of succession needs to be more established.

Such concerns led to the passage of the Twenty-fifth Amendment to the Constitution. The Twenty-fifth Amendment provides:

Section 1

In case of the removal of the President from office or of his death or resignation, the Vice President shall become President.

Section 2

Whenever there is a vacancy in the office of the Vice President, the President shall nominate a Vice President who shall take office upon confirmation by a majority vote of both Houses of Congress.

Section 3

Whenever the President transmits to the President pro tempore of the Senate and the Speaker of the House of Representatives his written declaration that he is unable to discharge the powers and duties of his office, and until he transmits to them a written declaration to the contrary, such powers and duties shall be discharged by the Vice President as Acting President.

Section 1 clarifies that the vice president becomes president upon the removal of the president, and Section 2 clarifies that the president can put someone else in the office of vice president if the vice president leaves office. Section 3 refers to what happens when the president becomes disabled and cannot perform the functions of the office. It provides that the vice president shall then handle the duties of the presidency until the president is fit to return to office.

# Compensation and Emoluments Clause

The President shall, at stated times, receive for his services, a compensation, which shall neither be increased nor diminished during the period for which he shall have been elected, and he shall not receive within that period any other emolument from the United States, or any of them.

The most recent example of a vice president taking over from an incapacitated president was in 2007, when Vice President Dick Cheney briefly took over while President George W. Bush was undergoing a hospital procedure.

This passage indicates that the president shall receive a set compensation for duties performed as president and that this salary shall not change while the president is in office. The United States Code provides that the president's salary is $400,000 a year, though the president also receives a $50,000 annual expense account and a $100,000 travel account.

The passage also prohibits so-called emoluments—defined as a profit or gain. The purpose of the so-called Domestic Emoluments Clause is to preserve the president's independence from Congress. Under the clause, Congress may neither increase nor decrease the president's compensation during his term. This prevents the Legislature from having any possible financial influence or pressure over the sitting president.

The clause did not receive significant attention until the presidency of Donald J. Trump, who was a wealthy businessman and real estate magnate before entering politics. Lawsuits were filed alleging that Trump violated this clause because some of his properties did business with the federal government. For example, one lawsuit alleged that Trump International Hotel violated the Domestic Emolument Clause because it had a continuing contract with the General Services Administration while Trump was the sitting president. The lawsuit was declared moot (or no longer live) after Trump left office.

# Commander-in-Chief Power

> The President shall be Commander in Chief of the Army and Navy of the United States, and of the Militia of the several States, when called into the actual Service of the United States.

Article II, Section 2 begins with one of the more frequently invoked phrases in American constitutional law and popular culture alike—that the president is "Commander in Chief." This means that the president is the leader of the armed forces of the United States—the Army and Navy by text and also the Marines and Air Force by extension. An acting U.S. attorney general wrote in a 1947 memo that "the phrase 'Army and Navy' is used in the Constitution as a means of describing all the armed forces of the United States." Thus, the president of the United States is the leader of the most powerful military in the world. That is an awesome responsibility.

The Founding Fathers wanted the president in charge of the armed forces even over the military commanders. Recall that the Founding Fathers were quite concerned about standing armies and the potential ability of the military to overthrow the government. The Constitution gives Congress the power to declare war, but oftentimes presidents have acted quickly in cases of military conflict or when military force was necessary. Founding Father James Madison (1751–1836) had warned that the president, more so than Congress, might be more prone to declare war than a more deliberative body. In other words, according to Madison, the president was "most interested in war & most prone to use it."

Some scholars assert that the commander-in-chief power means that the president is head of the armed forces, and the clause does not provide the president with even more implied or inherent powers. Some point to Alexander Hamilton's (c. 1755–1804) language in *Federalist Papers,* No. 69, when he wrote that that the commander-in-chief power is "nothing more than the supreme command and direction of the military and naval forces, as first general and admiral of the confederacy."

The Supreme Court seemingly interpreted the Commander-in-Chief Clause as giving powers to the president to act militarily when Congress is not available. In 1861, President Abraham Lincoln (1809–1865)—facing secession from the South and the beginning of the U.S Civil War—ordered the blockade of Southern ports. The Supreme Court in the *Prize Cases* (1863) noted that Congress ultimately approved of President Lincoln's actions when Congress was not in session but also seemed to suggest that Lincoln could have acted without congressional approval, because the nation was at war. The Court majority, per Justice Robert Cooper Grier (1794–1870), wrote that "the President was bound to meet [the Civil War] in the shape it presented itself, without waiting for Congress to baptize it with a name."

One of the more interesting conflicts in American constitutional law involves the division of power between the president and Congress in times of war. Presidents have engaged in bombing without seeking prior authorization from Congress, as they are supposed to do under the War Powers Act/Resolution of 1973. Congress passed this law largely as a result of the aggressive presidency of Richard M. Nixon, who had extended the Vietnam War into Laos and Cambodia. In fact, Congress passed the law over the veto of the War Powers Act.

Recent presidents have received significant criticism for their broad use of the commander-in-chief powers. President George W. Bush's administration, or at least some parts of his administration, pushed for an increase in presidential power during the so-called War on Terror. Congress responded with the USA PATRIOT Act a mere 45 days after the terrorist strikes of September 11, 2001. During the Bush presidency, the federal government engaged in warrantless electronic surveillance in the United States of persons suspected of having involvement with or ties to terrorists or enemy combatants. The government defended the program in part on the Commander-in-Chief Clause of the Constitution.

President Barack Obama pushed the envelope on commander-in-chief powers when he reasoned that he did not need authorization from Congress to conduct drone strikes in Libya and elsewhere. This earned him the derisive moniker "the drone president" in some circles. Greg Miller of the *Washington Post* wrote in June 2016 that President Obama was supposed to be the president who reined in the Central Intelligence Agency, but "[f]or all he did to check the CIA's powers, Obama will more likely be remembered as the president who unleashed the agency's fleet of armed drones."

Obama's successor, President Donald J. Trump, at times expanded the use of drone strikes. He also received significant criticism for threatening to use the military on a widespread scale to quell social justice protests around the country.

Critics charge that the War Powers Act does little to constrain aggressive presidents who often act through executive orders with increasing frequency and act unilaterally at least for the first 60 days, the amount of time before the president must obtain congressional approval. For example, political scientist Corey Brettschneider writes in his book *The Oath and the Office: A Guide to the Constitution for Future Presidents* (2018) that "it is long past time for Congress to pass a new war powers bill—one that would restore the original balance between Congress's power and the president's."

# Pardon Power

and he shall have Power to grant Reprieves and Pardons for Offenses against the United States, except in Cases of Impeachment.

Article II, Section II contains the president's pardon power, a power traced back to early Greece and Rome and, in more modern times, English law and early colonial law. The pardon power extends only to federal crimes, not state crimes. Furthermore, the president cannot pardon impeachment convictions or issue pardons to cover conduct that has not yet been committed. However, the pardon power otherwise is quite broad—too broad some critics say.

There are different types of pardons, including full pardons for individuals, amnesties for groups of persons, and commutations, which reduce the penalties associated with convictions. Note that the Constitution itself speaks of "Reprieves and Pardons." There are also remission of fines and forfeitures and reprieves.

The full pardon—what Chief Justice John Marshall (1755–1835) in 1833 called "an act of grace"—is by far the most expansive type of pardon. It releases the person from wrongdoing and restores the person's civil rights without qualification. This means that a person pardoned of a felony offense can vote in elections or possess a firearm. The Supreme Court explained in *Ex parte Garland* (1866) that "a pardon reaches both the punishment prescribed for the offense and the guilt of the offender; and when the pardon is full, it releases the punishment and blots out of existence the guilt, so that in the eye of the law the offender is as innocent as if he had never committed the offense."

Despite the far-reaching impact of a full pardon, a person pardoned may still have some collateral effects from the previous conviction. The fact that the person committed the crime may be considered in subsequent proceedings against the individual or may prohibit the recipient of the pardon from participating in certain activities, such as practicing law or medicine.

Amnesty is similar in scope to the full pardon except it applies to a class of people rather

One of the most famous examples of a U.S. president pardoning someone was when President Gerald R. Ford (shown here at a House Judiciary Subcommittee meeting on the matter) pardoned Richard M. Nixon, who had resigned to avoid impeachment, in 1974. Many objected to this move, but Ford felt it was needed to heal the country after the Watergate scandal.

than an individual. President Jimmy Carter (1924–), for example, granted amnesty to a class of people who had evaded the draft for the Vietnam War in violation of the Selective Service Act.

*Commutation is an example of a president issuing a reduced form of punishment to a convicted individual. Similarly, the president can reduce criminal fines, penalties, and all types of forfeitures.*

Commutation is an example of a president issuing a reduced form of punishment to a convicted individual. Similarly, the president can reduce criminal fines, penalties, and all types of forfeitures. Sometimes a president will issue a reprieve that delays punishment. For example, President Bill Clinton (1946–) granted a reprieve to death-row inmate Juan Raul Garza (1956–2001), delaying his execution for six months—though he later was executed when President George W. Bush was in office. Clinton granted the reprieve not so much to examine whether Garza was guilty or innocent but to give time to the Department of Justice to study racial disparities in the implementation of the federal death penalty system.

## Controversial Pardons

Questions surface over the broad nature of the pardon power. Throughout American history, there have been some very controversial pardons. Perhaps the most controversial was President Andrew Johnson (1808–1875), a Southerner from Tennessee, issuing a blanket pardon to all Confederate troops who were willing to pledge their allegiance to the United States of America. In 1977, President Jimmy Carter issued a pardon to many persons who dodged the draft to avoid military service during the Vietnam War. The next year, Carter issued a posthumous pardon to former Confederate president Jefferson Davis (1808–1889), saying that the country needed to heal.

In 2001, President Bill Clinton—in his last day in office—pardoned his half-brother Roger Clinton (1956–), who had a cocaine trafficking conviction from the 1980s. However, it was Clinton's pardon of billionaire financier Marc Rich (1934–2013) on Clinton's last day in office that shocked many people across the political spectrum. The *New York Times* called the pardon "a shocking abuse of presidential power."

An interesting issue that has never been resolved is whether a president may issue a self-pardon. No president has ever done this. The issue came into sharper focus when in 2018 President Donald J. Trump stated that he had "the absolute right" to issue a self-pardon. This occurred the year before he was impeached for the first time (he was impeached a second time in 2021). Trump was not the only president involved in this discussion, as the topic had surfaced during the presidencies of Nixon and Clinton—two other presidents who were subject to impeachment.

Congress cannot limit the president's pardon power. Back in *Ex parte Garland*, the Supreme Court wrote that "the power of the President [to issue a pardon] is not subject to legislative control" and that "Congress can neither limit the effect of his pardon, nor exclude from its exercise any class of offenders."

Several provisions in recent years have been introduced to limit the president's pardon power. These include proposed constitutional amendments to prohibit presidents from issuing self-pardons or pardoning family members or former members of the president's campaign or administration. None of these proposals has gained much traction, and to date, the president's pardon power remains quite broad.

# Treaty Power

He shall have Power, by and with the Advice and Consent of the Senate, to make Treaties....

The Treaty Clause allows presidents to enter international agreements on behalf of the United States. President Donald Trump is shown here at a treaty signing in 2020. Pictured left to right (seated) are Minister of Foreign Affairs Dr. Abdullatif bin Rashid Al Zayani of Bahrain, Prime Minister Benjamin Netanyahu of Israel, President Donald Trump, and Minister of Foreign Affairs Abdullah bin Zayed Al Nahyan of the United Arab Emirates.

The Treaty Clause provides that presidents can enter into treaties or international agreements with other countries but that such treaties must be approved by two-thirds of the Senate. The clause's "advice and consent" language seems to indicate that the Senate has an "advice" role before the president can enter into a treaty. However, in practice the Senate's role primarily has been one of approving or rejecting a treaty entered into by a president.

The great majority—90 percent, according to experts—of international agreements entered into by presidents, however, are not treaties but are rather executive agreements. Such international agreements are not submitted to the Senate for its advice and consent. Presidents have entered into such executive agreements with far greater frequency in the post–World War II era.

# Appointment Power

... and he shall nominate, and by and with the Advice and Consent of the Senate, shall appoint Ambassadors, other public Ministers and Consuls, Judges of the supreme Court, and all other Officers of the United States, whose Appointments are not herein otherwise provided for, and which shall be established by Law: but the Congress may by Law vest the Appointment of such inferior Officers, as they think proper, in the President alone, in the Courts of Law, or in the Heads of Departments.

The president can nominate and appoint various officers to the federal government, including ambassadors, public ministers and consuls, justices of the Supreme Court, and all other officers of the United States. The Senate then confirms these presidential appointments. Congress does have the power to appoint so-called inferior officers—a subject that has led to much litigation over who is a principal officer and who is an inferior officer.

This represents a key example of the separation of powers concept dividing power between the president and Congress. Some early presidents often took the advice and consent language referring to senatorial power more literally. For example, President George Washington believed that prenomination advice from the Senate was allowable but not required. Some presidents through the years have informally sought advice from members of Congress, but by far the more standard model has been the president nominating and the Senate confirming. In other words, the term "advice and consent" has devolved into just the word "consent" or the lack of consent.

## Removal Power

The Constitution does not specifically mention that the president may remove officers, but this power has been deemed to be a corollary of the Appointment

Clause. The thinking is that if the president can appoint an officer, the president can remove that officer too. The U.S. Supreme Court explained this removal power in 2020 by invoking President Harry Truman's (1884–1972) famous line that "the buck stops" with the president: "Without such power, the President could not be held fully accountable for discharging his own responsibilities; the buck would stop somewhere else."

The Supreme Court addressed the reach of the president's removal power in a case involving an agency created by Congress called the Consumer Financial Protection Bureau. Under the structure of this agency, Congress provided that its director could not be removed by the president absent inefficiency, neglect, or malfeasance.

The Court reasoned that Congress violated the principle of separation of powers by creating an independent agency and installing a director who essentially was free from the reach of the president, the head of the executive branch. Chief Justice John Roberts (1955–) reasoned that "[s]uch an agency lacks a foundation in historical practice and clashes with constitutional structure by concentrating power in a unilateral actor insulated from Presidential control."

# Recess Appointments

> The President shall have Power to fill up all Vacancies that may happen during the Recess of the Senate, by granting Commissions which shall expire at the End of their next Session.

Presidents can make recess appointments when the Senate is not in session. This clause was not considered controversial by the Framers at the 1787 Convention. Presumably, the idea was that there needs to be an additional way to make sure that the government operates smoothly, so if the Senate is not in session, there must be some way to get things done. Alexander Hamilton advanced the idea of recess appointments in *The Federalist Papers*, indicating that they were necessary to ensure the government operated efficiently.

Sometimes, however, presidents have used the recess power strategically. For example, a president could use it to appoint a person that he or she thinks the Senate will not approve. Some presidents used the recess power quite frequently. President Bill Clinton made 139 recess appointments, while his successor, President George W. Bush, made 171.

A recess is a break in Senate or House proceedings. The Twentieth Amendment says that Congress shall begin its session on January 3rd of each year. It may end sometime in the fall. Thus, there may be a so-called intersession recess between

when Congress formally ends its session and begins another. However, there are also smaller breaks called "intrasession recesses" when Congress breaks for shorter periods of time.

In 2014, the U.S. Supreme Court examined the president's recess powers to determine whether several recess appointments by President Barack Obama were constitutional. The Court held that recess appointments include both intersession and intrasession recesses. The Court determined that a recess period occurs only when the Senate is not in session for 10 days or longer. President Obama had sought to use the recess power to make appointments during Senate breaks of as few as three days. Congress deemed this unconstitutional. Congress also held that for purposes of the Recess Appointments Clause, "the Senate is in session when it says it is, provided that, under its own rules, it retains the capacity to transact Senate business."

President George W. Bush (pictured) made 171 recess appointments during his administration, which seems like a lot, but President Ronald Reagan beat that with 240.

Presidents use the recess power to fill all types of positions. Some of the more high-profile uses of recess appointments concern appointments to the federal bench. For example, President George W. Bush used his recess appointment power to nominate Charles W. Pickering (1937–) to the U.S. Court of Appeals for the Fifth Circuit in 2004. Pickering had previously served as a federal district court judge since 1990. Bush used the recess power because earlier, when he had tried to nominate Pickering to the Court of Appeals, Senate Democrats had strongly opposed Pickering for his views on abortion and because of opposition from some civil rights groups. Ultimately, Pickering retired from the bench just before his recess appointment ended.

# State of the Union Addresses

He shall from time to time give to the Congress Information of the State of the Union, and recommend to their Consideration such Measures as he shall judge necessary and expedient....

The President's State of the Union address consists of a summary of the year's developments, often focusing on the positive, and a recommendation to Congress for certain proposals that the president thinks necessary or beneficial for the public. Presidents George Washington and John Adams delivered their State of the Union addresses before Congress. Washington gave his initial address on January 8, 1790. Originally, the State of the Union address was known as the Annual Address.

However, the third president, Thomas Jefferson, balked at this practice and sent his State of the Union addresses in written form. Jefferson felt the practice of having the president deliver an address before Congress was akin to the British practice of a "speech from the throne." Subsequent presidents followed Jefferson's practice until President Woodrow Wilson (1856–1924) appeared before Congress in 1913.

President Franklin Delano Roosevelt also appeared before Congress and delivered his message to the nation. It has become common for presidents to deliver the annual State of the Union message before both houses of Congress in either January or February. Since 1947, when President Harry Truman delivered a State of the Union address, the addresses have been televised.

Some presidents do not deliver a State of the Union address in their first year on the job because it falls so close to their Inauguration Address, and some presidents do not give a State of the Union address right before they leave office in late January. President William Henry Harrison, the ninth president, did not give a State of the Union address because he died 32 days into his inauguration. The only other president not to give a State of the Union address was James Garfield (1831–1881), who was assassinated in his first year in office.

In 1982, President Ronald Reagan (1911–2004) started a tradition by acknowledging federal employee Lenny Skutnik (1953–), who was cheered for saving the life of Priscilla Tirado, a passenger on an airplane that had crash-landed in the icy Potomac River. Since Reagan's heartwarming gesture, subsequent presidents have honored a variety of humanitarians and other inspiriting figures. These individuals are sometimes called "the Lenny Skutniks." President Clinton pointed to civil rights heroine Rosa Parks, the woman who started the Montgomery Bus Boycott in the late 1950s by refusing to give up her seat to a white passenger.

Since 1966, there has been a tradition of a so-called opposition response to the president's State of the Union address. This began when Senator Everett Dirksen (1896–1969) and Representative Gerald Ford (1913–2066), both Republicans, delivered a message contrary to the message offered by then Democratic president Lyndon Baines Johnson (1908–1973).

# Convening Congress on Special Occasions

…[H]e may, on extraordinary Occasions, convene both Houses, or either of them, and in Case of Disagreement between them, with Respect to the Time of Adjournment, he may adjourn them to such Time as he shall think proper.

Supreme Court justice Joseph Story was the author of *Commentaries on the Constitution of the United States* (1833), which is still considered an early classic work on law in America.

The president has the power to convene Congress—either both houses or just one—on "extraordinary occasions." This usually occurs when the president has called on Congress to declare war, declare an emergency, or ask Congress to consider important appointments. U.S. Supreme Court justice Joseph Story (1779–1845) wrote in his influential *Commentaries on the Constitution* that "the power to convene congress on extraordinary occasions is indispensable to the proper operations, and even safety of the government." In 1948, President Harry Truman convened both houses of Congress to consider thorny questions of inflation and foreign aid.

It was more common in early American history for the president to convene Congress, or at least the Senate. President George Washington convened the Senate to consider several of his appointments. He also convened the Senate to consider the Jay Treaty.

The last clause grants the president the authority to adjourn Congress whenever the chambers cannot agree when to adjourn. Congress has agreed when to adjourn nearly all the time over the years. Thus, this is a presidential power that has never been exercised.

# The Take Care Clause

[H]e shall take Care that the Laws be faithfully executed, and shall Commission all the Officers of the United States.

The Take Care Clause is one of the more controversial clauses in the Constitution in the sense that it is subject to widely varying interpretations. It has a Janus-like character because some view it primarily as a limitation on presidential power, while other scholars and historians view it as a major source of presidential power.

The limitation view interprets the clause as saying that the president should enforce the laws that Congress makes. In other words, the president must follow the directives of Congress in ensuring that the law is enforced. However, the more expansive view interprets the clause as empowering the president to enforce federal law.

The Supreme Court has seemingly emphasized that the Take Care Clause means that the president cannot alter the law but has a constitutional obligation to make sure that the executive department follows the law. The Court at least implied this during its seminal opinion *Marbury v. Madison* (1803), when the Court reasoned that when the executive branch fails to enforce the law or perform a duty, a person can file a writ of mandamus, ordering the executive official, even the president, to comply with the law.

The interpretation of the clause comes into focus, or becomes a major issue, when the executive branch decides not to enforce certain federal laws. For example, during the Obama administration, federal prosecutors were instructed not to enforce the Controlled Substances Act when it came to the criminalization of marijuana and not to enforce certain aspects of the nation's immigration laws. The Obama administration believed that marijuana should not be prosecuted, particularly when used for medicinal purposes. The administration also believed that the immigration laws should not be used to deport those individuals who came to the United States when they were children and had not run afoul of the criminal laws. These were examples of the executive branch exercising its prosecutorial discretion under the power of the Take Care Clause. Critics charged that it was an example of the executive branch flouting the will of Congress and a segment of the population. For example, Todd Garvey of the Congressional Research Service writes in a white paper that "some Members of Congress have asserted that these unilateral Presidential non-enforcement determinations upset the separation of powers, harm Congress as an institution and a coordinate branch of government, and are in direct violation of the President's constitutional obligation to 'take Care that the Laws be faithfully executed.'"

The powers of the president came into clear focus during the administration of President Harry Truman, who asserted that he had the power under both the Vesting Clause and the Take Care Clause to seize the nation's steel mills amid a major strike. Truman reasoned that he had the authority to do this to ensure that steel production, which was necessary for the war effort, would not dissipate and cause national defense and security problems.

Truman's legal team argued that he had these powers in the aggregate when one combined the powers of the president under the Vesting Clause, the Commander in Chief Clause, and the Take Care Clause. The Supreme Court rejected the idea that the Take Care Clause gave

President Harry S. Truman declared that the Vesting and Take Care Clauses gave him the right to seize steel mills during a labor strike, but the Supreme Court declared it an unconstitutional action.

the president the power to assume a lawmaking power. The Court explained: "We could not sanction the seizures and condemnations of the steel plants in this case without reading Article II as giving the President not only the power to execute the laws but to make some. Such a step would most assuredly alter the pattern of the Constitution."

Chief Justice Fred Vinson (1890–1953) dissented in the Youngstown Steel case, noting that presidents thoroughout American history had taken certain actions even if not authorized by Congress. He noted the action of President Thomas Jefferson with the Louisiana Purchase, a purchase of a significant amount of land in our current country from France in 1803. Presidential scholars Cliff Sloan, Louis Fisher, and Moshe Spinowitz write that the Louisiana Purchase revealed "an executive who, without explicit constitutional authority, was willing to exercise broad presidential power to secure long-term benefits to the country."

Jefferson was not alone among our chief executives at taking swift action when necessity and emergency called. Consider that President Abraham Lincoln seized Confederate ships and ordered the naval blockade of such ships without congressional authorization.

|| *Roosevelt wrote in his autobiography that "the executive [is] subject only to the people, and, under the Constitution, bound to serve the people affirmatively in cases where the Constitution does not explicitly forbid him to render the service."* ||

Providing benefits to the country motivated President Theodore Roosevelt to propose what he called the "stewardship" theory of the executive branch. Roosevelt wrote in his autobiography that he followed the course "of regarding the executive as subject only to the people, and, under the Constitution, bound to serve the people affirmatively in cases where the Constitution does not explicitly forbid him to render the service."

# Executive Orders

The Constitution does not specifically mention executive orders. However, all presidents (except William Henry Harrison, who only served in office 32 days) from George Washington to Joe Biden (1942–) have issued executive orders. It is considered a part of what is termed inherent presidential power. Much of that inherent power derives from the Take Care Clause.

Executive orders must derive either from one of the president's congressional powers (such as the Take Care Clause) or from a statutory directive from Congress. In other words, its authority must stem from the Constitution or an act of Congress. Thus, an executive order can exceed the president's power if not rooted or closely connected to one of the president's Article II powers either singularly or in the aggregate, or at the direction of Congress. Like laws and statutes, the courts can review the constitutionality of executive orders. For example, the Supreme Court invalidated President Truman's executive order seizing the nation's steel mills in the Youngstown Steel case.

Some Presidential executive orders are quite famous in American history, such as President Franklin Delano Roosevelt's Executive Order 9066 in 1942, which created internment camps on American soil for Japanese American citizens, or President Truman's Executive Order 9981 in 1948, which ordered the desegregation of the American armed forces. Truman contended that the authority for this executive order stemmed from his authority as commander in chief.

Presidents can sometimes modify or revise previous executive orders with new executive orders. This sometimes happens when a new president takes office and has fundamentally different policy ideas or preferences than his predecessor. Many believe that the presidents have issued too many executive orders, arrogating themselves the ability to issue executive orders to address a wide range of issues. Cato Institute scholar Michael Tucker refers to it as "Presidents Gone Wild—with Executive Orders."

The ability of the U.S. president to sign directives called "executive orders" is derived from Article II of the U.S. Constitution.

# Executive Privilege

Another power of the presidency not found in the Constitution is executive privilege—the ability of the president to keep secret conversations or written memos from advisors. Presidents have claimed the need for executive privilege in order to give and receive candid advice from advisors and members of the cabinet. Presidents also have claimed that executive privilege is necessary for national security issues.

Probably the most infamous example of executive privilege occurred in the wake of the Watergate scandal. In June 1972, a burglary occurred at the headquarters of the Democratic National Headquarters at the Watergate building in Washington, D.C. The burglars were connected to the Committee for the Re-election of the President, and high-level White House officials were involved. During Senate committee hearings, presidential aide Alexander Butterfield (1926–) revealed that there was a secret taping system in the White House. This caused Attorney General Elliott Richardson (1920–1999) to appoint a special prosecutor, Archibald Cox (1912–2004), to investigate.

Cox then issued a subpoena for the White House tapes, which President Nixon resisted on the grounds of executive privilege. This led to Nixon demanding that Attorney General Richardson fire Cox. Richardson and his deputy, William Ruckelshaus (1932–2019), refused to fire Cox and instead resigned from office in an event called the Saturday Night Massacre. The third in command, solicitor general Robert Bork (1927–2012), eventually followed Nixon's order.

Eventually, a new special prosecutor, Leon Jaworski (1905–1982), sought a grand jury indictment of several White House officials, and President Nixon was named an "unindicted co-conspirator." Jaworski issued a subpoena duces tecum (a subpoena to produce documents) to hand over the tapes. Once again, Nixon claimed executive privilege and sought to quash the subpoena.

Ultimately, the case went to the U.S. Supreme Court, which unanimously ruled that the president did not have an absolute privilege to withhold the tapes. Chief Justice Warren Burger (1907–1995) wrote the opinion for the Court denying the privilege and ordering that the subpoena must be followed. Chief Justice Burger emphasized that the president's invocation of executive privilege was not tied to "military or diplomatic secrets"—areas that might justify executive privilege. Instead, the president's "generalized interest in confidentiality" was trumped by the particularized need for this evidence in a criminal case. Burger wrote that "the allowance of the privilege to withhold evidence that is demonstrably relevant in a criminal trial would cut deeply into the guarantee of due process of law and gravely impair the basic function of the courts." He concluded that the president's generalized interest in confidentiality "cannot prevail over the fundamental demands of due process of law in the fair administration of criminal justice."

# Impeachment

The President, Vice President and all civil officers of the United States, shall be removed from office on impeachment for, and conviction of, treason, bribery, or other high crimes and misdemeanors.

The ultimate check against the president and other civil officers of the United States is the impeachment power found in Congress. It is a crucial check to ensure that the president and other officials comport themselves within the confines of the law. As we read last chapter, Article I provides that the House has the sole power of impeachment, and impeachment trials are held in the Senate. Article I, Section 3 provides that "no Person shall be convicted without the Concurrence of two thirds of the Members present."

Impeachment has a long history in law. The English Parliament used the power of impeachment to police political offenses against the government. The American colonies also had impeachment as a tool at their disposal. It normally was confined to misconduct committed while in office.

A key textual question is what "high crimes and misdemeanors" are. It is clear what treason and bribery are, but what rises to the level of "high crimes and misdemeanors"? Some believe that this means the president must commit a felony-type offense that poses a grave threat to the security of the nation. Others take a much broader view as to what actions constitute impeachable offenses.

There is no right to a jury trial in an impeachment proceeding. However, the president or other officials have a legal team that defends and presents evidence before the senators. The chief justice of the United States normally presides over these proceedings. The Senate has very broad discretion in setting the procedures to be used during the impeachment proceedings.

Four presidents have faced impeachment: Andrew Johnson, Richard Nixon, Bill Clinton, and Donald Trump. Johnson, who assumed the presidency after the assassination of Abraham Lincoln, was the first president to be impeached. Johnson got into hot water for firing Secretary of War Edwin Stanton (1814–1869) in violation of a federal law known as the Tenure in Office Act. Congress had passed this law in an effort to prevent Johnson, a Southerner, from firing members of Lincoln's cabinet. Though the Supreme Court declared the Tenure in Office Act unconstitutional, Congress still impeached Johnson, though he was not convicted in the Senate.

There was not another case of presidential impeachment until Richard Nixon. The House Judiciary Committee voted on articles of impeachment for Nixon, but the president resigned before the case reached the full House.

More recently, President Bill Clinton was impeached by the House for obstruction of justice and perjury. Clinton had allegedly lied during a deposition in a civil suit brought by a woman named Paula Jones (1966–), who alleged that Clinton had sexually harassed her when he was the governor of Arkansas. During a deposition in the civil case, Clinton told Jones's attorneys that he never had an extramarital affair with White House intern Monica Lewinsky (1973–) and that he did not have sex with her.

Attorney General Janet Reno (1938–2016) appointed independent counsel Kenneth Starr (1946–) to investigate whether Clinton lied in the deposition and the grand jury. The investigation also examined a wide variety of possible other misdeeds. This led to a behemoth report called the Starr Report.

President Bill Clinton (left) was impeached in 1998 based on sexual misconduct charges with then-intern Monica Lewinski (pictured). The president was accused of obstructing justice and lying under oath, but he was not found guilty.

The Constitution Explained

President Donald Trump was the first president to be impeached twice, but both attempts failed, proving just how difficult it is to successfully toss a president out of office.

The House voted on two articles of impeachment against Clinton. In the Senate, Chief Justice William Rehnquist (1924–2005) presided over the impeachment trial. The Senate did not convict Clinton by the necessary two-thirds majority.

Then came the presidency of Donald J. Trump. The House impeached Trump twice—the first time in December 2019 and then again in January 2021. Each time there were not enough votes in the Senate to convict Trump. The first impeachment of Trump consisted of two articles: (1) abuse of power and (2) obstruction of Congress. The first impeachment began after there was some evidence that President Trump had enlisted foreign aid from the Ukraine in his reelection bid in 2020. The Senate acquitted Trump of both charges in February 2020. The votes were 48–52 and 47–53.

In an unprecedented move, the House once again impeached Trump on charges of "inciting an insurrection." The allegation was that President Trump had incited a riot on January 6th when he urged many of his supporters to march to the Capitol and make their voices heard. For a couple months, since the November 2020 election, Trump had said that the election was "rigged" and stolen by the Democrats. On January 6th, Trump told a throng of people: "You don't concede when there's theft involved. Our country has had enough. We're not going to take it any more.... If you don't fight like hell, you're not going to have a country anymore."

Though Trump didn't specifically tell his supporters to storm the Capitol and cause a riot, House Democrats believed that he was responsible for fanning the flames of discontent that boiled over on January 6, 2021, when a mob overran the Capitol and occupied houses of Congress, committing acts of vandalism.

The second impeachment trial conducted in the Senate led to a final result of 57–43. While a majority of senators voted for the impeachment of President Trump, the vote fell ten votes short of the necessary two-thirds majority. Trump remained defiant after his second acquittal, calling the proceedings "the latest witch hunt in the history of our country."

The second impeachment trial was unprecedented as it took place after President Trump already had left the presidency. Some argue that impeachment proceedings should extend only to those officials who are still in office, as the plain text of the Constitution reads "current officials" can be impeached, not former officials. Others argue that the impeachment process can continue once the official leaves office, as long as the impeachment is for conduct that the official committed while in office.

Ultimately, impeachment remains a highly partisan matter. The impeachment processes of all four presidents occurred during highly partisan times.

# Article III and the U.S. Supreme Court

## Section 1

> The judicial power of the United States, shall be vested in one supreme Court, and in such inferior Courts as the Congress may from time to time ordain and establish. The judges, both of the supreme and inferior Courts, shall hold their Offices during good Behavior, and shall, at stated Times, receive for their Services a Compensation which shall not be diminished during their Continuance in Office.

Today, the U.S. Supreme Court universally is considered the body that interprets the Constitution. Though listed after the legislative and executive branches, this third branch of government has become in the eyes of some the "most dangerous" branch, as Supreme Court justices with lifetime appointments decide so many important issues in American society. Consider that the Supreme Court ultimately decided whether a woman had a constitutional right to an abortion, whether corporations are persons for purposes of constitutional law, and even the 2000 presidential election.

It makes sense that the judicial branch is listed last. After all, the legislative branch is listed first, as it passes laws. The executive branch is listed second, as it implements the laws. The judicial branch is listed third, as it interprets the laws. However, the Constitution is silent on the power of the judicial branch to declare laws unconstitutional. One of the great achievements of Chief Justice John Marshall (1755–1835), who served in that role from 1801 to 1835, was to famously declare in *Marbury v. Madison* (1803) that "it is emphatically the province and duty of the judicial department to declare what the law is." Marshall claimed for the judicial branch the so-called power of judicial review.

In fairness, Marshall did not pluck this power out of thin air. A few state supreme court jurists had exercised the power of judicial review. Sir Edward Coke (1552–1634), an English jurist, had declared that judges had the power to review the constitutionality of laws way back in 1610, but Marshall put the Supreme Court on the map in terms of carving out the power of judicial review.

## *Marbury v. Madison* and the Power of Judicial Review

Judicial review is second nature to us today, as the Supreme Court has determined the validity of the death penalty, the right to die, abortion, the right to advertise legal services, the right of universities to consider race as a key admissions factor, and many other important concepts. However, in 1803, when the Court decided *Marbury v. Madison*, it was not a settled principle at least in terms of the U.S. Supreme Court.

The controversy began over an early attempt at court packing by the Federalist Party. John Adams (1735–1826), a Federalist, had just lost the presidential election to his longtime rival—and amazingly, his vice president—Thomas Jefferson (1743–1826), a Democratic-Republican. Adams and the Federalist-dominated Congress sought to pack the Courts with Federalist judges. Congress passed a law that authorized the creation of judges in the District of Columbia, so-called justices of the peace. Around this time, Adams also nominated his sitting secretary of state, John Marshall, to be chief justice of the United States. Congress easily confirmed Marshall, a fellow Federalist, but Marshall still had work as secretary of state. He was supposed to sign and have commissions delivered for these justices of the peace.

Marshall signed the commissions, but some of them were not delivered by the time Jefferson took office as president. Jefferson ordered his secretary of state, James Madison (1751–1836), to not deliver the commissions. One of the individuals prevented from assuming his position was William Marbury (1762–1835), who filed suit directly in the U.S. Supreme Court. Marbury sued Madison and sought the Supreme Court to order Madison to deliver his commission.

Marbury sued in December 1801, but the Supreme Court did not hear the case until 1803, because Congress had passed a law that abolished the Supreme

Court's terms in 1802—an astonishing act of political power that would be considered patently unconstitutional and unauthorized today. However, eventually the Court heard the case.

Chief Justice Marshall wrote the Court's unanimous opinion in *Marbury v. Madison*, a case that Erwin Chemerinsky calls "the single most important decision in American constitutional law." Marshall asked several questions, including:

- Does William Marbury have a right to his commission for judicial office?
- Does the law provide Marbury with a remedy?
- If Marbury has a remedy, can the court issue a writ of mandamus ordering the delivery of the commission?

Marshall first determined that, yes, Marbury had a right to his commission. The Court said yes, because President Adams had signed the commission that appointed Marbury to the position. Thomas Jefferson disputed this point, noting that "delivery is one of the essentials to

Chief Justice John Marshall wrote the 4–0 Supreme Court opinion that James Madison did not have the right to withhold delivery of Marbury's commission.

the validity of the deed," a principle he called "never yet contradicted." However, Marshall reasoned that Congress had passed the law and the president had signed the commission. That was enough such that Marbury had a right. This makes intuitive sense. Think of an employer giving you a job, you having a signed contract, and then the employer just arbitrarily reneges and takes the job away.

The next question Marshall grappled with was whether Marbury had a remedy. Marshall said yes and wrote in oft-quoted language: "The very essence of civil liberty certainly consists in the right of every individual to claim the protection of the laws, whenever he receives an injury." The issue was a little more complicated because Marbury was suing the executive branch of government—the secretary of state and, essentially, the president. However, Marshall explained that "[t]he government of the United States has been emphatically termed a government of laws, and not of men." In other words, even the executive branch and the president are not above the law.

The next question for Marshall was whether the Court could issue a writ of mandamus forcing the other branches of government to do or not do something. This was a delicate but also deliciously important point of *Marbury v. Madison*. Marshall reasoned that there was a difference between political acts, for which the executive branch has discretion, and ministerial acts, where the executive branch must perform certain actions.

A Maryland businessman and Federalist Party member, William Marbury was one of the "Midnight Judges" appointed by President John Adams before leaving office.

Marshall said that purely political questions are beyond the purview of the Court. This is called the political question doctrine, a matter discussed earlier in the chapter on the powers of the executive branch. However, Marshall wrote that where the executive "is directed by law to do a certain act affecting the absolute rights of individuals," the court can declare a remedy for the harmed individual.

Thus, so far, Marbury appeared to be winning the case. He had a right to the position, he deserved a legal remedy, and the Court had the power to issue the remedy. So why did he ultimately lose the case?

He lost because Chief Justice Marshall determined that a section of the Judiciary Act of 1789 was unconstitutional. Marbury had reasoned that he had a right to sue directly in the U.S. Supreme Court, because Section 13 of the Judiciary Act of 1789 gave him this right. Marshall reasoned that Section 13 of the Judiciary Act of 1789 was unconstitutional because it conflicted with Article III of the Constitution, which did *not* give Marbury the right to sue directly in the U.S. Supreme Court.

In other words, Section 13 of the Judiciary Act of 1789 gave the Supreme Court more types of original jurisdiction than did the language in Article III. Thus, Marshall reasoned that when a statute or law conflicts with the Constitution, the Constitution prevails. Marshall explained that Marbury should have filed in a lower federal court, not directly in the Supreme Court, writing, "the jurisdiction had to be appellate, not original."

The importance of *Marbury v. Madison* is that Marshall established that the judicial branch, most notably the U.S. Supreme Court, has the power to determine the constitutionality of the laws. In other words, a law repugnant to the Constitution is void and cannot be enforced or applied. This is the venerated power of judicial review.

# Power of Judicial Review

> It is emphatically the province and duty of the judicial department to declare what the law is.
>
> —Chief Justice Marshall in *Marbury v. Madison* (1803)

Legal scholars disagree over whether Marshall was correct with regard to the unconstitutionality of the provision of the Judiciary Act of 1789. However, there is nearly universal agreement that his opinion was a brilliant political move that assured the judicial branch much-needed respect in the American constitutional structure. Marshall ruled in favor of President Thomas Jefferson, his distant cousin and political enemy, but he scored a huge victory for the Supreme Court and the judicial branch in general. In the words of constitutional scholar Erwin Chemerinsky, "The brilliance of Marshall's opinion cannot be overstated."

The Supreme Court in Marshall's time did not exercise its power of judicial review and strike down laws very often. In fact, the U.S. Supreme Court did not strike down another federal law until its dreaded ruling in *Dred Scott v. Sanford* in 1857, a decision that sanctioned slavery and helped plunge the country into a bloody civil war.

However, Marshall and his colleagues on the Supreme Court also established the power of the Supreme Court to review the constitutionality of state court decisions in *Martin v. Hunter's Lessee* (1816) and *Cohens v. Virginia* (1821). The chief justice upheld Section 25 of the Judiciary Act of 1789, which gave the Court the power to hear cases appealed from a state high court. The cases involved attempts by the Virginia state courts to ignore the rights of those who had held land and were loyal to the British government. The Virginia government had confiscated the lands unilaterally pursuant to state laws that justified such confiscations.

The U.S. Supreme Court declared that state laws can violate the U.S. Constitution just as much as federal laws. This time Justice Joseph Story (1779–1845)—the youngest person ever appointed to the U.S. Supreme Court and a founder of the Harvard Law School—wrote the Court's opinion. Chief Justice Marshall could

Mendes J. Cohen (pictured) and Philip J. Cohen were brothers convicted of selling lottery tickets in Virginia. Their appeal went to the U.S. Supreme Court in *Cohens v. Virginia*, resulting in the Court establishing that it had the power to review state supreme court cases when constitutional rights were an issue.

not write the Court's opinion because he had to recuse himself since his brother, James Marshall (1764–1848), had purchased land from one of the parties in the Supreme Court litigation.

# Life Tenure

The judges, both of the supreme and inferior courts, shall hold their offices during good behaviour;

U.S. Supreme Court justices have life tenure, as do all Article III federal judges—federal district court and federal appeals court judges. The Framers gave life tenure to federal judges to ensure an independent judiciary. Many state court jurists were elected, meaning that they were more beholden to political pressures than life-tenured federal judges. Alexander Hamilton (c. 1755–1804) explained this in *Federalist Papers*, No. 78, when he wrote, "The complete independence of the courts of justice is peculiarly essential in a limited Constitution."

Supporters of lifetime appointments emphasize the need for an independent judiciary, often called a "crown jewel" in our Constitution. For example, it was the heroic federal judges of the U.S. Court of Appeals for the Fifth Circuit who had the temerity and force of will to strike down many segregation laws and policies that were quite popular among many whites in the Southern states. Author Jack Bass famously wrote about jurists like Elbert Tuttle (1897–1996) and John Minor Wisdom (1905–1999) in his book *The Unlikely Heroes*.

Others believe that Supreme Court justices serve too long at times. Justice William O. Douglas (1898–1980), for example, served on the Court for more than 36 years, from 1939 until his retirement in 1975. His failing health in his last years was a cause for concern among his colleagues and others. Sixteen justices have served more than 30 years on the Court.

## SUPREME COURT JUSTICES SERVING OVER 30 YEARS

| Justice | Years Served |
| --- | --- |
| William O. Douglas | 36 (1939–1975) |
| John Paul Stevens | 35 (1975–2010) |
| John Marshall | 34 (1801–1835) |
| Stephen J. Field | 34 (1863–1897) |
| John Marshall Harlan | 34 (1877–1911) |
| Hugo Black | 34 (1937–1971) |
| William Brennan | 34 (1956–1990) |
| Joseph Story | 33 (1812–1845) |

| Justice | Years Served |
|---|---|
| William Rehnquist | 33 (1972–2005) |
| James Wayne | 32 (1835–1867) |
| Bushrod Washington | 31 (1798–1829) |
| John McLean | 31 (1830–1861) |
| Bryon White | 31 (1962–1993) |
| Clarence Thomas | 31+ (1991–present) |
| William Johnson | 30 (1804–1834) |
| Anthony Kennedy | 30 (1988–2018) |

Opponents counter that the terms are simply too long, with some justices or judges staying on long after they can physically or mentally handle the job. Some federal judges on the lower courts have served until they were more than 100 years old. For example, Judges Wesley Brown (1907–2012), a federal district court judge in Kansas, and William Woodrough (1873–1977), of the U.S. Court of Appeals for the Eighth Circuit, both served on the bench until their deaths at the age of 104. Others contend that the lifetime appointments have created emperors in robes who wield too much power.

## "Good Behavior"

The Constitution does not automatically guarantee life tenure no matter what. If an Article I federal judge commits bribery, for example—a felony and a crime of dishonesty—that federal judge can lose his or her life tenure. Federal judges can be subject to impeachment.

However, judges may not be removed simply because government officials do not like their rulings. This caused Ruth Bader Ginsburg (1933–2020) to write in 1983— before she was on the federal bench—that the clause was intended to serve not as a constraint but "a guarantee of independence." Thus, a federal judge can be removed from the bench through impeachment for serious crimes, not for rulings that upset members of Congress or the general public. The Good Behavior Clause therefore relates to judges being subject only to criminal laws and not to political whims.

## Creating the Supreme Court and the Federal Judiciary

Article III, Section 1 provides for the creation of the U.S. Supreme Court, the highest court in the federal judiciary, and such lower courts as Congress deems necessary. Because the size of the Supreme Court has remained constant since 1869, many assume the Constitution sets the number at nine, but the Constitution makes no provision for the composition of the Supreme Court in terms of number of justices. This means Congress has the power to set that number.

The Constitution mentions the judicial powers shall be "in one supreme court," but the actual formation of the Court came when Congress passed the Judiciary Act of 1789. This law not only created the Court but also established its jurisdiction, or authority to hear certain types of cases. Justice Sandra Day O'Connor (1930–) in her book *The Majesty of the Law: Reflections of a Supreme Court Justice* called this law "the single most important legislative enactment of the nation's founding years." In essence, the Judiciary Act of 1789 filled in the blanks left by Article III of the Constitution.

The 1789 law called for six justices to serve on the U.S. Supreme Court—a chief justice and five associate justices. When the Supreme Court first met, the Court's six justices were Chief Justice John Jay (1745–1829) and five other associate justices: John Rutledge (1739–1800), William Cushing (1732–1810), James Wilson (1742–1798), John Blair (1732–1800), and James Iredell (1751–1799). Washington had originally nominated Robert H. Harrison (1745–1790) as one of the first six justices, but Harrison, suffering from poor health, declined.

The number of Supreme Court justices has fluctuated over time from six to ten justices. Consider the following:

## NUMBER OF SUPREME COURT JUSTICES

| Justices | During the Years |
|:---:|:---:|
| 6 | 1789–1807 |
| 7 | 1807–37 |
| 9 | 1837–63 |
| 10 | 1863–66 |
| 7 | 1866–69 |
| 9 | 1869– |

Again, Congress set the number of Supreme Court justices at nine in 1869 and this number has remained constant. The Judiciary Act of 1869 was the law that created the current number of nine justices. Congress thought that there should be one U.S. Supreme Court for every circuit court of appeals. Since there were nine circuit courts, it made sense to have nine Supreme Court justices.

## Debate on Life Tenure and Number of Justices

Currently, Congress is mulling over whether to expand the U.S. Supreme Court. There has been talk that the Court should be expanded to 13 justices since there are now 13 federal circuit courts of appeals. House and Senate Democrats introduced a bill, titled the Judiciary Act of 2021, to increase the number of justices from 9 to 13.

In response, Rep. Doug LaMalfa (1960–) from Texas stated in Congress that "the absurd proposal brought forth now to pack the U.S. Supreme Court out of thin air with four new Justices is the latest in a breathtaking effort to seize and seal power for Democrats." He and fellow representative Dusty Johnson (1976–) of South Dakota introduced a proposal, called "Save the 9," to amend the Constitution to keep the number at nine.

Justice Stephen Breyer (1938–), who has been on the Supreme Court since 1994, warned against court-packing plans in a speech delivered at Harvard Law School in April 2021. He said that congressional efforts to expand the Court would erode public trust in the Court as a body of independent jurists. Breyer warned that "if the public sees judges as politicians in robes, its confidence in the courts, and in the rule of law itself, can only diminish, diminishing the Court's power, including its power to act as a 'check' on the other branches."

The current debate about changing the size of the Court is nothing new. A few times, there have been proposals to change the composition of the Supreme Court. The most infamous of these occurred in 1937 when President Franklin Delano Roosevelt (1882–1945) introduced his

When the first chief justice, John Jay, led the Supreme Court, there were only six justices serving. This later increased to seven and then the current nine justices. Some people are now proposing we have 13 justices on the bench.

"court-packing" plan that would have increased the Court's size to as many as 15 members. Roosevelt was incensed that the Supreme Court—led by a group of older justices known as the "Four Horsemen"—had invalidated many pieces of his New Deal legislation he thought necessary to jump-start the flagging American economy still trying to recover from the ravages of the Great Depression. For example, the Court had struck down a minimum wage law in New York in a 1936 decision. However, the very next year—right after President Roosevelt introduced his plan to add new justices to the Court—the Court upheld a Washington State minimum wage law. Justice Owen Roberts (1875–1855) allegedly "switched his vote" by voting to strike down the New York minimum wage law in 1936 but to uphold the Washington minimum wage law in 1937. This was famously called the "switch in time that saved nine."

The Court has had a membership of nine since 1869. The stability of the Court may be well served by keeping its number at nine. After all, every state high court has either five, seven, or nine justices. Furthermore, there would appear to be no stopping point to packing the Court. What if a political party in control of Congress believes that the Court is filled with justices aligned with the other party? Can it expand the Court from 13 to 15 to 17 to 19 to 21?

Meanwhile, President Joe Biden issued an executive order in April 2021 establishing a commission to study Supreme Court reform. The commission presumably will examine not only the size of the Court but also whether federal judges should retain life tenure or, as some have proposed, have 20-year terms. In other words, it appears many are taking aim at the Constitution's provision of lifetime appointments for Supreme Court justices.

# Original Jurisdiction

The Supreme Court shall have original and exclusive jurisdiction of all controversies between two or more States. The Supreme Court shall have original but not exclusive jurisdiction of (1) All actions or proceedings to which ambassadors, other public ministers, conculs, or vice consuls of foreign states are parties; (2) All controversies between the United States and a State; (3) All actions or proceedings by a State against the citizens of another State or against aliens.

The U.S. Supreme Court has two types of jurisdiction: original and appellate. Original jurisdiction means that the Supreme Court has the power to hear the case immediately, or the case is filed first directly in the Supreme Court. Appellate jurisdiction means that a higher court has the power to review judgments by a lower court. In other words, the losing party in a case can appeal to the U.S. Supreme Court, asking the high court to hear the case.

A key example of the Court using its original jurisdiction occurs when one state sues another state. The Court exercised its original jurisdiction to settle a border dispute between two states in *Virginia v. Tennessee* (1893). This is the type of case that can be brought originally in the Supreme Court.

Appellate jurisdiction means that a higher court has the power to review judgments by a lower court. The U.S. Supreme Court has appellate jurisdiction in the vast majority of the cases that are appealed to it. The Court has appellate jurisdiction over all decisions of the federal courts of appeals, decisions by the highest state courts (usually called state supreme courts) that involve a federal or constitutional question, and decisions by special panels of three judges in federal district courts.

## The Lower Federal Courts

Originally, the Judiciary Act of 1789 created 13 lower federal courts called district courts. They were divided into three circuits—the Eastern, the Middle, and the Southern. Thus, litigants in federal court initially would have their case heard before one federal district court judge. The law also provided for circuit courts, which were composed of three judges. The three judges were one sitting federal district court judge and two justices of the U.S. Supreme Court. This meant that

Supreme Court justices had to serve in courts around the country. They literally had to travel across the country to hear cases. The practice was known as "circuit duty" or, more commonly, "riding circuit."

Some Supreme Court justices actually resigned because of the arduous nature of "riding circuit." For example, U.S. Supreme Court Justice Thomas Johnson (1732–1819) of Maryland resigned after serving on the high court for little more than a year because of the required travel. After Johnson resigned, Congress passed a law that required circuit courts to consist of only one U.S. Supreme Court justice. However, Supreme Court justices rode circuit until 1891.

Congress then created 16 judgeships in six circuit courts in the Judiciary Act of 1801. However, politics reared its ugly head, and the Democratic-Republican Party repealed the Judiciary Act of 1801 in the Judiciary Act of 1802. This new law retained the structure of six circuit courts but abolished the extra judgeships because these judges were appointed by Federalist president John Adams.

Finally, Congress created the U.S. Courts of Appeals that exist today in the Judiciary Act of 1891. This law was called the Evarts Act, after U.S. senator William Evarts (1818–1901) of New York. Each one of these circuit courts would have its own judges. Thus, there were now three levels of federal judges: (1) federal district court judges; (2) federal appeals court judges; and (3) U.S. Supreme Court justices.

This three-tiered model still exists today. Most federal cases are heard directly before one federal district court judge. If a litigant loses before that federal district court judge, the party can appeal to the U.S. Court of Appeals, which generally hears cases in panels of three judges. Stated another way, the federal district courts are the trial courts, where witnesses testify and jurors often decide cases. Federal judges on the U.S. Courts of Appeals are intermediate appellate court judges. They only hear arguments from attorneys and read various written submissions from attorneys.

If a party loses before a U.S. Circuit Court of Appeals, the party can petition for what is known as en banc, or full panel review. While panel decisions are in front of three judges, the en banc court consists of all active full-time members of the particular circuit. Thus, an en banc decision could consist of 15 judges or even more depending upon the number of judges.

U.S. Senator William Evarts of New York sponsored the Judiciary Act of 1891 (the Evarts Act) that importantly created the U.S. Court of Appeals.

# COURT HIERARCHY

1. U.S. Supreme Court (final appellate court)
2. U.S. Circuit Court of Appeals (intermediate appellate courts)
3. Federal District Courts (trial courts)

A losing party before a three-judge panel at the circuit court level does not have to seek en banc review. Instead, they can file a document known as a petition for writ of certiorari to the U.S. Supreme Court. The cert petition explains why the case is important enough to merit review by the U.S. Supreme Court.

The U.S. Supreme Court does not have to take the appeals that are filed before it. The Court has a vast amount of so-called discretionary jurisdiction. This means it can pick and choose the cases it wants to hear. And the Supreme Court is very selective about the cases that it hears. In a typical Supreme Court term, there are about 8,000 petitions to the High Court, and the Court grants only about 70 to 80 cases a year.

Since at least 1924, the Court has operated under what is known as the Rule of Four. This means that if four justices agree to hear a case, the case is placed on the Court's docket. There are several factors as to why the justices might want to review a particular case. Rule 10 of the Supreme Court rules explains that a key factor is when the lower courts disagree on an important point of law. The lower court disagreement most relevant to this is when the U.S. Circuit Courts of Appeals disagree on a point law. This is called a circuit split. The idea is that the law should be at least relatively uniform—there should not be wide variances on the law in different circuits.

Another common reason that justices take a case is when a lower federal court strikes down a federal law or statute as unconstitutional. In fact, Congress sometimes will build into a law a provision for expedited review of a law if it is struck down. For example, when Congress passed the Communications Decency Act of 1996, part of a larger telecommunications bill, Congress had a special provision in the law providing that if the law is challenged in court, that a special three-judge federal district court should hear the case. This came to pass when numerous civil liberties groups challenged on First Amendment grounds a part of the Communications

William Howard Taft, who had previously served as president of the United States from 1909 to 1913, was chief justice from 1921 to 1930.

Decency Act that criminalized the online transmission of patently offensive or indecent communications. A special three-judge panel struck down the law. The government then appealed directly to the U.S. Supreme Court, which affirmed the lower court decision in *Reno v. ACLU* (1997).

Years ago, the U.S. Supreme Court had a much more brutal caseload, but Chief Justice William Howard Taft (1857–1930), who served in that capacity from 1921 until his death in 1930, successfully lobbied Congress to give the Court greater control over its docket. Congress responded with the Judiciary Act of 1925. Taft also successfully petitioned Congress for the funds to build a new building for the Supreme Court—a beautiful marble structure known as the Marble Palace. In her book *Majesty of the Law*, Justice Sandra Day O'Connor writes of Taft: "another great Chief Justice … who perhaps deserves almost as much credit as [John] Marshall for the Court's modern-day role but who does not often get the recognition: William Howard Taft."

Taft was effective in part because he was a former president of the United States. He remains the only person to have served both as president and as a justice on the U.S. Supreme Court.

# Impeachment

While Article III federal judges enjoy life terms, they are not insulated from removal because of the power of impeachment. Federal judges can be impeached, or removed from office, for "Treason, Bribery, or other high crimes and misdemeanors." This means that federal judges receive lifetime appointments but can be removed from office for bad conduct. Recall from discussions of Article I that the U.S. House of Representatives has the "sole power of impeachment" and the U.S. Senate has "the sole power to try all impeachments."

To remove a federal judge or other official subject to impeachment, the official must have committed a serious crime. According to the Federal Judicial Center, 15 federal judges through the years have been impeached. All but one were federal district court judges. For example, the first federal judge to be impeached was John Pickering (1737–1835), a federal district court judge from New Hampshire who was impeached in 1803. Only one U.S. Supreme Court Justice has ever been impeached—Samuel Chase (1741–1811), who was then acquitted in the Senate.

The following judges have been impeached and removed from office (adapted from the Federal Judicial Center, "Impeachments of Federal Judges." https://www .fjc.gov/history/judges/impeachments-federal-judges).

- John Pickering, U.S. District Court for the District of New Hampshire: Impeached by the U.S. House of Representatives, March 2, 1803, on charges of mental instability and intoxication on the bench; convicted by the U.S. Senate and removed from office, March 12, 1804.

- Samuel Chase, Associate Justice, Supreme Court of the United States: Impeached by the U.S. House of Representatives, March 12, 1804, on charges of arbitrary and oppressive conduct of trials; acquitted by the U.S. Senate, March 1, 1805.

- James H. Peck (1790–1836), U.S. District Court for the District of Missouri: Impeached by the U.S. House of Representatives, April 24, 1830, on charges of abuse of the contempt power; acquitted by the U.S. Senate, January 31, 1831.

- West H. Humphreys (1806–1882), U.S. District Court for the Middle, Eastern, and Western Districts of Tennessee: Impeached by the U.S. House of Representatives, May 6, 1862, on charges of refusing to hold court and waging war against the U.S. government; convicted by the U.S. Senate and removed from office, June 26, 1862.

- Mark W. Delahay (1828–1879), U.S. District Court for the District of Kansas: Impeached by the U.S. House of Representatives, February 28, 1873, on charges of intoxication on the bench; resigned from office, December 12, 1873, before opening of trial in the U.S. Senate.

- Charles Swayne (1842–1907), U.S. District Court for the Northern District of Florida: Impeached by the U.S. House of Representatives, December 13, 1904, on charges of abuse of contempt power and other misuses of office; acquitted by the U.S. Senate, February 27, 1905.

- Robert W. Archbald (1848–1926), Commerce Court and U.S. Court of Appeals for the Third Circuit: Impeached by the U.S. House of Representatives, July 11, 1912, on charges of improper business relationship with litigants; convicted by the U.S. Senate and removed from office, January 13, 1913.

- George W. English (1866–1941), U.S. District Court for the Eastern District of Illinois: Impeached by the U.S. House of Representatives, April 1, 1926, on charges of abuse of power; resigned from office November 4, 1926; Senate Court of Impeachment adjourned to December 13, 1926, when, on request of the House manager, impeachment proceedings were dismissed.

- Harold Louderback (1881–1941), U.S. District Court for the Northern District of California: Impeached by the U.S. House of Representatives, February 24, 1933, on charges of favoritism in the appointment of bankruptcy receivers; acquitted by the U.S. Senate, May 24, 1933.

- Halsted L. Ritter (1868–1951), U.S. District Court for the Southern District of Florida: Impeached by the U.S. House of Representatives, March 2,

1936, on charges of favoritism in the appointment of bankruptcy receivers and practicing law while sitting as a judge; convicted by the U.S. Senate and removed from office, April 17, 1936.

- Harry E. Claiborne (1917–2004), U.S. District Court for the District of Nevada: Impeached by the U.S. House of Representatives, July 22, 1986, on charges of income tax evasion and of remaining on the bench following criminal conviction; convicted by the U.S. Senate and removed from office, October 9, 1986.

- Alcee L. Hastings (1936–2021), U.S. District Court for the Southern District of Florida: Impeached by the U.S. House of Representatives, August 3, 1988, on charges of perjury and conspiring to solicit a bribe; convicted by the U.S. Senate and removed from office, October 20, 1989.

Judge Harry E. Claiborne, a U.S. district judge from Nevada, was impeached on charges of tax evasion and removed from office in 1986.

- Walter L. Nixon (1928–), U.S. District Court for the Southern District of Mississippi: Impeached by the U.S. House of Representatives, May 10, 1989, on charges of perjury before a federal grand jury; convicted by the U.S. Senate and removed from office, November 3, 1989.

- Samuel B. Kent (1949–), U.S. District Court for the Southern District of Texas: Impeached by the U.S. House of Representatives, June 19, 2009, on charges of sexual assault, obstructing and impeding an official proceeding, and making false and misleading statements; resigned from office, June 30, 2009. On July 20, 2009, the U.S. House of Representatives agreed to a resolution not to pursue further the articles of impeachment, and on July 22, 2009, the Senate, sitting as a court of impeachment, dismissed the articles.

- G. Thomas Porteous Jr. (1946–), U.S. District Court for the Eastern District of Louisiana: Impeached by the U.S. House of Representatives, March 11, 2010, on charges of accepting bribes and making false statements under penalty of perjury; convicted by the U.S. Senate and removed from office, December 8, 2010.

# Supreme Court Operations

The party that seeks Supreme Court review is known as the petitioner. The party that responds to the petitioner's request is known as the respondent. If the Court decides to hear a case, it notifies both parties, and then each side must write a brief before the Court. The term "brief" is a bit of a misnomer, because Supreme Court briefs are not short. They typically range anywhere from 30 to 50 pages in length.

The petitioner files a brief first, and then the respondent files a brief. The petitioner then has an opportunity to file a reply brief. The parties are not the only ones who file briefs before the U.S. Supreme Court. Interested groups, businesses, professors, or others often file what are known as "amicus" or "friend-of-the-court" briefs. The purpose of an amicus brief is to provide insight to the justices on a particular issue or area of law. In some cases, there are more than 100 amicus briefs filed. For example, when the U.S. Supreme Court was reviewing the constitutionality of so-called affirmative action policies for the University of Michigan undergraduate and law schools, there were amicus briefs filed by all sorts of groups in the business world who generally supported the idea of promoting diversity. However, there were many other groups who opposed the policies.

Amicus briefs sometimes can have an impact on the Court. An interesting example occurred in the famous First Amendment case *Hustler Magazine Co. v. Falwell* (1988), a case sometimes billed as the Preacher v. the Pornographer. Jerry Falwell (1933–2007), a well-known televangelist and head of a political organization called the Moral Majority, had sued Larry Flynt (1942–2021), the publisher of *Hustler* magazine, for intentional infliction of emotional distress after *Hustler* had published a parody of some liquor ads of the time that featured celebrities talking about their "first times"—the first time they had tasted the drink but with an obvious sexual double entendre. Flynt published a parody ad in which Falwell described his first time as a "drunken rendezvous with his mother in an outhouse." This greatly upset Falwell, who filed a lawsuit and won a sizeable jury verdict.

*Hustler* appealed all the way to the U.S. Supreme Court. One of the amicus briefs in the case was filed by the Association of American Editorial Cartoonists and written by Roslyn Mazer (1949–). Mazer and fellow attorney George Kaufman had compiled an impressive list of historical examples of cartoons, arguing that cartoonists needed leeway for their expressive work. At the time, many in the press were worried how the case might turn out. It just so happened that Chief Justice William Rehnquist was a greater collector of political cartoons, and he found the amicus brief very persuasive.

Rehnquist wrote the opinion for a unanimous court and cited much information that was mentioned in the amicus brief. "Despite their sometimes caustic nature, from the early cartoon portraying George Washington as an ass down to the present day, graphic depictions and satirical cartoons have played a prominent role in public and political debate," Rehnquist wrote. This is just one of many examples in which amicus briefs played a role.

After the parties file their briefs, there is a process known as oral argument. In oral argument, each side receives 30 minutes. During this process, the attorney begins with an opening statement, and the justices fire questions at the attorney. The process is incredibly demanding, as the justices generally are very active in their questioning. During the Covid-19 pandemic, each justice would ask questions in order, starting with Chief Justice John Roberts Jr. (1955–) and followed by each associate justice in terms of seniority. Thus, Justice Clarence Thomas (1948–), who has served on the Court the longest, would ask his questions next, and the last would be Justice Amy Coney Barrett (1972–), the newest justice on the Supreme Court.

There are attorneys who specialize in Supreme Court arguments. Daniel Webster (1782–1852), a U.S. congressman and attorney from Massachusetts, argued nearly 250 cases before the U.S. Supreme Court, but, believe it or not, he doesn't hold the record. Walter Jones (1745–1815) of Virginia argued 317 cases before the Supreme Court over a nearly 50-year span from 1801 to 1850.

## Supreme Court Opinions

After the Supreme Court hears oral arguments, they meet in conference to discuss the case. At this time, the justices take a vote on the case. If the chief justice is in the majority, he or she gets to assign which justice writes the opinion. This is known as the assignment power. If the chief justice is not in the majority, then the senior associate justice in the majority gets to assign the opinion.

There are several different types of opinions. If there is only one opinion for all the justices, this is a unanimous opinion. For example, Chief Justice Earl Warren (1891–1974) wrote the Court's unanimous opinion in *Brown v. Board of Education* (1954), ruling that segregated public schools violated the Equal Protection Clause of the Fourteenth Amendment. However, if the justices are split, then there is either a majority or plurality opinion for the Court. A majority opinion is an opinion that five or more justices sign. The majority opinion is the force of law; it has precedential value. So, if all nine justices participate in a case, a majority opinion would have five or more justices agree to it. A plurality opinion is the main opinion of the Court but one that does not have a majority of five justices who sign their name to it. For example, let's say that a Court splits 7–2 but the seven justices are split into an opinion of four and an opinion of three. The opinion for the four justices is called a plurality opinion.

Justices also write concurring opinions. A concurring opinion is one that agrees with the result of the majority opinion but not necessarily its reasoning. Sometimes, concurring opinions become more influential with the passage of time. For example, in *Katz v. United States* (1967), the Supreme Court determined that the government violated the Fourth Amendment right to be free from unreasonable searches and seizures when it bugged a public pay phone and eavesdropped on the conversations of bookie Charles Katz. Justice Potter Stewart (1915–1985) wrote the majority opinion for the Court, but it was Justice John Marshall Harlan II's (1899–1971) concurring opinion that has proven to be more important. In that

Associate Justice Potter Stewart served in the Supreme Court from 1958 to 1981. He famously stated in the *Jacobellis v. Ohio* case that, when it comes to judging a film as pornography, "I know when I see it."

opinion, Justice Harlan created what is known as the "reasonable expectation of privacy" test—a test still used today by judges to determine whether the government has violated the Fourth Amendment.

Speaking of Stewart, he was known for his concurring opinion in an obscenity case before the Court in 1964. In *Jacobellis v. Ohio*, the Court was grappling with whether a French movie, *Les Amants* (The Lovers) was legally obscene. Stewart wrote a concurring opinion that included the following memorable passage: "I shall not today attempt further to define the kinds of material I understand to be embraced within that shorthand description; and perhaps I could never succeed in intelligibly doing so. But I know when I see it, and the motion picture involved in this case is not that."

When justices disagree with the result of a majority opinion, they may file a dissenting opinion. Dissents can be important or even prophetic. Consider that in 1896, the U.S. Supreme Court legalized segregation in *Plessy v. Ferguson*, upholding a Louisiana law that mandated separate railway accommodations on the basis of race. Only one justice dissented—Justice John Marshall Harlan I (1877–1911), the so-called "Great Dissenter." Harlan famously wrote:

> But, in view of the Constitution, in the eye of the law, there is in this country no superior, dominant ruling class of citizens. There is no caste here. Our Constitution is color-blind and neither knows nor tolerates classes among citizens. In respect of civil rights, all citizens are equal before the law. The humblest is the peer of the most powerful. The law regards man as man, and takes no account of his surroundings or of his color when his civil rights as guaranteed by the supreme law of the land are involved.

Harlan was all alone in his dissent in 1896, but 58 years later in *Brown v. Board of Education*, the Supreme Court adopted his color-blind position and ruled against the noxious "separate but equal" doctrine of *Plessy v. Ferguson*. The *New York Times* wrote that "this is an instance of which the voice crying in the wilderness finally becomes an expression of the people's will." Chief Justice Charles Evans Hughes (1862–1948) echoed a similar theme as to the importance of a dissenting opinion when he wrote: "A dissent in a court of last resort is an appeal to the brooding spirit of the law, to the intelligence of a future day, when a later decision may possibly correct the error into which the dissenting judge believes the court to have been betrayed."

Indeed, sometimes a dissenting opinion later becomes the law of the land. However, even if a dissenting opinion never commands a majority, that does not lessen its importance. Justice Antonin Scalia (1936–2016), famous for his strongly worded dissents, once said that "dissents augment rather than diminish the prestige of the Court."

## Chief Justices

Article III does not mention a chief justice, but the Constitution in Article I, Section 3 provides that "when the President is tried for impeachment, the Chief Justice shall preside." For example, when the Senate tried President Bill Clinton (1946–), Chief Justice William Rehnquist presided over this trial. Similarly, when the Senate held the impeachment trial of President Andrew Johnson (1808–1875) back in 1869, Chief Justice Salmon P. Chase (1808–

Justice John Marshall Harlan II was nicknamed "the Great Dissenter" for the many times he dissented on rulings in which the Supreme Court ruled in favor of restricting civil liberties.

1873) presided over the trial. Donald Trump (1946–) was unique among American presidents in that he faced two impeachment trials. Chief Justice John Roberts Jr. presided over the first trial, but Senate pro tem leader Patrick Leahy (1940–) presided over Trump's second trial. Roberts apparently reasoned that he was not constitutionally required to preside over this second trial, as it took place after Trump was no longer president.

The United States has had 17 chief justices—from John Jay to John G. Roberts Jr. It is common to refer to distinct Supreme Court periods by the last name of the sitting chief justice, such as the Warren Court, the Burger Court, or the Roberts Court.

John Jay served as the Court's original chief justice from 1789 until 1795 when he left the Court to become governor of New York. President George Washington (1732–1799) originally had offered Jay the position of secretary of state, but Jay declined. Washington then nominated him to serve as chief justice. The second chief justice, John Rutledge, only served for five months in 1795. He was a so-called recess appointment, meaning that Washington nominated him when the Senate was not in session to confirm the nomination. When the Senate reconvened, they voted against Rutledge by a vote of 14–10. Rutledge left the Court to become chief justice of the South Carolina Supreme Court.

Earl Warren was considered one of the great chief justices of the Supreme Court. He famously led the Warren Commission that investigated the assassination of President John F. Kennedy.

The third chief justice was Oliver Ellsworth (1745–1807), the primary architect of the Judiciary Act of 1789. He served as chief justice from 1796 to 1800. It was the fourth chief justice, John Marshall, who is still considered today as the most powerful and significant chief justice in American history. In his biography of Marshall, Jean Edward Smith called him "the Definer of the Nation." He served on the Court for 34 years, from 1801 to 1835. He remains the longest-serving chief justice in American history.

President John Adams nominated Marshall, his secretary of state, to replace Ellsworth. In fact, for a couple of remarkable years, Marshall technically served as both secretary of state and chief justice of the United States. Today, this could not happen, as it would be seen as a clear conflict of interest. Marshall's early opinions established the power of the judicial branch, including the concept of judicial review—the power to review whether acts of the legislative or executive branch are constitutional. Marshall declared in the famous case *Marbury v. Madison* (1803) that "it is emphatically the province and duty of the judicial department to declare what the law is." He also carved out broad powers of Congress to pass laws that were deemed necessary and proper in *McCullough v. Maryland* (1819) and broadly defined commerce in *Gibbons v. Ogden* (1824).

Another chief justice known for his great leadership was Earl Warren, who guided the Court from 1953 until 1969. Surprisingly to modern Court observers, Warren had never served as a judge before President Dwight D. Eisenhower (1890–1969) nominated him to replace the vacant chief justiceship after Fred Vinson (1890–1953) died. Warren served as a deputy city attorney for Oakland, district attorney for Alameda County, California attorney general, and governor of California. Warren initially sought the Republican nomination for president in 1952 but withdrew and gave his support to Eisenhower, who returned the favor and later elevated Warren to chief justice.

Warren receives praise from historians for marshaling a unanimous Court in *Brown v. Board of Education* (1954). Previously, the Court was divided over the question of segregation when it was initially argued in 1952, but Warren knew that the country needed the Court to do the right thing. Warren wrote that "in the field of public education, the doctrine of separate but equal has no place" and that "separate educational facilities are inherently unequal."

The Warren Court upheld the constitutionality of the Civil Rights Act of 1964, reasoning that Congress had the power under the Commerce Clause to pass a law that prohibited hotels from denying service to African Americans in *Heart of Atlanta Moel v. United States* and to prohibit a restaurant in Atlanta from denying African Americans the right to eat inside the restaurant in *Katzenbach v. McClung*.

The Warren Court also was known for expanding the Bill of Rights when it came to criminal defendants with cases such as *Gideon v. Wainwright* (1963), ensuring that poor defendants facing felony charges are entitled to an attorney; *Miranda v. Arizona* (1966), mandating that those arrested be read their rights by police before questioning and custodial interrogation; and *Mapp v. Ohio* (1961), ensuring that the exclusionary rule applied in state criminal prosecutions.

Chief Justice John G. Roberts Jr. is the current chief justice and has been since his nomination to replace his former boss, Chief Justice William Rehnquist, in 2005. After serving as a law clerk to Rehnquist in 1980–81, Roberts worked in private practice in Washington, D.C., and served as deputy solicitor general, a position from which he argued many cases before the U.S. Supreme Court. Roberts also served as a judge on the U.S. Court of Appeals for the District of Columbia Circuit from 2003 until being elevated to the Supreme Court.

## CHIEF JUSTICES

| Name | Years as Chief Justice |
| --- | --- |
| John Jay | 1789–1795 |
| John Rutledge | 1795 |
| Oliver Ellsworth | 1795–1800 |
| John Marshall | 1801–1835 |
| Roger B. Taney | 1836–1864 |
| Salmon P. Chase | 1864–1873 |
| Morrison Waite | 1874–1888 |
| Melville Fuller | 1888–1910 |
| Edward White | 1910–1921 |
| William Howard Taft | 1921–1930 |
| Charles Evans Hughes | 1930–1941 |
| Harlan Fiske Stone | 1941–1946 |
| Fred Vinson | 1946–1953 |
| Earl Warren | 1953–1969 |
| Warren Burger | 1969–1986 |
| William Rehnquist | 1986–2005 |
| John G. Roberts Jr. | 2005– |

# The Confirmation Controversy

Article II, Section 2 provides that the president of the United States shall have the power to nominate "Judges of the Supreme Court." That same part of the Constitution also provides that the president shall have the power to nominate "all other Officers of the United States, whose Appointments are not herein otherwise provided for, and which shall be established by Law." This means that the president has the power to nominate all federal judges.

The Constitution also provides that the U.S. Senate shall provide "Advice and Consent." This means that the president's judicial nominees must be confirmed by the Senate. The process has become even more politicized in recent years, with senators often voting along party lines. After the president nominates a candidate to the U.S. Supreme Court, the U.S. Senate either confirms or denies the nominee. The Senate Judiciary Committee gathers extensive information about the nominee, holds hearings, and eventually votes on whether to move the candidate on for a full Senate vote. The confirmation process can be quite difficult and lengthy depending on how controversial the candidate is deemed to be by Congress or, in recent years, whether a controversy erupts that threatens the candidate.

Twelve times the Senate rejected judicial appointments. Other times, candidates voluntarily withdrew their name from consideration. Here are the 12 Supreme Court nominees who had losing vote tallies in the Senate.

## REJECTED JUDICIAL APPOINTMENTS

| Candidate | Year Rejected | Vote (N–Y) |
|---|---|---|
| John Rutledge | 1795 | 14–10 |
| Alexander Wolcott | 1811 | 24–9 |
| John C. Spencer | 1843 | 26–21 |
| George W. Woodward | 1845 | 29–20 |
| Jeremiah Black | 1860 | 26–25 |
| Ebenezer R. Hoar | 1870 | 33–24 |
| William B. Hornblower | 1893 | 30–24 |
| Wheeler Peckham | 1894 | 41–32 |
| John J. Parker | 1930 | 41–39 |
| Clement F. Haynesworth Jr. | 1969 | 55–45 |
| G. Harold Carswell | 1970 | 51–45 |
| Robert Bork | 1987 | 58–42 |

Two of the more contentious confirmation hearings in recent memory were the confirmations of Justice Clarence Thomas and Justice Brett Kavanaugh (1965–). Thomas was confirmed by a vote of 52–48, and Kavanaugh was confirmed by an

Many Americans were troubled and upset by the confirmation of Brett Kavanaugh as a Supreme Court justice. He was narrowly confirmed by a 50–48–1 vote.

equally narrow margin of 50–48–1. Both justices faced allegations of sexual misconduct. Thomas had previously been the supervisor of Anita Hill (1956–) at both the Department of Education and the Equal Employment Opportunity Commission. Hill—who later became a law professor—accused Thomas of sexual harassment. The allegations were controversial, however, in part because Hill initiated the charges years after the fact, on the eve of Thomas's confirmation. Thomas vehemently denied the allegations, and famously referred to the Senate's inquiry into the harassment allegations as a "high-tech lynching."

Justice Kavanaugh faced even tougher allegations when a college psychology professor named Christine Blasey Ford (1966–) accused him of sexually assaulting her with another teenager at a high school party when she was 15 and he was 17. Ford testified as to her allegations, and Kavanaugh responded indignantly that the accusations were falsehoods.

## Qualifications of Supreme Court Justices

The Constitution does not provide or list any qualifications for federal judges, including Supreme Court justices. Technically, a nonlawyer with no prior judicial experience could be appointed to the U.S. Supreme Court. In fact, some very effective U.S. Supreme Court justices—Chief Justices Earl Warren and William Rehnquist, to name two—had never served as judges before being nominated to serve on the U.S. Supreme Court.

In practice, however, Supreme Court justices have very high levels of professional accomplishments in their legal careers. Congress and the Department of Justice vet the candidates, and the American Bar Association, the nation's largest association of lawyers, issues a rating of whether a judge is "highly qualified," "qualified," or "not qualified" to serve on the high court.

Most Supreme Court justices in recent memory previously served on a federal court of appeals. Consider the current Supreme Court justices. Eight of the nine current justices (as of 2022) have prior judicial experience:

- Chief Justice John Roberts (2005–) previously served on the U.S. Circuit Court of Appeals for the District of Columbia.
- Justice Clarence Thomas (1992–) previously served on the U.S. Circuit Court of Appeals for the District of Columbia.
- Justice Stephen Breyer (1994–) previously served on the U.S. Circuit Court of Appeals for the First Circuit.
- Justice Samuel A. Alito Jr. (2006–) previously served on the U.S. Circuit Court of Appeals for the Third Circuit.
- Justice Sonia Sotomayor (2009–) previously served on the U.S. Circuit Court of Appeals for the Second Circuit.
- Justice Neil Gorsuch (2017–) previously served on the U.S. Circuit Court of Appeals for the Tenth Circuit.
- Justice Brett Kavanaugh (2018–) previously served on the U.S. Circuit Court of Appeals for the D.C. Circuit.
- Justice Amy Coney Barrett (2020–) previously served on the U.S. Circuit Court of Appeals for the Seventh Circuit.

The only current justice who did not have prior judicial experience is Justice Elena Kagan (1960–), who has served on the U.S. Supreme Court since 2010. However, Justice Kagan has had an incredible legal career that includes serving as the dean of the Harvard Law School and as U.S. solicitor general. Only one current justice—Sonia Sotomayor (1954–)—has served on both the federal district court and the federal appeals court level.

# Articles IV–VIII

W̶e have discussed the three major articles of the U.S. Constitution—Article I and the legislative branch, Article II and the executive branch, and Article III and the judicial branch. However, the Constitution has seven articles—though collectively they are much shorter than any of the first three articles.

## Article IV: Full Faith and Credit Clause

> Full Faith and Credit shall be given in each State to the public Acts, Records, and judicial Proceedings of every other State. And the Congress may by general Laws prescribe the Manner in which such Acts, Records and Proceedings shall be proved, and the Effect thereof.

Most of the U.S. Constitution deals with the powers of the federal government and its three branches. That certainly is what the first three Articles are all about. However, Article IV is fundamentally different. It deals with how states deal with each other. Scholars sometimes refer to this as horizontal federalism, as compared to the traditional federalism between the federal and state governments.

The Full Faith and Credit Clause means that states generally should respect and honor judgments and rulings in other state courts. In other words, if a party is divorced in the state of California, that judgment of divorce is recognized in the state of Tennessee.

## 28 U.S.C. 1738

The Acts of the legislature of any State, Territory, or Possession of the United States, or copies thereof, shall be authenticated by affixing the seal of such State, Territory or Possession thereto.

The records and judicial proceedings of any court of any such State, Territory or Possession, or copies thereof, shall be proved or admitted in other courts within the United States and its Territories and Possessions by the attestation of the clerk and seal of the court annexed, if a seal exists, together with a certificate of a judge of the court that the said attestation is in proper form.

Such Acts, records and judicial proceedings or copies thereof, so authenticated, shall have the same full faith and credit in every court within the United States and its Territories and Possessions as they have by law or usage in the courts of such State, Territory or Possession from which they are taken.

Pride parade attendees celebrate the 2013 U.S. Supreme Court decision to allow same-sex marriage in this 2013 photo taken in Manhattan. The Supreme Court ruled that bans on gay marriage violated Due Process and Equal Protection Clauses in the Constitution.

This issue came into the forefront of public consciousness in another aspect of family law—marriage. The issue percolated because some states recognized the validity of same-sex marriages and other states did not. Congress further muddied matters by passing a federal law known as the Defense of Marriage Act (DOMA). The U.S. Supreme Court essentially obviated this problem by ruling that bans on same-sex marriage violated both the Due Process and Equal Protection Clauses.

## Privileges and Immunities Clause

> The Citizens of each State shall be entitled to all Privileges and Immunities of Citizens in the several States.

The Privileges and Immunities Clause prohibits states from discriminating against out-of-state persons with regard to fundamental rights and the ability to make a living. The clause prohibits "a state from discriminating against citizens of other States in favor of them." A classic case involved a state law that charged out-of-staters $2,500 for a shrimp fishing boat license but only $25.27 for such a license for an in-state fisherman. This is patent and obvious state discrimination.

An interesting Supreme Court case involving the Privileges and Immunities Clause was *Piper v. New Hampshire* (1985). In this case, the state of New Hampshire had a rule that attorneys must live in New Hampshire to be members of the New Hampshire Bar. Kathryn Piper, a resident of Vermont who lived only 400 yards from the New Hampshire border, applied for the ability to take the New Hampshire bar exam—the necessary test that law school graduates must pass to become licensed attorneys. Piper took and passed the exam, but the New Hampshire authorities would not give her a New Hampshire license because she did not live in the state.

*The Privileges and Immunities Clause prohibits states from discriminating against out-of-state persons with regard to fundamental rights and the ability to make a living.*

Piper sued, alleging several constitutional claims. Her primary claim was based on the Privileges and Immunities Clause. "The lawyer's role in the national economy is not the only reason that the opportunity to practice law should be considered a 'fundamental right,'" wrote Justice Lewis Powell Jr. (1907–1998) for the Supreme Court. "We believe that the legal profession has a noncommercial role and duty that reinforce the view that the practice of law falls within the ambit of the Privileges and Immunities Clause."

The state of New Hampshire advanced four reasons in favor of its rigid residency requirement, including that (1) out-of-state lawyers will not learn New Hampshire court rules as well as in-state lawyers; (2) out-of-state lawyers may act less ethically; (3) out-of-state lawyers may have a more difficult time being ready for court hearings and proceedings; and (4) out-of-state lawyers will not do as many pro bono hours (providing legal services for free).

The Court considered and rejected each one of these arguments. The Court said there was no evidence that out-of-state lawyers would not study New Hampshire rules or act less ethically than in-state lawyers. The one interest that gave the Court more pause was that out-of-state lawyers may not be as accessible to court hearings, especially ones on short notice. However, the Court reasoned that an out-of-state lawyer could associate or work with an in-state lawyer if necessary. The Court also felt that out-of-state lawyers could be just as concerned with access to justice issues than in-state lawyers. The Court concluded that New Hampshire violated the Privileges and Immunities Clause.

The Privileges and Immunities Clause of Article IV is similar to the Dormant Commerce Clause in that both deal with discriminatory state laws. In fact, often state laws will violate both clauses, but there are some key differences between the two. First, the Privileges and Immunities Clause only applies to discrimination against out-of-staters. Second, only citizens can sue under the Privileges and Immunities Clause, while corporations and noncitizens can sue under the Dormant Commerce Clause. Third, there are a couple of exceptions to the Dormant Commerce Clause—such as congressional approval and the so-called market participant exception—that do not apply to the Privileges and Immunities Clause.

To determine whether a law violates the Privileges and Immunities Clause, the first issue is whether the state has discriminated against out-of-staters vis-à-vis in-staters. Second, if there is such differential treatment, the question is whether the state has a sufficient justification for the discrimination.

## Extradition Clause

A Person charged in any State with Treason, Felony, or other Crime, who shall flee from Justice, and be found in another State, shall on Demand of the executive Authority of the State from which he fled, be delivered up, to be removed to the State having Jurisdiction of the Crime.

The Extradition Clause means that persons charged with crimes in one state will be extradited, or moved back, to the state that is charging them. This is a type of interstate compact that is necessary for states to operate efficiently and effectively. If there was not an Extradition Clause, a person could avoid criminal charges in Tennessee by moving to Kentucky and staying there.

## Fugitive Slave Clause

No Person held to Service or Labour in one State, under the Laws thereof, escaping into another, shall, in Consequence of any Law or Regulation therein, be discharged from such Service or Labour, but shall be delivered up on Claim of the Party to whom such Service or Labour may be due.

The Fugitive Slave Clause is a relic from the awful institution of slavery. It was a protection for slaveowners who wanted a way to be able to obtain any of their human chattel that fled and escaped. This noxious clause—like the Three-Fifths Clause—shows who slavery was reflected in the U.S. Constitution even though the word "slavery" was not mentioned.

Fortunately, the 39th Congress passed the Thirteenth Amendment, which outlawed slavery or involuntary servitude.

An 1872 illustration depicts fugitive slaves fighting off slave catchers. Unfortunately, the Fugitive Slave Clause of the Constitution was designed to protect the "property" of slaveowners in the South. The clause was overturned in 1865 by the Thirteenth Amendment.

## Admissions Clause

New States may be admitted by the Congress into this Union; but no new State shall be formed or erected within the Jurisdiction of any other State; nor any State be formed by the Junction of two or more States, or Parts of States, without the Consent of the Legislatures of the States concerned as well as of the Congress.

This provision in Article IV provides for the admission of new states to the United States. Most states formerly were territories and then at some point made the move from territory to state. The last two states admitted to the Union were Alaska and Hawaii—both admitted in 1959. Only three other states—Oklahoma, New Mexico, and Arizona—were admitted in the twentieth century.

The most likely possibilities for a 51st state include either the District of Columbia or Puerto Rico.

The Congress shall have Power to dispose of and make all needful Rules and Regulations respecting the Territory or other Property belonging to the United States; and nothing in this Constitution shall be so construed as to Prejudice any Claims of the United States, or of any particular State.

The next clause in Article IV gives Congress broad powers to make necessary rules and regulations for different territories. Congress did this with the Northwest Ordinance of 1787, passed the same year as the Constitutional Convention. This allowed Congress to prohibit slavery in newly admitted states in the early nineteenth century. However, it technically gives Congress the power to sell off national land, including parks.

## Guarantee Clause

The United States shall guarantee to every State in this Union a Republican Form of Government, and shall protect each of them against Invasion; and on Application of the Legislature, or of the Executive (when the Legislature cannot be convened) against domestic Violence.

This provision guarantees to the states the protection of the federal government. It also promotes the concept of majority rule. The Framers included the term "domestic Violence" in the Clause to refer to internal uprisings in a state. The Framers probably were thinking about Shays' Rebellion, when a group of economically distressed farmers rose up in armed rebellion.

# Article V

The Congress, whenever two thirds of both Houses shall deem it necessary, shall propose Amendments to this Constitution, or, on the Application of the Legislatures of two thirds of the several States, shall call a Convention for proposing Amendments, which, in either Case, shall be valid to all Intents and Purposes, as Part of this Constitution, when ratified by the Legislatures of three fourths of the several States, or by Conventions in three fourths thereof, as the one or the other Mode of Ratification may be proposed by the Congress; Provided that no Amendment which may be made prior to the Year One thousand eight hundred and eight shall in any Manner affect the first and fourth Clauses in the Ninth Section of the first Article; and that no State, without its Consent, shall be deprived of its equal Suffrage in the Senate.

The Framers realized that changes would need to be made to the Constitution. Thus, in Article V, they provided a process by which the Constitution can be amended or modified. For an amendment to go to the states, it first must be passed by both houses of Congress by a two-thirds majority vote. If a measure passes through two-thirds vote in both houses of Congress, then it goes to the states for potential ratification. Three-fourths of the states must then approve the measure for it be added to the Constitution. This is how all the amendments to the Constitution have been added. The other method is through state conventions. If two-thirds of state conventions call for an amendment, then the amendment can pass if three-fourths of states pass the measure.

It is difficult to amend the U.S. Constitution. There have been only 27 amendments. Some others have come very close. For example, the Equal Rights Amendment (ERA) passed Congress by the necessary supermajorities and was sent to the states for ratification. But not enough states ratified the measure in the requisite ten-year period.

The Equal Rights Amendment states:

Section 1. Equality of rights under the law shall not be denied or abridged by the United States or by any State on account of sex.

Section 2. The Congress shall have the power to enforce, by appropriate legislation, the provisions of this article.

Section 3. This amendment shall take effect two years after the date of ratification.

# AMENDING THE U.S. CONSTITUTION

**Both houses of Congress must adopt a proposed amendment with a 2/3 vote**

*or*

**A convention of the states, duly called by Congress under Article V, must adopt a proposed amendment**

**3/4 of state legislatures must ratify the amendment**

*or*

as proposed by Congress

**Ratifying conventions in 3/4 of the states must ratify the amendment**

The ratifying convention option has been used only once, for the Twenty-first Amendment.

On all but two occasions since 1917, Congress has limited the length of time the states have to ratify an amendment.
An amendment must be ratified by the requisite number of states within the stated period in order to become operative.

33 constitutional amendments have been adopted by both houses of Congress and sent to the states for ratification since 1789. Of those, only 27 have been ratified by the requisite number of states and became valid as part of the United States Constitution.

The Founders, under Article V, made it possible—but difficult—to amend the Constitution because they didn't want frivolous changes to be made to the document.

# Article VI

## Debts

> All Debts contracted and Engagements entered into, before the Adoption of this Constitution, shall be as valid against the United States under this Constitution, as under the Confederation.

This provision ensured that the new Constitution would not cancel out preexisting debts. In other words, the new Constitution did not grant a massive, whole-scale bankruptcy.

## Supremacy Clause

> This Constitution, and the Laws of the United States which shall be made in Pursuance thereof; and all Treaties made, or which shall be made, under the Authority of the United States, shall be the supreme Law of the Land; and the Judges in every State shall be bound thereby, any Thing in the Constitution or Laws of any State to the Contrary notwithstanding.

Article VI contains one of the most important clauses in the entire Constitution—the Supremacy Clause. This provides that the U.S. Constitution is the supreme law of the land. However, the Supremacy Clause also means that when a federal and state law conflict, the federal law trumps.

The Supremacy Clause is the basis for the preemption doctrine. This doctrine means that state laws that conflict with federal law have no effect. However, there are different types of preemption: (1) express preemption and (2) implied preemption. Sometimes a federal law will contain a provision that explicitly says that it preempts state law. However, other times it is implied that federal law preempts state law. If federal law dominates or occupies the field, then federal law controls. This is called field preemption. For example, state laws impacting immigration likely will be preempted, because immigration is an area in which the federal government occupies the field. The Supreme Court explained in *United States v. Arizona* (2012) that "State law must also give way to federal law in at least two other circumstances. First, the States are precluded from regulating conduct in a field that Congress, acting within its proper authority, has determined must be regulated by its exclusive governance."

## No Religious Tests

The Senators and Representatives before mentioned, and the Members of the several State Legislatures, and all executive and judicial Officers, both of the United States and of the several States, shall be bound by Oath or Affirmation, to support this Constitution; but no religious Test shall ever be required as a Qualification to any Office or public Trust under the United States.

This provision requires U.S. officers to pledge or affirm that they will support the U.S. Constitution. It also includes a provision that does not require religious tests to serve the country. This provision fulfills the spirit of freedom of religion, something protected even more in the First Amendment of the U.S. Constitution.

# Article VII

The Ratification of the Conventions of nine States, shall be sufficient for the Establishment of this Constitution between the States so ratifying the Same.

Article VII requires that nine states must ratify the Constitution for it go into effect. The nine states that ratified the Constitution are:

| State | Ratification Date |
| --- | --- |
| Delaware | December 7, 1787 |
| Pennsylvania | December 12, 1787 |
| New Jersey | December 18, 1787 |
| Georgia | January 2, 1788 |
| Connecticut | January 9, 1788 |
| Massachusetts | February 6, 1788 |
| Maryland | April 28, 1788 |
| South Carolina | May 23, 1788 |
| New Hampshire | June 21, 1788 |

# The First Amendment

Congress shall make no law respecting an establishment of religion, or prohibiting the free exercise thereof, or abridging the freedom of speech, or of the press, or the right of the people peaceably to assemble and to petition the government for a redress of grievances.

The First Amendment consists of the first 45 words of the Bill of Rights and consists of five freedoms: (1) religion, (2) speech, (3) press, (4) assembly, and (5) petition. Additionally, the U.S. Supreme Court also ruled in *NAACP v. Alabama* (1958) that the First Amendment protects the related freedom of association.

The First Amendment serves as our blueprint for personal freedom. It ensures that we live in an open society. The First Amendment contains five freedoms: religion, speech, press, assembly, and petition. Without the First Amendment, religious minorities could be persecuted, or the government could establish a single, national religion. The press could not criticize government, and citizens could not mobilize for social change. This would mean we would lose our individual freedom.

# Freedom of Religion

The first two clauses of the First Amendment—"respecting an establishment of religion or prohibiting the free exercise thereof"—are the religion clauses. The first is the Establishment Clause. The second is the Free Exercise Clause. Together, these clauses require that the government act in a neutral manner when it comes to religion.

The Establishment Clause provides that church and state remain separate to a certain degree. In a letter to the Danbury Baptists in 1802, President Thomas Jefferson (1743–1826) used the phrase a "wall of separation between church and state." The U.S. Supreme Court later used Jefferson's "wall of separation" metaphor to describe the meaning of the Establishment Clause and rule that state-mandated prayer in public schools violated the Establishment Clause.

The concern over separation between church and state was significant to several of the Framers, notably James Madison (1751–1836) and Thomas Jefferson. They and some others desired to place some distance between church and state to prevent American political leaders from acting like English monarchs who were intolerant of other religious views.

King Henry VIII (1491–1547) of England was a prime example of what can happen when there is not a sufficient barrier between church and state. King Henry broke away from the Catholic Church in 1531 after Pope Clement VII (1478–1534) refused to support his divorce from Catherine of Aragon (1485–1536). Henry established the Protestant Church of England. In 1534, the English Parliament passed the Act of Supremacy, establishing Henry as the head of the Church of England. This was a disaster for religious freedom.

Later, Parliament passed the Treason Act, which effectively silenced anyone who spoke out against the king. The act was used to silence religious dissenters. Religious intolerance seemed to be the standard in much of Europe, including England. Many people fled England to settle in America and the New World because of religious persecution. Religious dissenters in England were ostracized, punished, and imprisoned.

As noted, in the 1960s, the U.S. Supreme Court ruled that public school officials violated the Establishment Clause when they led students in prayer. The Court's ruling arose from the efforts of a man named Steven Engel, who ob-

When the Constitution stipulates that Americans have freedom of religion, this means *all* religions, including some that might not be popular with some Americans.

jected to his school requiring his elementary school kids to recite prayers in school. In 1958, the school district in Engel's area adopted a 22-word prayer developed and encouraged by the New York Board of Regents: "Almighty God, we acknowledge our dependence upon Thee, and we beg Thy blessings upon us, our parents, our teachers, and our Country."

Engel believed that public school officials should not be dictating what prayers a student should utter. He believed it was a private matter and objected to what he called a "one-size-fits-all" prayer. He and four other sets of parents filed a lawsuit contending that the mandatory prayer in public schools violated the First Amendment.

Engel lost in the New York State court system. In fact, New York's highest court—the New York Court of Appeals—declared: "That the First Amendment was ever intended to forbid as an 'establishment of religion' a simple declaration of belief in God is so contrary to history as to be impossible of acceptance."

However, Engel—with assistance from the American Civil Liberties Union (ACLU)—appealed to the U.S. Supreme Court. In 1962, the Court ruled in *Engel v. Vitale* (1962) that the mandatory prayer requirement violated the Establishment Clause of the First Amendment.

|| *Justice Black wrote that one of the very reasons why the colonists fled England was to find a place more tolerant when it came to religious practices.* ||

"The New York laws officially prescribing the Regents' prayer are inconsistent both with the purposes of the Establishment Clause and with the Establishment Clause itself," Justice Hugo Black (1886–1971) wrote for the Court majority. "It is neither sacrilegious nor antireligious to say that each separate government in this country should stay out of the business of writing or sanctioning official prayers and leave that purely religious function to the people themselves and to those the people choose to look to for religious guidance."

Justice Black wrote that one of the very reasons why the colonists fled England was to find a place more tolerant when it came to religious practices. He explained: "It is a matter of history that this very practice of establishing governmentally composed prayers for religious services was one of the reasons which caused many of our early colonists to leave England and seek religious freedom in America."

There was only one dissenter in the landmark case, Justice Potter Stewart (1915–1985). He believed his colleagues on the Court had "misapplied a great constitutional principle." Stewart pointed out that in 1954, Congress had added the phrase "one Nation under God, indivisible, with liberty and justice for all" to the Pledge of Allegiance. He also noted other common instances of religion in public life, such as that, since 1865, U.S. coins bore the words "In God We Trust."

The Supreme Court's decision in *Engel v. Vitale*—though controversial and criticized at times—remains good law. In several subsequent decisions, the Court has reaffirmed its core holding, as in *Abington School District v. Schempp* (1963), *Wallace v. Jaffree* (1985), *Lee v. Weisman* (1992), and *Santa Fe Independent Community School District v. Doe* (2000).

The Santa Fe case involved a Texas high school district's practice of allowing prayers over the loudspeaker at high school football games. Little is more important in Texas than high school football. Think *Friday Night Lights*. Many people in the community supported these prayers.

However, the ACLU challenged the practice on behalf of two students who objected to the practice. These students felt that they were a captive audience and faced coercive pressure to conform to majoritarian practices. The school district countered that the practice was constitutional because the students voted on the prayer practice. After all, majority rule is a fundamental principle of American government.

However, in terms of the freedoms in the First Amendment and the Bill of Rights, the rights of the minority are especially important. Some have called the Bill of Rights a counter-majoritarian document. In his majority opinion, Justice John Paul Stevens (1920–2019) addressed this concern, writing: "Here, however, Santa Fe's student election system ensures that only those messages deemed 'appropriate' under the District's policy may be delivered. That is, the majoritarian process implemented by the District guarantees, by definition, that minority candidates will never prevail and that their views will be effectively silenced."

Stevens also noted that the practice would be perceived by football game attendees as being endorsed or promoted by the school. To the majority, this was an unacceptable blurring of the lines between church and state.

Chief Justice William Rehnquist (1924–2005) wrote a dissenting opinion joined by two other justices. He accused the majority of "bristl[ing] with hostility to all things religious in public life." Rehnquist pointed out that many presidents had issued Thanksgiving Day prayers, the frieze in the U.S. Supreme Court contains a picture of Moses, and other religious references permeate American culture.

The differing views of the Establishment Clause between Justice Stevens and Chief Justice Rehnquist are emblematic of the fact that people simply differ on what the Establishment Clause actually means. The Supreme Court remains deeply divided over its meaning. Author Stephen Mansfield captured this difference quite well in his book *Ten Tortured Words*—referring to the 10 words "Congress shall make no law respecting an establishment of religion."

It is still debatable when governmental action violates the Establishment Clause. Consider two decisions that the Supreme Court issued on June 27, 2005—the last day of the Court's term that year—*Van Orden v. Perry* and *McCreary County v. ACLU of Kentucky*. Both cases involved public displays of the Ten Commandments. The *Van Orden* case involved a Ten Commandments monument placed in a Texas public park forty years prior. It remained unchallenged until a homeless man—who once was a lawyer, Thomas Van Orden—challenged the constitutionality of its placement. The McCreary County case involved two Ten Commandment displays placed in county courthouses.

The challengers to the Ten Commandment displays in both cases argued that the Ten Commandments are primarily a set of religious documents, and the government may not promote or endorse that religious message. Instead, the government must remain neutral toward religion. The government officials in both cases countered that the Ten Commandments serve as the foundation for our moral and legal systems and should be respected. For example, many of the Ten Commandments—such as "Thou shalt not kill" and "Thou shalt not steal"—are principles codified in our criminal law codes.

The 10 Commandments are on this stone display installed at a parking lot in Cuero, Texas.

The Supreme Court ruled 5–4 in both decisions but reached different results. In *Van Orden,* the Court ruled 5–4 that the Ten Commandments monument in the Texas public park was constitutional and could remain there, but the Court ruled by the same split that the Ten Commandments displays in the Kentucky case had to be removed.

Admittedly, there were some differences between the two cases. A display in a public park is different from a display in a courthouse. Many people might have to go to a courthouse, but they could avoid the park if they were deeply offended by the display. However, these differences did not matter to eight of the nine Supreme Court justices. Four justices ruled in favor of the displays in both cases, and four justices ruled against the displays in both cases. Only Justice Stephen Breyer (1938–)—who had been on the Court since 1994—switched sides in the two cases. Breyer proposed what is called the "legal judgment" test. Breyer explained: "If the relation between government and religion is one of separation, but not of mutual hostility and suspicion, one will inevitably find difficult borderline cases. And in such cases, I see no test-related substitute for the exercise of legal judgment." Breyer wrote that this test is not one of "personal judgment" but requires the justices to consider the underlying purposes of the Establishment Clause and consider "context and consequence."

What does that mean? If you are scratching your head at Breyer's language, don't worry, you are not alone. Many trained legal scholars don't understand Breyer's "legal judgment" test.

# Establishment Clause Tests

Speaking of tests, the Supreme Court has come up with a dizzying array of them to try to decipher whether a governmental display, rule, or regulation offends the Establishment Clause. The most common test is called the Lemon test. This comes from a 1971 Supreme Court decision called *Lemon v. Kurtzman*. It involved a challenge to a Pennsylvania law that provided subsidies for textbooks at schools, including religious schools. The Court established a three-part test to determine whether a government action violates the Establishment Clause. The test requires that (1) the action must have a secular purpose; (2) its primary effect must not advance or inhibit religion; and (3) there must be no excessive entanglement between church and state.

The Court has applied the Lemon test in many cases through the years but has reached inconsistent results, calling on several justices to criticize the test as too malleable and flexible. Justice Antonin Scalia (1936–2016) once even called it "a nightmarish ghoul … that still stalks our Establishment Clause jurisprudence."

Justice Stephen Breyer used a touchstone he calls "legal judgment" to justify why he is the only justice to have waffled on the issue of displays of the 10 Commandments government property.

In 1984, Justice Sandra Day O'Connor (1930–) proposed what she called a "refinement" of the Lemon test called the endorsement test. Under this view, from the perspective of a reasonable observer, the question becomes whether this reasonable person believes that the governmental display or practice involves the government endorsing or promoting religion.

In 1989, Justice Anthony Kennedy (1936–), in a concurring opinion, proposed still another test—called the coercion test. Kennedy focused on the indirect coercive pressure placed upon religious minorities when the government aligns with a majoritarian religious practice. Kennedy reasoned in *Lee v. Weisman* (1992) that a public middle school's practice of having rabbi-led prayer at a graduation ceremony violated the Establishment Clause because it placed such coercive pressure upon religious minorities. In response, Justice Scalia referred to Kennedy's test as "a boundless, and boundlessly manipulable, test of psychological coercion" and accused the majority opinion of taking readers on a "psychojourney."

> *Kennedy reasoned in* Lee v. Weisman *(1992) that a public middle school's practice of having rabbi-led prayer at a graduation ceremony violated the Establishment Clause because it placed such coercive pressure upon religious minorities.*

At other times, the Court applies what is sometimes referred to as a "history and tradition" analysis. The idea is that if a religious-based practice has been done for a long time, it has acquired the force of history and tradition and perhaps even been secularized to a certain extent. The Court applied this type of analysis in a case called *Marsh v. Chambers* (1983), when Nebraska state senator Ernest Chambers challenged the legislature's then 107-year-old practice of having chaplain-led prayer before legislative sessions. The Court applied a similar analysis in upholding a New York town's practice of opening town meetings with a prayer in *Town of Greece v. Galloway* (2014).

Whatever one's feelings on the Establishment Clause, it is hard to argue with Justice Clarence Thomas's (1948–) assessment that much clarification is needed of the Court's jurisprudence in this area. The results appear inconsistent and even puzzling.

# The Free Exercise Clause

The second religion clause of the First Amendment is the Free Exercise Clause. It protects a person's right to practice religion freely or to practice no religion at all. The First Amendment protects both the religiously devout and the fiercely atheistic.

There is absolute protection for freedom of belief under the Free Exercise Clause. A person can belief in God, Buddha, Allah, or the Flying Spaghetti Monster. In fact, courts are not supposed to determine free-exercise cases based on whether a religious practice is orthodox or a commonly practice religion.

However, there is not absolute protection for religious-based conduct that may conflict with a neutral and generally applicable law that applies across the board. In fact, the level of free exercise protection has diminished somewhat over the years, because of a difference in approach from the U.S. Supreme Court.

Take the example of an Arizona man who was stopped by the police carrying 38 pounds of marijuana in his car. Authorities charged him with drug possession and distribution. The man claimed that he was a high priest in the Church of Marijuana and had a divine duty to distribute as much marijuana as he could. The court rejected his defense.

The Supreme Court's height of protecting religious practices under the Free Exercise Clause was in the 1960s and 1970s. In 1963, the Court ruled in *Sherbert v.*

An Arizona man was not able to get away with carrying 38 pounds of marijuana by saying he was a priest in the Church of Marijuana. Too bad for him he didn't claim to be a member of the actual International Church of Cannabis in Denver, Colorado (pictured), which is the home of Elevationism, a registered religion.

*Verner* that South Carolina officials violated the free-exercise rights of Adele Sherbert, a Seventh-Day Adventist who was fired from her job and denied unemployment benefits because she would not work on Saturdays. Seventh-Day Adventists believe that the day of worship is Saturday, not Sunday. Sherbert argued that the state violated her freedom of conscience by denying her unemployment benefits simply because she refused to work on Saturdays.

The state courts in South Carolina rejected Sherbert's free-exercise claims, finding that she could still practice her religious faith at different times. The U.S. Supreme Court reversed, finding that the state infringed on her religious liberty rights and that the state could not justify such an infringement by a compelling, or strong, state interest. "Significantly, South Carolina expressly saves the Sunday worshipper from having to make the kind of choice which we here hold infringes the Sabbatarian's religious liberty," Justice William Brennan Jr. (1906–1997) wrote for the Court.

In legal terms, the Supreme Court in the Adele Sherbert case applied the highest form of judicial review—strict scrutiny—to determine whether South Carolina violated her religious liberty rights. Under strict scrutiny, the government can infringe on religious liberty only if the government advances a compelling governmental interest in a very narrowly drawn way. The state of South Carolina had argued that the denial of unemployment benefits was justified because the state had a compelling interest in preventing fraudulent claims for benefits. However, the U.S. Supreme Court ruled that South Carolina had failed to carry its burden of showing a danger of such claims.

The Court continued this pattern of applying strict scrutiny to free-exercise claims when a litigant was able to show that a governmental entity had substantially burdened its religious liberty rights, but that all changed in 1990. That year, the Court decided a case involving a similar issue. In *Employment Division v. Smith,* two Native American drug counselors from Oregon claimed their First Amendment rights were violated when they were denied unemployment benefits after they were fired for drug use. The individuals had ingested peyote—a hallucinogenic drug—for religious reasons. The two individuals argued that their religious rights, like that of Sherbert, were being punished.

The Court ruled in favor of the state and against the two former drug counselors. The high court wrote that the state's criminal law against drug use was a neutral law of general applicability. The Court found there was no religious exemption to fail to comply with the state's drug laws.

Now, the key question in Free Exercise Clause cases is whether the government is directly targeting a religious practice. If the law is not neutral and is targeting a specific religion, then strict scrutiny still applies. But after *Employment Division v. Smith*, if a law is neutral and of general applicability, then the Court applies a much more deferential standard of review for the government—something called rational basis.

Critics charged that the Court unnecessarily lowered the level of religious liberty protection for free exercise in *Employment Division v. Smith*. The Court, however, has never overruled the *Smith* decision. Instead, Congress has responded by passing two laws—the Religious Freedom Restoration Act (RFRA) of 1993 and the Religious Land Use and Institutionalized Persons Act (RLUIPA) of 2000.

What this means is that individuals generally have greater rights under these statutes or laws than they do under the Free Exercise Clause of the Constitution. Many believe that the Court's decision in *Employment Division v. Smith* should be revisited and overruled, but as we learned when discussing the Supreme Court in the judiciary chapter, it often takes decades for the Court to overrule a prior decision, if ever.

# Freedom of Speech

The First Amendment also protects the right of free speech, but this seemingly simple concept has created a labyrinthine body of law full of different rules, tests,

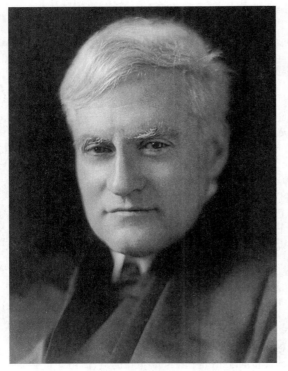

An associate justice during the 1930s, Benjamin Cardozo asserted that free speech as provided by the First Amendment is "the indispensable condition" of a free society.

exceptions, and doctrines. What is clear is its importance. The First Amendment and its protection of free speech is what Justice Benjamin Cardozo (1870–1938) once called "the matrix, the indispensable condition, of nearly every other freedom." Without freedom of speech, individuals could not criticize government, speak out against abuses, achieve individual self-fulfillment, or participate in the process of democratic self-government.

Initially, it was clear that the First Amendment applied when the government sought to prevent speech from ever occurring—what are called "prior restraints" on expression. An example of this was the dreaded English Licensing Law of 1643, which required printing houses to obtain licenses from the Crown before they could print. The great English legal historian William Blackstone (1723–1780) warned against prior restraints on expression, as did the great poet John Milton (1608–1674), who wrote a tract titled *Areogatica* against the licensing law. He famously wrote:

Tho all the winds of doctrine were let loose to play upon the fields, whoever knew truth put to the worse in a free and open encounter. Let Her and Falsehood grapple … whoever knew truth put to the worse in a free and open encounter.

Our early leaders, known as the Founding Fathers, spoke out mightily against arbitrary actions by the king of England and the English Parliament, such as tax increases. They wanted to ensure that Americans would have the right to criticize their government.

## Early Free-Speech Battle

James Madison included the First Amendment in the Bill of Rights in his "great rights of mankind" speech as we talked about earlier in the chapter on Article I. The Founding Father era was marked by bitter divisions between the Federalist Party and the Democratic-Republican Party. The leaders, and their newspaper editor surrogates, ruthlessly attacked each other with harsh political speech. One would have thought that the lessons from England would have forged in the colonists a healthy respect for free speech.

However, in a bitter irony, many of the same persons who voted to ratify the First Amendment also voted to ratify the Sedition Act of 1798, a law used by the Federalist Party to silence political opposition and dissent. The two-party system led to bitter political rancor, something President George Washington (1732–1799) had warned about in his Farewell Address. "Let me now take a more comprehensive view, and warn you in the most solemn manner against the baneful effects of the spirit of party generally," Washington told the country. "The alternate domination of one faction over another, sharpened by the spirit of revenge, natural to party dissension, which in different ages and countries has perpetrated the most horrid enormities, is itself a frightful despotism."

Despite Washington's warnings, the country plunged into deep conflict. Most notably, there was a split between Washington's former vice president, John Adams (1735–1826), and his former secretary of state, Thomas Jefferson. Adams became the leader of the Federalist Party, while Jefferson became the leader of the Democratic-Republican Party.

After George Washington left office, his former vice president, John Adams (pictured), rose to head the Federalist Party. The Federalists were supportive of Great Britain and were not exactly champions of free speech.

The parties differed most notably in their support of different superpowers. The Federalists aligned more with Great Britain, while the Democratic-Republicans aligned with France. To make matters worse, Adams and Jefferson ran against each other for president in 1796, with Adams narrowly prevailing.

However, there was no Twelfth Amendment to the Constitution in 1796, which ensures that the president and vice president run together from the same party. At that time, the highest vote-getter became the president, and the second-highest vote-getter became the vice president. Think of the prospect of a team of President Donald Trump (1946–) and Vice President Hillary Clinton (1947–), or President Joe Biden (1942–) and Vice President Donald Trump. It just did not work very well.

The Adams administration had great difficulty dealing with France. The situation worsened when some French naval vessels attacked American ships. The so-called "Quasi-War" with France ensued. Meanwhile, the Jefferson-led Democratic-Republicans criticized the Adams administration.

The Federalist-dominated Congress responded with a draconian assault on free-speech—the Sedition Act of 1798. It provided in part:

*SEC. 2. And be it further enacted,* That if any person shall write, print, utter or publish, or shall cause or procure to be written, printed, uttered or published, or shall knowingly and willingly assist or aid in writing, printing, uttering or publishing any false, scandalous and malicious writing or writings against the government of the United States, or either house of the Congress of the United States, or the President of the United States, with intent to defame the said government, or either house of the said Congress, or the said President, or to bring them, or either of them, into contempt or disrepute; or to excite against them, or either or any of them, the hatred of the good people of the United States, or to stir up sedition within the United States, or to excite any unlawful combinations therein, for opposing or resisting any law of the United States, or any act of the President of the United States, done in pursuance of any such law, or of the powers in him vested by the constitution of the United States, or to resist, oppose, or defeat any such law or act, or to aid, encourage or abet any hostile designs of any foreign nation against United States, their people or government, then such person, being thereof convicted before any court of the United States having jurisdiction thereof, shall be punished by a fine not exceeding two thousand dollars, and by imprisonment not exceeding two years.

‖ *The Sedition Act of 1798 turned the First Amendment on its head by criminalizing political* ‖
*speech—the type of speech that inspired the drafting of the provision in the first place.*

The law, especially Section 2, essentially criminalized harsh political criticism, treating it as defaming the government. The Sedition Act of 1798 turned the First Amendment on its head by criminalizing political speech—the type of speech that inspired the drafting of the provision in the first place. Sadly, many of the Framers did not see a problem in silencing their political opposition. Even members of the U.S. Supreme Court were actively involved in this process, because of the unusual dual role that these jurists served in the early days of the country, which included riding circuit. Justice Samuel Chase (1741–1811) was later impeached (though acquitted) for this poor conduct during the Sedition Act trial of journalist James Callender (1758–1803).

Ultimately, the country survived the Sedition Act ordeal when Jefferson became president, as he pardoned all those who had been convicted under it.

# Development of First Amendment Law

First Amendment free-speech law developed during the time of World War I. Historian and law professor Paul Murphy explained this well in his *World War I and the Origin of Civil Liberties in the United States*. The United States often suppressed the speech of political dissidents like anarchists and socialists.

In an act perilously like the Sedition Act of 1798, Congress passed the Espionage Act of 1917 and an amendment to it called the Sedition Act of 1918. These laws were used to prosecute political opponents. The Espionage Act criminalized attempting to cause insubordination to the war effort, willfully attempting to cause insurrection, and obstructing the recruitment or enlistment of potential volunteers. The Sedition Act of 1918 was a more direct assault on free speech. It criminalized:

> Uttering, printing, writing, or publishing any disloyal, profane, scurrilous, or abusive language intended to cause contempt, scorn … as regards the form of government of the United States or Constitution, or the flag or the uniform of the Army or Navy … urging any curtailment of the war with intent to hinder its prosecution; advocating, teaching, defending, or acts supporting or favoring the cause of any country at war with the United States, or opposing the cause of the United States.

Eugene V. Debs was a founding member of the Industrial Workers of the World and ran five times for the presidency under the Socialist Party ticket. In *Debs v. United States*, (1919) he was accused of violating the Espionage Act.

Literally thousands of people were prosecuted under these laws. Even famed labor organizer and frequent presidential hopeful Eugene Debs (1855–1826) was imprisoned for violating the Espionage Act after he criticized the draft. Debs had famously stated in a speech that "you need to know that you are fit for something better than slavery and common fodder."

## Clear and Present Danger

The U.S. Supreme Court decided some of these cases, including *Schenck v. United States* (1919). Socialists Charles Schenck and Elizabeth Baer had been prosecuted in U.S. District Court for distributing leaflets critical of the U.S. war effort, but the U.S. Supreme Court unanimously upheld their convictions, emphasizing that what can be said in times of peace often cannot be said in times of war. Writing for a unanimous Court, Justice Oliver Wendell Holmes Jr. (1841–1935) colorfully explained that the First Amendment does not protect all speech, writing: "The most stringent protection of free speech would not protect a man in falsely shouting fire in a theatre and causing a panic." Holmes's "shouting fire in a theatre" soon entered the cultural lexicon.

Holmes then created what became known as the clear and present danger test, writing:

The question in every case is whether the words used are used in such circumstances and are of such a nature as to create a *clear and present danger* that they will bring about the substantive evils that Congress has a right to prevent. It is a question of proximity and degree. When a nation is at war many things that might be said in time of peace are such a hindrance to its effort that their utterance will not be endured so long as men fight, and that no Court could regard them as protected by any constitutional right.

Holmes did indicate at least that the First Amendment free-speech clause did apply to more than prior restraints but also subsequent punishments on a speaker, writing: "It may well be that the prohibition of laws abridging the freedom of speech is not confined to previous restraints."

The Court reached similar decisions in *Frohwerk v. United States* (1919) and *Debs v. United States* (1919) with Holmes writing again. The *Schenck-Frohwerk-Debs* trilogy showed Holmes leading a Supreme Court that did not protect free speech.

However, something profound happened during the summer of 1919. Justice Holmes took a broader view of free speech. Several legal scholars and the great jurist Learned Hand (1872–1961) counseled Holmes on the importance of free speech. This resulted, in the fall of 1919, in Holmes breaking ranks with his fellow jurists, aside from Justice Louis Brandeis (1856–1941).

The case *Abrams v. United States* (1919) featured the prosecution of five Russian immigrants who disseminated leaflets critical of U.S. foreign policy toward Russia. The Supreme Court upheld their convictions by a 7–2 vote. Justice John Hessin Clarke (1857–1945), writing for the majority, applied what is sometimes pejoratively called "the bad-tendency test"—that speech can be prosecuted if it has negative consequences.

This time Justice Holmes wrote what Seton Hall law professor Thomas Healy has called "the Great Dissent." Holmes intensified his "clear and present danger" test, writing that "it is only the present danger of immediate evil or an intent to bring it about that warrants Congress in setting a limit to the expression of opinion where private rights are not concerned."

Associate Justice Oliver Wendell Holmes Jr. was one of the most influential justices in Supreme Court history, and his opinions continue to be cited today in court cases.

Holmes also introduced what has become known as the "marketplace of ideas" metaphor in free speech law. He wrote:

But when men have realized that time has upset many fighting faiths, they may come to believe even more that they believe the very foundations of their own conduct that the ultimate good desired is better reached by free trade in ideas—that the best test of truth is the power of the thought to get itself accepted in the competition of the market, and that truth is the only ground upon which their wishes safely can be carried out.

For much of the 1920s, Holmes and Brandeis dissented in free-speech cases. They recognized, as Holmes wrote in *Gitlow v. New York* (1925), that "every idea is an incitement."

# Free Speech and the Jehovah's Witnesses Cases

The composition of the Supreme Court changed when Charles Evans Hughes (1862–1948) joined the Court as chief justice in 1930. In 1931, for the first time, the Court protected an individual in a free-speech case. *Stromberg v. California* involved the prosecution of 19-year-old Yetta Stromberg, who every morning at a Communist Youth camp near San Bernardino, California, displayed a red flag to honor the working class.

A raid of the camp led to Stromberg being charged under a law that criminalized the display of the red flag "as a sign, symbol, or emblem of opposition to organized government or as an invitation or stimulus to anarchistic action or as an aid to propaganda that is of a seditious character."

A jury convicted Stromberg largely based on Communist literature in her possession. Chief Justice Hughes reversed her conviction, noting that people have the right to "free political discussion." He concluded that the California law was "too vague and indefinite" and could be used to convict many who advocated for political change by peaceful means.

The *Stromberg* case not only marked the first time the Court had struck down a law on First Amendment grounds, but it also established the principle that the First Amendment protects forms of symbolic speech. In later years, the Court ruled that wearing black peace armbands and even burning the American flag as a form of political protest are forms of symbolic speech or expressive conduct.

Later in the 1930s, the Court for the first time in *Herndon v. Lowry* (1937) invalidated a sedition-type prosecution, finding that a young African American Communist named Angelo Herndon (1913–1997) could not be convicted under an inciting insurrection law simply for trying to increase membership in the Communist Party in Georgia. The Court ruled that Herndon's "membership in the Communist

Party and his solicitation of a few members wholly fails to establish an attempt to incite others to insurrection."

*A jury convicted Stromberg largely based on Communist literature in her possession. Chief Justice Hughes reversed her conviction, noting that people have the right to "free political discussion."*

In the 1930s and 1940s, the Supreme Court protected First Amendment principles largely in a group of cases filed by the Jehovah's Witnesses, who often ran afoul of city officials for their insistence on distributing religious literature even in the face of prosecution and persecution. A notable example was an African American man named Roscoe Jones who was prosecuted in Opelika, Alabama, for selling religious literature without a license and nearly beaten to death in La Grange, Georgia.

Free-speech freedoms took a nose-dive during World War II and the era of the 1950s known as the "Red Scare" or "McCarthyism"—a terrifying period in American history when U.S. senator Joseph McCarthy (1908–1957) led Torquemada-style verbal interrogations of persons suspected of sympathizing with Communists. Guilt by association became standard operating procedure in American society. During this time, as University of Chicago law professor Geoffrey Stone explains, "hundreds, if not thousands, of innocent individuals ... ha[d] their reputations destroyed."

However, the 1960s witnessed a period of flourishing for First Amendment freedoms, as the U.S. Supreme Court, led by Chief Justice Earl Warren (1891–1974), reached its apex of power and decided a litany of free-expression cases that arose out of the Civil Rights Movement. In civil rights cases during the 1960s, the Court breathed First Amendment life into libel law, invalidated discriminatory permit denials for civil rights protestors, overturned breach-of-the-peace convictions for peaceful protests on state capitol grounds, and invalidated a conviction for peaceful sit-ins at segregated lunch counters and libraries.

When the Warren Court ended with the retirement of Chief Justice Warren in 1969, many feared that the Court would retract or reduce constitutional freedoms, including the freedom of speech. However, in the free-speech arena, the Court under Chief Justice Warren E. Burger (1907–1995) expanded First Amendment doctrine in numerous ways. The Court narrowed several unprotected categories of speech, protecting for the first time advertising or commercial speech, and warned against the government discriminating against speech based on the content or message of the speaker. This expansion of free-speech doctrine continued even more in the subsequent decades under Courts headed by Chief Justices William H. Rehnquist and his former law clerk, John G. Roberts Jr. (1955–).

In 2019, Roberts declared in an interview with Belmont University College of Law dean and former U.S. attorney general Alberto Gonzales (1955–): "I'm probably the most aggressive defender of the First Amendment. Most people might think that doesn't quite fit with my jurisprudence in other areas."

# Fundamental Free-Speech Principles

Free-speech law is an intricate area, but there are numerous fundamental principles that can help readers navigate it.

1. *The First Amendment protects the ability of people to criticize the government.*

The essence of the First Amendment is the ability of individuals to criticize the government. The Supreme Court defended this principle most notably in *New York Times Co. v. Sullivan* (1964), ruling that an editorial advertisement published in the *New York Times* that spoke of rights abuses perpetrated by Southern officials in Montgomery, Alabama, did not subject the newspaper or principal creators of the ad to liability for defamation. Montgomery police commissioner L. B. Sullivan had sued the *Times* and four African American clergymen who created the ad for defamation, even though he was not specifically identified.

An all-white, state-court jury in Alabama had awarded Sullivan $500,000 in damages, a verdict upheld by the Alabama Supreme Court. The *Times* appealed to the U.S. Supreme Court, and the fate of media entities to report on civil rights abuse hung in the balance.

Justice William Brennan memorably wrote that "there is a profound national commitment that debate on public issues should be robust, uninhibited, and wide-open and may well include vehement, caustic and unpleasantly sharp attacks on public officials."

Many years later, the Supreme Court reaffirmed the ability of individuals to criticize the government in a case involving a gay rights activist in Houston who had challenged the authority of police officers. Raymond Wayne Hill (1940–2018), the head of the Gay Rights Caucus, saw one of his friends being hassled by a police officer. Hill believed that the police were treating his friend unfairly, so he approached the officer and said, "Hey, why don't you pick on somebody your own size?"

For his brazenness at accosting the police officer, the officer arrested Hill and charged him with violating an ordinance prohibiting individuals from interrupting the official duties of po-

Published on March 29, 1960, in the *New York Times,* this ad, which was full of factual errors, resulted in a lawsuit by Police Commissioner L. B. Sullivan of Montgomery, Alabama.

lice officers. The ordinance read: "It shall be unlawful for any person to assault, strike or in any manner oppose, molest, abuse or interrupt any policeman in the execution of his duty, or any person summoned to aid in making an arrest."

A municipal court acquitted Hill of the charges. Hill then turned around and filed a federal civil rights lawsuit against the city and the officer, alleging that the law under which he was arrested was unconstitutional because it prohibited his right to free speech. The case went all the way to the U.S. Supreme Court, and the Court ruled in favor of Hill, finding that the law was overbroad because it criminalized a substantial amount of protected speech.

*Justice Brennan reiterated the right of individuals to challenge police authorities. "The First Amendment protects a significant amount of verbal criticism and challenge directed at police officers."*

Once again, Justice Brennan reiterated the right of individuals to challenge police authorities. "The First Amendment protects a significant amount of verbal criticism and challenge directed at police officers," he wrote, adding that the "freedom of individuals verbally to oppose or challenge police action without thereby risking arrest is one of the principal characteristics by which we distinguish a free nation from a police state."

The case resonates today in the wake of massive social justice protests in the wake of the deaths of George Floyd (1973–2020), Breonna Taylor (1993–2020), and other African Americans at the hands of police officers around the country. The First Amendment would be empty parchment if citizens did not have the ability to engage in dissident political speech and criticize government officials.

2.    *The First Amendment generally prohibits content and viewpoint discrimination by the government against private speakers.*

Content discrimination refers to the fact that government officials generally should not censor speech based on its content or message. The concern is that the government might engage in thought control, and freedom of thought is the beginning of freedom of speech.

Laws that restrict speech based on content are treated differently—as more suspect—than laws that do not. The key terms in First Amendment law are "content-based" and "content-neutral." A content-based law is one that discriminates against speech based on content. A content-neutral law is one that applies across the board to *all* forms of speech or is passed without reference to the content of the speech.

For example, let's say that a city ordinance prohibits all political signs but allows religious and commercial signs. This ordinance is content-based because it treats political signs worse that other types of signs. However, if a city prohibited all signs, that law would be content-neutral. A city ordinance banning all signs is unconstitutional, because it is too broad and forecloses an important medium of speech, but it would be considered content-neutral. Another way of expressing this concept is that the government applies greater scrutiny to a content-based law than a content-neutral law.

One may question why a content-based law is considered worse than a content-neutral law. The reason given is that, in a free society, we do not want the government telling us what to say, listen to, or believe. In other words, we don't want the government picking and choosing the messages that private citizens may hear.

The case of Earl Mosley illustrates this principle well. Mosley was a federal postal employee who worked in Chicago. Mosley believed that Jones Comprehensive High School was engaging in racial discrimination. For example, he believed the school needed to hire more African American teachers. Mosley took it upon himself to go near the school on his off-hours and picket peacefully by himself. He carried signs that read "Jones High School practices black discrimination" and "Jones High School has a black quota."

"There were very few commercial high schools in those days, teaching kids a trade," one of Mosley's lawyers, Harvey Barnett, said. "Mr. Mosley believed that black kids need an opportunity to go to commercial schools to get ahead in life."

Chicago had an ordinance that prohibited picketing within 150 feet of a school but had an exemption for labor picketing. In other words, picketing was not allowed with 150 feet of the school, but those involved in a labor union dispute could protest.

> *Mosley's lawyers ... contended that the Chicago ordinance was unconstitutional because it involved impermissible content discrimination.*

Mosley's lawyers, including Barnett, who argued the case before the U.S. Supreme Court at the age of 28, contended that the Chicago ordinance was unconstitutional because it involved impermissible content discrimination. It discriminated against Mosley based on the content or message of his speech.

The U.S. Supreme Court agreed and ruled in favor of the lone picketer in *Chicago Police Department v. Mosley* (1972). Writing for the Court, Justice Thurgood Marshall (1908–1993) explained in memorable language: "But above all else, the First Amendment means that the government may not restrict speech because of its message, ideas, subject matter, or its content."

Think of this as the "MISC" concept—message, ideas, subject matter, or content. The principle of content discrimination generally means that the government should not be discriminating against certain types of speech or speakers.

Content discrimination is bad, but so-called viewpoint discrimination is worse. Content discrimination refers to broad subject matter discrimination, while viewpoint discrimination goes deeper by restricting particular ideas. The discrimination against ideas is even stronger. For example, a law that allows commercial speakers but not political speakers represents a form of content discrimination. However, a law that allows the Republican Party speaker but not the Democratic Party speaker is a more focused and more intense type of speech discrimination.

*Content discrimination is bad, but so-called viewpoint discrimination is worse. Content discrimination refers to broad subject matter discrimination, while viewpoint discrimination goes deeper by restricting particular ideas.*

The difference between content and viewpoint discrimination may seem difficult to discern, but it really is not upon close inspection. For example, if a city prohibits all political speeches in a public park, that constitutes content discrimination, as the city policy clearly regulates speech based on its subject matter. However, let's say that the city then allows a speaker from one political party but not another. City officials seemingly prefer the viewpoint of the Republican Party over the Democratic Party—or vice versa. Here, the city has engaged in viewpoint discrimination, a subset of content discrimination.

The Supreme Court addressed the difference between viewpoint and content discrimination in *Rosenberger v. University of Virginia* (1995). The case involved a Christian-based student publication, *Wide Awake*, that was denied funding by the University of Virginia even though the university had approved funding for student groups of other religions. The challenged students argued that the university had discriminated against the religious viewpoint of their publication.

The Supreme Court agreed, with Justice Anthony Kennedy explaining the key difference between viewpoint and content discrimination:

> When the government targets not subject matter but particular views taken by speakers on a subject, the violation of the First Amendment is all the more blatant. Viewpoint discrimination is thus an egregious form of content discrimination. The government must abstain from regulating speech when the specific motivating ideology or the opinion or perspective of the speaker is the rationale for the restriction.

Another example of viewpoint discrimination occurred years earlier at a public school in Iowa. Several students, including siblings John Tinker and Mary Beth Tinker (1952–), wore black armbands to school to protest U.S. involvement in the Vietnam War. School officials had learned of the impending armband activism and hastily passed a school rule banning the wearing of armbands. The rule was problematic because school officials allowed students to wear other symbols, such as Iron Crosses or political campaign buttons. Thus, school officials ostensibly targeted a specific symbol associated with a particular political viewpoint. This is viewpoint discrimination.

3. *The First Amendment applies to a wide range of symbolic speech or expressive conduct.*

The First Amendment clearly applies to the spoken and written word, but the reach of the First Amendment extends to a wide range of symbolic speech and so-called expressive conduct. For example, the Supreme Court ruled that then-19-year-old Yetta Stromberg had a free-speech right to display a red flag at a Communist youth camp.

John and Mary Beth Tinker had a First Amendment right to wear black peace armbands to protest U.S. involvement in the Vietnam War at the schools they attended. The Court protected their symbolic speech, calling it "akin to pure speech."

More controversially, the First Amendment also protected the right of political protestor Gregory Lee Johnson (1956–), who burned an American flag as part of a protest against policies of the Ronald Reagan (1911–2004) administration. Prosecuted for violating a Texas flag desecration law, the Court found that the Johnson's act was a form of pure speech.

The difficult task is determining when expressive conduct is "expressive" enough to merit First Amendment review. The Supreme Court has examined this in a variety of contexts. One of its efforts came from the unusual expression of a student named Spence, who flew an upside down flag outside his dormitory room as a way to express his displeasure at the U.S. bombing of Cambodia. The Court created what has become known as "the Spence test." First, there must be an intent to convey a particularized message, and second, that message must be reasonably understood by others. The test is not as protective of First Amendment rights as it should be. After all, not all messages are particularized—nor should they be. Furthermore, First Amendment freedoms should not necessarily depend on the understanding of third parties.

However, it remains true that—as Chief Justice William Rehnquist once wrote—there are a lot of things out there with a "kernel of free expression," but they are not sufficiently expressive enough to merit protection. Some of the First Amendment claims can border on the bizarre. Take the case of the Indiana man who claimed he had a First Amendment–based right to grow the grass in his yard as high as he wanted to protest the overly authoritarian nature of city officials. Or the Minnesota man who claimed he had a First Amendment right to throw a pie in the face of a city councilman whose policies he detested.

4. *The First Amendment protects a great deal of offensive and even repugnant speech.*

Gregory Lee Johnson (right) is shown here with attorney William Kunstler in 1989. The Supreme Court ruled that Johnson's burning of an American flag as a political protest was a form of free speech.

The flagburner, the hatemonger, and the funeral protestor all have benefited from the generosity of the First Amendment's broad coverage. Justice William Brennan expressed the point quite succinctly in *Texas v. Johnson* (1989), writing, "If there is a bedrock principle underlying the First Amendment, it is that the government may not prohibit the expression of an idea simply because society finds it offensive or disagreeable."

The Court continued that principle with its ruling in *Snyder v. Phelps* (2011), protecting members of the Westboro Baptist Church from liability. The group, located in Topeka, Kansas, believes that God is punishing the United States because it tolerates homosexuality. The church and its followers began a practice of protesting at the funerals of slain members of the military. Church members hold up the most hurtful and hateful of signs evincing flagrant bias against gay persons.

The group protested outside the funeral of slain Marine Matthew Snyder near Westminster, Maryland. The protestors acted peacefully and complied with police orders but still engaged in their repugnant speech. Snyder's father, Albert, learned of the protest and sued the Westboro Baptist Church and its founder, Fred Phelps (1929–2014), for intentional infliction of emotional distress and other torts. A federal jury had rendered a whopping verdict of nearly $11 million, but both the Fourth U.S. Circuit Court of Appeals and the U.S. Supreme Court reversed and ruled in favor of the unpopular group. Chief Justice John Roberts famously wrote:

> Speech is powerful. It can stir people to action, move them to both tears of joy and sorrow, and—as it did here—inflict great pain. On the facts before us, we cannot react to that pain by punishing the speaker. As a Nation we have chosen a different course—to protect even hurtful speech on public issues to ensure that we do not stifle public debate. That choice requires that we shield Westboro from tort liability for its picketing in this case.

This fundamental principle has been under attack for quite some time, especially in the last several decades. Many people often act—to quote the late, great, longtime *Village Voice* columnist Nat Hentoff (1925–2017)—in a spirit of "Free Speech for Me, but Not for Thee." In other words, people claim they support freedom of speech in theory but when push comes to shove, they quickly can identify speech that ought to be censored. Activist Jonathan Rauch (1960–) warned of this back in the early 1990s, writing: "A very dangerous principle is now being established as a social right: Thou shall not hurt others with words. This principle is a menace—and not just to civil liberties. At bottom it threatens liberal inquiry—that is, science itself."

5.  *The First Amendment does not protect all forms of speech.*

The text of the First Amendment is absolute: "Congress shall make no law … abridging the freedom of speech." In the words of the late Justice Hugo Black—in certain contexts at least—"no law" meant no law, but the freedom of speech is not absolute. You don't have a First Amendment right to perjure yourself in court or extort money from another person. There are a host of other examples of unprotected categories of speech. Some of the more common are obscenity, incitement to imminent lawless action, true threats, obscenity, child pornography, and fighting words.

Thus, a key part of First Amendment free-speech law is determining whether speech falls into one of these narrowly unprotected categories of speech. Justice Frank Murphy (1890–1949) explained this in his now famous (or infamous) opinion in the classic "fighting words" opinion *Chaplinsky v. New Hampshire* (1942) when he wrote:

> There are certain well-defined and narrowly limited classes of speech, the prevention and punishment of which have never been thought to raise any Constitutional problem. These include the lewd and obscene, the profane, the libelous, and the insulting or "fighting" words—those which by their very utterance inflict injury and cause an immediate breach of the peace.

There are several narrowly unprotected categories of speech not entitled to First Amendment protection. Some of the more common are incitement, fighting words, true threats, child pornography, obscenity, and defamation.

These unprotected categories often started as quite broad, but then have narrowed over time. Take fighting words, for example. It used to mean that a person could not utter profanity at a law enforcement official, as Jehovah's Witnesses member Walter Chaplinsky did to Rochester, New York, marshal James Bowering after Bowering had called him a "damned Fascist and racketeer." However, now there is significant precedent protecting the profane speaker or even the middle-digit posturer. The Supreme Court famously narrowed the fighting words doctrine in the celebrated free-speech decision *Cohen v. California* (1971) to purely face-to-face personal insults.

Paul Robert Cohen faced criminal charges for breach of the peace when he wore a jacket bearing the words "Fuck the Draft" in a Los Angeles County Courthouse. Cohen argued that his passive act of wearing a jacket with a message was free speech. The state argued that the profane message was a form of fighting words, like those of Chaplinsky's decades earlier.

Another unprotected category of speech is incitement to imminent lawless action. The Court examined this in *Brandenburg v. Ohio* (1969),

Are profane gestures such as giving someone "the finger" considered free speech? According to court interpretations, yes!

a case involving a Ku Klux Klan leader named Clarence Brandenburg who burned a cross with about a dozen fellow Klansmen in the presence of a television reporter near Cincinnati, Ohio. Brandenburg then proclaimed that if the politicians in Washington, D.C., did not start listening to the people, "some revengeance [sic]" might have to be taken.

Brandenburg faced criminal charges in state court for violating the Ohio Criminal Syndicalism law, which prohibited the advocacy of "crime, sabotage, violence or unlawful methods of terrorism as a means of accomplishing industrial or political reform." He was convicted. Ohio appellate courts affirmed his conviction, but he appealed to the U.S. Supreme Court.

The Court determined in *Brandenburg* that "the constitutional guarantees of free speech and free press do not permit a State to forbid or proscribe advocacy of the use of force or of law violation except where such advocacy is directed to inciting or producing imminent lawless action and is likely to incite or produce such action." This has proven to be a very speech-protective standard.

A key question in early 2021 concerned whether outgoing president Donald J. Trump incited imminent lawless action when he spoke near the White House and urged supporters to march on the Capitol where members of Congress were certi-

When President Donald Trump made his speech on January 6, 2021, in Washington, D.C., many interpreted his words as inciting the attack on the Capitol that followed soon after. Was his speech protected under the Constitution since he never explicitly called for an attack?

fying the results of the 2020 presidential election. "We're going to walk down, and I'll be there with you," he said. "You'll never take back our country with weakness. You have to show strength, and you have to be strong."

Following his remarks, thousands of Trump supporters marched to the U.S. Capitol grounds. Several hundred members stormed the Capitol and committed acts of violence. In the resulting chaos, several people died. Critics charged that Trump incited violence with his speech. Others disagreed, pointing out that Trump never explicitly called for violence.

Obscenity is another salient example of an unprotected category of speech. There used to be obscenity prosecutions for booksellers who sold James Joyce (1882–1941) and D. H. Lawrence (1885–1930) novels. Now obscenity prosecutions are generally reserved for traffickers in sexually violent materials. However, the standards for obscenity are difficult to discern and seem to have a disturbing eye-of-the-beholder aspect to them. The Supreme Court developed the test for obscenity in *Miller v. California* (1973), and it has three parts.

To be legally obscene, material first must appeal predominately to a prurient interest in sex. Prurient is defined as morbid or shameful. Second, the material must depict sexual material in a "patently offensive" way. Both these prongs of the *Miller* test are considered under community standards—which essentially means whatever a local jury decides. Third, the material must have no serious literary, artistic, political, or scientific value. This last prong prohibits an overly puritanical prosecutor and community from criminalizing sexual material that really ought to be considered protected speech.

Periodically, government officials will argue that the Supreme Court should create new unprotected categories of speech. For example, the government argued in *United States v. Stevens* (2010) that images of animal cruelty were so bad that they were always unprotected—that is, not protected as free speech. Federal prosecutors had charged a man named Robert Stevens for marketing videos that featured pit bull dogs. A segment of the video showed pit bulls mauling to death another animal.

The Supreme Court resisted the government's argument to create a new unprotected category. Chief Justice Roberts warned that the government's argument was "startling and dangerous." He explained that the government does not have "freewheeling authority" to create new categories of unprotected speech. The Court in recent years also has rejected government officials' attempts to create new unprotected categories for violent video games, funeral protests, and false speech. Each time the Supreme Court has rebuffed this and taken the side of free speech.

6.  *The First Amendment often depends on the status of the speakers.*

At times, discrimination against speakers—so-called speaker discrimination—can be a form of impermissible content discrimination, but certainly not all the time.

Instead, the Court has carved out separate tests and bodies of law for four types of speakers—public employees, public school students, prisoners, and members of the military.

None of these types of speakers forfeit their rights when they enter the schoolhouse gate, the workplace, the jail cell, or the military base, but they certainly don't retain the level of rights they would receive outside of their context or status. For example, the Supreme Court ruled in *Garcetti v. Ceballos* (2006) that when public employees engage in official, job-duty speech, they have no free-speech protection—no matter how important the speech is.

*School officials can prohibit student speech in school that substantially disrupts school activities, is vulgar or lewd, or promotes the illegal use of drugs.*

Similarly, the Court has ruled that public school students don't "shed" all of their free-speech rights at the "schoolhouse gate," but that those rights must be interpreted "in light of the special characteristics of the school environment." School officials can prohibit student speech in school that substantially disrupts school activities, is vulgar or lewd, or promotes the illegal use of drugs.

Likewise, prisoners retain some First Amendment rights behind bars. Justice Sandra Day O'Connor once wrote that "prison walls do not form a barrier separating inmates from the protections of the Constitution" but then gave prison officials much deference to limit prisoner expression to further legitimate safety or rehabilitative goals.

Finally, members of the military have reduced free-speech rights as well. The Court has recognized the military's strong interest in establishing esprit-de-corps among the enlisted.

7.    *The First Amendment also protects the right not to speak.*

When one traditionally thinks of freedom of speech or even First Amendment cases, we think of a person engaging in speech that offends, annoys, or disturbs others—and then the government reacts by punishing the speaker. However, the First Amendment also applies when the government attempts to force or compel someone to speak.

The classic example comes from the Court's famous flag-salute opinion *West Virginia State Board of Education v. Barnette*, rendered on Flag Day in 1943—during World War II. West Virginia had a law that required public school students to salute the flag and recite the Pledge of Allegiance. Those who failed to conform faced expulsion from school and their parents potentially a 30-day jail sentence. Three years earlier, in *Minersville School District v. Gobitis*, the Supreme Court had upheld a similar flag salute law that had been challenged by Jehovah's Witness students Lillian and Billy Gobitis. The Court ruled 8–1 in favor of the state, elevating political authority over religious liberty and freedom of conscience.

This decision helped unleash a wave of violence against Jehovah's Witnesses in the thousands. Three justices—Hugo Black, William O. Douglas (1898–1980), and Frank Murphy—took the unusual step of announcing that they were wrong in another Jehovah's Witness case. The Court was actively looking for another student flag-salute case. They got it in *Barnette* and ruled 6–3 to overrule *Gobitis* and protect freedom of conscience.

Justice Robert Jackson (1892–1954) emphasized that the First Amendment protected the right of the Jehovah's Witness students to freedom of conscience—that these students had an individual sphere of liberty that the government could not infringe. He famously referred to this as a "fixed star in our constitutional constellation."

The no-compelled-speech doctrine means that the government cannot force us to say certain things or post certain messages. We are not automatons or the purveyors of only government-supported messages.

8.   *First Amendment rights at times are limited by the reaction of onlookers.*

One would think that a person should have the ability to speak at all times if the person speaks peacefully and offers their commentary, but the First Amendment ideal does not match the real world. The reality is that our First Amendment free-speech rights often depend upon the actions of others.

Take public school students, for example. The leading standard in First Amendment free-speech law is that student speech is protected by the First Amendment unless school officials can reasonably forecast that the speech will cause a substantial disruption.

A student speaker could speak in an entirely peaceful manner, but onlookers could react to that speech with unruly behavior and create a substantial disruption. This happened in a case in California where several students wore T-shirts with pictures of the American flag on Cinco de Mayo. This upset another body of students, who believed that the students wearing the T-shirts with American flags were disrespecting Latino students. An assistant principal, fearing possible violence between the student groups, forbade the students from wearing those T-shirts even though they were acting peacefully.

Even though they were committing no violent acts, students at one public school were forbidden to wear shirts with American flags on them during a Cinco de Mayo event because it was perceived as deliberately inflammatory by school officials.

9.   *Free speech rights are always fragile—especially in times of real or supposed emergencies.*

First Amendment rights are always fragile—especially during supposed times of crisis. Consider the massive restriction on free-speech rights when the United States was in a quasi-war with France. The Federalist Congress passed the Sedition Act of 1798, which led to the suppression of speech from the opposite political party. Consider the time of World War I when the suppression of civil liberties became a patriotic duty.

Early in the twenty-first century, look what happened after the terrorist attacks on September 11, 2001. We got the USA PATRIOT Act, which led to the suppression of much critical speech once again. In 2020, a worldwide pandemic caused by COVID-19 led to government-ordered lockdowns and restrictions on public gatherings. Many contended that such swift government action was needed to protect public health, safety, and welfare. Others countered that the measures often resulted in a sharp restriction on First Amendment freedoms.

## Freedom of the Press

Thomas Jefferson once said that if he had to choose between a government without newspapers or newspapers without government, he would not hesitate to "choose the latter." A free press is the heart of the First Amendment. The press has historically served as a check upon the government. The press is sometimes referred to as the "Fourth Estate" because of its important position in society in examining the three branches of government—the executive, legislative, and judicial. The press in England was not free. English officials passed licensing laws that forced writers and publishers to obtain prior approval of their works from the Crown before publication.

The English monarchy established this system of prior restraint to prevent criticism of the king. English courts, including the secret court known as the Star Chamber, punished those who engaged in seditious libel. In theory, seditious libel referred to speech that called for treason against the government. In practice, seditious libel referred to speech criticizing the king.

The 1735 trial of John Peter Zenger for libel remains a landmark case for freedom of the press. Zenger, who was publisher of the *New York Weekly Journal*, was accused for criticizing New York governor William Cosby.

In the United States, the tradition of press freedom began with the celebrated case in 1735 of John Peter Zenger (1697–1746), who was prosecuted for criminal libel for criticizing the royal governor of New York, William Cosby (1690–1736). In a landmark legal moment, a jury ignored the prevailing law at the time and determined that truth was a defense to a libel action. Under current law, a statement cannot be considered libelous if it is true.

More than two hundred years later, in 1964, the U.S. Supreme Court afforded the press much greater freedom in *New York Times Co. v.*

*Sullivan.* In this case, the *New York Times* printed an editorial advertisement by the Committee to Defend Martin Luther King and the Struggle for Freedom in the South.

The ad criticized the actions of certain "Southern violators" and accused them of violating the civil rights of African American students in Montgomery, Alabama. The ad read: "Again and again the Southern violators have answered Dr. King's peaceful protests with intimidation and violence. They have bombed his home almost killing his wife and child. They have assaulted his person. They have arrested him seven times."

Even though he was not named specifically in the ad, L. B. Sullivan, the Montgomery, Alabama, police commissioner, sued the newspaper for libel (publishing false statements of facts about someone) in the amount of $500,000. The article contained certain misstatements. For example, Martin Luther King Jr. (1929–1968) had been arrested only four times, not seven.

> *The Court wrote that "debate on public issues should be uninhibited, robust, and wide-open, and ... may well include vehement, caustic, and sometimes unpleasantly sharp attacks on government and public officials."*

An Alabama jury awarded Sullivan $500,000. However, the U.S. Supreme Court reversed the jury verdict against the newspaper. The decision "transformed American libel law." The Court wrote that "debate on public issues should be uninhibited, robust, and wide-open, and ... may well include vehement, caustic, and sometimes unpleasantly sharp attacks on government and public officials."

The Court created a new standard that gives the press quite a bit of protection when it is sued for libel by a public official or public figure. That standard requires the plaintiff (the person suing) to show that the newspaper printed the material with "actual malice," defined as knowing the material was false or acting in "reckless disregard" as to whether the material is true or false.

In recent years, Justice Clarence Thomas has called for the Court to revisit its decision in *Times v. Sullivan* and subsequent decisions that extended the actual malice standard. Thomas contends that the decisions "were policy-driven decisions masquerading as constitutional law." He added that "[t]he constitutional libel rules adopted by this Court in *New York Times* and its progeny broke sharply from the common law of libel, and there are sound reasons to question whether the First and Fourteenth Amendments displaced this body of common law."

# Freedom of Assembly and Petition

The last two freedoms of the First Amendment ensure that citizens can assemble and directly petition the government to call public attention to a certain cause. There has been less case law on these last two freedoms in the First Amendment, as they often are viewed as appendages or extensions to freedom of speech. After all, when persons assemble to protest, they also are speaking or expressing their opposition. Similarly, a petition to the government is a form of speech.

Over the course of American history, striking workers, civil rights advocates, antiwar demonstrators, and Ku Klux Klan marchers have sought the protections of the First Amendment. They sought the right to freely assemble and petition the government for a redress of grievances. Sometimes these efforts have galvanized public support or changed public perceptions. The freedom of assembly was essential to both the Civil Rights Movement of the 1950s and 1960s and the women's suffrage movement.

Perhaps the most eloquent example of this occurred in March 1961, when nearly 200 African American students met at Zion Baptist Church and marched down to the state capital in Columbia, South Carolina. Among these protestors was future U.S. representative James Clyburn (1940–).

Carrying placards reading "Down with Segregation" and similar messages, the students walked single and double file for approximately 45 minutes, attracting a crowd of 200 to 300 onlookers, when the police gave them 15 minutes to disperse. Instead of leaving, the students chanted patriotic and religious songs. At the end of the 15 minutes, police officers arrested the students. A magistrate court convicted 187 students, subjecting them to fines and jail time. The South Carolina Supreme Court affirmed the convictions.

Citizens have the right to gather signatures on petitions in support of getting issues or candidates on ballots or otherwise solicit the government to enact changes.

However, the students appealed to the U.S. Supreme Court, which reversed the convictions. In the majority opinion for the Supreme Court, Justice Potter Stewart wrote that the students' actions "reflect an exercise of these basic constitutional rights [to speech, assembly, and petition] in their most pristine and classic form." Stewart emphasized that the students acted peaceably and never threatened violence or harm. He concluded that the First and Fourteenth Amendments do not "permit a State to make criminal the peaceful expression of unpopular views."

In recent years, a massive outpouring of social justice protests has taken place across the country over deaths like that of George Floyd, who was murdered by a Minneapolis police officer on May 25, 2020. The death of Floyd and others killed by the police seared the collective conscience of many and led to an increase in social activism. Many of the protests have remained peaceful, though some were marred by violence. The First Amendment protects the right to assemble peacefully but does not protect violence, looting, and other criminal conduct.

Citizens also have a right to petition the government to correct injustices, or in the words of the First Amendment, for a "redress of grievances." Though probably the least known clause of the First Amendment, it arguably has deeper historical roots than any other First Amendment freedom. Consider that two of history's most venerated documents—the Magna Carta and the Declaration of Independence—were petitions to kings of England. Each document petitioned the ruler with various complaints.

# The Second Amendment

A well regulated militia being necessary to the security of a free state, the right of the people to keep and bear arms shall not be infringed.

The most oddly worded provision in the entire Bill of Rights is the Second Amendment, which speaks of both a "well-regulated militia" and "the right of the people to keep and bear arms." For many years, the U.S. Supreme Court interpreted the Second Amendment as protecting only the right of the states to have a militia. In other words, the thinking was that the Second Amendment protected the collective right of the people as a whole to have a militia. Under this interpretation, a person only has a right to keep and bear arms if used in militia service.

The U.S. Supreme Court seemingly adopted the collectivist interpretation of the Second Amendment in *Miller v. United States* (1939), ruling that Jack Miller and Frank Layton violated the National Firearms Act of 1934 by transporting a double-barrel shotgun across state lines from Arkansas to Oklahoma. The Supreme Court, per Justice James McReynolds (1862–1946), determined that there was no reasonable relationship between such a weapon and militia service, and thus, there was no Second Amendment defense to prosecution. Many interpreted the decision as reasoning that the Second Amendment protected militia service, not an individual right to carry weapons. The Ninth Circuit in *Silveira v. Lockyer* (2002) wrote that "[w]hat *Miller* does strongly imply, however, is that the Supreme Court rejects the traditional individual rights view."

Many courts through the years also adopted this collectivist, militia interpretation of the Second Amendment. The Sixth U.S. Circuit Court of Appeals wrote in *Stevens v. United States* (1971): "Since the Second Amendment right 'to keep and bear Arms' applies only to the right of the State to maintain a militia and not to the individual's right to bear arms, there can be no serious claim to any express constitutional right of an individual to possess a firearm." Similarly, the Eighth U.S. Circuit Court of Appeals wrote in *State v. Nelsen* (1988) that "Nelsen claims to find a fundamental right to keep and bear arms in that amendment, but this has not been the law for at least 100 years."

# History of the Right to Keep and Bear Arms

There is historic support for the idea that the Second Amendment protects an individual right. Justice Joseph Story (1779–1845) wrote in his influential *Commentaries* that the right to keep and bear arms "has justly been considered, as the palladium of the liberties of a republic." St. George Tucker (1752–1827) similarly wrote that the Second Amendment "may be seen as the true palladium of liberty" and that "the right of self defence is the first law of nature."

Several early versions of state constitutions also seemingly support an individual rights interpretation. For example, Pennsylvania's Declaration of Rights in 1776 provided that "the people have a right to bear arms for the defense of themselves and the state." Massachusetts's Constitution in 1780 provided that "the people have a right to keep and bear arms for the common defence."

‖ *This begs the question what is meant by the "common defence." A person could read that as protecting the right to bear arms only if done in conjunction with others, as in a militia.* ‖

This begs the question what is meant by the "common defence." A person could read that as protecting the right to bear arms only if done in conjunction with others, as in a militia. However, important in understanding the militia was that during the days of the colonial government, every citizen was potentially part of the militia. Richard Henry Lee (1732–1794), writing under the pseudonym "the Federal Farmer," wrote that "A militia when properly formed, are in fact the people themselves, and render regular troops in great measure unnecessary."

James Madison (1751–1836) himself—"the Father of the Bill of Rights"— wrote in *Federalist Papers*, No. 46 about "the advantage of being armed, which the Americans possess over the people of almost every other nature."

White protestors at a Black Lives Matter rally in Dayton, Ohio, are shown here carrying guns. The jury is still out on this type of behavior. Are they carrying guns in self-defense? This appears to be more an act of intimidation, yet it is completely legal.

It was not until 2008 that the U.S. Supreme Court fundamentally changed course and ruled that the Second Amendment protects an individual right to keep and bear arms in *District of Columbia v. Heller* (2008). Two years later, the Court ruled that the Second Amendment right also limited state and local governments' ability to restrict or regulate gun possession in *McDonald v. City of Chicago* (2010).

Controversy continues, particularly as people virulently disagree over the merits of various forms of gun control. With each mass shooting, continued pressure percolates to increase the regulation of firearms.

# Second Amendment Protects an Individual Right

The District of Columbia had a stringent law on guns, prohibiting even operable firearms in individual homes. The challengers to the law included Dick Heller, who provided security at the Thurgood Marshall Judicial Center as a special police officer with the District of Columbia police force. Heller had to carry a gun at this job but could not have an operable firearm at his home, which was directly across from abandoned public housing. Originally, the first listed plaintiff was Shelly Parker, who had challenged drug dealers in her neighborhood. The complaint in the case read: "As a consequence of trying to make her neighborhood a better place to live, Ms. Parker has been threatened by drug dealers."

Other plaintiffs included Tom Palmer, a gay man who previously had successfully defended himself from an assault with a handgun. He contended that as a gay man he needed the weapon to deal with antigay violence. The other three plaintiffs were Gillian St. Lawrence, Tracey Ambeau, and George Lyon. All three wanted to have firearms in their home for self-defense purposes.

Common to all six plaintiffs was a genuine belief that they should have the ability to own a firearm to defend themselves. However, the District of Columbia filed a motion to dismiss the complaint, arguing that the Second Amendment simply did not protect an individual right to keep and bear arms. Instead, the District argued that the Second Amendment was written for fear that the federal government might disarm state militias.

U.S. District Court judge Emmet G. Sullivan (1947–) noted that there were three views of the Second Amendment: (1) a collective right of the states to arm the militia; (2) a limited individual right to bear arms but only as a member of the state militia; or (3) a free-standing individual right to keep and bear arms.

> *U.S. District Court judge Emmet G. Sullivan (1947–) noted that there were three views of the Second Amendment: (1) a collective right of the states to arm the militia; (2) a limited individual right to bear arms but only as a member of the state militia; or (3) a free-standing individual right to keep and bear arms.*

Judge Sullivan reasoned that there was no individual right to keep and bear arms "separate and apart from Militia use." Sullivan cited a litany of federal appeals court opinions that accorded with this interpretation of the Second Amendment. At the time, only one federal appeals court decision—the Fifth Circuit in *United States v. Emerson* (2001)—had found the Second Amendment to protect an individual right. Judge Sullivan questioned the *Emerson* decision, noting that the majority of the three-judge panel that decided *Emerson* seemingly ignored earlier Fifth Circuit rulings. Sullivan termed this "troubling." Sullivan concluded: "While plaintiffs extol many thought-provoking and historically interesting arguments for finding an individual right, this Court would be in error to overlook sixty-five years of unchanged Supreme Court precedent and the deluge of circuit case law rejecting an individual right to bear arms not in conjunction with service in the Militia."

The plaintiffs appealed Judge Sullivan's dismissal to the U.S. Court of Appeals for the District of Columbia. A three-judge panel of the D.C. Circuit reversed 2–1 in *Parker v. District of Columbia* and found an individual right to keep and bear arms. Judge Laurence Silberman (1935–) wrote for the two-member majority and he focused first on the question of standing—whether these six plaintiffs had a sufficient stake in the litigation, a preenforcement challenge to the D.C. handgun ordinance. Silberman reasoned that only Dick Heller had standing to pursue the litigation, but he was the lone plaintiff who had applied and been denied a license to own a handgun. "The denial of the gun license is significant," Silberman wrote. "It constitutes an injury independent of the District's prospective enforcement of its gun laws."

Silberman thus proceeded to an analysis of whether the D.C. ordinance violated the Second Amendment. Silberman termed the militia clause "prefatory" and the operative clause "operative."

Silberman also rejected the District's argument that the Second Amendment was drafted because of a fear that the federal government would disarm the state militias. If that was the case, according to Silberman, then the Founding Fathers would have written amendments that read, "Congress shall make no law disarming the state militias" or "States have a right to a well-regulated militia."

Silberman focused on the word "people," calling it "the most important word" in the Second Amendment. He noted that other constitutional amendments, such as the First, Fourth, Ninth, and Tenth Amendments, also used similar terminology and several focused on protecting individuals from infringement by the government.

Silberman reasoned that nearly all of the Bill of Rights—save for the Tenth Amendment—protect against government infringement of individual rights. Thus, the Second Amendment also protects against governmental intrusion against an individual right to keep and bear arms.

Silberman also indicated that "the correspondence and political dialogue of the founding era indicate that arms were kept for lawful use in self-defense and hunting." The District also had argued that the use of the words "keep and bear" were military terms and, thus, fit more closely with the idea that the Second Amendment protects militia's use of firearms, not individuals. However, Silberman wrote that the word "bear" in this context is merely just a synonym of "carry."

Silberman concluded that "the operative clause, properly read, protects the ownership and use of weaponry beyond that needed to preserve the state militias." One judge on the panel, Judge Karen LeCraft Henderson (1944–), dissented. She focused on the fact that the Second Amendment applies only to the militias of the states and the District of Columbia is not a state. She also contended that the *United States v. Miller* decision

A circuit judge for the Washington, D.C., Court of Appeals and a recipient of the Presidential Medal of Freedom, Judge Laurence Hirsch Silberman has interpreted the Second Amendment as applying to individuals, not militias, because of the language used in the amendment.

supported the collectivist model of the Second Amendment more so than an individual-rights model.

The District of Columbia then appealed to the U.S. Supreme Court, which granted review. The Court took the case and in a landmark opinion ruled 5–4 that the Second Amendment protected an individual right to keep and bear arms. Justice Antonin Scalia (1936–2016), in his majority opinion, agreed with Judge Silberman and adopted a similar approach by describing the Amendment as being divided into a prefatory clause (the militia clause) and an operative clause (the right to keep and bear arms). This phrasing was once again adept, as Scalia elevated the right to keep and bear arms over the militia clause.

*Justice Scalia adopted Judge Silberman's division of the Second Amendment into a prefatory clause (the militia clause) and the operative clause (the right to keep and bear arms).*

Scalia relied heavily on the fact that the Second Amendment mentions "the right of the people." Scalia noted that the Bill of Rights contains three other mentions of the right of the people—(1) the right of the people to peaceably assemble in the First Amendment; (2) the right of the people to be free from unreasonable searches and seizures in the Fourth Amendment; and (3) the Ninth Amendment, which uses similar language—"retained by the people." Scalia explained: "All three of these instances unambiguously refer to individual rights, not collective rights, or rights that may be exercised only through participation in some corporate body."

Scalia then turned his attention to the language of the operative clause—"the right of the people to keep and bear arms." He reasoned that the phrase "keep arms" meant to have weapons in one's home. The right to keep arms means that an individual has the right to store firearms in his or her house for self-defense purposes. Scalia also determined that the words "bear arms" referred to the right of individual people to carry weapons outside of organized militia service. He wrote that the right to bear arms was "unambigiously used to refer to the carrying of weapons outside of an organized militia."

Scalia then turned to the history of the Second Amendment and the right to keep and bear arms. He first focused attention on what occurred in late-seventeenth-century England when the Stuart kings sought to consolidate and expand their power base by disarming their enemies. The heavy hand of the Stuart kings led ultimately to the Glorious Revolution and the adoption of the English Bill of Rights of 1689, which included specific protection for the right to keep and bear arms.

Scalia also focused attention on the plight of the colonists under the heavy reign of British king George III (1738–1820) who sought to disarm the colonists to ensure that they would comply with increasingly oppressive tax laws.

In his conclusion, Scalia recognized that handgun violence presented a serious problem in society and said that the District of Columbia had other tools to address

this. However, he continued: "But the enshrine-
ment of constitutional rights necessarily takes
certain policy choices off the table. These include the absolute prohibition of handguns held
and used for self-defense in the home."

Justice John Paul Stevens (1920–2019) and
Stephen Breyer (1938–) both authored dissenting
opinions. Stevens read the history much differently
than Justice Scalia. He viewed the Second Amendment as primarily about the militia. "The Second
Amendment was adopted to protect the right of
the people of each of the several States to maintain a well-regulated militia," he wrote. "It was a
response to concerns raised during the ratification
of the Constitution that the power of Congress
to disarm the state militias and create a national
standing army posed an intolerable threat to the
sovereignty of the several States."

While Justice Stevens sparred with Justice
Scalia and offered a different view of Second
Amendment history, Justice Breyer focused on
the level of handgun violence in the United
States. He viewed the D.C. ordinance banning
handguns as "a permissible legislative response
to a serious, indeed life-threatening, problem."

The late Supreme Court justice Antonin Scalia concluded
that the Founding Fathers intended for private citizens to
keep and bear arms based on the language used and also
taking into account the historical context in which the Constitution was written.

Breyer emphasized that many cities in the Founding Era limited firearms within city
limits. He also quoted quite a few statistics about gun-related violence in the United
States, such as "[f]rom 1993 to 1997, there were 180,533 firearm-related deaths in
the United States, an average of over 36,000 per year."

# Incorporating the Second Amendment

Two years after *Heller*, the U.S. Supreme Court incorporated the Second Amendment and held that it applied to limit state and local governments in *McDonald v. City
of Chicago*. The City of Chicago had a virtual flat ban on handgun possession. Otis
McDonald (1933–2014), an antigang activist in his 70s, was one of several individuals
who challenged the ban. McDonald said he needed a handgun for self-defense, because
several gang members had threatened him for his antigang activity. Another plaintiff
was Colleen Lawson, another Chicago resident, whose home had been burglarized.
She, like McDonald, said that she needed a handgun for self-defense purposes.

The same five-member majority in *Heller* also ruled that the Second Amendment and the right of self-defense was important enough to also limit state and

local governments. In his majority opinion, Justice Samuel Alito Jr. (1950–) framed the question as whether the right to keep and bear arms was "essential to our scheme of ordered liberty" or "deeply rooted in this Nation's history and tradition."

Alito reasoned that the core concept of the Second Amendment—and why it is so vitally important in a free society—is that it enables individuals to engage in self-defense of their homes. He reasoned that those who drafted and ratified the Bill of Rights considered the Second Amendment right to keep and bear arms to be seminally important. The fear of many of the Framers, according to Justice Alito, was that a standing army supported by the federal government would disarm the citizenry and subject them to the whims of the government. Alito added that both the Federalists and Anti-Federalists, the two major founding political parties at the nation's beginning, both agreed on how fundamental the right to keep and bear arms was.

> *Alito reasoned that the core concept of the Second Amendment—and why it is so vitally important in a free society—is that it enables individuals to engage in self-defense of their homes.*

Alito recounted how after the Civil War, groups of ex-Confederate soldiers roamed the South to disarm recently freed African Americans and attempted to keep them in a position of subjugation. Senator Henry Wilson (1812–1875) of Massachusetts, during the 39th Congress, warned that "There is one unbroken chain of testimony from all people that are loyal to this country, that the greatest outrages are perpetrated by armed men who go up and down the country searching houses, disarming people, committing outrages of every kind and description."

In fact, an 1866 federal law—called the Freedmen's Bureau Act of 1866—provided that "the right ... to have full and equal benefit of all laws and proceedings concerning personal liberty, personal security, and the acquisition, enjoyment, and disposition of estate, real and personal, *including the constitutional right to bear arms*, shall be secured to and enjoyed by all the citizens ... without respect to race or color, or previous condition of slavery."

Influential U.S. representative Thaddeus Stevens (1792–1868) of Pennsylvania warned: "Disarm a community and you rob them of the means of defending life. Take away their weapons of defense and you take away the inalienable right of defending liberty."

The City of Chicago had argued that while the right to keep and bear arms is in the Constitution, it should not be incorporated because the Second Amendment—and guns in particular—has an important impact on public safety. However, Justice Alito noted that many other important freedoms found in the Bill of Rights also impact public safety, such as the exclusionary rule of the Fourth Amendment, the privilege against self-incrimination under the Fifth Amendment, and the speedy trial right of the Sixth Amendment. Under these amendments, criminal defendants—even ones who are guilty—may go free because of constitutional violations committed by government officials.

Justice Alito wrote that history and tradition supported the notion that this basic right of self-defense undergirding the Second Amendment established its seminal importance. Alito relied on early legal commentators, such as Joseph Story and St. George Tucker, early state constitutional provisions, and efforts by the 39th Congress during the post–Civil War period deploring the attempts to disarm the 180,000 black troops who had served the Union during the conflict. In fact, Alito cited sources showing that many abolititionists supported the right to keep and bear arms because they faced hostile slaveowners bent on disarming the abolitionists. Senator Samuel C. Pomeroy (1816–1891) of Kansas stated in 1866:

> Every man ... should have the right to bear arms for the defense of himself and family and his homestead. And if the cabin door of the freedman is broken open and the intruder enters for purposes as vile as were known to slavery, then should a well-loaded musket be in the hand of the occupant to send the polluted wretch to another world, where his wretchedness will forever remain complete.

Congressman Thaddeus Stevens of Pennsylvania was an ardent abolitionist and Radical Republican who asserted that Americans must be allowed to possess the means to defend their liberties and homes.

Alito concluded: "In sum, it is clear that the Framers and ratifiers of the Fourteenth Amendment counted the right to keep and bear arms among those fundamental rights necessary to our system of ordered liberty."

# Second Amendment Litigation

*Heller* ruled that the Second Amendment protected an individual right, and *McDonald* ruled that this right was incorporated to limit state and local governments. However, even the majority opinion in *Heller* did not argue that the Second Amendment was an absolute right. Scalia acknowledged that "nothing in our opinion should be taken to cast doubt on longstanding prohibitions on the possession of firearms by felons and the mentally ill, or laws forbidding the carrying of firearms in sensitive places such as schools and government buildings, or laws imposing conditions and qualifications on the commercial sale of a firearm."

However, the Supreme Court decision in *Heller* did not specifically identify what standard of review—what level of scrutiny—should apply to various gun regulations and laws. Staunch Second Amendment supporters assert that because the right to keep and bear arms is a fundamental right protected in the Bill of Rights, any gun legislation must meet strict scrutiny—the highest level of constitutional scrutiny. These individuals assert that the right to keep and bear arms in the Second Amendment is just as important as freedom of speech in the First Amendment.

However, most lawyers examining Second Amendment challenges to various gun laws have reviewed the legislation under a version of intermediate scrutiny—the mid-level form of scrutiny between the high standard of strict scrutiny and the low standard of rational basis.

*Because Second Amendment jurisprudence is in its infancy, many courts are looking to First Amendment free-speech jurisprudence for guidance. For example, several judges have drawn the obvious parallel that just as the First Amendment does not protect all forms of speech, the Second Amendment does not protect all types of weapons.*

The first question to ask is whether a challenged restriction impacts conduct within the scope of the Second Amendment. If it does not, then the restriction is constitutional. If the restriction does impact Second Amendment conduct, then the question is whether the weapons in question are (1) in common usage; and (2) in typical usage by law-abiding citizens for lawful purposes, such as for hunting or self-defense. Other courts state the test a bit differently. Their rule is that the Second Amendment protects weapons unless they are dangerous and unusual.

Because Second Amendment jurisprudence is in its infancy, many courts are looking to First Amendment free-speech jurisprudence for guidance. For example, several judges have drawn the obvious parallel that just as the First Amendment does not protect all forms of speech, the Second Amendment does not protect all types of weapons. A federal appeals court used a different First Amendment analogy that protected the right to own certain types of guns. The case involved a Second Amendment challenge to a Maryland law that banned semiautomatic rifles.

The appeals court analogized to the First Amendment principle that bans on entire mediums of speech are constitutionally suspect. The U.S. Supreme Court identified this principle in *City of Ladue v. Gilleo* (1994), a case involving a ban on yard signs. "Our prior decisions have voiced particular concern with laws that foreclose an entire medium of expression," the Supreme Court explained in the yard-sign case.

The Fourth Circuit majority adopted this rationale in interpreting the Second Amendment right to "keep and bear arms," writing that Maryland's law banning semiautomatic rifles was "akin" to a law that bans an entire medium of speech.

Courts have examined and developed, over nearly a 100-year period, a complex and intricate body of First Amendment law. However, Second Amendment law is in its nascent phase. Because Second Amendment law is in its incipient phases, expect

The Constitution Explained

to see more courts drawing analogies to First Amendment precedent. Also, expect to see more and more Second Amendment challenges to more and more gun regulations, which are likely to increase as the number of mass shootings increases.

# The Fourth Amendment

The right of the people to be secure in their persons, houses, papers and effects, against unreasonable searches and seizures, shall not be violated, and no Warrants shall issue, but upon probable cause, supported by Oath or affirmation, and particularly describing the place to be searched, and the persons or things to be seized.

If you ask Americans what right they cherish the most, some may answer freedom of speech, because they like to speak their minds. Others who are religious likely will refer to freedom of religion. However, a good number of people may emphasize the right to privacy—specifically in their home. If they are more well versed in constitutional lingo, they might even mention the right to be free from unreasonable searches and seizures. That's right, the Fourth Amendment is one of the most cherished individual freedoms in the Bill of Rights. Justice Louis Brandeis (1856–1941) once wrote in a dissenting opinion back in 1928 that this freedom is "the right to be let alone—the most comprehensive of rights and the right most valued by civilized men."

The Framers appreciated this right, as they or people they knew had experience with British officials searching their goods or materials with broad, fishing-expedition types of warrants called writs of assistance. British officials sought these writs of assistance to make sure that the colonists were not avoiding import duties and smuggling in materials without paying taxes. The first legal challenge brought against such writs of assistance was in 1761 in Boston, Massachusetts. A lawyer named James Otis Jr. (1725–1783) waxed eloquent in his language against the dreaded writs:

> I will to my dying day oppose, with all the powers and faculties God has given me, all such instruments of slavery on the one hand, and villainy on the other, as this writ of assistance is. It appears to me … the worst instrument of arbitrary power, the most destructive of English liberty, and the fundamental principles of the constitution, what was ever found in an English-law book.

Otis further intoned that the writs of assistance "place the liberty of every man in the hands of every petty officer." Spectators and later historians declared that it was one of the most impassioned and celebrated speeches in the history of American law. One of those who was most moved was a 25-year-old lawyer named John Adams (1735–1826)—the future second president of the United States. Adams later wrote that Otis's argument "breathed into this nation the breath of life" and that "American independence was then and there born."

Because of the colonial experience with writs of assistance and the related general warrants—warrants that were not particular but quite broad—several states included provisions in their state constitutions prohibiting unreasonable searches and seizures. Virginia's Declaration of Rights declared that "general warrants … are grievous and oppressive, and ought not to be granted." Pennsylvania's Declaration of Rights contained a similar provision that provided people should be "free from search and seizure" if there was not a warrant drafted with "sufficient foundation" and particularly described what was to be searched. Delaware, Maryland, Massachusetts, and New Hampshire also adopted provisions in their state constitutions prohibiting writs of assistance and general warrants. These state constitutional provisions were key precursors to the Fourth Amendment.

Attorney, pamphleteer, and legislator James Otis Jr. is often remembered for his quote "Taxation without Representation is tyranny."

Fourth Amendment scholar Phillip A. Hubbart writes that the Fourth Amendment was drafted "to protect an almost sacred right that the colonists felt about their privacy, particularly the privacy of their homes, but also their persons, businesses, and other private premises."

Notice the first clause of the Fourth Amendment mentions "the right of the people to be secure in their persons, houses, papers, and effects." People don't want the police to search their bodies and rummage through their homes. A popular saying is a man's home is his castle. The Constitution safeguards this concept of privacy in the Fourth Amendment. This amendment protects people from government invasions into their homes and bodies.

During the colonial period, the aforementioned writs of assistance allowed British customs officials to inspect all of a colonist's cargo to prevent smuggling of goods that were to be taxed. These writs of assistance allowed the officials to search and seize whatever property they desired without prior approval by a judge or magistrate.

In response, the Founding Fathers adopted the Fourth Amendment. This amendment prohibits "unreasonable searches and seizures." This means that not all searches and seizures are prohibited. Only those that are unreasonable violate the Fourth Amendment.

## What Is Reasonable and Unreasonable?

The key question is, "When is a search reasonable?" because the Fourth Amendment only prohibits "unreasonable searches and seizures." The Fourth Amendment gives one example in its text as to when a search is reasonable—when the police have a warrant that is backed up by probable cause and particularity.

Probable cause means more than just a hunch. The police must point to specified evidence showing that the person likely is carrying certain material. Probable cause means that the police have individualized suspicion that a person is carrying illegal contraband or harboring illegal material in his or her home. Probable cause essentially means that the police have a reasonable and probable belief that someone is carrying contraband or engaging in illegal activities. "In dealing with probable cause, however, as the very name implies, we deal with probabilities," the U.S. Supreme Court explained in *Brinegar v. United States* (1949). "These are not technical; they are the factual and practical considerations of everyday life on which reasonable and prudent men, not legal technicians, act."

The Court in *Brinegar* further explained that there is a difference between "mere suspicion" and "probable cause." Mere suspicion is not enough. The police must have some basis grounded in fact, not speculation, that someone is engaging in illegal activity. The Court explained:

The Constitution protects U.S. citizens from unreasonable search and seizures, but there are cases when a police officer can search your home or vehicle without a warrant.

The rule of probable cause is a practical, nontechnical conception affording the best compromise that has been found for accommodating these often opposing interests. Requiring more would unduly hamper law enforcement. To allow less would be to leave law-abiding citizens at the mercy of the officers' whim or caprice.

Thus, the police must have probable cause, but that is not all. They also must obtain a warrant from a judge, and the warrant on its fact must indicate to the judge that there is probable cause. There is a principle called the "four corners" rule. This means that the probable cause must be apparent in the warrant itself, not from extraneous factors not set out in the warrant.

## Neutral and Detached Magistrate

The warrant must be signed by a judge or magistrate who is "neutral and detached." This means that the magistrate must be independent, not a mere shill for the police. The term often used is a "rubber stamp." A magistrate who always approves of warrants no matter what they say is not neutral and detached; he or she is merely a rubber stamp for law enforcement.

The Supreme Court has explained that to be neutral and detached, a magistrate must be independent from law enforcement. A magistrate is not neutral and detached if he or she works in some capacity with law enforcement. "Whatever else neutrality and detachment might entail, it is clear that they require severance and disengagement from activities of law enforcement," the Supreme Court wrote in *Shadwick v. City of Tampa* (1972).

The Supreme Court once invalidated a Georgia scheme that provided that justices of the peace would be paid for search warrants that they authorized and not paid for search warrants they denied. Testimony revealed that a justice of the peace had issued some 10,000 warrants and never denied one. The Court reasoned in *Connally v. Georgia* (1977) that this scheme violated the key Fourth Amendment principle of having a "neutral and detached magistrate." The justices of the peace were not neutral and detached, because they had a clear financial incentive under this Georgia law to approve, not deny, warrants.

## Particularity Requirement

The Fourth Amendment concludes with the language "particularly describing the place to be searched, and the persons or things to be seized." This language is known as the particularity requirement. Under this requirement, the warrant also must explain what particular items or places are to be searched. Otherwise, the warrant authorizes a roving or fishing net type of search. The warrant must also state what material is being targeted in the search. The British would often use so-called "general warrants" when searching colonists' property. A general warrant allowed authorities to search all of a person's property. The Fourth Amendment generally forbids the use of general warrants. It requires the police to state specifically what items they expect to find.

> *Under this requirement, the warrant also must explain what particular items or places are to be searched. Otherwise, the warrant authorizes a roving or fishing net type of search. The warrant must also state what material is being targeted in the search.*

The Supreme Court invalidated a search based on the particularity requirement in *Lo-Ji Sales, Inc. v. New York* (1979), where a warrant identified two allegedly obscene films at a New York adult bookstore. However, the warrant also contained a conclusory statement that other similar material likely would be found at the bookstore. Law enforcement officials then conducted a roving, fishing-net type of search and found other materials they deemed to be legally obscene.

The U.S. Supreme Court ruled that this practice violated the particularity requirement of the Fourth Amendment. "This search warrant and what followed the entry on petitioner's premises are reminiscent of the general warrant or writ of assistance of the 18th century against which the Fourth Amendment was intended to protect," Chief Justice Warren Burger (1907–1995) wrote for a unanimous Court.

## Exceptions to the Warrant Requirement

We know that a warrant backed up by probable cause is an example of a reasonable search under the Fourth Amendment. Warrantless searches are presumed unconstitutional unless they fit into one of several exceptions that the courts have developed through the years. It is this part of Fourth Amendment—whether a certain exception to the warrant requirement applies—that makes search and seizure law deliciously complex and interesting.

## The Automobile Exception

One of the key exceptions concerns automobiles. In fact, it is called the automobile exception. The idea behind the automobile exception is that due to the inherent mobility of automobiles, there is not sufficient time for law enforcement officials to obtain a warrant to search the contents of an automobile. The Supreme Court created the automobile exception to the Fourth Amendment in *Carroll v. United States* (1925). The Court examined whether the police could stop a vehicle on the highway that officers reasonably believed was carrying illegal liquor. The Court upheld the warrantless stop and search of the vehicle because of what it identified as a "necessary difference" between searching "a store, dwelling house or other structure" and searching "a ship, motorboat, wagon or automobile." The difference, according to the Court, was that a "vehicle can be quickly moved out of the locality or jurisdiction in which the warrant must be sought."

Here, a clear contrast exists between the treatment of the home and the car. Homes are not inherently mobile—unless, perhaps, we are talking about a mobile home. However, most homes are fixed and cannot be moved. Thus, the police must obtain a warrant before searching a home. The Supreme Court declared in *Payton v. New York* (1979) that "[i]t is a basic principle of Fourth Amendment law that searches and seizures inside a home without a warrant are presumptively unconstitutional."

*The Supreme Court declared in* Payton v. New York *(1979) that "[i]t is a basic principle of Fourth Amendment law that searches and seizures inside a home without a warrant are presumptively unconstitutional."*

The home exception even extends to the land immediately outside your home—called the curtilage. The idea behind the special protections for the home and curtilage is that individuals have a clear and reasonable expectation of privacy in their homes and the area just outside their homes. In 2018, the Court applied the curtilage exception to prohibit the warrantless search of a motorcycle parked on the defendant's driveway. Wait a second, you probably are saying—you just wrote that individuals have a reduced level of Fourth Amendment protection for vehicles, such as cars or motorcycles.

Yes, that is true, but the motorcycle was parked right outside the home. Here, the curtilage concept trumped the automobile exception. "When a law enforcement officer physically intrudes on the curtilage to gather evidence, a search within the meaning of the Fourth Amendment has occurred," the Court wrote in *Collins v. Virginia* (2018). "Such conduct thus is presumptively unreasonable absent a warrant."

However, automobiles not only have "ready mobility" that justify differential treatment but are also subject to what the Supreme Court has called "pervasive and continuing governmental regulation and controls." For example, automobile owners must obtain new registration every year for their vehicles, and in many locales, they must also have the vehicle undergo an emissions inspection. Thus, the police do not need a warrant to stop an automobile.

However, the police still must have some level of individualized suspicion to stop a vehicle. The police cannot just willy-nilly stop your automobile for no reason. They need to have reasonable suspicion—a level of individualized suspicion not quite as rigid as probable cause—rather than a general hunch. For example, most of the time, the police pull over vehicles because a person was speeding, violated a traffic ordinance, or has out-of-date vehicle registration plates.

When the police pull over your vehicle, the officer may then ask you to produce your license and registration. This is standard operating procedure. This does not give the police officer carte blanch to search your automobile. In other words, the police generally need probable cause to search your vehicle—this means that they have some clear indication or evidence that there is illegal contraband in your vehicle.

However, the police might obtain the necessary level of probable cause to search your vehicle through yet another Fourth Amendment concept called the "plain smell" doctrine. Under the plain smell doctrine, if the police smell the distinct odor of marijuana in your vehicle, the police can search the vehicle for evidence of marijuana. This doctrine, however, loses its force to the extent that an increasing number of states have legalized marijuana, including for recreational use.

## Plain View Doctrine

The plain smell doctrine actually emanates from another, even more well-established exception to the warrant requirement of the Fourth Amendment—the plain view doctrine. Under this doctrine, if the police are in a lawful vantage point—a place where they have a lawful right to be—and then inadvertently come across a piece of incriminating evidence, the police have not violated the Fourth Amendment.

If police see something illegal in plain sight, they do not need a search warrant to use it as evidence in an arrest.

For example, let's say that the police have a valid search warrant to search a home for certain illegal weapons. As the police are searching the home, they inadvertently see a large pile of cocaine sitting on a table. The police do not violate the Fourth Amendment just because they did not file a warrant to search for the cocaine, because the cocaine clearly was in "plain view" of the officers, and these officers were lawfully present in the home already due to a valid search warrant.

Contrast that with a police officer who suspects that a person is trafficking in illegal drugs in a home. The officer walks up to a window in the home, peers through the window, and sees the cocaine on the kitchen table. The officer then claims "plain view." This conduct violates the Fourth Amendment, because the officer did not have a valid search warrant to search the home. The officer was not in a lawful vantage point when he or she saw the cocaine. Thus, the plain view doctrine is inapplicable.

## Exigent Circumstances

A glaring exception to the warrant requirement is when the police are confronted with emergency circumstances and need to act quickly—even enter a home without a warrant. Generally, entering a home without a warrant is a Fourth Amendment violation, but not if there are so-called exigent circumstances. Again, the rationale behind the exigent circumstances doctrine is that the police are confronted with emergency circumstances and do not have time to go get a warrant.

There are three major areas in which the exigent circumstances doctrine applies—(1) hot pursuit of a fleeing felon; (2) life-threatening or very dangerous circumstances; and (3) the imminent destruction of evidence. The hot pursuit variant of exigent circumstances applies when the police are pursuing a person who they have probable cause to believe committed a felony and the person enters a

One case in which a police officer does not need a search warrant is when they are in pursuit of a felon who is running or driving away to avoid capture.

home for which the police have no valid search warrant. Because the police officers are in hot pursuit, they are deemed to be under exigent circumstances and can enter the home to capture the fleeing individual.

The most common application of exigent circumstances applies when the police are confronted with life-threatening circumstances. For example, if the police reasonably believe that a homicide has been committed in the home, they may enter that home without a warrant under the exigent circumstances rationale. Or if there is credible evidence that a person has harmed or is about to harm himself or others inside the home, the police likely have exigent circumstances to enter the home to prevent the harm.

The last exception refers to the immediate destruction of evidence. This can be a troubling application of the exigent circumstances rationale—and the Supreme Court has been quite loath to recognize this variant—but it has been mentioned in dicta several times that this type of exigent circumstances can exist.

## Stop and Frisk

Another major exception to the warrant requirement is the stop and frisk, sometimes called a "Terry stop" because the Court sanctioned the use of the practice in the case of *Terry v. Ohio* (1968). In this case, Martin McFadden, a more than 30-year veteran of the Cleveland police department, observed two men repeatedly walking back and forth past a jewelry store and peering through the store's window. The two men then met a third man and conversed with him on the street. McFadden approached the men, including defendant John Terry, frisked him, and found a weapon. Terry argued that the officer lacked any individualized suspicion to pat him down. The Supreme Court disagreed, reasoning that if a police officer reasonably believes that individuals pose a safety risk to the officer or to the general public, the officer may "conduct a carefully limited search of the outer clothing of such persons in an attempt to discover weapons which might be used to assault him."

Only Justice William O. Douglas (1898–1980) dissented in *Terry v. Ohio*. He believed that the police should not be able to search an individual unless the officer possesses probable cause that the individual has engaged in wrongdoing. He famously wrote:

> To give the police greater power than a magistrate is to take a long step down the totalitarian path. Perhaps such a step is desirable to cope with

modern forms of lawlessness. But if it is taken, it should be the deliberate choice of the people through a constitutional amendment. Until the Fourth Amendment, which is closely allied with the Fifth, is rewritten, the person and the effects of the individual are beyond the reach of all government agencies until there are reasonable grounds to believe (probable cause) that a criminal venture has been launched or about to be launched.

The "Terry stop," or stop-and-frisk exception, allows police to search a person in a public place if they have any suspicion of wrongdoing.

The Court extended the reach of the *Terry* decision decades later in *Minnesota v. Dickerson* (1993), when the Court upheld a police officer patting down a suspect and finding illegal drugs. The Court held that when the officer conducted a lawful Terry stop and felt a lump in the defendant's jacket that appeared to be contraband, the officer did not violate the Fourth Amendment. Some refer to the Court's decision in *Dickerson* as an expansion of the plain view doctrine to the "plain feel" or "plain touch" doctrine.

Interestingly, the Court avoided the issue of race when it decided *Terry v. Ohio* even though Officer McFadden was white and two of the men he stopped and frisked, including John Terry, were African American. At trial, defense attorney Louis Stokes (1925–2015), who later became a member of Congress, cross-examined McFadden about why he began watching Terry and Chilton. McFadden did not mention their race but did mention that the two men then went and spoke to a white man. Perhaps the Court did not want to get involved in the explosive issue of race, given that the country had witnessed a series of disturbances in cities across the United States.

However, decades later, the issue of race stood front and center before a reviewing federal court in New York City. The stop-and-frisk exception has been criticized because at least in certain circumstances it has devolved into racial profiling. The New York City Police Department implemented an aggressive and far-reaching stop-and-frisk policy that included more than 685,000 stops in 2011 alone. A federal judge ruled in 2013 that the policy, which was used far more often on African Americans and Latinos, was a form of "indirect racial profiling" that violated the Fourth Amendment and the Equal Protection Clause of the Fourteenth Amendment.

## Search Incident to Arrest

Law enforcement officials also do not need a warrant to conduct what is called a search incident to a lawful arrest, also known as a search incident to arrest (SITA). This means that when the police lawfully arrest a person, they may search that person and the nearby physical area within the person's wingspan. There are two primary rationales for this exception to the warrant requirement—to protect the safety of officers and to prevent the destruction of evidence. In fact, there is a pressing need to search a person who has been or is about to be arrested. The police need to make sure the person is not armed and dangerous and need to preserve evidence.

> *A key requirement for a lawful search incident to a lawful arrest is that the search must be contemporaneous with the arrest; that is. it must take place about the very same time as the arrest.*

A key requirement for a lawful search incident to arrest is that the search must be contemporaneous with the arrest; that is, it must take place about the very same time as the arrest. This reduces the likelihood that any resulting search is pretextual or subject to abuse.

## School Searches

Another exception to the warrant requirement is searches in the public schools. The idea is that school officials do not need probable cause and a warrant every time they have some individualized suspicion that a student is carrying contraband. In *New Jersey v. T.L.O.* (1985), the Supreme Court ruled that public school officials can conduct searches of students based upon a reasonableness standard rather than the traditional standard of probable cause. The case involved the search of a female student's purse by an assistant school principal who suspected the student and another student of smoking in the school's bathroom. The assistant principal then searched the girl's purse and found evidence that she was trafficking in small amounts of marijuana.

The student argued that the assistant principal violated the Fourth Amendment, but the Court disagreed, writing that "the constitutional rights of minors are not automatically coextensive" with those of adults. The Court also applauded the reasonableness standard as one that would give public school officials and administrators needed flexibility, writing that it will "spare teachers and school administrators the necessity of schooling themselves in the niceties of probable cause and permit them to regulate their conduct according to the dictates of reason and common sense." Under this reasonableness standard, the school official must show that the initial search is justified at its inception and that any resulting or continuing search not be too intrusive.

Years later, the Supreme Court ruled in *Safford Unified School District v. Redding* (2009), however, that strip searches of public-school students are generally too intrusive. The case concerned a 13-year-old girl subject to a strip search because another student (falsely, it turned out) told school officials she was selling prescription pills at school. School officials subjected the student to a strip search, which revealed nothing. The Court emphasized that the degree of intrusion did not match the low level of individualized suspicion that the student may have had prescription pills on her person.

## Border Searches

Yet another well-recognized exception to the warrant requirement is border searches. U.S. Customs officials may search persons at the border without individualized suspicion of wrongdoing. Such searches must take place at the international border or its basic equivalent. The idea is traced to the idea of national sovereignty—that the United States and its officials have greater power to conduct searches to protect the integrity of its borders.

There are some lower court cases, however, that have required customs officials to have a degree of individualized suspicion—reasonable suspicion—before conducting strip searches at the border.

Searches at international borders can be conducted without the person being under suspicion of a crime.

## Community Caretaking

There was an idea that police officers should not be subject to Fourth Amendment constraints if they are acting more as community caretakers than as enforcers of laws. For example, if an officer spots a vehicle with an abnormally low tire, he or she may decide to pull that vehicle over to warn the vehicle's driver of the impending traffic danger that the driver could have a blowout. In that instance, the officer does not need a law enforcement–type reason to pull over the vehicle. The officer is not pulling over the vehicle as a pretext to search for criminal wrongdoing.

The Court implicitly recognized this community caretaking exception in an automobile Fourth Amendment case, *Cady v. Dombrowski* (1973), in which the Court recognized that officers often have "community caretaking functions" such as responding to disabled vehicles or checking on pedestrians stranded on a highway.

Lower courts for many years were divided on whether this community caretaking exception could be used to justify warrantless searches of homes or whether this community caretaking exception was confined to automobiles. In May 2021, the U.S. Supreme Court reasoned in *Caniglia v. Strom* that the community caretaking exception does not apply to the warrantless searches of houses.

The case involved a man who was believed to be distraught, and his wife asked the police to conduct a search of the house to see if the man was okay. The police entered the home without a warrant to conduct a welfare check on the man but also removed his firearms. The man later argued that the police had violated the

Fourth Amendment when they entered his home without a warrant and removed his firearms.

The police argued that they were acting merely as community caretakers. A federal appeals court reasoned that the community caretaking exception can apply to homes and cars, writing that "threats to individual and community safety are not confined to the highways."

The Supreme Court unanimously reversed and refused to sanction the warrantless search of a home under the guise of the community caretaking rationale. "What is reasonable for vehicles is different from what is reasonable for homes," wrote Justice Clarence Thomas (1948–). In his concurring opinion, Justice Samuel Alito (1950–) wrote that "there is no special Fourth Amendment rule for a broad category of cases involving community caretaking." In fact, Alito noted that the Court back in *Cady v. Dombrowski* had simply used the term "community caretaking" in passing.

This was a welcome decision from the Supreme Court and a victory for those who care about privacy, particularly in the home.

# Technology and the Fourth Amendment

A major concern is that with certain technological advancements, Fourth Amendment rights can be violated, and people's privacy rights can be lost. An early example of this was wiretapping—the use of electronic surveillance to target suspected criminal targets. Back in 1928, the Supreme Court ruled 5–4 in *Olmstead v. United States* (1928) that Prohibition officials did not violate the Fourth Amendment when they surreptitiously listened to the telephone conversations of Roy Olmstead (1866–1966), head of an illegal liquor distribution ring. The Court reasoned that listening to telephone conversations was not a search. "Here we have testimony only of voluntary conversations secretly overheard," Chief Justice William Howard Taft (1857–1930) wrote for the majority. "There was no searching. There was no seizure. The evidence was secured by the use of the sense of hearing and that only." Taft emphasized that there was no physical trespass.

|| *A major concern is that with certain technological advancements, Fourth Amendment rights can be violated, and people's privacy rights can be lost.* ||

It took about four decades for the Supreme Court to overrule its decision in *Olmstead* and take a broader view of what constitutes a search in *Katz v. United States* (1967). In this case, law enforcement wiretapped a public phone booth to record the phone calls of bookie Charles Katz. The FBI wiretapped the phone without a warrant and argued there was no Fourth Amendment violation because there was no physical trespass.

The Supreme Court sided with Katz, reasoning that he had a right to privacy in his telephone conversations even if they took place in a public pay phone booth.

"The Fourth Amendment protects people, not places," Justice Potter Stewart (1915–1985) wrote for the majority. "What a person knowingly exposes to the public, even in his own home or office, is not a subject of Fourth Amendment protection. But what he seeks to preserve as private, even in an area accessible to the public, may be constitutionally protected."

In a concurring opinion, Justice John Marshall Harlan II (1899–1971) proposed what is called the "reasonable expectation of privacy" test—as Harlan described it, "first that a person have exhibited an actual subjective expectation of privacy and, second, that the expectation be one that society is prepared to recognize as reasonable." The bottom line is that FBI agents should have applied to get a warrant rather than listen in on Katz's private conversations.

In recent years, the Court has utilized the *Katz* reasonable expectation of privacy test in different cases that involve enhanced technology. For example, in *Kyllo v. United States* (2001), the Court ruled that the use of a thermal imager to detect hotspots was a search within the meaning of the Fourth Amendment. This means that the government cannot use a thermal imager to scan a home for hotspots without a warrant. Justice Antonin Scalia (1936–2016), often a great defender of Fourth Amendment freedoms, wrote for the majority: "We think that obtaining by sense-enhancing technology any information regarding the interior of the home that could not otherwise have been obtained without physical intrusion into a constitutionally protected area constitutes a search—at least where (as here) the technology in question is not in general use."

A little more than a decade later, the Supreme Court again showed sensitivity to how the use of enhanced technology could threaten privacy rights under the Fourth Amendment in *United States v. Jones* (2012). The case concerned the government's use of a Global Positioning System (GPS) tracking device that law enforcement placed on the vehicle of Antoine Jones, a Washington, D.C., nightclub owner who law enforcement suspected of running a cocaine distribution ring. The government placed the device on Jones's car and monitored his movements for 28 days.

The Supreme Court unanimously ruled that this warrantless action violated the Fourth Amendment. Once again, Justice Scalia was at the forefront of protecting Fourth Amendment freedoms. "It is important to be clear about what occurred in this case," Scalia wrote. "The government physically occupied private property for

Like his grandfather, John Marshall Harlan I (1833–1911), John Marshall Harlan II was an associate justice of the Supreme Court, serving from 1955 to 1971. It was Harlan II who first proposed the "reasonable expectation of privacy" test.

the purpose of obtaining information. We have no doubt that such a physical intrusion would have been considered a 'search' within the meaning of the Fourth Amendment when it was adopted."

Justice Sonia Sotomayor (1954–) authored a concurring opinion in which she agreed that there was a physical trespassory violation of the Fourth Amendment but reiterated that such a trespass was not necessary to find a Fourth Amendment violation. In other words, surveillance without a physical invasion is enough to violate the Fourth Amendment. Sotomayor also questioned the so-called third-party doctrine in Fourth Amendment cases—that there is no Fourth Amendment violation when a person voluntarily discloses information to a third party, such as banks or phone companies.

"People disclose the phone numbers that they dial or text to their cellular providers; the URLs that they visit and the e-mail addresses with which they correspond to their Internet service providers; and the books, groceries and medications they purchase to online retailers," she wrote. "I, for one, doubt that people would accept without complaint the warrantless disclosure to the government of a list of every Web site they had visited in the last week, or month, or year." It is not surprising that Sotomayor sees the problems with the third-party doctrine and wants to protect Fourth Amendment values even more. In her tenure on the Court, she has consistently emerged as the Supreme Court's premier defender of Fourth Amendment values on the Court.

The Supreme Court continued its protection of Fourth Amendment values with regard to digital privacy in a case involving cell phone searches in *Riley v. California* (2014). San Diego police had stopped a vehicle driven by Leon Riley and then later searched his cell phone without a warrant trying to find information to connect him to a gang shooting. At that time, lower courts were divided on whether police needed a search warrant to search the cell phone of someone who was arrested. The theory used by law enforcement was the search incident to a lawful arrest as applied to cell phones. Other lower courts held that the police needed a warrant to search cell phones.

*The Court emphasized the ubiquity of cell phones in modern life, writing that they were "such a pervasive and insistent part of daily life that the proverbial visitor from Mars might conclude they were an important feature of human anatomy."*

The Court ruled that, generally, police need a warrant. The Court emphasized the ubiquity of cell phones in modern life, writing that they were "such a pervasive and insistent part of daily life that the proverbial visitor from Mars might conclude they were an important feature of human anatomy." Chief Justice John Roberts Jr. (1955–) also emphasized how much private information people carry on their cellphones and noted that the term "cell phone" may be a misnomer—that they "could just as easily be called cameras, video players, rolodexes, calendars, tape recorders, libraries, diaries, albums, televisions, maps, or newspapers."

Roberts also blasted the use of the search incident to a lawful arrest rationale used to search cell phones without a warrant. Recall that the search incident to a lawful arrest relies on the rationale that officers need to search to protect themselves. Roberts explained: "Digital data stored on a cell phone cannot itself be used as a weapon to harm an arresting officer or to effectuate the arrestee's escape. Law enforcement officers remain free to examine the physical aspects of a phone to ensure that it will not be used as a weapon—say, to determine whether there is a razor blade hidden between the phone and its case. Once an officer has secured a phone and eliminated any potential physical threats, however, data on the phone can endanger no one."

Adam Liptak of the *New York Times* called the *Riley* decision a "sweeping victory for privacy rights in the digital age." It is hard to argue with the sage Supreme Court reporter.

The Court continued its sensitivity to the need for digital privacy and prevented the government from having unfettered access to a person's cell phone data and locational information without a warrant. Thus, the government generally needs a warrant for cell tower phone information. "We decline to grant the state unrestricted access to a wireless carrier's database of physical location information," Chief Justice John G. Roberts Jr. wrote for the majority.

The Court's decisions in *Riley* and *Carpenter* show a U.S. Supreme Court that is sensitive to digital privacy and the amount of private information that people store in their cell phones. In the future, perhaps the Court will show a similar level of solicitude for the sheer amount of surveillance through data that takes place in modern society. Some have even coined the term "dataveillance" to recognize this foreboding phenomenon.

## What Is a Seizure?

So far, we have focused our discussion on unreasonable searches, but the Fourth Amendment also prohibits unreasonable seizures of persons. A common definition of a seizure is that a person is seized when he or she, in light of all the surrounding circumstances, reasonably believes that he or she is not free to leave. For example, if a group of police officers approaches you and surrounds you, and one of them draws his weapon, you have been seized for purposes of the Fourth Amendment. If the police arrest you, you have been seized. If a police officer shoots you, you have been seized. If the police come up to your home and fire their weapons through your windows, you have been seized.

Much of Fourth Amendment jurisprudence concerns itself with whether a search warrant is valid or whether an exception to the warrant requirement applies in Fourth Amendment law. However, the question of what constitutes a seizure is also very important. Certainly, there is a seizure when a government agent physically restrains a person and prohibits them from leaving. Thus, an arrest is a seizure for purposes of the Fourth Amendment.

The government's conduct must be intentional, not accidental. The Supreme Court has explained that "a Fourth Amendment seizure does not occur [unless] ...

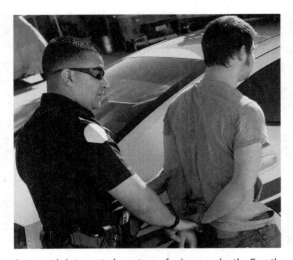

An arrest is interpreted as a type of seizure under the Fourth Amendment.

there is a governmental termination of [an individual's] freedom of movement through means intentionally applied." The Supreme Court used to employ what is known as "the free to leave" test. The Supreme Court described other instances of facts that lean toward a finding of a seizure, including things such as the "threatening presence of several officers, some physical touching of the person of the citizen, or the use of language or tone of voice indicating that compliance with the officer's request might be compelled."

The Supreme Court took a restrictive view of what constitutes a seizure in a case called *California v. Hodari D.* (1991), a case involving a police officer chasing a young man who refused to yield to the police officer's yell of "Stop." Instead, Hodari D. kept running but allegedly dropped a rock of cocaine. The officer picked up the cocaine and later charged Hodari D., who argued that he was unlawfully seized.

However, the U.S. Supreme Court held that Hodari D. was not seized because he did not submit to the officer's show of authority but instead kept running. The Court reasoned that a seizure involves the application of force but not to someone running away. "That is no seizure," the Court wrote.

The reality is that police officers can come up to individual citizens and ask them questions without it being classified as a seizure. The Court declared in *Florida v. Bostick* (1991) that "our cases make clear that a seizure does not occur simply because a police officer approaches an individual and asks a few questions."

This makes sense, because there are myriad police-citizen interactions every day that do not involve hostile questioning or anything remotely approaching a custodial interrogation. If every conversation between a police officer and a citizen were considered a seizure, then police officers could not do their jobs or even speak to crime victims.

What is also true is that a consensual encounter between a police officer and a citizen can devolve into a seizure or detention that triggers Fourth Amendment protections. For example, a police officer might come up to a person and ask that person to accompany them to the police station. This looks much more like a seizure than a consensual police-citizen encounter.

## Drug Courier Profile

When it comes to seizures, police officers are not supposed to engage in racial profiling, but what if they come up with a profile of those who traffic in illegal drugs? That is what the Drug Enforcement Agency did in the 1970s as a way to target and slow down the trafficking of illegal drugs through the airports. Common elements of the profile typically included the age of the person (20–35), flying to and from a source city for drugs, paying for airline tickets in cash, false callback numbers given to airlines, using a fake driver's license or other identity document, being either the first or last person to deplane the aircraft, appearing nervous, traveling alone, wearing lots of jewelry and expensive clothes, and sometimes race.

*In* Reid v. Georgia *(1980), the Court held that U.S. Drug Enforcement Administration (DEA) agents violated the Fourth Amendment by relying solely on the drug courier profile to identify two men coming off an airplane.*

The U.S. Supreme Court once called the drug courier profile "a somewhat informal compilation of characteristics believed to be typical of persons unlawfully carrying narcotics." In *Reid v. Georgia* (1980), the Court held that U.S. Drug Enforcement Administration (DEA) agents violated the Fourth Amendment by relying solely on the drug courier profile to identify two men coming off an airplane. The Court focused on the lack of reasonable suspicion in the case, as the agents had little more to go on than the two men had similar luggage and one looked furtively at another in the terminal.

However, nearly ten years later, the Court at least implicitly approved of the drug courier profile in *United States v. Sokolow* (1989). The DEA had the following information that fit the profile: (1) Sokolow had just returned from Miami, a source city for drugs; (2) he paid for his ticket in cash, a wad of twenty dollar bills at that; (3) he did not check any luggage; (4) he changed planes en route to Hawaii; (5) he dressed in a black jumpsuit and wore lots of jewelry; and (6) he gave a false callback name to the airlines. The majority approved of the seizure and held that the agents had reasonable suspicion, writing:

Any one of these factors is not by itself proof of any illegal conduct and is quite consistent with innocent travel. But we think taken together they amount to reasonable suspicion....

We do not agree with respondent that our analysis is somehow changed by the agents' belief that his behavior was consistent with one of the DEA's "drug courier profiles." A court sitting to determine the existence of reasonable suspicion must require the agent to articulate the factors leading to that conclusion, but the fact that these factors may be set forth in a "profile" does not somehow detract from their evidentiary significance as seen by a trained agent.

In more recent years, there has been a concern that race played too large a role in the implementation of the drug courier profile, that it was an excuse to pull over or stop a greater percentage of black and brown persons. As a consequence, courts generally require more than just drug courier profile characteristics to provide

Concern that police were using courier profiles to target minorities has led courts to decide that simply fitting a profile is not enough to target someone in a drug investigation.

reasonable suspicion. The problem, of course, is that many of the alleged characteristics associated with the drug courier profile are, by themselves, innocent behavior. It certainly is not a crime to pay for things in cash, wear lots of jewelry, or travel to large cities that are called source cities for drugs. The profile may be useful as an additional factor in a close case, but law enforcement is better served by coming up with individual suspicious behavior rather than the loose factors associated with the drug courier profile.

# The Exclusionary Rule

Controversy surrounds the Fourth Amendment because sometimes the police will violate the rights of a person who is carrying contraband, such as illegal drugs. A common example is when a police officer discovers drugs on a person—but only after an unreasonable search or seizure. The defendant's defense attorney then files a motion to suppress the evidence of the drugs as a result of an alleged unconstitutional search. The idea is that the resulting evidence from an improper search is fruit of a poisonous tree.

Our Constitution allows a person illegally searched to file a motion to suppress the evidence. This is called the exclusionary rule. Judge Benjamin Cardozo (1870–1938) expressed this concept when he said, "The criminal is free to go because the constable has blundered." The rationale behind the exclusionary rule is to require law enforcement officials to obey the law.

The Supreme Court ruled that the exclusionary rule applied in federal criminal cases way back in *Weeks v. United States* (1913). However, it took the Court several decades to hold that the exclusionary rule also applied in state criminal proceedings. The case involved a Cleveland woman named Dollree Mapp (1923–2014), who was charged by the police with possession of obscene materials.

Three Cleveland police officers arrived at Mapp's home, claiming that they had a search warrant. Police alleged that they had information that Mapp's home was harboring a suspect who was possibly involved in a bombing. Mapp struggled with one of the officers after she allegedly grabbed a piece of paper from the officer that purportedly was the search warrant. The officers then searched nearly the entire home, including Mapp's bedroom and her basement. In a trunk in the basement, officers found several pornographic materials.

Ultimately, Mapp's case reached the U.S. Supreme Court, which ruled in her favor that the police had violated the Fourth Amendment in conducting a roving search without having a valid search warrant or perhaps any search warrant at all.

"There is no war between the Constitution and common sense," Justice Tom C. Clark (1899–1977) wrote for the Court. "Presently, a federal prosecutor may make no use of evidence illegally seized, but a State's attorney across the street may, although he supposedly is operating under the enforceable prohibitions of the same Amendment. Thus, the State, by admitting evidence unlawfully seized, serves to encourage disobedience to the Federal Constitution which it is bound to uphold."

Justice Clark then responded to Justice Cardozo's famous criticism of the exclusionary rule—"the criminal goes free because the constable has blundered"—with the memorable line: "The criminal goes free, if he must, but it is the law that sets him free. Nothing can destroy a government more quickly than its failure to observe its own laws, or worse, its disregard of the charter of its own existence."

|| *The exclusionary rule remains a staple of modern Fourth Amendment jurisprudence. It serves as a powerful deterrent to encourage police officers to follow the law.* ||

The exclusionary rule remains a staple of modern Fourth Amendment jurisprudence. It serves as a powerful deterrent to encourage police officers to follow the law. Criminal defense attorneys routinely file motions to suppress evidence, contending that police searches were invalid, overbroad, or otherwise unconstitutional. The government often counters that the search warrant was drafted narrowly enough and contained sufficient indicia of probable cause.

## Good Faith Exception

While the exclusionary rule remains a staple of Fourth Amendment jurisprudence, the Supreme Court has created a significant exception to the rule called the good faith exception. The idea behind the good faith exception is that the exclusionary rule should not apply when the police acted in objective good faith that they were acting pursuant to a valid search warrant that is later deemed invalid. In *United States v. Leon* (1984), the Court wrote:

> In most such cases, there is no police illegality and thus nothing to deter. It is the magistrate's responsibility to determine whether the officer's allegations establish probable cause and, if so, to issue a warrant comporting in form with the requirements of the Fourth Amendment. In the ordinary case, an officer cannot be expected to question the magistrate's probable-cause determination or his judgment that the form of the warrant is technically sufficient.

The Court extended the good faith exception to the exclusionary rule in certain cases that involve mistakes by clerical employees. The case of Bennie Dean Herring is quite instructive. A police investigator learned that Herring, no stranger to law enforcement in Coffee County, Alabama, had come to a police-impound lot to recover something from his truck. The investigator then asked a clerical employee to run a check to see if Herring had any outstanding warrants. When the employee found no outstanding warrants, the investigator then asked the employee to check with her counterpart in a neighboring county. The police employee from another county mistakenly said that Herring had an outstanding warrant. That was a mistake, as the warrant had been recalled five months earlier.

Believing the information to be true, the investigator followed Herring as he left the police lot. They pulled over his vehicle and found him with methamphetamine in his pocket and a pistol in his car. Police charged Herring with possession of illegal drugs and being a felon in possession of a firearm. Herring argued that the police lacked probable cause to stop him, because he had no active warrant. Herring was correct that he had no active warrant, but the Supreme Court refused to apply the exclusionary rule.

|| *The Court reasoned that the exclusionary rule should not apply when it does not appreciably deter unlawful conduct by the police.* ||

The Court reasoned that the exclusionary rule should not apply when it does not appreciably deter unlawful conduct by the police. Here, the Coffee County police officers did nothing wrong. They made no intentional mistakes. Instead, the mistake was an act of negligence from an employee in a neighboring county. Chief Justice Roberts reasoned that the exclusionary rule arose from cases involving "intentional conduct that was patently unconstitutional." Chief Justice Roberts explained:

> To trigger the exclusionary rule, police conduct must be sufficiently deliberate that exclusion can meaningfully deter it, and sufficiently culpable that such deterrence is worth the price paid by the justice system. As laid out in our cases, the exclusionary rule serves to deter deliberate, reckless, or grossly negligent conduct, or in some circumstances recurring or systemic negligence. The error in this case does not rise to that level.

Justice Ruth Bader Ginsburg (1933–2020) wrote a dissenting opinion that was joined by three of her colleagues. "Petitioner Bennie Dean Herring was arrested, and subjected to a search incident to his arrest, although no warrant was outstanding against him, and the police lacked probable cause to believe he was engaged in criminal activity," she began her opinion. She explained the exclusionary rule serves purposes other than to deter police misconduct. For example, she reasoned that the rule also prohibits the government from profiting from unlawful misconduct and enables the judicial branch to avoid any taint of governmental misconduct. She also stressed that the exclusionary rule is often the only way to redress a Fourth Amendment violation.

She also explained that the failure to apply the exclusionary rule in this case would enable police departments and other law enforcement agencies to be negligent in their recordkeeping. "Inaccuracies in expansive, interconnected collections of electronic information raise grave concerns for individual liberty," she wrote.

In fairness, there are exceptions to the good faith exception. For example, if the affidavit in question is truly a so-called "bare bones" affidavit, then the good faith exception does not apply. The good faith exception also would not apply if the officer knew that the search warrant affidavit contained false information.

A broad application of the good faith exception to the exclusionary rule is dangerous for individual liberty. Judge Thomas Woodall, a former judge on the Tennessee Court of Criminal Appeals, expressed it well: "It is obvious that a constitutional right without an effective remedy for violation of that right is nothing more than an unenforceable objective on a piece of paper."

## Bivens Actions and Section 1983 Suits

The exclusionary rule is not the only remedy that can be used to counteract Fourth Amendment violations. The Supreme Court provided another remedy in the case *Bivens v. Six Unknown Named Agents of Federal Bureau of Narcotics* (1971). This is a remedy for individuals to assert Fourth Amendment claims for misconduct committed by federal agents. A federal statute, 42 U.S.C. § 1983 (usually called Section 1983), provides that individuals have the right to sue state or local government officials for violations of their constitutional rights.

The late Justice Ruth Bader Ginsburg, defending the exclusionary rule, asserted that ignoring it in certain cases would encourage police to be lax in their recordkeeping, which could result in violating people's rights.

The more controversial of these is the *Bivens* case, since the Court created a remedy even though there was no specific statute that provided for a cause of action. However, the facts of the *Bivens* case provided the Court with an opportunity to provide a vehicle for redress. Six federal agents entered Webster Bivens's home for suspected narcotics violations, arrested him in front of his wife and children, took him to the police station, and strip-searched him.

He sued the officers for violating his constitutional rights and using excessive force against him. An excessive force claim is rooted in the Fourth Amendment—that an officer exceeded his authority in effecting an arrest or seizure of a person. Both a federal district court and a federal appeals court ruled against Bivens.

However, the U.S. Supreme Court reversed. The Court wrote that "the Fourth Amendment operates as a limitation upon the exercise of federal power regardless of whether the State in whose jurisdiction that power is exercised would prohibit or penalize the identical act if engaged in by a private citizen."

In his opinion, Justice William J. Brennan Jr. (1906–1997) quoted Chief Justice John Marshall's (1755–1835) famous words in *Marbury v. Madison* (1803): "The very essence of civil liberty certainly consists in the right of every individual to claim the protection of the laws, whenever he receives an injury."

The reality is that individuals need some recourse if they are injured grievously by federal, state, or local government officials. These officials should not be able to engage in excessive force. The Court recognized this in cases such as *Tennessee v. Garner* (1984), where the Court ruled that a police officer engaged in excessive force when he shot and killed an unarmed fleeing teenager who had just committed a house robbery.

While government officials should be liable for constitutional violations, they have a doctrine—qualified immunity—that provides them with a great deal of protection. The idea behind qualified immunity is that government officials often must make split-second decisions and should not be subject to monetary liability unless they violated clearly established constitutional or statutory law.

|| *The idea behind qualified immunity is that government officials often must make split-second decisions and should not be subject to monetary liability unless they violated clearly established constitutional or statutory law.* ||

In many qualified immunity cases, courts must ask two questions: (1) first, whether there was a violation of constitutional rights; and (2) if so, whether that right was clearly established. In a 2009 decision, the Supreme Court gave federal trial court judges the option of proceeding to the second part of the test first and dismissing lawsuits based on qualified immunity if the constitutional right in question was not clearly established.

The qualified immunity doctrine has come under increased fire in recent years. Many believe it allows government officials to get off the hook for really bad behavior. If a civil rights plaintiff is not able to point to a previous case nearly on point, the danger is always present that a government official may escape liability under the qualified immunity doctrine.

A good example of the qualified immunity doctrine comes from the student strip-search case discussed previously—*Safford Unified School District v. Redding* (2009). Recall that the Court found that public school officials violated the Fourth Amendment when they strip-searched student Savana Redding on mere rumors that she had prescription pills. However, what was also true was that the Supreme Court granted school officials qualified immunity.

The criticism of the doctrine covers the ideological spectrum. For example, Jay Schweikert of the Cato Institute calls qualified immunity a failure:

> Qualified immunity has also been disastrous as a matter of policy. Victims of egregious misconduct are often left without any legal remedy

simply because there does not happen to be a prior case on the books involving the exact same sort of misconduct. By undermining public accountability at a structural level, the doctrine also hurts the law enforcement community by denying police the degree of public trust and confidence they need to do their jobs safely and effectively.

## Conclusion

Reasonable minds may differ on the merits or lack thereof of qualified immunity, but there is nearly universal understanding that the Fourth Amendment is of vital importance. Most people revere the amendment's protection of privacy, particularly for their personage and their home. As Justice Louis Brandeis wrote years ago, it truly is "the most comprehensive of rights" and "the one most valued by mankind."

# The Fifth Amendment

No person shall be held to answer for a capital, or otherwise infamous crime, unless on a presentment or indictment of a grand jury, except in cases arising in the land or naval forces, or in the militia, when in actual service in time of war or public danger; nor shall any person be subject for the same offense to be twice put in jeopardy of life or limb; nor shall be compelled in any criminal case to be a witness against himself, nor be deprived of life, liberty, or property, without due process of law; nor shall private property be taken for public use, without just compensation.

The longest amendment in the Bill of Rights is the Fifth Amendment. It contains several freedoms, including (1) the right to a grand jury; (2) the right to be free from double jeopardy; (3) privilege against self-incrimination; (4) due process; and (5) just compensation. Linda Monk writes in her book *The Words We Live By* that "the Fifth Amendment is a hodgepodge of provisions affecting both criminal law and civil law." The bulk of the amendment deals with freedoms for those charged with crimes, but the right to due process applies in the civil context too, as does the right to just compensation.

# Grand Jury

No person shall be held to answer for a capital, or otherwise infamous crime, unless on presentment or indictment of a grand jury …

A grand jury is a body of citizens, usually in groups of 16 to 23, who decide whether a prosecutor has presented enough evidence to obtain an indictment of an individual. Grand juries are designed to serve as a type of buffer between the prosecution and the defendant. Critics charge that grand juries—more often than not—do not serve this ideal buffering function and instead serve as a rubber stamp for the prosecution. There is a famous saying about grand juries that reflects this sentiment—"a grand jury will indict a ham sandwich."

Grand juries are distinct from trial juries—also called petit juries—which usually consist of 12 people. Sometimes prosecutors use the grand jury method of initiating criminal charges against individuals rather than filing an accusatory document—called an information—and proceeding with a preliminary hearing. The

The Fifth Amendment guarantees that a grand jury must determine whether or not there is enough evidence to bring charges against an accused party for certain crimes.

grand jury serves as a screening mechanism to determine whether the prosecutor has enough evidence to obtain what is known as a true bill. If the grand jury decides there is not evidence, it would issue what is called a no bill. Grand juries are used in federal court and in some states. Most states explain the operational workings and functions of the grand jury in their rules of criminal procedure.

The right to a grand jury is the most prominent right that is not incorporated or extended to the states by the Due Process Clause. This means that states do not have to provide a grand jury for individuals before prosecution.

Most states allow prosecutors to file an information, which is a document that includes an accusation of formal charges of criminal conduct against a defendant. In the information, the prosecutor includes a sworn statement that there is enough evidence to try the defendant. It is a common method of introducing criminal charges against defendants in many states. The prosecution files the information, and a judge considers the information at a preliminary hearing. This is the most common method of proceeding with the prosecution of criminal cases in many states and differs greatly from the grand jury process. In many states, a prosecutor has the option of proceeding with an information or with a grand jury indictment.

Perhaps the most distinguishing feature of a grand jury is its secrecy. Grand jury proceedings are not public, and grand jurors are required to take an oath about secrecy. Another distinguishing feature is that traditional rules of evidence do not apply in the grand jury setting. Prosecutors can present evidence that might be excluded at trial for being hearsay. Grand juries also have the power to compel witnesses to testify.

The grand jury usually is composed of more citizens than the petit jury. In Texas, however, grand jurors are composed of 12 jurors. Second, the grand jury only hears from the prosecutor, not the defense. The prosecutor decides what witnesses to call and which individuals receive immunity for their grand jury testimony. The subject or target of a grand jury is not allowed to bring an attorney and present evidence. The grand jury has broad powers to subpoena witnesses, including the defendant. The defendant can assert his or her Fifth Amendment right against self-incrimination at the grand jury proceeding.

# Double Jeopardy

… nor shall any person be subject for the same offense to be twice put in jeopardy of life or limb

The Double Jeopardy Clause serves as a constraint on both prosecutors and courts. It provides three constitutional protections: (1) no reprosecution for the same offense after a defendant has been acquitted; (2) no second prosecution for the same offense after a conviction; and (3) a limit on multiple punishments for the same offense.

The most common conception of double jeopardy concerns no second prosecution after a defendant has been acquitted. In the words of the U.S. Supreme Court, "an acquittal is afforded special weight." The idea is that a person should not be subjected to the embarrassment, harassment, and stresses of a second prosecution after a jury or judge has rendered an acquittal or not-guilty verdict. If this were not the case, then the government could keep subjecting a defendant to trial after trial until the prosecution obtained a favorable verdict.

*The idea is that a person should not be subjected to the embarrassment, harassment, and stresses of a second prosecution after a jury or judge has rendered an acquittal or not-guilty verdict.*

A lesser-known conception of double jeopardy concerns a second prosecution after the defendant already has been convicted. That would amount to unnecessary and excessive punishments, as the defendant already has been punished.

The final conception of double jeopardy is the one that comes up the most often in litigation—multiple punishments for the same offense. How this plays out is that a prosecutor charges an individual under multiple statutes for the same offense. The prosecutor in effect is seeking cumulative punishments by charging violations under different laws. This may violate the Double Jeopardy Clause if the conduct arises out of the same offense.

Sometimes, prosecutors can charge a defendant with violating multiple crimes coming out of the same criminal act without violating double jeopardy.

The test used is the "Blockburger test," which comes from the U.S. Supreme Court's decision in *Blockburger v. United States* (1932). Under the Blockburger test, the first question is whether the different charges arise out of the same act or transaction. If so, then the next question is whether each law has a distinct element that is not found in the other law. If the charges arise out of the same act and there is not a distinct element in one law not found in the other, then there is a double jeopardy problem.

It is a complicated test. Take the case of *Brown v. Ohio* (1977), which reached the U.S. Supreme Court. A defendant stole a car in East Cleveland, Ohio, and nine days later was caught in Wickliffe, Ohio. The defendant pled guilty to joyriding in Wickliffe, but prosecutors later charged him with both auto theft and joyriding in East Cleveland. The Court found that joyriding was a lesser-included offense of auto theft under Ohio law, and thus prosecutors could not charge him again with either joyriding or auto theft because the defendant already had pled guilty to joyriding in another Ohio county.

To the Court, joyriding and auto theft were "the same statutory offense," and thus, prosecutors could not add on successive and cumulative punishments for conduct for which the defendant already had pled guilty.

There are exceptions to the principle against double jeopardy. Two key exceptions are (1) that a person can be charged criminally and then sued civilly for the same conduct; and (2) that a person can be charged in state and federal courts under different criminal laws.

The first exception applies when a person is tried for the crime of murder and then is sued by the harmed family for wrongful death. A person can be charged in separate criminal and civil trials. For example, retired football star O. J. Simpson (1947–) faced criminal murder charges for the deaths of his ex-wife Nicole Brown Simpson (1959–1994) and her companion Ronald Goldman (1968–1994). After the completion of the criminal case, the victims' families sued Simpson in civil court.

Double jeopardy means that someone cannot be charged twice for the same crime. Two exceptions are that someone can face a criminal and then a civil charge for the same crime, and they can also be charged in a state and then a federal court.

In a criminal case, the state brings charges against an individual to confine that person in prison. In a civil suit, normally one private party sues another private party for money. Another exception, shown by the trial of four Los Angeles Police Department officers for beating motorist Rodney King (1965–2012), is that a criminal defendant can sometimes be charged criminally in state court and then in federal court. The officers were charged with different crimes. In state court, they faced assault charges. In federal court, they faced federal civil rights charges.

## Privilege against Self-Incrimination: The Miranda Warning

Arguably, the most well-known freedom found in the Fifth Amendment is the privilege against self-incrimination. This means that the government cannot force a person to testify against themselves in court. When somebody says, "I take the Fifth," it means they are taking their Fifth Amendment constitutional right not to incriminate themselves.

The privilege applies even more frequently when the police arrest and place a person in custody. When a police officer arrests a suspect, the officer is supposed to read the suspect their rights. The officer warns the suspect: "You have the right to remain silent. Anything you say can and will be used against you."

Ernesto Miranda was convicted of kidnapping and rape in 1963, but the Supreme Court overturned the decision in 1966 because he was not informed of his right to an attorney. He was convicted again the next year.

Unfortunately, some law enforcement officers ignored this constitutional right and would beat confessions out of defendants. In a 1966 decision, the U.S. Supreme Court voided the conviction of a young Latino man in part because the police had not informed him of his right to remain silent.

In March 1963, Phoenix police arrested Ernesto Miranda (1941–1976) at his home on charges of rape and kidnapping. A witness identified Miranda as her assailant. The police then took him to an interrogation room, where he was questioned for two hours straight by two police officers. The officers emerged from the interrogation room with a typed, signed confession from Miranda.

At his jury trial, the prosecution introduced his confession into evidence. The police officers also testified as to Miranda's oral confession. The jury convicted him of both kidnapping and rape. He was sentenced to 20 to 30 years in prison. The Arizona state courts upheld his conviction, finding that Miranda did not ask for an attorney during his police questioning.

The U.S. Supreme Court reversed the decision, however, focusing on the failure of the officers to advise Miranda of his right to an attorney and his right to have an attorney present during his questioning. "Without these warnings the statements were inadmissible," Chief Justice Earl Warren (1891–1974) wrote in his majority opinion. "The mere fact that he signed a statement which contained a typed-in clause stating that he had 'full knowledge' of his 'legal rights' does not approach the knowing and intelligent waiver required to relinquish constitutional rights."

Chief Justice Warren explained in his majority opinion:

Today, then, there can be no doubt that the Fifth Amendment privilege is available outside of criminal court proceedings and serves to protect persons in all settings in which their freedom of action is curtailed in any significant way from being compelled to incriminate themselves. We have concluded that without proper safeguards the process of in-custody interrogation of persons suspected or accused of crime contains inherently compelling pressures which work to undermine the individual's will to resist and to compel him to speak where he would not otherwise do so freely. In order to combat these pressures and to permit a full opportunity to exercise the privilege against self-incrimination, the accused must be adequately and effectively apprised of his rights and the exercise of those rights must be fully honored.

Some defended the *Miranda* decision as the absolute correct decision, including former U.S. attorney general Ramsey Clark (1927–2021) in his book *Crime in America: Observations on Its Nature, Causes, Prevention, and Control.* Clark wrote: "All *Miranda* means is that we must not take advantage of the poor, the ignorant and the distracted—that government will be fair and has self-confidence. Are the rights of the poor and uneducated so unimportant that they are not to be accorded what others cannot be denied?"

As for Ernesto Miranda, his conviction was reversed, but he was retried and reconvicted. Sentenced to 20 years, he managed to obtain parole in 1972. He later carried cards in his pocket that featured the "Miranda Rights" that his case championed. However, he was stabbed to death in January 1976 in a bar fight. When the police searched his clothing, they found his Miranda cards. They read the Miranda rights to his assailant.

Opposition to *Miranda* was fierce. Constitutional amendments were introduced to overturn it and place it in the dustbin of history. Police unions and others argued that the Supreme Court acted like a super-legislature in creating the Miranda rights out of thin air. Congress seemingly opposed *Miranda,* at least in part, because shortly after the decision, it passed a law that provided that whether a suspect's statements were admissible depended solely on whether they were made voluntarily. Thus, the federal statute, in effect, was a legislative overruling, or ignoring, of *Miranda.* The law provided in part:

> The trial judge in determining the issue of voluntariness shall take into consideration all the circumstances surrounding the giving of the confession, including (1) the time elapsing between arrest and arraignment of the defendant making the confession, if it was made after arrest and before arraignment, (2) whether such defendant knew the nature of the offense with which he was charged or of which he was suspected at the time of making the confession, (3) whether or not such defendant was advised or knew that he was not required to make any statement and that any such statement could be used against him, (4) whether or not such defendant had been advised prior to questioning of his right to the assistance of counsel; and (5) whether or not such defendant was without the assistance of counsel when questioned and when giving such confession.

Thus, under the federal law, a confession could still be considered voluntary even if police did not read a suspect his Miranda rights.

The statute largely lay dormant for a few decades until the case of *Dickerson v. United States* (2000). Charles Dickerson was indicted for robbing banks and a conspiracy charge. FBI agents interrogated him and produced a confession. However, Dickerson argued that his Fifth Amendment rights were violated because FBI agents had interrogated him without reading him his Miranda rights. Dickerson filed a motion to suppress evidence of the confession, contending that because he wasn't read his Miranda rights, his confession should be thrown out.

A federal district court granted his motion to suppress, but the Fourth U.S. Circuit Court of Appeals reversed, based on the federal law. According to the appeals court, the federal law mandated that the confession was valid if it was made voluntarily. The fact that Dickerson did not get his Miranda rights was a factor in voluntariness, but it was not outcome determinative.

The net result is that under the federal law, the confession was valid, while under the Miranda ruling, it was not. Dickerson then appealed to the U.S. Supreme Court. Many believed that the Supreme Court might finally overturn *Miranda*.

The day the Court announced the decision, Chief Justice William Rehnquist (1924–2005) announced that he was the author of the opinion in *Dickerson v. United States*. Supreme Court observers, including seasoned *New York Times* reporter Linda Greenhouse, thought *Miranda* was about to get overruled. There was credibility for this viewpoint, as Rehnquist long had criticized the *Miranda* decision as judicial policymaking from the bench. Greenhouse recounted in a *Times* article: "There was considerable drama in the courtroom today as the chief justice announced that he would deliver the decision in the case, *Dickerson v. United States*, No. 99-5525. The announcement meant that he was the majority opinion's author. Given his statements over more than 25 years about *Miranda*'s lack of constitutional foundation, there was the distinct possibility that he was about to announce that *Miranda* had been overruled."

Linda Greenhouse is a Pulitzer Prize–winning journalist for the *New York Times* who specializes in covering the U.S. Supreme Court. She is also president of the American Philosophical Society.

But to the surprise of Greenhouse and others, Rehnquist's opinion protected the *Miranda* decision and invalidated the federal law as inconsistent with the decision. "But Congress may not legislatively supersede our decisions interpreting and applying the Constitution," Rehnquist wrote.

Rehnquist explained that Chief Justice Warren's opinion in *Miranda* is "replete" with statements that the Court was announcing a new constitutional rule. "We do not think there is such justification for overruling *Miranda*," Rehnquist wrote. "*Miranda* has become embedded in routine police practice to the point where the warnings have become part of our national culture."

Attorney Alfred Knight in his book *The Life of the Law* explains the importance of the

Fifth Amendment. He writes that "[d]espite the scorn that has been heaped upon it, the privilege against self-incrimination seems neither irrational nor silly when viewed objectively. Its essence is a citizen, arms folded, confronting the state and saying, 'Prove it.'"

# Due Process

Due process is one of the greatest rights Americans possess. One eminent legal historian has said the right of due process has "served as the basis for the constitutional protection of the rights of Americans."

Due process has often been divided into two basic categories: procedural due process and substantive due process. Procedural due process means that the government must guarantee a fair process before taking away an individual's life, liberty, or property. The basic elements to procedural due process are notice and the right to a fair hearing. This prevents the government from arbitrarily taking away someone's job or freedom.

Substantive due process means that laws must advance a legitimate, governmental objective. Normally, a law must be justified on a rational basis. It must be rationally related to a legitimate goal. Due process applies in both the criminal and civil law realm.

The Fifth Amendment, unlike the Fourteenth Amendment, does not contain an explicit equal protection clause. However, the U.S. Supreme Court in *Bolling v. Sharpe* (1954) interpreted the Fifth Amendment as containing the right of equal protection with the Due Process Clause. *Bolling* involved a claim that the public schools in the District of Columbia were segregated, and such segregation violated basic principles of equal protection. *Bolling* was decided the same day as the more well-known *Brown v. Board of Education* (1954), in which the Supreme Court invalidated the practice of segregation in public schools in Kansas, Virginia, South Carolina, and Delaware.

# Just Compensation

The last clause of the Fifth Amendment provides that "nor shall private property be taken for public use without just compensation." This means that the government cannot simply take a citizen's land without paying for it.

The government does possess the power of eminent domain, or the right to take private property for public use. However, the Due Process Clause of the Fifth Amendment and the Fourteenth Amendment require that the government give "just compensation" before invoking this sovereign power.

There are two basic types of takings—possessory takings and regulatory takings. Possessory takings mean that the government—or another approved entity—takes over all or part of your land and you do not have the right to possess that land anymore. It is similar to voluntarily selling your property—once the deed changes hands, you would be trespassing if you went onto that property to use the land again.

*The government does possess the power of eminent domain, or the right to take private property for public use. However, ... the government [must] give "just compensation" before invoking this sovereign power.*

Possessory takings can involve all of your land, which will require you to completely relocate yourself, your family, or even your business. In other situations, only a partial possessory taking will occur. Often, you can remain in your home or business—you just will not be able to use the seized part of your land.

There are also nonpossessory takings, as not all takings mean that someone has the right to move in and take over your land. A prime example of this is an easement, which gives a party a right to occupy and use part of your land. This can include installing and maintaining power lines or constructing a pipeline underground. The company can come onto your land in accordance with the easement while you remain on your land as well. Easements can often diminish property value and sometimes lead to litigation.

Regulatory takings occur when a governmental entity, such as a city or town, passes a law or regulation that limits your use of the land. A prime example of a regulatory taking could be a zoning ordinance that prohibits you from operating a building as a commercial property. Regulatory takings often involve changes to zoning and land use laws, and it can be difficult to prove that a taking truly occurred and that you deserve just compensation.

Many takings are relatively straightforward, as the government acknowledges that it is taking public property. The only issue in these situations is how much money, or "just compensation," the government will pay for taking your property.

To constitute a valid taking, the taking must be for a "public use." This is one of the more controversial parts of the Fifth Amendment's Taking Clause. A key question is whether the taking of private property from one owner and granting it to another private property owner can ever constitute "public use." An example of a taking for public use would be when the government exercises its power of eminent domain and takes land to build a railroad. The idea is that giving land for railroad construction is a "public use."

This controversy surfaced in the Supreme Court's decision in *Kelo v. City of New London* (2005). The city of New London, Connecticut, approved of a development plan that allegedly would bring 1,000 new jobs to the economically distressed city. The development plan focused on pharmaceutical giant Pfizer's decision to build a new research center in the Fort Trumbull area of New London.

The New London Development Corporation went on a mission to acquire the necessary land for the development of this new complex. However, several homeowners—including Susette Kelo—refused to sell their land. Kelo loved her house and its location and wanted to remain there.

The city instituted inverse condemnation proceedings to acquire title to her land and force her to give up her home. Kelo and others challenged this action in court as an unlawful taking in violation of the Fifth Amendment. The case proceeded all the way to the U.S. Supreme Court, which ruled 5–4 against Kelo.

The government can exercise eminent domain rights for public projects such as freeways or railroads. This allows the government to take possession of private property provided that adequate compensation is given to the owners.

Writing for the majority, Justice John Paul Stevens (1920–2019) wrote that the city's "determination that the area was sufficiently distressed to justify a program of economic rejuvenation is entitled to our deference." The majority reasoned that the economic redevelopment was a "public use" under the Takings Clause.

Justice Sandra Day O'Connor (1930–) wrote a blistering dissent. She warned: "Any property may now be taken for the benefit of another private party, but the fallout from this decision will not be random. The beneficiaries are likely to be those citizens with disproportionate influence and power in the political process, including large corporations and development firms. As for the victims, the government now has license to transfer property from those with fewer resources to those with more."

Justice Clarence Thomas (1948–) also wrote a dissenting opinion in the case, and he pointed out that the government's use of the condemnation power often fell heavily upon African Americans. He explained that "Urban renewal projects have long been associated with the displacement of blacks; in cities across the country, urban renewal came to be known as 'Negro removal.'"

Justice Stevens himself later remarked after his retirement that the *Kelo* decision was his "most unpopular decision, no doubt about it." Reaction to the *Kelo* decision was swift in state legislatures. At least 43 states adopted more limits on the power of eminent domain, some of them by amending their own state constitutions. Alabama quickly passed a state law that prohibits the use of economic redevelopment for eminent domain except in cases of blight. Florida passed a constitutional amendment that provided: "Private property taken by eminent domain may not be conveyed to a natural person or private entity except as provided by general law passed by a three-fifths vote of the membership of each house of the Legislature." Louisiana also passed a constitutional amendment that placed even more restrictions on the power of eminent domain.

# The Sixth Amendment

"In all criminal prosecutions, the accused shall enjoy the right to a speedy and public trial, by an impartial jury of the state and district wherein the crime shall have been committed, which district shall have been previously ascertained by law, and to be informed of the nature and cause of the accusation; to be confronted with the witnesses against him; to have compulsory process for obtaining witnesses in his favor, and to have the assistance of counsel for his defense."

## Speedy Trial

The right to a speedy trial ensures that a criminal defendant will not sit in jail for too long before having a trial. In the old criminal justice saying, "justice delayed is justice denied." The Speedy Trial Clause seeks to ensure that criminal defendants don't languish in jail while the legal process moves along at a glacial pace. This clause prevents officials from keeping a defendant imprisoned for a lengthy period of time before a trial. If there was no provision for a "speedy" trial, an accused's defense could suffer. People's memories could wane, and so-called exculpatory evidence (evidence showing defendant's innocence) could be lost.

The Court ruled in *Klopfer v. North Carolina* (1967) that the right to a speedy trial was a fundamental right that is important enough that it is extended and applied at the state court level. The case involved a situation in which a prosecutor brought misdemeanor criminal trespass charges against Peter Klopfer, but the case ended in a mistrial. Instead of seeking a retrial, the prosecutor employed a procedure known as "nolle prosequi with leave." Under this procedure, the defendant is released from custody, but the prosecutor at some indefinite point of time in the future may elect to prosecute the defendant again.

|| *The Supreme Court ruled in favor of Klopfer, reasoning that to put Klopfer to indefinite delay would cause unnecessary anxiety.* ||

Klopfer argued that this prosecutorial device violated his constitutional right to a speedy trial. He argued that he had the right to know if and when he was going to be tried again for this misdemeanor offense of criminal trespass. The Supreme Court ruled in favor of Klopfer, reasoning that to put Klopfer to indefinite delay would cause unnecessary anxiety. Chief Justice Earl Warren explained: "The pendency of the indictment may subject him to public scorn and deprive him of employment, and almost certainly will force curtailment of his speech, associations and participation in unpopular causes. By indefinitely prolonging this oppression, as well as the 'anxiety and concern accompanying public accusation,' the criminal procedure condoned in this case by the Supreme Court of North Carolina clearly denies the petitioner the right to a speedy trial which we hold is guaranteed to him by the Sixth Amendment of the Constitution of the United States."

The Court addressed the speedy trial right at length in a case involving the delayed murder prosecution of Kentucky inmate Willie Barker in the case *Barker v. Wingo* (1972). The Court identified several factors important to determining whether there was a violation of the right to a speedy trial. These factors are (1) length of the delay; (2) the reason for the delay; (3) whether the defendant asserted his or her speedy trial rights; and (4) prejudice to the defendant.

The Court explained that the length of the delay was "the triggering mechanism" in that if there is not a significant delay, then there is no need to address the other factors. If there is a significant delay, then a reviewing court must balance the other factors. The next factor is the government's reason for the delay. In other words, was there a legitimate reason for the delay, or was the prosecution playing games or engaging in some improper motive in delaying the matter? The third factor also is important—whether the defendant asserted his or her speedy trial rights. The Court noted that "failure to assert the right will make it difficult for a defendant to prove that he was denied a speedy trial." Finally, the fourth factor—prejudice—is perhaps the most important factor. The Court identified three concerns regarding a long delay: (i) to prevent oppressive pretrial incarceration; (ii) to minimize anxiety and concern of the accused; and (iii) to limit the possibility that the defense will be impaired. The last concern is the most significant, as a defendant could be prejudiced by a long delay because his witnesses may be lost or have died or lose recall of significant events. In other words, a long delay could impair a defendant's right to put on an effective defense.

About twenty years later, the U.S. Supreme Court ruled in *Doggett v. United States* (1992) that an accused's Sixth Amendment right to a speedy trial was violated by an eight-and-a-half-year gap between his indictment and arrest. The Court determined that the defendant would be prejudiced in trying to defend himself against charges filed years ago of which he was unaware.

# Public Trial

The Sixth Amendment begins with the words, "In all criminal prosecutions, the accused shall enjoy a right to a speedy and public trial." The Sixth Amendment right to a public trial ensures that defendants are not tried in secret, as was the case in, for instance, the Spanish Inquisition and the dreaded English Star Chamber. The Star Chamber was an English court dissolved by Parliament in 1641 that was known for its secretive judicial meetings and harsh sentences. It would convict and punish individuals without providing them with any protections comparable to those found in our Bill of Rights.

These practices are anathema to a free and open society. People facing criminal charges have the right to have their case heard in an open court of law. Justice Hugo Black (1886–1971) forcefully wrote in *In Re Oliver* (1948) that "the guarantee [of a public trial] has always been recognized as a safeguard against any attempt to employ our courts as instruments of persecution."

However, the Sixth Amendment right to a public trial does not give the press any special access to court proceedings. The U.S. Supreme Court clarified this in *Nixon v. Warner Communications* (1978), writing that while the constitutional right to a public trial is important, "it confers no special benefit upon the press." There, the Court explained that the Sixth Amendment does not mandate that criminal trial proceedings be broadcast. Rather, the Sixth Amendment is satisfied if the public and press can attend criminal trial proceedings.

Justice Hugo Black served on the Supreme Court bench from 1937 to 1971. Nominated by Franklin D. Roosevelt, Black believed the Fourteenth Amendment clarified that the liberties provided by the Bill of Rights must be adhered to by the states.

The Sixth Amendment right to public access is not absolute. The court may need to close a courtroom to protect a witness or prohibit the disclosure of extremely sensitive information. However, generally, a judge can close a courtroom only when there is an overriding interest for closure and the closure is no greater than necessary. A judge must make particularized findings to support the closure, which again must be narrowly tailored to the specific situation.

The Sixth Amendment right to a public trial is not to be confused with the First Amendment right of access to court proceedings. The key difference is that the criminal defendant has the Sixth Amendment right to a public trial, while the press and the public have the qualified First Amendment right of access to court proceedings.

# Impartial Jury

An impartial jury must also judge every person charged with a crime. Sometimes, a judge will pick a jury from another county than the one in which the defendant allegedly committed the crime. In our legal system, this is called a change of venue. A judge will change venue if a defendant would be prejudiced (that is, adversely affected by prejudgment). This potential problem occurs when a high-profile criminal case receives a lot of pretrial publicity. Judges have a duty to ensure that a defendant will not be prejudged by the jury.

*This potential problem occurs when a high-profile criminal case receives a lot of pretrial publicity. Judges have a duty to ensure that a defendant will not be prejudged by the jury.*

The process of selecting a jury is called *voir dire*. In this process, attorneys from each side ask the prospective jurors in the box a series of questions. Attorneys then have two types of challenges to attempt to remove jurors they do not think will be good for their client or case. These two types of challenges are for-cause challenges and peremptory challenges. For-cause challenges are used for when a prospective juror is clearly biased. For example, let's say there is an assault case, and the chief prosecution witness is a police officer. If, during *voir dire*, a prospective juror tells one of the questioning attorneys, "I hate police officers and I would never trust a word that comes out of a police officer's mouth," such a person cannot be impartial and would be dismissed with a for-cause challenge.

Peremptory challenges are much different. Peremptory challenges are used because attorneys often have a hunch that a person would not make a good juror for their side. In different types of cases, each side has a set number of peremptory challenges. The most peremptory challenges are available in death penalty cases because of what is at stake. The Supreme Court has ruled that attorneys may not exercise their peremptory challenges in a manner or in a way that discriminates on the basis of race or gender. Most litigation centers on the subject of race.

The Supreme Court also has held that in a criminal case, the Sixth Amendment requires that the jury be unanimous. This did not used to be the rule, as the Supreme Court in 1972 had upheld the state of Louisiana's practice of allowing convictions based on a 10–2 jury vote. However, in *Ramos v. Louisiana* (2020), the Supreme Court changed course.

### Notice: "to be informed of the nature and cause of the accusation"

The Sixth Amendment also provides that a defendant must have notice of the charges filed against them. Individuals need to know what charges they face so that they can prepare a defense to those charges. If defendants do not know the criminal charges they face, it is impossible to prepare a defense to those charges. It would run counter to the system of fairness that the Bill of Rights tries to provide for defendants to not have notice.

# Confrontation Clause

The Confrontation Clause of the Sixth Amendment provides: "In all criminal prosecutions, the accused shall enjoy the right … to be confronted with the witnesses against him." This clause ensures that a criminal defendant can cross-examine those who testify against him. U.S. Supreme Court justice Antonin Scalia (1936–2016) wrote: "The perception that confrontation is essential to fairness has persisted over the centuries because there is much truth to it.… It is always more difficult to tell a lie about a person 'to his face' than 'behind his back.'"

The U.S. Supreme Court has recognized that face-to-face confrontation ensures greater reliability by reducing the risk that an innocent person will be convicted. The Confrontation Clause ensures that a witness must face cross-examination—a process by which a witness must answer questions by an attorney from the other side. The Court has referred to cross-examination as the "greatest legal engine ever invented for the discovery of truth."

However, the Court has relaxed the requirements of the Confrontation Clause in child-abuse cases. In *Maryland v. Craig*, the U.S. Supreme Court ruled constitutional a Maryland law allowing child-abuse victims to testify by a one-way closed-circuit television. The Court reasoned that the state's interest in the physical and psychological well-being of children could outweigh a defendant's Sixth Amendment rights.

The key to determining whether a defendant's rights under the Confrontation Clause have been violated is whether the evidence submitted is testimonial or nontestimonial. If the evidence is testimonial, then the Confrontation Clause generally requires the defendant have an opportunity to cross-examine the witness who made the testimonial statement. The Supreme Court has explained the difference between testimonial and nontestimonial statements as follows: "Statements are nontestimonial when made in the course of police interrogation under circumstances objectively indicating that the primary purpose of the interrogation is to enable police

The Confrontation Clause of the Sixth Amendment says that a defendant in court has the right to cross-examine a witness brought to the stand by the prosecution.

assistance to meet an ongoing emergency. They are testimonial when the circumstances objectively indicate that there is no such ongoing emergency, and that the primary purpose of the interrogation is to establish or prove past events potentially relevant to later criminal prosecution."

### Compulsory Process

The Sixth Amendment also provides that a criminal defendant can force witnesses to testify in the trial. Often, people do not want to get involved in a criminal trial. The Compulsory Witness Clause provides that a defendant can try to prove his or her case whether the witnesses want to get involved or not.

# Assistance of Counsel

The last freedom in the Sixth Amendment is the assistance of counsel. This means that those charged with crimes have the right to an attorney even if they cannot afford an attorney. The Supreme Court explained that there is too much at stake in the criminal process—liberty and sometimes even life—to not have a trained legal advocate on the defendant's side.

The reality of the criminal court system in the United States is that the vast majority of criminal defendants cannot afford to hire a high-priced criminal defense attorney. This means that these defendants are represented by public defenders or by private attorneys who are appointed by the courts. Many U.S. criminal defense attorneys make at least part of their living off of appointed cases. Many jurisdictions have appointment lists from which judges will select attorneys for representation.

If a defendant cannot afford an attorney, they are entitled to free legal counsel provided by the state.

The U.S. Supreme Court first ruled that a criminal defendant was entitled to an attorney in the death penalty case of the Scottsboro Boys—an infamous series of cases that reached the U.S. Supreme Court several times during a long, strange road.

The Scottsboro Boys was the name given to nine African American youth who were falsely accused of rape by two young white women on a train near Scottsboro, Alabama. Apparently, the Scottsboro Boys and a group of white youths got into a fight on a train. When the train came to a stop in Scottsboro, the police questioned the Scottsboro Boys about a possible assault. Two white women, Victoria Price and Ruby Bates, also accused the Scottsboro Boys of rape. At that time in Alabama, such a charge of interracial rape caused significant commotion.

An angry white mob surrounded the local jail, forcing the sheriff to call in the Alabama National Guard. Prosecutors hauled the defendants into court quickly. A local Tennessee lawyer from Chattanooga, Stephen Roddy, agreed to defend the Scottsboro Boys, and he requested assistance from an Alabama attorney. However, these attorneys did not have sufficient time to prepare a valid defense. The case proceeded to trial in April, and on April 9, 1932, the jury sentenced the defendants to death. Alabama courts affirmed the death sentence.

However, on appeal, the U.S. Supreme Court reversed in *Powell v. Alabama* (1932) in an opinion written by Justice George Sutherland (1862–1942). The Court focused on the fact that the rushed nature of the trial and the failure to appoint the defendants an experienced criminal defense attorney and give that attorney or attorneys time to prepare amounted to a denial of due process of law under the Fourteenth Amendment to the U.S. Constitution.

Justice Sutherland explained:

In the light of the facts outlined in the forepart of this opinion—the ignorance and illiteracy of the defendants, their youth, the circumstances of public hostility, the imprisonment and the close surveillance of the defendants by the military forces, the fact that their friends and families were all in other states and communication with them necessarily difficult, and above all that they stood in deadly peril of their lives—we think the failure of the trial court to give them reasonable time and opportunity to secure counsel was a clear denial of due process.

Sutherland added, "The necessity of counsel was so vital and imperative that the failure of the trial court to make an effective appointment of counsel was likewise a denial of due process within the meaning of the Fourteenth Amendment."

Several of the Scottsboro Boys were tried a second time and again convicted. In two subsequent decisions, *Patterson v. Alabama* (1935) and *Norris v. Alabama* (1935), the U.S. Supreme Court once again reversed the convictions based on the fact that African Americans were excluded from the jury.

Four of the Scottsboro Boys were released in 1937. Others were convicted and spent decades in prison. One of the Scottsboro Boys, Clarence Norris (1912–1989), remained in prison until 1976 when he received a pardon from Alabama governor George Wallace (1919–1998). In April 2013, Alabama governor Robert Bentley (1943–) signed legislation that officially pardoned and exonerated all nine of the Scottsboro Boys.

Justice George Sutherland, who served on the Supreme Court from 1922 to 1938, wrote the majority opinion on the *Powell v. Alabama* case.

A few years after *Powell*, the U.S. Supreme Court ruled in *Johnson v. Zerbst* (1938) that federal criminal court defendants had an absolute right to counsel. "The purpose of the constitutional guaranty of a right to counsel is to protect an accused from conviction resulting from his own ignorance of his legal and constitutional rights, and the guaranty would be nullified by a determination that an accused's ignorant failure to claim his rights removes the protection of the Constitution," the Court explained.

However, a few years later in *Betts v. Brady* (1942), the Supreme Court refused to extend that rule to all state court criminal defendants. The Court held that a state court criminal defendant was only entitled to an attorney if he or she could show special circumstances. One of the justices who dissented in that case was Justice Hugo Black, who fervently believed the right to counsel was too important not to provide to criminal defendants.

While the Supreme Court ruled that those facing the death penalty in state court were entitled to an attorney, the Court did not grant that right to state-court criminal defendants until the case of Clarence Earl Gideon (1910–1972), a Florida inmate who hand-wrote his own appeal to the U.S. Supreme Court, asking the Court to grant him a new trial and appoint him an attorney.

Gideon allegedly broke into a Florida pool hall to steal money. This criminal act earned him felony charges and later a conviction in Florida state court. In the beginning of the case, Gideon asked the court for a lawyer. The trial judge responded that under Florida law, the only criminal defendants entitled to a court-appointed lawyer were those defendants facing capital (death-penalty) charges. Gideon insisted that "the United States Supreme Court says I am entitled to be represented by Counsel."

The Florida trial judge disagreed and refused to appoint Gideon an attorney. He attempted to represent himself but was convicted. Gideon appealed his case all the way to the U.S. Supreme Court. The Court accepted his case for review and appointed him a Washington, D.C.–based attorney named Abe Fortas (1910–1982) to represent Gideon before the Court. Fortas later became a U.S. Supreme Court justice.

> *Writing for the Court, Justice Hugo Black reasoned that attorneys in criminal cases are "necessities, not luxuries."*

The Supreme Court ruled that Gideon had a constitutional right to an appointed attorney. Writing for the Court, Justice Hugo Black reasoned that attorneys in criminal cases are "necessities, not luxuries." He reasoned that the complexity of the criminal justice system often requires a person with experience and knowledge of the criminal law. In other words, fundamental fairness dictated that Clarence Earl Gideon ought to have a lawyer.

It was highly fitting that Justice Black, the justice who had dissented in *Betts v. Brady*, got to write the opinion overruling that decision. Black allegedly told a friend, "When *Betts v. Brady* was decided, I never thought I'd live to see it overruled."

Gideon was appointed an attorney, and in a new trial, he was found not guilty. Famed writer Anthony Lewis wrote a book about the case called *Gideon's Trumpet*. Lewis wrote: "The case of *Gideon v. Wainwright* is in part a testament to a single human being. Against all the odds of inertia and ignorance and fear of state power, Clarence Earl Gideon insisted that he had a right to a lawyer and kept on insisting all the way to the Supreme Court of the United States."

# Ineffective Assistance of Counsel

As noted, the last freedom in the Sixth Amendment of the U.S. Constitution provides for the "assistance of counsel" for those facing criminal charges. The U.S.

Supreme Court determined in *McMann v. Richardson* (1970) that the right to counsel means the right to reasonably effective assistance of counsel.

However, the Court did not set a clear standard for a line between effective assistance of counsel and ineffective assistance of counsel. Some lower courts applied what was known as the "farce and mockery" standard, meaning that a defendant had "assistance of counsel" as long as his or her trial was not a "farce and mockery." Other lower courts proclaimed that the applicable standard was that of a reasonably competent attorney.

The determination was vitally important because defendants who challenged their convictions in state post-conviction proceedings or federal *habeas corpus* proceedings often argued that their convictions should be set aside because they received so-called ineffective assistance of counsel. In other words, these defendants argued that they were deprived of their Sixth Amendment right to assistance of counsel. The defendants hope to convince a court to find that their attorney was so bad that that they deserve a new trial represented by competent counsel. It is a long shot, but some defendants have been successful at obtaining *habeas corpus* relief and earning another shot.

Sandra Day O'Connor—shown here in 2004 after retiring from the Supreme Court—argued that ineffective counsel resulted when an attorney was deficient in their representation of the client and that this deficiency prejudiced the defendant.

In 1984, the Supreme Court finally set the standard for ineffective assistance of counsel in *Strickland v. Washington,* a decision involving the death sentence of inmate David Washington. Washington had committed a string of murders and kidnappings allegedly to obtain money for his family.

Washington waived his right to a jury trial and admitted his involvement in the murders. He pled guilty and hoped for leniency from the trial judge. Washington's attorney offered little to nothing in the way of mitigating evidence, and the trial judge sentenced Washington to death.

Later, Washington filed a petition for *habeas corpus* relief in federal court, contending that his trial counsel committed ineffective assistance of counsel. A federal district court ruled against Washington, but a federal appeals court ruled in his favor. Thus, the state of Florida—through then prison superintendent Charles Strickland—sought review in the U.S. Supreme Court.

The U.S. Supreme Court established a two-part test for determining ineffective assistance of counsel. The first prong was deficiency—the inmate had to show that his trial attorney was deficient in his representation. This meant far below that of a reasonably competent attorney. In her majority opinion, Justice Sandra Day O'Connor wrote that "a fair assessment of attorney performance requires that every effort be made to eliminate the distorting effects of hindsight, to reconstruct the circumstances of counsel's challenged conduct, and to evaluate the conduct from counsel's perspective at the time."

The next prong is prejudice. The challenging inmate must show that the attorney's deficient performance prejudiced, or adversely affected, the defendant. "The defendant must show that there is a reasonable probability that, but for counsel's unprofessional errors, the result of the proceeding would have been different," O'Connor wrote. "A reasonable probability is a probability sufficient to undermine confidence in the outcome."

Applying this new standard, the majority reasoned that David Washington received the effective assistance of counsel. The majority reasoned that trial counsel followed a reasonable strategic choice in having his client accept responsibility for his crimes and that that acceptance of responsibility might cause the judge to not impose the death penalty.

With regard to prejudice, the majority also reasoned that the attorney's failure to offer mitigating evidence did not change the outcome of the proceeding. Justice O'Connor wrote: "Given the overwhelming aggravating factors, there is no reasonable probability that the omitted evidence would have changed the conclusion that the aggravating circumstances outweighed the mitigating circumstances and, hence, the sentence imposed."

Justice Thurgood Marshall (1908–1993) dissented, reasoning that if an attorney's performance was deficient, there was no need to show prejudice. Marshall also differed in his assessment of the facts of the case. He reasoned that Washington's trial attorney was deficient in failing to offer mitigating evidence and to have psychological testing of his client. "If counsel had investigated the availability of mitigating evidence, he might well have decided to present some such material at the hearing," Marshall wrote. "If he had done so, there is a significant chance that [Washington] would have been given a life sentence."

# The Eighth Amendment

"The basic concept underlying the Eighth Amendment is nothing less than the dignity of man."

—Chief Justice Earl Warren in *Trop v. Dulles* (1958)

Imagine a world in which you are cited for going 10 miles over the speed limit and are fined $5,000. Imagine that the government seeks to impose a civil forfeiture penalty and seize your vehicle, saying that not only were you speeding but that you had a little bit of contraband in the car. Imagine that you are charged with simple possession of marijuana, and a judge imposes a 10-year criminal sentence. Imagine that you are sentenced to death for felony assault.

Such a world would remind one of the Athenian ruler Draco, who inspired the word "draconian" for unusually harsh punishments. Fortunately, we have the Eighth Amendment to the U.S. Constitution, which seeks to ensure that punishments are proportional, not disproportional, to the actual offense committed.

The Eighth Amendment contains three freedoms: (1) no excessive bail; (2) no excessive fines; and (3) no cruel and unusual punishment. We will examine each one of these in turn.

# Excessive Bail

Excessive bail shall not be required, nor excessive fines imposed, nor cruel and unusual punishment inflicted.

Bail refers to money or security paid to the court to secure the temporary release of a defendant charged with a crime. The defendant—or the friend or family of the defendant—pays money to the court in the promise that he or she will reappear for the next court hearing in the case. Historically, bail did not require the delivery of money, but a person would serve as a surety and promise that the defendant would appear for later court dates.

A defendant can have a bail hearing at which he or she can argue that the setting of bail was too high—higher than what is normally imposed in similar cases. Thus, a defendant can file a motion to reduce bail.

Bail lessens or reduces the chances that innocent persons will be detained in jail. As Supreme Court justice Robert Jackson (1892–1954) wrote, "The spirit of the procedure [for bail] is to enable [defendants] to stay out of jail until a trial has found them guilty." Bail reduces hardship on the defendant and the defendant's family members. Bail gives a defendant the opportunity to get his or her affairs in order, hire a lawyer, and mount an effective defense. Bail also serves institutional purposes in that it can help to reduce overcrowding of jails.

Not every criminal defendant is entitled to bail. If a crime is serious enough or the defendant is considered a flight risk, a judge does not have to provide bail. This means that the defendant will stay detained pending the outcome of the criminal process.

The Eighth Amendment provides that bail shall not be excessive. A court examines whether the bail amount is much higher than the state interests involved in setting bail in the first place. As a practical matter, constitutional-based challenges to bail (arguing that the bail violates the Excessive Bail Clause of the Eighth Amendment) are not very successful. The more successful challenges are that a court did not follow the state or federal statute providing for bail. Under the federal law known as the Bail Reform Act of

Bails are not allowed to be excessive, but even so, often a defendant cannot afford to pay the full bail. A solution is to pay a bail bond, which is usually 10 percent of the full bail. A bondsman covers the bail in return for the percentage and, usually, additional fees.

2004, a judge "shall order the pretrial release of the person on personal recognizance, or upon execution of an unsecured appearance bond in an amount specified by the court ... unless the judicial officer determines that such release will not reasonably assure the appearance of the person as required or will endanger the safety of any other person or the community."

## Excessive Fines

The Eighth Amendment also prohibits excessive fines. This clause traces back to language in the venerable Magna Carta of 1215, which provided that "a Freeman shall not be amerced for a small fault, but after the manner of the fault; and for a great fault after the greatness thereof, saving to him his contenement."

This difficult English language meant that any economic penalties needed to be proportional to the wrong committed and not so large as to prohibit a "freeman" from earning a living. Despite the admonition in the Magna Carta, the notorious Star Chamber, an early English secret court of "justice," imposed heavy fines on the enemies of the English kings. Several English kings imposed exorbitant fines to raise funds for their causes. In fact, kings imposing excessive fines was one reason that led to King James II (1633–1701) being deposed in the Glorious Revolution of 1688.

Tellingly, the next year Parliament passed the English Bill of Rights, which contained a protection very similar to the Eighth Amendment: "excessive Bail ought not be required, nor excessive Fines imposed; nor cruel and unusual Punishments inflicted."

*In colonial America, several governments adopted a version of the English Bill of Rights' prohibition on excessive punishment.*

In colonial America, several governments adopted a version of the English Bill of Rights' prohibition on excessive punishment. For example, the Virginia Declaration of Rights provided: "Excessive bail shall not be required, nor excessive fines imposed, nor cruel and unusual punishments inflicted."

In the nineteenth century, state constitutions in nearly all the states prohibited excessive fines. Despite the near-universal condemnation of excessive fines, abuses continued. Southern states passed Black Codes to maintain white supremacy. One insidious method used was imposing exorbitant fines for relatively minor offenses. For example, a Mississippi law said that "freedmen, free negroes and mulatoes" with "no lawful employment" faced $50 fines for vagrancy. An Alabama law imposed a $50 fine and six months' imprisonment for loitering.

In more recent times, the focus of the Excessive Fines Clause has focused on situations in which the government may imprison someone but apply forfeiture laws and take a person's money. A good example is what happened to Hosef Bakajakian when he was attempting to fly to Italy from Los Angeles International Airport with his two daughters. Bakajakian was carrying more than $350,000 in cash. Federal law required persons to disclose if they were carrying more than $10,000 in currency on an airplane. He was charged with failure to report to the U.S. Customs officials, and the government kept his money.

Bakajakian pled guilty to failure to report, but the case proceeded to a bench trial on the question of forfeiture. The U.S. government wanted the entire amount of money to be forfeited. However, the U.S. Supreme Court ruled that such a forfeiture for failing to report amounted to a grossly excessive punishment in violation of the Eighth Amendment. "The touchstone of the constitutional inquiry under the Excessive Fines Clause is the principle of proportionality," wrote Justice Clarence Thomas (1948–) in *United States v. Bakajakian* (1998). "The amount of the forfeiture must bear some relationship to the gravity of the offense that it is designed to punish." Thomas reasoned that forfeiting more than $350,000 in money bore little resemblance to an offense that called for a maximum fine of $5,000.

While the *Bakajakian* case was a victory for those who felt that forfeiture laws were imposed in a draconian way, the Excessive Fines Clause at that time only limited the federal government, not state governments. That finally changed in the case of *Timbs v. Indiana* (2019).

## *Timbs v. Indiana*

Today, all 50 states have a constitutional provision in their state constitutions prohibiting excessive fines. As Justice Ruth Bader Ginsburg (1933–2020) wrote in *Timbs v. Indiana* (2019), "the protection against excessive fines has been a constant shield throughout American history." She explained that excessive funds can be used "to retaliate against or chill the speech of political enemies."

The U.S. Supreme Court did not incorporate the Excessive Fines Clause of the Eighth Amendment until 2019 in a case that showed the dangers of civil forfeiture proceedings. Tyson Timbs was arrested and later pleaded guilty in Indiana state court to dealing a controlled substance and conspiracy to commit theft.

*The U.S. Supreme Court did not incorporate the Excessive Fines Clause of the Eighth Amendment until 2019 in a case that showed the dangers of civil forfeiture proceedings.*

The sentence required Timbs to pay $1,203 in fees and court costs. The police also seized Timbs's Land Rover SUV at the time of his arrest. Timbs had purchased the $42,000 vehicle with money he had received from his father's life insurance policy. However, the state of Indiana—through a private law firm—brought a civil forfeiture action on Timbs, seeking confiscation of his Land Rover, which allegedly had been used to transport heroin.

A trial court rejected the forfeiture claim, noting that the SUV was bought for $42,000 and the maximum civil fine for Timbs's drug conviction was $10,000. The Indiana Court of Appeals affirmed, but the Indiana Supreme Court reversed, finding that the Excessive Fines Clause of the Eighth Amendment only limits the federal government, not state governments.

Timbs then appealed to the U.S. Supreme Court, which unanimously reversed in an opinion by Justice Ginsburg, who wrote that "the historical and logical case for concluding that the Fourteenth Amendment incorporates the Excessive Fines Clause is overwhelming." She reasoned that it was both "fundamental to our scheme of ordered liberty" and "deeply rooted in this Nation's history and tradition." In his concurring opinion, Justice Clarence Thomas was even more emphatic on the historical record against excessive fines, writing: "The right against excessive fines traces its lineage back in English law nearly a millennium, and from the founding of our country, it has been consistently recognized as a core right worthy of constitutional protection." The difference was that Thomas believes that the vehicle for incorporation is the Privileges and Immunities Clause of the Fourteenth Amendment, not the Due Process Clause.

Indiana argued that the Excessive Fines Clause doesn't apply to civil forfeitures, only criminal law penalties. However, the Court cited one of its earlier decisions holding that a civil forfeiture does trigger the Excessive Fines clause when the forfeiture is at least partially punitive.

# Cruel and Unusual Punishment

By far the most frequent source of the Eighth Amendment concerns what punishment is "cruel and unusual." The bulk of the most visible discussions involve whether the ultimate punishment—death—is cruel and unusual within the meaning of the Eighth Amendment. However, the Cruel and Unusual Punishment Clause applies to any form of criminal punishment that is grossly disproportionate to the underlying conduct that led to the conviction. There is not a strict proportionality requirement in Eighth Amendment law. In order to rise to the level of a constitutional violation, the punishment must be grossly disproportionate.

A stark example of a grossly disproportionate punishment occurred in *Robinson v. California* (1962). The case concerned a Los Angeles City ordinance that criminalized being addicted

Sentencing someone to a lengthy prison term for a minor offense is one example of "cruel and unusual" punishment.

to narcotics. The law did not require the charged person to use narcotics illegally. It simply stated that narcotics addiction itself was a crime. The Supreme Court determined that this was akin to punishing a person for having a venereal disease or a mental illness.

Another example would be a person jaywalking across a street and receiving a 10-year prison sentence. That punishment is clearly excessive and grossly disproportionate to the underlying offense, which is more of an infraction than a serious crime. Another example occurred in the celebrated case of *Weems v. United States* (1910). The case involved the dishonest actions of Paul Weems, an official with the Coast Guard serving in the Philippines, then a colony of the United States. Weems committed fraud by falsifying a document to obtain cash. He received a sentence of 15 years' imprisonment. The Supreme Court reasoned that such a severe penalty for a relatively minor offense violated the Eighth Amendment.

Most states have guidelines that classify criminal offenses as either felonies or misdemeanors, and then they have different classifications for gradations of those offenses.

However, the problem for criminal defendants comes into play when they are recidivist or repeat offenders. Some states refer to them as "career offenders." These repeat offenders can be subject to much higher forms of punishment because of their prior convictions. The U.S. Supreme Court even upheld California's "three-strikes" law that mandated a life sentence for any individual convicted of their third felony. The Court reasoned that the state has a very strong interest in protecting the public from habitual criminals who are likely to reoffend.

‖ *The U.S. Supreme Court even upheld California's "three-strikes" law that mandated a life sentence for any individual convicted of their third felony.* ‖

The problem with this approach is that it could lead to someone receiving a life sentence for conduct that does not even approach a life sentence by itself. In one case, a defendant received a life sentence for stealing a set of golf clubs. The problem for the defendant was that this was his third felony, so he received a life sentence. The Supreme Court upheld the life sentence and rejected the Eighth Amendment challenge.

# Evolving Standards of Decency

The Supreme Court has adopted a very important standard—or phrase—that is quite important to its Eighth Amendment jurisprudence. The phrase is "evolving standards of decency." The case involved a former soldier, Albert Trop, who had escaped from a stockade while he was serving as a private in the U.S. Army in the French Morocco. Trop was in the stockade for a previous breach of disciplinary rules.

The very next day, Trop and his companion who had escaped willingly surrendered to Army officials in a truck. He was turned over to military police and court-martialed for desertion even though he was gone for only one day. He was decommissioned and had to serve three years of hard labor.

Years later, in 1952, Trop applied for a passport and was denied on the grounds that under a federal law known as the Nationality Act of 1940, he had lost his citizenship because of his conviction for desertion. Trop then filed a federal lawsuit, seeking a court to declare that he was a U.S. citizen. Both a federal district court and federal appeals court ruled against him.

However, the U.S. Supreme Court reversed and ruled in Trop's favor. "Citizenship is not a license that expires upon misbehavior," Chief Justice Earl Warren (1891–1974) wrote for the Court, adding that "citizenship is not lost every time a duty of citizenship is shirked." The chief justice focused on the fact that Albert Trop never renounced his citizenship and never abandoned his citizenship.

Chief Justice Warren believed that the loss of citizenship was too great a punishment against a person who did what Trop did. In other words, the punishment was way too excessive. He wrote in oft-cited language that "the [Eighth] Amendment must draw its meaning from the evolving standards of decency that mark the progress of a maturing society."

Applying this concept, Warren reasoned that taking away a person's citizenship represents "the total destruction of the individual's status in organized society." He compared the punishment to a form of torture that simply went beyond the pale. He also added that "[w]hen the Government acts to take away the fundamental right of citizenship, the safeguards of the Constitution should be examined with special diligence."

Under the evolving standards of decency, the Court examines trends in state legislatures and essentially adopts a majoritarian view of punishment. For example, when the Supreme Court invalidated the death penalty in 2002, it found that there was an evolving standard of decency that surfaced with regard to the execution of defendants who were intellectually disabled. More and more states—and countries around the world—began to view it as fundamentally wrong to execute a person even for the awful crime of murder.

Some criticize the evolving standards of decency test as a vehicle by which justices and judges can impose their own personal predilections into the Constitution. Perhaps the most consistent critic of the concept of evolving standards of decency was Justice Antonin Scalia (1936–2016), who referred to *Trop v. Dulles* in a most pejorative way, writing: "That case has caused more mischief to our jurisprudence, to our federal system, and to our society than any other that comes to mind." Scalia views the Court as ignoring the will of the people and the text of the Constitution when it comes to interpreting the Eighth Amendment, particularly with regard to capital punishment.

# The Death Penalty

Speaking of capital punishment, debate over this controversial issue continues to dominate debate over whether the ultimate punishment is "cruel and unusual." As the Supreme Court stated in 1976, "Death is different." For some, the question of whether the death penalty is cruel and unusual punishment and in violation of the Eighth Amendment is an easy question. They point to the beginning clause in the Fifth Amendment, which reads, "No person shall be held to answer for a capital, or otherwise infamous crime." The Due Process Clause of the Fifth Amendment also mentions "no deprivation of life … without due process of law." As Justice Scalia wrote, "the very text of the [Constitution] recognizes that the death penalty is a permissible legislative choice."

However, others point to the idea that society's ideals of what punishments are permissible change and evolve over time. Initially, the death penalty featured public hangings, spectacles that featured tens of thousands of attendees and fiery religious sermons about the evils of sin and debauchery.

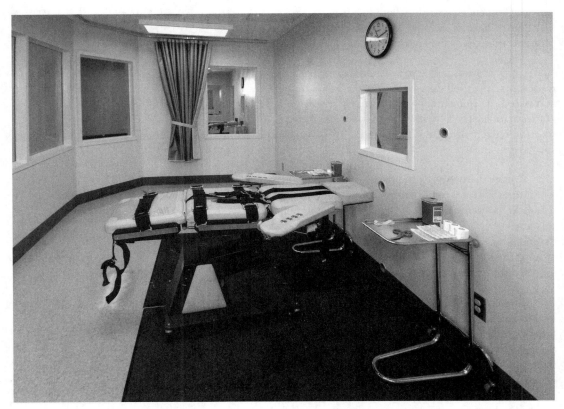

This is the room at San Quentin State Prison in California where prisoners sentenced to death are given a lethal injection. Some have argued that this procedure can cause great pain and therefore qualifies as cruel and unusual punishment.

The death penalty was a standard punishment for all sorts of crimes both in England and colonial America. Many colonies put people to death for relatively minor crimes. Counterfeiting was punishable by death in Pennsylvania in the early part of the eighteenth century. Adultery was a capital crime in three colonies: Connecticut, Massachusetts, and New Hampshire. Smuggling tobacco in Virginia was a capital offense. In Virginia, slaves could be killed by the state for administering medicine.

Beginning in the nineteenth century, two significant developments occurred with the death penalty. First, many states—beginning with Connecticut in 1830—began ending executions as mass public events and conducting them in jailyards out of public view. Second, states began to seriously consider different ways of executing criminals. The idea was that hanging was too brutal and often resulted in prolonged suffering for the condemned person. Authors Robert Linton and Greg Mitchell describe this as the search for "the ultimate oxymoron—the humane killing."

In 1879, the U.S. Supreme Court approved of death by firing squad in Utah, and in 1890, the Supreme Court upheld the process of electrocution—the term created by combining the words "electricity" and "execution." The Court ruled that these two methods were not cruel and unusual punishment. In 1921, Nevada became the first state to adopt the gas chamber. Later in the twentieth century, lethal injection became a common method of execution. Today, most states that still have the death penalty use the lethal injection process—though controversies abound today on whether the administration of specific combinations of drugs truly provide a less painful death.

The death penalty surged in popularity during times of crises, such as Prohibition, World War I, and the Great Depression. Many states seemed to be affected by a fear of armed gangsters. However, in the 1950s and 1960s, the pendulum began to swing the other day. There were some controversial executions, such as those involving Julius Rosenberg (1918–1953) and Ethel Rosenberg (1915–1953) for allegedly spying for the Soviet Union. California inmate Caryl Chessman (1921–1960) became a celebrity of sorts, writing several books until his eventual execution in 1960.

In 1966, a Gallup poll showed for the first time that more people disfavored the death penalty than favored it—47 percent to 42 percent. In 1965, the U.S. Department of Justice called for the abolition of the death penalty.

Meanwhile, many other countries began to abolish the death penalty. For example, Canada did so in 1967, and two years later, Great Britain followed suit. Abolitionists gained steam, led by

The espionage case of American civilians Ethel and Julius Rosenberg that resulted in their being executed in 1953 led to greater opposition to the death penalty in America because many people felt the Rosenbergs were innocent.

the legal efforts of the NAACP Legal Defense Fund. Ultimately, the U.S. Supreme Court confronted the constitutionality of the death penalty in *Furman v. Georgia* (1972).

## Invalidating the Death Penalty

On June 29, 1972, the U.S. Supreme Court effectively ended capital punishment in the United States with its opinion in *Furman v. Georgia*. The Court was sharply divided, 5–4, and all nice justices wrote a separate opinion, totaling 238 pages in all. At the time, the *Furman* decision was the longest in the history of the Court. (This record was later broken in the campaign finance decision a few years later in *Buckley v. Valeo* in 1976.)

The five justices who ended capital punishment did so for different reasons. The five justices in the majority were Justices William Brennan (1906–1997), Thurgood Marshall (1908–1993), William O. Douglas (1898–1980), Byron White (1917–2002), and Potter Stewart (1915–1985). Justices Brennan and Marshall wrote that the death penalty—in any form—violated the Eighth Amendment and constituted cruel and unusual punishment. For the remainder of their tenures on the Court, these two justices dissented from every death penalty case that favored the ultimate punishment.

Justice Brennan reasoned that the death penalty was a barbaric practice that was "degrading to human dignity." He also noted that this ultimate punishment was imposed arbitrarily on only a few individuals charged and convicted of murder.

‖ *Justice Brennan reasoned that the death penalty was a barbaric practice that was "degrading to human dignity" … [and] was imposed arbitrarily on only a few individuals charged and convicted of murder.* ‖

Justice Marshall in his concurring opinion also concluded that the death penalty was *per se* unconstitutional in violation of the Eighth Amendment. He did a historical analysis, examining the death penalty from the Middle Ages to colonial America to modern times. He noted that at the time of the decision, 41 states authorized the death penalty. All of those states authorized the death penalty for murder, and 16 states authorized execution for the crime of rape.

However, Marshall determined that the traditional justifications for the death penalty—retribution and deterrence—did not support the death penalty. He argued that neither retribution nor vengeance was an appropriate consideration for the government. As for deterrence, Marshall cited statistics showing that the crime rate for serious crimes was just as high or higher in those states with the death penalty as it was in states without the death penalty. He also called the death penalty "morally unacceptable."

Justice Douglas took a different approach. He focused on the fact that the death penalty was imposed far more frequently on African American defendants than on Caucasian defendants for the same crimes. He viewed this as fundamentally incompatible with the Equal Protection Clause of the Fourteenth Amendment, which is designed to ensure that similarly situated persons are treated the same. Douglas wrote that the death penalty laws at issue in *Furman* and the two companion cases with it were "pregnant with discrimination."

The remaining two justices in the five-member majority—Potter Stewart and Byron White—did not find the death penalty *per se* unconstitutional in all applications. Instead, they focused on the specific death penalty laws at issue in *Furman* and whether these laws provided enough guidance to jury members to decide whether a defendant should receive a death sentence.

Justice Stewart issued the most oft-cited quote in all of *Furman*'s 238 pages when he wrote: "These death sentences are cruel and unusual in the same way that being struck by lightning is cruel and unusual. For, of all the people convicted of rapes and murders in 1967 and 1968, many just as reprehensible as these, the petitioners are among a capriciously selected random handful upon whom the sentence of death has in fact been imposed." Stewart concluded that the death penalty could not be so "freakishly and wantonly" applied.

Byron White also wrote a narrow concurring opinion. He—like some of his colleagues—emphasized how rarely the death penalty was imposed even on first-degree murderers. He concluded that "the penalty is so infrequently imposed that the threat of execution is too attenuated to be of substantial service to criminal justice."

Four justices dissented, including Chief Justice Warren Burger (1907–1995). The impact of the *Furman* decision was immediate, as the more than 600 death row inmates essentially had their death sentences commuted to life imprisonment sentences.

## Swift Legislative Action and a Supreme Reversal

After *Furman*, 35 states reworked their death penalty statutes to provide more guidance to juries in its application in sentencing. Some adopted so-called aggravating and mitigating factors for jurors to consider when deliberating during a death pen-

Justice Byron White served on the Supreme Court from 1962 to 1993. White felt that because the death penalty was only used very rarely, it did not serve as an effective deterrent to crime.

alty case. An aggravating factor is something that makes the crime of murder look more heinous. For example, typical aggravating factors include that the victim was a law enforcement officer or first responder, or the victim was especially young or old.

Mitigating factors are those factors that might cause a jury to consider that the defendant—even though guilty of a terrible crime—deserves a punishment less than death. Typical mitigating factors include that the defendant was relatively young, the defendant did not have a significant history of criminal activity, or the defendant was under duress from another individual.

In 1976, the U.S. Supreme Court ruled in *Gregg v. Georgia*, 428 U.S. 153, that the revised death penalty laws that provided more guidance to juries were constitutional. These statutes provided juries with aggravating and mitigating circumstances to consider when determining whether to apply a death sentence. Lawmakers argued that by considering aggravating and mitigating circumstances, death sentences would become less arbitrary.

Under this new statutory model, before jurors could impose a sentence of death, they had to find that there was at least an aggravating factor present. In *Gregg*, the Supreme Court examined Georgia's new death penalty statute. Justice Potter Stewart, who had voted against the state's death penalty law in *Furman*, wrote the opinion finding the amended Georgia law constitutional. He noted that the new law focused the jury's attention on "the particularized nature of the crime and the particularized characteristics of the individual defendant." He also wrote that because of the consideration of the aggravating and mitigating factors, "[n]o longer can a jury wantonly and freakishly impose the death sentence; it is always circumscribed by the legislative guidelines."

The *Gregg* decision provided a blueprint for other states to tinker with their death penalty laws to make sure they provided appropriate guidance to jurors in capital cases. The Court in *Gregg* also focused on another aspect of Georgia's law—that the state supreme court had to review every death sentence to make sure it was imposed properly. This is a process sometimes known as comparative proportionality.

‖ *The Gregg decision provided a blueprint for other states to tinker with their death penalty* ‖
*laws to make sure they provided appropriate guidance to jurors in capital cases.*

Justice Stewart explained that this process provided an additional safeguard to ensure that a jury's sentence of death was not aberrant: "The provision for appellate review in the Georgia capital-sentencing system serves as a check against the random or arbitrary imposition of the death penalty. In particular, the proportionality review substantially eliminates the possibility that a person will be sentenced to die by the action of an aberrant jury."

The *Gregg* decision established that the death penalty *per se* does not violate the Eighth Amendment. Since *Gregg*, the focus has turned to whether particular forms of punishment are unconstitutional or whether it is unconstitutional to apply the death penalty to particular types of defendants, such as those who are under 18 or who are intellectually disabled.

# Ineligible Defendants for the Death Penalty

The Supreme Court has ruled that the death penalty cannot be imposed upon defendants with certain characteristics or conditions. These include inmates who are (1) insane; (2) intellectually disabled; or (3) juveniles when they committed their crime.

## Insane

The Court first determined that it would violate the Eighth Amendment and the concept of the "evolving standards of decency" to execute an inmate who truly was insane. The case involved a defendant named Alvin Bernard Ford, who when he was convicted of murder in 1984 did not exhibit signs of insanity. However, in later years on death row, Ford's mental condition deteriorated significantly. He referred to himself as the pope, began speaking in code, and became obsessed with a delusion that the Ku Klux Klan and numerous guards were conspiring against him.

His attorneys had Ford evaluated by a psychiatrist, who determined that Ford suffered from paranoid schizophrenia and delusional thinking. Florida law at the time required the Florida governor to appoint three psychological experts to evaluate the inmate to determine his sanity.

The three state experts all evaluated Ford and deemed him competent. However, their examinations were relatively cursory. Ford's attorneys managed to obtain an evidentiary hearing to determine Ford's sanity. A federal district court ruled against Ford, but a federal appeals court reversed.

On further appeal, the U.S. Supreme Court unanimously ruled that the state of Florida could not execute Ford, because it violates the Eighth Amendment to execute the insane. Writing for the Court, Justice Thurgood Marshall noted that there was a longstanding history in English common law against executing the insane.

Justice Marshall also noted that the Florida law in this case that provided for the appoint-

When mental illness is so severe that a defendant is judged incompetent to stand trial, the Eighth Amendmentís establishment of standards of decency protect the accused from an unjust prison term. Instead, mental health treatment would be in order.

ment of three medical experts was problematic. First, the law did not allow any cross-examination of the three experts. Even worse, the Florida statute allowed the state governor to appoint the experts instead of individuals who might be more naturally impartial. In sum, the Florida law did not provide enough safeguards to ensure that the evaluation of the inmate would be an accurate factfinding mission.

Instead, the Court reasoned that the statute was deficient, writing: "Rather, consistent with the heightened concern for fairness and accuracy that has characterized our review of the process requisite to the taking of a human life, we believe that any procedure that precludes the prisoner or his counsel from presenting material relevant to his sanity or bars consideration of that material by the factfinder is necessarily inadequate."

Justice Marshall also emphasized that it offended humanity to execute an inmate who was insane. "Similarly, the natural abhorrence civilized societies feel at killing one who has no capacity to come to grips with his own conscience or deity is still vivid today," he wrote. "And the intuition that such an execution simply offends humanity is evidently shared across this Nation. Faced with such widespread evidence of a restriction upon sovereign power, this Court is compelled to conclude that the Eighth Amendment prohibits a State from carrying out a sentence of death upon a prisoner who is insane."

## Intellectually Disabled

In 2002, the Supreme Court ruled that it violated the Eighth Amendment to execute an inmate who was mentally retarded, a term the Court has replaced with "intellectually disabled." The idea is that a defendant who is intellectually disabled is not able to appreciate the gravity of his or her wrongdoing as much as a normally functioning individual.

This was not always the Court's position. Back in 1989, the Court ruled in *Penry v. Lynaugh* (1989) that it did not violate the Eighth Amendment to execute an inmate who was mentally retarded. This decision paved the way for the state of Texas to execute Johnny Paul Penry (1956–) even though he had a very low IQ. Fortunately for Penry, a further appeal led to another decision by the Court, *Penry v. Johnson* (2001), which held that the trial court's instructions on mitigating evidence was inadequate. Later, Penry pled guilty to three life sentences, and he remains on death row.

However, the Court's earlier decision still allowed for the execution of inmates who were intellectually disabled. That all changed in the case of Virginia inmate Daryl Renard Atkins, who had a tested IQ of only 59—well below the line for intellectual disability. His lawyers did not argue that his low level of intellectual functioning justified his criminal actions. Rather, they argued that his low IQ should prohibit the state of Virginia from executing him.

The Supreme Court ruled 6–3 that it violates the Eighth Amendment to execute those who truly are intellectually disabled. In his majority opinion, Justice John Paul Stevens (1920–2019) reasoned that there was an emerging legislative trend in the states to prohibit the execution of those who are intellectually disabled. Since the Court's decision in *Penry* in 1989, at least 16 different states had amended their death penalty laws to prohibit such executions.

> *Stevens explained that those who are intellectually disabled are less able to appreciate the gravity of harm their criminal actions cause.*

Stevens explained that those who are intellectually disabled are less able to appreciate the gravity of harm their criminal actions cause. He also explained that intellectually disabled defendants are less able to assist their attorneys, express remorse for their actions, or understand the court proceedings, and are more likely to be subject to wrongful executions.

The Court's decision ultimately led to Daryl Atkins's (1977–) death sentence to be commuted to a life sentence. The Court's decision also spawned a new array of litigation over whether inmates truly are intellectually disabled. Predictably, after the Court's decision in Atkins, a host of other inmates filed petitions arguing that they also should be removed from death row because they are intellectually disabled.

The *Atkins* decision led to a flood of death penalty litigation over whether certain inmates fell into this category. One such inmate who filed a claim was Freddie Lee Hall (1945–) from Florida. Hall apparently suffered from intellectual deficits his entire life. However, he had a tested IQ of 71—one point above the cutoff score of 70 under Florida law. Because Hall's IQ was 71, he was not considered intellectually disabled even though his attorneys testified that he had the mental capacity of a young child.

The U.S. Supreme Court invalidated Florida's law in *Hall v. Florida* (2014). The Court emphasized that Hall's IQ score was within the standard error of measurement (SEM). The Court also reiterated that medical experts had testified that whether a person is intellectually disabled must be determined by several factors—the IQ test merely being one of the methods.

"The death penalty is the gravest sentence our society may impose," Justice Anthony Kennedy (1936–) wrote for the majority in a 5–4 decision. "Persons facing that most severe sanction must have a fair opportunity to show that the Constitution prohibits their execution. Florida's law contravenes our nation's commitment to dignity and its duty to teach human decency as the mark of a civilized world."

## Juvenile Offenders

Three years after the *Atkins* decision, the Court also ruled that those who commit murder while a juvenile cannot be executed. The idea is similar—that juveniles are less mature and less fully developed than adults and may not appreciate the gravity of the harm they cause to the same extent.

Back in 1989, the Supreme Court had ruled in *Stanford v. Kentucky* that 17-year-old murderer Kevin Stanford (1963–) could be executed for his crime even though he was a juvenile at the time of his offense.

However, the Court overruled the *Stanford* decision years later in a case styled *Roper v. Simmons* (2005). The case involved a brutal murder committed by 17-year-old Christopher Simmons (1976–) in Missouri. He kidnapped a woman, tied her up, and then took her to a bridge and dumped her into the water on September 9, 1993. The crime undoubtedly was horrific, and prosecutors sought the death penalty.

A jury sentenced Simmons to death in 1994. His attorneys filed a variety of appeals through the years. The one argument that ultimately resonated with first the Missouri Supreme Court and then the U.S. Supreme Court was that juvenile murderers should not be executed.

The U.S. Supreme Court agreed with this position in its decision in *Roper v. Simmons*. Writing for the majority, Justice Anthony Kennedy noted that juveniles were different from adults in three significant ways: (1) juveniles are less mature than adults; (2) juveniles are more susceptible to peer pressure than adults; and (3) the character of juveniles is not as well developed as that of adults.

Juveniles—those under 18 years of age—are judged under different standards than adults because they tend to lack emotional and intellectual maturity.

Kennedy also focused on the fact that very few executions of juvenile murderers took place in the United States. The far more common penalty was life imprisonment. Kennedy identified a clear trend in the states disfavoring the imposition of the death penalty on those who committed murder before the age of 18. In other words, Kennedy sought something approaching a national consensus emerging against such executions. This was similar to what the Court had found a few years earlier with regard to the execution of intellectually disabled inmates in *Atkins v. Virginia* (2002).

Finally, and somewhat more controversially to some (including Justice Scalia in dissent), Kennedy emphasized that the United States was about the only country in the world that regularly executed those who committed murder as juveniles. Kennedy wrote that since 1990 only seven other countries—Iran, Pakistan, Saudi Arabia, Yemen, Nigeria, the Democratic Republic of Congo, and China—have executed defendants who were juveniles at the time of their crime. That this was not exactly a list that the United States should be on was the clear implication in Kennedy's ruling.

Kennedy acknowledged that the line at age 18 might seem arbitrary to some, but it was a familiar line in society. "The age of 18 is the point where society draws the line for many purposes between childhood and adulthood," Kennedy wrote. "It is, we conclude, the age at which the line for death eligibility ought to rest."

The Court's decision in *Roper v. Simmons* has led to an array of other Eighth Amendment challenges to sentences for juveniles other than the death penalty. Led by gifted attorney Bryan Stevenson (1959–) of the Equal Justice Initiative, challenges were filed against state laws that imposed mandatory sentences of life without the possibility of parole (LWOP) for juvenile offenders. In *Graham v. Florida* (2010), the Supreme Court reasoned that such LWOP sentences for juveniles was cruel and unusual punishment for juveniles who did not commit the crime of murder. The case involved a 16-year-old sentenced to life imprisonment for the crimes of armed burglary and attempted armed robbery. "Life without parole is an especially harsh punishment for a juvenile," wrote Justice Kennedy for the majority. "Under this sentence a juvenile offender will on average serve more years and a greater percentage of his life in prison than an adult offender."

Two years later, the Court also invalidated an Alabama state law that imposed a mandatory LWOP sentence for two 14-year-old juveniles convicted of murder. The Court held in *Miller v. Alabama* (2012) that "the Eighth Amendment forbids a sentencing scheme that mandates life in prison without possibility of parole for juvenile offenders."

## No Death Penalty for Rape

The Supreme Court also has limited the types of crime that can lead to the imposition of the death penalty. In 1977—only one year after the Court had reinstituted the death penalty in *Gregg*—the Court ruled in *Coker v. Georgia* (1977) that it violated the Eighth Amendment to sentence someone to death for the crime of rape.

> *In 1977 … the Court ruled in Coker v. Georgia (1977) that it violated the Eighth Amendment to sentence someone to death for the crime of rape.*

The case involved Georgia inmate Ehrlich Anthony Coker, who had raped and killed a woman in December 1971. He then kidnapped, raped, and beat another woman nearly to death. He was sentenced to three life terms. Three years later in 1974, Coker escaped from prison and kidnapped another woman. He was caught and charged with another crime of rape. He ultimately was sentenced to death under a Georgia law that allowed for jurors to sentence defendants to the death penalty if there were sufficient aggravating circumstances. Coker had aggravating circumstances, as he had previous convictions for rape and violence.

The NAACP Legal Defense Fund agreed to represent Coker, because it viewed the Georgia statute as a remnant of racism. Indeed, the law traditionally was used to target African American men who had allegedly raped white women. Coker's lawyer, David Kendall (1944–) argued his cause before the High Court. Interestingly, the Court's plurality opinion in *Coker* was written by Justice Byron White, the justice for whom Kendall used to serve as a law clerk.

In *Coker*, the U.S. Supreme Court emphasized that very few states had similar statutes that allowed a jury to sentence a defendant to death for rape. In fact, in 1925, only 25 states allowed such sentences. Then, in the 1970s, the number had been reduced to 16.

White reasoned that the clear legislative trend was that the crime of rape—no doubt a horrifying crime—was not a death penalty crime. White explained:

> Rape is without doubt deserving of serious punishment; but in terms of moral depravity and of the injury to the person and to the public, it does not compare with murder, which does involve the unjustified taking of human life. Although it may be accompanied by another crime, rape, by definition, does not include the death of or even the serious injury to another person.

Nearly four decades after the *Coker* decision, the Supreme Court also ruled in *Kennedy v. Louisiana* (2008) that even child rapists cannot be executed if their victim lives. The argument for extending the death penalty to child rapists focuses on the age of the victims and the lasting and sometimes permanent harm inflicted upon those who are most vulnerable.

The case involved defendant Patrick Kennedy, who was charged with and convicted of raping his own stepdaughter and then blaming the crime on two neighborhood boys. Louisiana was one of the few states at the time that allowed for the death penalty for the crime of child rape.

‖ *The argument for extending the death penalty to child rapists focuses on the age of the victims and the lasting and sometimes permanent harm inflicted upon those who are most vulnerable.* ‖

The Court explained that between 1930 and 1964, there were more than 450 persons executed for the crime of child rape. However, the last execution of someone for the awful crime was in 1964. Furthermore, in 1925, there were 18 states that had laws on the books that made the crime of child rape a death-eligible crime. In 2008, there were only six states that had such laws on the books. Perhaps even more telling to the Court's majority, there were only two defendants in the United States—Patrick Kennedy and one other man—on death row for the crime of child rape.

The Court was sharply divided 5–4 in this decision. Writing for the dissenters, Justice Samuel Alito (1950–) explained: "The harm that is caused to the victims and to society at large by the worst child rapists is grave. It is the judgment of the Louisiana lawmakers and those in an increasing number of other States that these harms justify the death penalty. The Court provides no cogent explanation why this legislative judgment should be overridden. Conclusory references to 'decency,' 'moderation,' 'restraint,' 'full progress,' and 'moral judgment' are not enough."

Alito criticized the Court for concluding that there was an emerging national consensus emerging against imposing death sentences for child rapists. Alito pointed out that several states had passed such laws in recent years and that bills had been introduced to make child rape a death-eligible crime in several other state legislatures.

Politicians all across the political aisle also criticized the Court's decision in *Kennedy v. Louisiana*. Barack Obama (1961–), then a U.S. senator from Illinois and a presidential candidate, expressed his disagreement with the Court's decision. "I have said repeatedly that I think that the death penalty should be applied in very narrow circumstances for the most egregious of crimes," Obama said at a news conference in Chicago. "I think that the rape of a small child, six or eight years old, is a heinous crime and if a state makes a decision that under narrow, limited, well-defined circumstances the death penalty is at least potentially applicable, that that does not violate our Constitution."

# Challenging the Methods of Execution

Current challenges to the death penalty focus on the pain caused by lethal injection—the most common form of execution in the United States. This is somewhat similar to challenges in the late nineteenth century when challenges were made to death by shooting in *Wilkerson v. Utah* (1879) and to electrocution in *In Re Kemmler* (1890).

So far, challenges to the lethal injection system have been unsuccessful. The Court in *Baze v. Rees* (2008) upheld Kentucky's three-drug protocol for executions that required the administration of three drugs to the inmate facing execution: (1) sodium thiopental or Pentathol; (2) pancuronium bromide or Pavulon; and (3) potassium chloride.

"This Court has never invalidated a State's chosen procedure for carrying out a sentence of death as the infliction of cruel and unusual punishment," Chief Justice John G. Roberts Jr. (1955–) wrote for the majority.

Several years later, the Court examined the lethal injection protocol of the state of Oklahoma. Oklahoma's lethal injection protocol consisted of three drugs: (1) midazolam; (2) vecuronium bromide; and (3) potassium chloride. It was the use of midazolam that was controversial, as there was evidence that it inflicted pain on inmates. For example, in *Glossip v. Gross,* one of Richard Glossip's (1963–) coplaintiffs, Charles Warner—executed in Oklahoma in 2015—stated as he was being executed: "My body is on fire. No one should go through this. I'm not afraid to die."

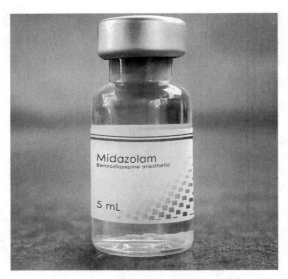

Midazolam (brand name, Versed) is a drug most often used to treat sleep disorders, agitation, and seizures, and as an anesthetic. Sometimes, when used with other drugs in an execution, it can cause painful side effects.

The Court ruled 5–4 that Oklahoma's lethal injection protocol did not violate the Eighth Amendment. Writing for the majority, Justice Samuel Alito wrote: "The District Court did not commit clear error when it found that midazolam is highly likely to render a person unable to feel pain during an execution."

Four justices dissented, with two of them—Sonia Sotomayor (1954–) and Stephen Breyer (1938–)—writing dissenting opinions. Justice Sotomayor's dissent focused on Oklahoma's lethal injection process and criticized the use of midazolam. For his part, Justice Breyer took aim at the entire death penalty.

Breyer's dissent focused on several problems with the death penalty, including: "(1) serious unreliability; (2) arbitrariness in application; and (3) unconscionably long delays that undermine the death penalty's penological purpose." Justice Breyer noted that evidence shows that at least a few innocent persons have been executed and that many more innocent persons were barely spared the death penalty, literally being days away from execution before exoneration.

He also warned that the death penalty system does not provide adequate guidance on which convicted murders are the worst of the worse, or the ones that truly deserve the ultimate punishment. This is the rationale that caused the Court to strike down the death penalty years earlier in *Furman v. Georgia* (1972).

> *Justice Breyer noted that evidence shows that at least a few innocent persons have been executed and that many more innocent persons were barely spared the death penalty....*

Breyer's dissent attracted immediate attention and caused many in the abolitionist movement to hope that perhaps the Supreme Court would examine the constitutionality of capital punishment. Richard Dieter, the head of the Death Penalty Information Center, stated: "I think this case [*Glossip v. Gross*] will be remembered more for that dissent than for the decision itself."

Justice Breyer continued his critique of the death penalty in another case that his colleagues chose not to review—*Jordan v. Mississippi* (2018). The case involves a Mississippi inmate named Richard Gerald Jordan, who was 72 at the time he filed his latest challenge to his death conviction for murdering a woman in 1976.

Even for death penalty cases, Jordan's case is a bit unusual, as he has had four death sentences. The first three between 1977 and 1986 were overturned for different legal reasons. His fourth sentence was imposed in 1998. He has filed numerous legal challenges to his latest death sentence.

Jordan's attorneys' challenge presented the fact that it is cruel and unusual to make someone sit on death row for more than 40 years. The Court declined to hear the case, but Breyer found that the petition raised some meritorious issues, including the lengthy delays between the sentence of death and the execution and the geographic disparities of the death penalty.

Regarding the length of time, Breyer noted that Jordan is the oldest person on death row in Mississippi and has spent more than half his life on death row: "In my view, the conditions in which Jordan appears to have been confined over the past four decades reinforce the Eighth Amendment concern raised in his petition."

Justice Breyer identified another issue that he thought merited the full Court's attention—the abject geographic disparities in the death penalty. There are only a few counties in the country that actually execute inmates. "This geographic concentration reflects a nationwide trend," Breyer writes. "Death sentences, while declining in number, have become increasingly concentrated in an ever-smaller number of counties."

Today, there are 27 states that still have the death penalty. In 2020, there were 17 executions. There were 11 in 2021. Perhaps the death penalty is on the decline. On the other hand, the death penalty is still constitutional, according to the U.S. Supreme Court since its decision in *Gregg v. Georgia* in 1976.

# The Ninth and Tenth Amendments

The first eight amendments to the U.S. Constitution set out very specific freedoms, such as freedom of speech and religion in the First Amendment, the right to keep and bear arms in the Second Amendment, and the right to be free from unreasonable searches and seizures in the Fourth Amendment.

The last two amendments in the Bill of Rights—the Ninth and Tenth Amendments—are different. They are written in very different language. The Ninth Amendment reads like a catch-all provision that just because something is not enumerated, or listed, doesn't mean the Bill of Rights doesn't protect it. The Tenth Amendment recognizes the rights of states, or the fact that if the federal government does not have certain powers, then the rights are reserved to the states.

Another way of saying this is that the first eight amendments to the U.S. Constitution are designed to protect individuals from abuse by federal government officials. They specifically list out various freedoms. However, the ninth and tenth are different; they point out the division of powers between the federal government and various state governments.

# The Ninth Amendment

The enumeration in the Constitution, of certain rights, shall not be construed to deny or disparage others retained by the people.

One common objection to the Bill of Rights when it was first considered was that listing, or enumerating, certain rights would mean that those were the only rights the people possessed.

To answer this concern, Congress adopted the Ninth Amendment. It implies that people retain other rights not specifically listed in the Bill of Rights. Historian Leonard Levy writes that "the Ninth Amendment could also serve to draw the sting from any criticism that the catalog of personal freedoms was incomplete."

For 175 years, the Ninth Amendment "lay dormant" and was what has been called a "constitutional curiosity." The Supreme Court first delved into the Ninth Amendment with any detail in a case called *Griswold v. Connecticut* (1965). The case involved two Connecticut laws that prohibited medical providers from providing contraceptives to people and that prohibited people from using contraceptives. The two laws in question provided:

> Any person who uses any drug, medicinal article or instrument for the purpose of preventing conception shall be fined not less than fifty dollars or imprisoned not less than sixty days nor more than one year or be both fined and imprisoned.

> Any person who assists, abets, counsels, causes, hires or commands another to commit any offense may be prosecuted and punished as if he were the principal offender.

Estelle T. Griswold (1900–1981), executive director of the Planned Parenthood group in Connecticut, and C. Lee Buxton (1904–1969), a medical doctor at Yale Medical School, challenged the law. A few years earlier in *Poe v. Ullman* (1961), the U.S. Supreme Court had determined that a similar challenge was not ripe.

However, four years later, the Court delved into the constitutionality of these laws. In his majority opinion, Justice William O. Douglas (1898–1980) mentioned that the Bill of Rights not only protected specific freedoms listed in them, but they also contained "penumbras formed by emanations" that protect additional related freedoms. "Penumbras by emanations" may be the strangest, most bizarre language in the annals of Supreme Court history, but Douglas has a point.

For example, he pointed out that the First Amendment textually protects the freedoms of religion, speech, press, assembly, and petition. However, the Supreme

Court has interpreted the First Amendment to also protect the right to expressive association in *NAACP v. Alabama* (1958)—protecting the right of the civil rights group the National Association for the Advancement of Colored People (NAACP) to refuse to disclose its rank-and-file membership list to the state of Alabama. In other words, the Supreme Court was protecting the privacy rights of the NAACP members through the First Amendment even though privacy is not mentioned in the First Amendment.

Similarly, Douglas mentioned that the Third Amendment, which prohibits the government from quartering troops in private homes, protects homeowner privacy even though the word "privacy" is not found in the Third Amendment.

Douglas also specifically mentioned the Ninth Amendment and quoted its 21 words. Douglas was saying that the Ninth Amendment also protects a right to privacy. Douglas concluded: "We deal with a right of privacy older than the Bill of Rights—older than our political parties, older than our school system. Marriage is a coming together for better or for worse, hopefully enduring, and intimate to the degree of being sacred. It is an association that promotes a way of life, not causes; a harmony in living, not political faiths; a bilateral loyalty, not commercial or social projects. Yet it is an association for as noble a purpose as any involved in our prior decisions."

Serving on the U.S. Supreme Court from 1939 to 1975, Justice William Douglas was one of the most progressive justices in its history. He wrote the court opinion on *Griswold v. Connecticut,* saying that married couples had a right to contraceptives without government restrictions.

However, it was Justice Arthur Goldberg (1908–1990) who wrote much more extensively about the Ninth Amendment in his concurring opinion. Goldberg explained that the clear purpose of the Ninth Amendment was to ensure that there are constitutional rights that are not explicitly listed in the Bill of Rights. He emphasized that the marriage relationship was one that demanded and required privacy.

Goldberg wrote that the Ninth Amendment "is surely relevant in showing the existence of other fundamental personal rights, now protected from state, as well as federal, infringement." He added that "the Ninth Amendment simply lends strong support to the view that the "liberty" protected by the Fifth and Fourteenth Amendments from infringement by the Federal Government or the States is not restricted to rights specifically mentioned in the first eight amendments."

Justice Potter Stewart (1915–1985) dissented and questioned the reliance on the Ninth Amendment. Stewart wrote in memorable language that "to say that the

Ninth Amendment has anything to do with this case is to turn somersaults with history." To Stewart, the Ninth Amendment simply reflected a "truism" that not all rights are specifically mentioned in the Bill of Rights.

*The Supreme Court also used the Ninth Amendment in an auxiliary manner in* Roe v. Wade *(1973), ruling that a woman's right to terminate her pregnancy was protected by the Constitution.*

The Supreme Court also used the Ninth Amendment in an auxiliary manner in *Roe v. Wade* (1973), ruling that a woman's right to terminate her pregnancy was protected by the Constitution. Justice Harry Blackmun (1908–1999) explained: "This right of privacy, whether it be founded in the Fourteenth Amendment's concept of personal liberty and restrictions upon state action, as we feel it is, or, as the District Court determined, in the Ninth Amendment's reservation of rights to the people, is broad enough to encompass a woman's decision whether or not to terminate her pregnancy."

Since *Griswold* and *Roe*, the U.S. Supreme Court has mentioned the Ninth Amendment in several cases but without significant discussion. It remains to be seen whether the Ninth Amendment will protect other constitutional rights. It is possible that courts could use the Ninth Amendment to find greater protection to informational privacy or even ground the right to travel and vote—other fundamental rights—at least partly in the Ninth Amendment.

There is much to the view put forth by legal scholar Randy Barrett, who writes: "*In short,* the Amendment is what it appears to be: a meaningful check on federal power and a significant guarantee of individual *liberty.*"

# The Tenth Amendment

The powers not delegated to the United States by the Constitution, nor prohibited by it to the States, are reserved to the States respectively, or to the people.

The Anti-Federalists, the political party opposed to a strong central government, opposed the Constitution because they feared a federal government could swallow up the rights of states and individuals. Those who think the federal government is invading the decision making of state officials will cite the Tenth Amendment and "states' rights."

Remember that states have general police powers; they have the power to pass laws for the general health, safety, and welfare of their residents. The federal government, on the other hand, does not have general police powers. The federal government is only empowered to act when it is conducting itself pursuant to one of its enumerated powers found in Article I, Section 8 of the Constitution. It is the Tenth Amendment that restates the basic constitutional equation—that powers not specifically listed to the federal government are "reserved to the States." Justice Clarence Thomas (1948–) explained this principle well in one of his dissenting opinions when he wrote: "The Federal Government and the States thus face different default rules: Where the Constitution is silent about the exercise of a particular power—that is, where the Constitution does not speak either expressly or by necessary implication—the Federal Government lacks that power and the States enjoy it."

Justice Clarence Thomas has been on the Supreme Court since 1991 after Thurgood Marshall retired.

# The Fourteenth Amendment:
# The Second Bill of Rights

## Section I:

All persons born or naturalized in the United States, and subject to the jurisdiction thereof, are citizens of the United States and of the State wherein they reside. No State shall make or enforce any law which shall abridge the privileges and immunities of citizens of the United States; nor shall any State deprive any person of life, liberty, or property, without due process of law; nor deny to any person within its jurisdiction the equal protection of the laws.

The heart of the Fourteenth Amendment is its first section. This section contains perhaps the two most important phrases in American constitutional law—due process and equal protection. Due process means that the government must act according to the law. Equal protection means that people will be treated equally under the law.

Fairness and equality—those concepts resonate in people's understanding of the United States of America, the Declaration of Independence, and the U.S. Constitution. The Declaration of Independence famously proclaims that "all men are created equal"—leaving women out of the equation and conveniently ignoring the noxious practice of slavery. Likewise, the Constitution begins with the words "We the People."

The lofty rhetoric from these historic documents did not represent reality, particularly for African Americans and women. Historian Eric Foner writes: "Over the course of our history, American freedom has been a reality and a mythic ideal—a living truth for millions of Americans; a cruel mockery for others." In America, all men may have been created equal, but all men were not treated equally. All people did not come to our country on their own free will. Beginning in 1619, Africans were brought to North America in chains and treated as the property of white men.

The Constitution explicitly sanctioned slavery in at least three places. First, it prohibited Congress from abolishing the slave trade until 1807. Second, it provided that a slave who escaped to another state had to be returned to his or her owner. Third, another provision provided that slaves counted as three-fifths of a free person when determining the number of congressional seats for the House of Representatives and the number of electoral votes for president a state possessed.

The Declaration of Independence and the U.S. Constitution did not live up to these ideals of equality and protecting all people. However, after a bloody Civil War, Congress passed three amendments during the period of Reconstruction that sought to provide for a more just society. The most important of these was the Fourteenth Amendment.

U.S. Supreme Court justice John Paul Stevens (1920–2019) said the Fourteenth Amendment and its two related Civil War amendments "breathed new life into the entire document" of the Constitution. The Fourteenth Amendment has been called a second Bill of Rights and a second American Revolution. It is that significant in our constitutional history.

The Bill of Rights begins with the words "Congress shall make no law" and applies technically only to the U.S. Congress. Very early on, the Bill of Rights was understood to apply to not just Congress but also the other branches of the federal government. It did not, however, apply to state and local governments.

However, as we will discuss in more detail shortly, the Bill of Rights only restrained the federal government, not the various state and local governments. Most citizens come into greater contact with various state and local officials than

One of the longest-serving justices on the Supreme Court (1975 to 2010), Justice John Paul Stevens was a conservative judge who, by the end of his tenure, was considered to have strongly liberal ideas.

federal officials. This was especially true in early American history when the federal government was much smaller than it is now.

To put this into perspective, think about how many times you have seen or spoken with a local police officer. Compare that with how many times you have seen a member of the Federal Bureau of Investigation or the Central Intelligence Agency. The answer is obvious. By far, most people come into more contact with state and local officials than federal officials. Yet, prior to the Fourteenth Amendment, the Constitution only provided protection from the federal government.

> *By far, most people come into more contact with state and local officials than federal officials. Yet, prior to the Fourteenth Amendment, the Constitution only provided protection from the federal government.*

Let's return to the language of the Fourteenth Amendment. The first sentence reads: "All persons born or naturalized in the United States, and subject to the jurisdiction thereof, are citizens of the United States and of the State wherein they reside." The first sentence defines citizenship. It overturned the U.S. Supreme Court's 1857 decision in *Dred Scott v. Sandford*, which had ruled that blacks were not and could not be citizens and "had no rights that the white man was bound to respect."

The second clause contains the so-called Privileges and Immunities Clause. It provides: "No State shall make or enforce any law which shall abridge the privileges or immunities of citizens of the United States." The meaning of this clause has been the subject of intense debate among legal scholars. Two scholars have written that it is "impossible now to look back and conclusively prove what exactly the framers of the Fourteenth Amendment had in mind when they wrote these words." Some argue that the phrase "privileges and immunities" meant to extend the provisions in the Bill of Rights to the states. Others view the clause as far more limited.

In 1873, in the so-called *Slaughter-House Cases*, the U.S. Supreme Court interpreted the Privileges and Immunities Clause very narrowly. The High Court ruled that the Privileges and Immunities Clause applied only to certain rights people had as citizens of the federal government, or national citizens. The Court ruled that the states did not have to provide its citizens the same "privileges and immunities" as the federal government provided national citizens. The net effect of this ruling was that the Fourteenth Amendment did not automatically extend the protections of the Bill of Rights to the states. It would take Supreme Court decisions throughout the twentieth century to undo the damage caused by this decision.

The last two clauses of the first section of the Fourteenth Amendment carry enormous significance. They are the Due Process and Equal Protection Clauses. Due process, a principle that came from English law, means that the government must obey the law and act in a reasonable fashion. Today due process is divided into two concepts: procedural due process and substantive due process.

Procedural due process means that the state must use fair procedures when limiting a person's life, liberty, or property interests. Substantive due process means that the substance of law limiting these interests must be reasonable. Meanwhile, equal protection generally means that the government may not pass a law that discriminates against an individual or certain segment of society. For example, a law prohibiting interracial marriages treats people differently based on race and violates the Equal Protection Clause.

# No Protections against State Governments

The key significance of the Fourteenth Amendment is that it extends the vast majority of the freedoms found in the Bill of Rights to the states. In other words, it serves as the vehicle through which the Bill of Rights applies not just to the federal government but also to state and local governments.

Recall that in 1791, the states ratified, or officially approved, ten amendments to the U.S. Constitution known as the Bill of Rights. However, Congress did not adopt all of the proposals submitted by Representative James Madison (1751–1836). One key omission was the amendment that Madison had called "the most worthy." It read:

> No state shall violate the equal rights of conscience, or the freedom of the press, or the trial by jury in criminal cases.

*The key significance of the Fourteenth Amendment is that it extends the vast majority of the freedoms found in the Bill of Rights to the states.*

Madison had considered this proposal the most important because he feared that state governments would be far more likely to violate individual liberties than the federal government. Madison's amendment had passed the House, but it did not clear the Senate. The Senate's action in dropping this amendment on September 7, 1789, meant that the only individual liberty protections individuals possessed came from their state constitutions—and these were often interpreted by elected state judges, not federal judges with life tenure.

The reality that the Bill of Rights offered no protection from state officials was shone to light in the Supreme Court's decision in *Barron v. Baltimore* (1833). The case involved a wharf owner named John Barron, who had purchased a dock and harbor in Fell's Point in Baltimore, a harbor that had been home to the country's first naval ships. The wharves of Barron and other owners were hurt by the road-building and soil-excavating activities approved of by city officials.

The city's excavating activities damaged Barron's wharf, and he wasn't happy about it. He hired a lawyer in 1822 to take legal action against what he deemed the destruction of his wharf. A few years later, Barron's lawyer alleged in a lawsuit that the city officials had violated the Fifth Amendment of the U.S. Constitution by taking away Barron's property without just compensation. Recall that the last sentence in the Fifth Amendment reads: "nor shall private property be taken for public use, without just compensation."

Barron wanted the city to pay for the damage to his dock. The city officials countered that they were acting for the general welfare of the city by improving the city streets. Barron won before a jury, who awarded him $4,500 in damages—a whopping sum of money in 1828. However, an appeals court reversed the jury's verdict. Barron appealed all the way to the U.S. Supreme Court in what would become the first test case of the U.S. Bill of Rights.

Chief Justice John Marshall (1908–1993) ruled for the city of Baltimore, which coincidentally was represented by Marshall's ultimate successor—Roger B. Taney (1777–1864). Marshall wrote that the question of whether the Bill of Rights limited state or local governments was of "great importance, but not of much difficulty." Marshall pointed out that each state had its own constitution limiting the powers of government, but, unfortunately for Barron, there was no takings clause in the Maryland Constitution similar to what was found in the Fifth Amendment.

Marshall also reasoned that if the First Congress and the Founding Fathers had intended for the Bill of Rights to apply to the states, then "they would have declared this purpose in plain and intelligible language." He concluded that the Fifth Amendment is "intended solely as a limitation on the exercise of power by the government of the United States and is not applicable to the legislation of the states."

*Barron v. Baltimore* meant that citizens could sue for constitutional violations only if the violators were federal government officials. This would not change until a civil war, the adoption of the Fourteenth Amendment, and another century of judicial reasoning.

## The *Dred Scott* Decision

If the *Barron* case did not show the obvious need for something like the Fourteenth Amendment, then the *Dred Scott* decision certainly did. The Declaration of Independence stated that "all men are created equal." Unfortunately, this lofty principle did not equate with the horrible reality of slavery. Beginning in 1619, enslaved Africans were imported into North

In the 1857 *Dred Scott v. Sanford* case, Scott sued for his freedom and that of his wife and children based on the fact that they had lived in a free state for four years. The U.S. Supreme Court ruled against him on the basis that Scott was considered property.

America. Slavery became a staple of early American life, particularly in the South. It also became a huge issue when new states sought to be admitted into the Union. The question was whether they would be admitted as slave states or free states.

Famed U.S. representative Henry Clay (1777–1852) helped forge the so-called Missouri Compromise of 1820. Under this proposal, Missouri would become a slave state and Maine would enter as a free state. The Missouri Compromise sought to maintain a balance between slave and free states. Under the measure, slavery was prohibited in lands above Missouri's southern border.

Abolitionism gained momentum during this time period, as many more people grew to appreciate the inhumanity of slavery. African American social reformer Frederick Douglass (1818–1895), who rose out of slavery to become a leading abolitionist, said that the U.S. Constitution was "conceived in sin and shaped in iniquity."

The debate over slavery reached the U.S. Supreme Court with the case of a slave named Dred Scott (1799–1858). Peter Blow (1777–1832), Scott's owner, moved from Alabama to Missouri in 1832. After his death, Blow's executor sold Scott to Dr. John Emerson (1803–1843), an army doctor, in St. Louis, Missouri. In 1834, Emerson moved his family and Scott to Illinois, which unlike Missouri, was a free state. Later, Emerson relocated to what was then known as the Wisconsin Territory, which also outlawed slavery. Emerson later moved back to St. Louis in 1842 and died a year later. In 1846, Dred Scott and his wife, Harriet, filed suits in Missouri state courts, claiming that they had been emancipated, or freed, when Emerson had taken them into "free" territory.

The Scotts seemed to have the law on their side when they filed their suits, because the doctrine "once free, always free" was the law of the land. This meant that if an enslaved person moved to free territory, he or she was emancipated. However, Emerson's widow and her brother, John Sanford, opposed Scott in his petition for freedom. Even worse, the Missouri Supreme Court—with a majority of proslavery jurists—ruled against Scott.

Chief Justice Roger Taney (in office 1836 to 1864) considered African Americans so inferior to whites that the law was clearly not written to account for their rights or lack of rights.

On further appeal, the U.S. Supreme Court also ruled against Scott by a vote of 7–2. Chief Justice Roger Taney—the lawyer who had represented John Barron—wrote that Scott was part of "that unfortunate race" who were considered "so far inferior, that they had no rights which the white man was bound to respect."

In his opinion, Taney recognized the words of equality from the Declaration of Independence but reasoned that "it is too clear for dispute that the enslaved African race were not intended" to be covered by the Declaration. Justices John McLean (1785–1861) and Benjamin Robbins Curtiss (1809–1874) dissented. McLean pointed out that many blacks were "citizens of the New England States" and possessed the right to vote. For his part, Curtiss wrote that "under the Constitution of the United States, every free person born on the soil of a State, who is a citizen of that State by force of its Constitution or laws, is also a citizen of the United States." Curtiss was so upset at the decision of the Court that he resigned his position as associate justice.

The *Dred Scott* decision is viewed as a judicial and historical disaster that helped lead to the Civil War. It also led to the birth of the Fourteenth Amendment.

# The Birth of the Fourteenth Amendment

The nation plunged into a bloody Civil War a little more than a month after President Abraham Lincoln (1809–1865) assumed office. The war led to incredible carnage—some historians estimate up to 750,000 deaths—for more than four years until the South surrendered in December 1865.

After the Civil War, it fell to Congress to usher in a period of rebuilding the nation called Reconstruction. The members of the Thirty-ninth Congress were overwhelmingly Republicans from Northern states. These members were called the "Radical Republicans." Many members of the South had seceded from the Union to form the Confederacy. After the Union army prevailed and the North had won the Civil War, Congress had to figure out what to do about the Southern states and readmission to the Union.

The Thirty-ninth Congress passed three amendments and several laws designed to ensure that African Americans would receive some measure of equality. These laws sought to place African Americans in an environment free from slavery, terrorism, and indentured servitude.

First, Congress passed the Thirteenth Amendment, which outlawed slavery or involuntary servitude throughout the country. The amendment provided: "Neither slavery nor involuntary servitude, except as a punishment for crime whereof the party shall have been duly convicted, shall exist within the United States, or any place subject to their jurisdiction."

The amendment directly overruled the Court's decision in *Dred Scott*, which had safeguarded the institution of slavery. However, the amendment did not state

An 1865 illustration from *Harper's Weekly* depicts the celebration in Congress with the passage of the Thirteenth Amendment.

that African Americans could become citizens and enjoy equal rights as white Americans.

However, the Radical Republicans realized they needed to do more to protect the recently freed slaves, especially in the South. They wanted to ensure that the recently enslaved would become citizens. Unfortunately, many Southern states passed a series of laws, called Black Codes, designed to keep African Americans in a second-class position in society. These laws prevented blacks from voting, serving on juries, holding certain jobs, owning or carrying firearms, or assembling together after sunset.

The years immediately after the Civil War were violent ones for African Americans as angry white mobs lynched and killed thousands of African Americans. Many members of the Thirty-ninth Congress believed that something more was needed than the Thirteenth Amendment and civil rights laws to protect African Americans. This led to the Fourteenth Amendment.

In February, Rep. John Bingham (1815–1900)—known as the "Father of the Fourteenth Amendment"—introduced what would become section one of the Fourteenth Amendment with the intent "to enforce the bill of rights as it stands in the Constitution today." The Senate passed the Fourteenth Amendment on June 8, 1866. The House agreed to the Senate's changes on June 13, 1866.

President Andrew Johnson (1808–1875), who assumed the presidency after Lincoln was assassinated, opposed the Fourteenth Amendment, believing Congress had exceeded its power in adopting it.

The Radical Republicans expressly warned the Southern states that they would not be readmitted to the Union until they ratified the Fourteenth Amendment. In June 1868, Arkansas, Alabama, Florida, Georgia, Louisiana, North Carolina, and South Carolina finally ratified the Fourteenth Amendment and were readmitted to the Union.

## "Slaughtering" Part of the Fourteenth Amendment

The Radical Republicans of the Thirty-ninth Congress passed the Fourteenth Amendment largely to provide protection for African Americans. It is ironic then that the first test case of the Fourteenth Amendment in the Supreme Court involved an all-white butcher association who sued under the Fourteenth Amendment. These butcher companies challenged a state law that granted a monopoly on slaughterhouses to two companies in the city of New Orleans.

The law required all cattle dealers and butchers to conduct their business with the Crescent City Livestock Landing & Slaughterhouse Company. The challengers claimed that the state-granted monopoly deprived them of their constitutional rights under the Thirteenth and Fourteenth Amendments, creating an involuntary servitude in violation of the Thirteenth Amendment. They also argued the monopoly violated several sections of the Fourteenth Amendment, including violating their "privileges and immunities" as citizens of the United States, denying them equal protection of the laws, and due process.

In the *Slaughter-House Cases*, the U.S. Supreme Court rejected these arguments, ruling 5–4 that the act was constitutional. The five-member majority interpreted the Fourteenth Amendment's Privileges and Immunities Clause very narrowly to apply only to "fundamental" rights "which belong of right to the citizens of all free governments."

|| *The Court majority in effect read the Fourteenth Amendment in such a way that the Privileges and Immunities Clause of Section I of the Fourteenth Amendment became dead letter.* ||

The Court majority in effect read the Fourteenth Amendment in such a way that the Privileges and Immunities Clause of Section I of the Fourteenth Amendment became dead letter. The ruling meant that the key provisions in the Fourteenth Amendment became the Equal Protection and Due Process Clauses. The effect of this decision meant that it would not be until the twentieth century that the Fourteenth Amendment would nationalize the Bill of Rights to protect citizens from unconstitutional actions by state and local government officials.

Despite these statements, the Supreme Court interpreted the Privileges and Immunities Clause to render it a dead letter. The Court would later find another avenue to apply the protections of the Bill of Rights to the states through the Fourteenth Amendment: the Due Process Clause.

## The Incorporation Process—Total or Selective?

The Fourteenth Amendment is vitally important in American constitutional law because it provides the vehicle through which the freedoms found in the Bill of Rights are extended to apply to state and local government officials. This was not a foregone conclusion, particularly after the Supreme Court had interpreted the Privileges and Immunities Clause so narrowly. The legal question became whether the rights in the first eight amendments to the U.S. Constitution were "incorporated" into the Due Process Clause of the Fourteenth Amendment: "no state shall infringe on life, liberty, or property without due process of law."

Justice Hugo Black (1886–1971) argued vigorously in several cases that the Framers of the Fourteenth Amendment intended for Section 1 of the amendment to make the Bill of Rights applicable to the state. Black believed that Bingham, Thaddeus Stevens (1792–1868), and other members of the Committee of Fifteen had proclaimed as their purpose to overrule the decision in *Barron v. Baltimore*. Justice Black was an advocate of what is known as the "total incorporation" theory. This means that all freedoms in the Bill of Rights are incorporated via the Due Process Clause of the Fourteenth Amendment.

*The Fourteenth Amendment is vitally important in American constitutional law because it provides the vehicle through which the freedoms found in the Bill of Rights are extended to apply to state and local government officials.*

The majority of the Court never adopted Justice Black's total incorporation theory. Instead, the Court adopted what is known as selective incorporation—determining on a case-by-case basis that certain freedoms in the Bill of Rights were important enough to also apply to the states.

The Court began this process of selective incorporation in *Chicago, Burlington & Quincy Railroad Co. v. City of Chicago* (1897). The Court ruled that the Due Process Clause of the Fourteenth Amendment required a state government to compensate a railroad for taking part of its land for public use. "Due protection of the rights of property has been regarded as a vital principle of republican institutions," Justice John Marshall Harlan I (1877–1911) wrote for the majority.

It took many years, but in *Gitlow v. New York* (1925), the Court ruled that the First Amendment freedom of speech also applied to state and local governments. The case involved a socialist named Benjamin Gitlow (1891–1965), who was charged by New York state officials with violating a law prohibiting "advocacy of criminal anarchy." Gitlow had published writings known as "The Left Wing Manifesto" and "The Revolutionary Age" in which he advocated the overthrow of capitalist governments.

Gitlow argued that his conviction violated his First Amendment rights, because he was writing about abstract principles, not the violent overthrow of the government. The Court wrote that freedom of speech and press "are among the fundamental personal rights and 'liberties' protected by the due process clause of the Fourteenth Amendment from impairment by the States."

Throughout the rest of the twentieth century and the early part of the twenty-first century, the Court held that the vast majority of the freedoms in the Bill of Rights should apply to state and local governments, not just the federal government. The process requires the Court to determine whether a freedom in the Bill of Rights is important enough to extend to the states. Justice Benjamin Cardozo (1870–1938) famously wrote that the freedom must be "essential to a scheme of ordered liberty." That really is a fancy way of saying that the right is so important that it needs to limit state officials too.

Much of this occurred during the 1960s during the heyday of the Warren Court. For example, in *Mapp v. Ohio* (1961), the Warren Court ruled that if the state or local police violated the Fourth Amendment by engaging in an unreasonable search of a defendant's home to find contraband, then such incriminating evidence would have to be excluded from the defendant's trial. This is known as the exclusionary rule—that the material uncovered in an unconstitutional fashion must be excluded from trial.

> The Supreme Court had ruled that the exclusionary rule applied in federal prosecutions in Weeks v. United States *in 1913....*

The Supreme Court had ruled that the exclusionary rule applied in federal prosecutions in *Weeks v. United States* in 1913, but it took decades longer for the Court to finally find that the rule also limited state and local government officials.

## Right to a Jury Trial: *Duncan v. Louisiana*

The Warren Court also incorporated the Sixth Amendment right to a jury trial in a case out of Louisiana involving a young African American man named Gary Duncan. In *Duncan v. Louisiana* (1968), the U.S. Supreme Court ruled that the Fourteenth Amendment guaranteed a jury trial to an individual charged in state court of the crime of battery. Duncan was charged and convicted of simple battery for alleging slapping a white youth on the elbow.

Duncan sought a jury trial, but the trial judge denied the request. Duncan was convicted and sentenced to 60 days in jail and a $150 fine. He appealed his conviction, arguing that state officials violated his constitutional rights by denying him a jury trial. The state of Louisiana argued that the Constitution did not require the state to give any criminal defendant a jury trial in a state court.

The Supreme Court disagreed with the state of Louisiana, determining that the "Fourteenth Amendment guarantees a jury trial in all criminal cases which— were they tried in a federal court—would come within the Sixth Amendment's guarantee." The Court traced the right to a jury trial all the way back to the Magna Carta of 1215, a document signed by King John I (1166–1216) of England in which he promised not to violate certain rights of noblemen.

The state of Louisiana also argued that it did not violate Gary Duncan's constitutional rights because he was convicted of only a so-called "petty" crime and was sentenced to only 60 days in jail. In the federal court system, the courts had defined a petty crime as one that resulted in a jail sentence of less than six months. In *Duncan*, the Supreme Court refused to lay down a general definition as to what is a petty crime versus a serious crime. However, the High Court noted that Duncan's crime could have earned him up to two years in prison. The Court concluded that this was a "serious crime and not a petty offense."

In a concurring opinion, Justice Black reiterated his earlier position that the Fourteenth Amendment made all of the provisions of the Bill of Rights applicable to the states. However, Black said that "I am very happy to support this selective process through which our Court has … held most of the specific Bill of Rights' protections applicable to the States to the same extent they are applicable to the Federal Government."

Black wrote that "history conclusively demonstrates" that the purpose of section one of the Fourteenth Amendment was to "guarantee that thereafter no state could deprive its citizens of the privileges and protections of the Bill of Rights."

A majority of the Supreme Court never adopted Justice Black's total incorporation theory. However, the Supreme Court, through a process of selective incorporation, has made the vast majority of the freedoms of the first eight amendments of the Bill of Rights applicable to the states.

This process has continued in the twenty-first century. The Supreme Court, for example, incorporated the Second Amendment right to keep and bear arms in 2010 and the Excessive Fines Clause in 2019.

Through the process of selective incorporation, people in the United States are afforded nearly as much constitutional protections from state and local officials as from federal officials.

Justice Felix Frankenfurter, who served on the Supreme Court from 1939 to 1962, felt that following legal procedures was an essential part of protecting people's freedoms and liberty.

# Procedural Due Process

The Fourteenth Amendment consists of two types of due process: (1) procedural due process and (2) substantive due process. Procedural due process means that the government must act fairly and reasonably when it affects a person's interests in life, liberty, or property. Substantive due process means that the government has an adequate reason or justification before taking away a person's life, liberty, or property interests. In other words, procedural due process is about the process used, and substantive due process is about whether the government's action is either justified or irrational.

Procedural process is about having a fair procedure in place. Justice Felix Frankfurter (1882–1965) wrote in 1945 that "the history of freedom is, in no small measure, the history of procedure." For example, government officials must ensure that someone convicted of a crime receive a fair trial before a jury of his or her peers.

Many disputes involving procedural due process involve people charged with a crime. Several provisions of the Bill of Rights apply chiefly to those suspected of a crime, including the Fourth, Fifth, and Sixth Amendments. Procedural due process is obviously vitally important in a criminal case because a person's liberty and even life is at stake.

The Supreme Court has determined that the procedures that law enforcement officials engage in with regard to a suspect must ensure that the process is fair. If the conduct of the police officers is fundamentally unfair or "shocks the conscience," a conviction can be overturned.

## Fair Process in Criminal Cases

Consider the case of Antonio Richard Rochin in Los Angeles County, California. Three deputy sheriffs in Los Angeles County learned that Rochin might be trafficking in illegal drugs, so they went to his home on July 1, 1949. The officers entered the home, forced open Rochin's bedroom door on the second floor, and seized him half-naked. The officers saw drug capsules, which Rochin swallowed.

The deputies then forcibly removed Rochin from his home and took him to a local hospital. They ordered hospital personnel to pump his stomach with a tube to remove the capsules. The stomach pumping caused Rochin to vomit out the two capsules. The capsules contained morphine. The deputies then arrested Rochin for illegal possession of drugs. He was convicted and sentenced to 60 days in jail. During his trial, Rochin objected to the capsules being admitted into evidence.

‖ *The U.S. Supreme Court has ruled that the methods in which police obtain a confession from a suspect must be fair, or the confession cannot be admitted into evidence.* ‖

The U.S. Supreme Court reversed the conviction, finding that the conduct of the police violated the Due Process Clause. "This is conduct that shocks the conscience," the Court wrote. "Illegally breaking into the privacy of the petitioner, the struggle to open his mouth and remove what was there, the forcible extraction of his stomach's contents—this course of proceedings by agents of government to obtain evidence is bound to offend even hardened sensibilities."

## False confession

The U.S. Supreme Court has ruled that the methods by which police obtain a confession from a suspect must be fair, or the confession cannot be admitted into evidence. *Haley v. State of Ohio* (1948) concerned a case in which police arrested a 15-year-old African American youth, John Harvey Haley, and accused him of murder. The police alleged that he served as lookout for two other youths who robbed a grocery store and killed the owner. The police took Haley into custody, and five or six police officers questioned him for five straight hours. During the questioning, Haley was not allowed an attorney, advised of his right to an attorney, or allowed to make a phone call. Under duress and constant pressure, Haley signed a written confession.

After his confession was signed, a lawyer hired by his mother was twice denied admission to the jail. Police did not allow his mother to visit him until five days after his "confession." Prosecutors used the confession to obtain a first-degree murder conviction and a life sentence.

> *Douglas concluded that the police conduct during its intense questioning of Haley made an "empty form of the due process of law for which free men fought and died to obtain."*

The U.S. Supreme Court narrowly reversed the conviction by a 5–4 vote. "We do not think the methods used in obtaining this confession can be squared with that due process of law which the Fourteenth Amendment requires," wrote Justice William O. Douglas (1898–1980). The state had argued that the police did not violate Haley's due-process rights because they advised Haley of his rights when he signed his written confession. However, Douglas wrote that the conduct of the police was "darkly suspicious," especially given Haley's age. Douglas concluded that the police conduct during its intense questioning of Haley made an "empty form of the due process of law for which free men fought and died to obtain."

## Procedural Due Process Rights of Juveniles

Another important U.S. Supreme Court decision related to procedural due process rights involved a 15-year-old boy named Gerald Gault. Gault was arrested for making a lewd telephone call to a woman in his neighborhood. Six months earlier, Gault had gotten into trouble for being with a youth who had stolen a lady's wallet.

Officers took Gerald into custody on June 8, 1964, but they did not tell Gerald's parents that he was in custody until several days later. A juvenile judge held a hearing the very next day in his chambers. Gerald's parents only heard about the hearing from a friend of Gerald's who had been present when he was arrested.

After the hearing, Gerald was sent back to detention and was not released to his parents until a couple days later. His parents were not informed of the next hearing until the day of Gerald's release. The next hearing was held only a few days later, on June 15. The police sent a short, written notice of the date of the hearing.

At the June 15 hearing, probation officers filed a "referral report" about Gerald but did not disclose the report to Gerald's parents. The juvenile judge declared Gerald "delinquent" and ordered him sent to an "industrial school" until he turned 21. The woman who initially called the police about the lewd phone call was not even present. The judge relied on the testimony of the arresting police officer and the report by the probation officers.

His parents argued that they were not given sufficient notice and were not allowed to obtain an attorney for their son to combat the criminal charges. They filed a petition for a *habeas corpus* hearing in the Arizona Supreme Court to contest the juvenile court ruling. At that hearing, the juvenile judge testified he committed Gerald as a "delinquent" because he fit the definition of a "delinquent child," which was one who was "habitually involved in immoral matters."

Under the state's juvenile system, a youth did not have a right to an attorney, the right to confront and cross-examine witnesses, the right not to testify against himself, the right to a transcript of the hearing, and a right to appeal. The U.S. Supreme Court ruled that Arizona's juvenile court proceedings did not provide a sufficient level of procedural due process rights to juveniles facing delinquency proceedings.

The Supreme Court determined that Gault was denied the following rights: (1) the right of adequate notice; (2) the right to counsel; (3) the right to be informed of the privilege against self-incrimination; and (4) the right to cross-examine witnesses. The Court reversed the Arizona court's delinquency finding in part because the "confession" of Gault was obtained by a police officer "without counsel and without advising him of his right to silence."

"Under our constitution, the condition of being a boy does not justify a kangaroo court," the Court famously wrote, adding that the "essential difference between Gerald's case and a normal criminal case is that safeguards available to adults were discarded in Gerald's case because Gerald was 15 years of age instead of over 18."

## Procedural Due Process in Civil Cases

Procedural due process rights are not confined to the criminal arena; they also apply in civil cases. The Supreme Court has interpreted procedural due process to require that the government give notice and a hearing to those who may lose their life, liberty, and property interests in civil cases.

In 1970, the U.S. Supreme Court determined in *Goldberg v. Kelly* that the state of New York had to provide a hearing to someone before terminating their public assistance benefits. New York City allowed the Department of Social Services to terminate someone's welfare benefits without affording the person a chance to contest those findings. The city procedures did allow someone to contest the cancellation of benefits after they had already been terminated. This did not satisfy the constitutional requirements of procedural due process, according to the Supreme Court.

The Court determined that a welfare recipient must have "timely and adequate notice" of the reasons for the termination of benefits. The Court also said that the person must have "an effective opportunity" to contest the denial of benefits. "In almost every setting where important decisions turn on questions of fact, due process requires an opportunity to confront and cross-examine adverse witnesses," the Court wrote.

## Due Process Rights for Students

Public school students also possess due process rights. In 1975, the U.S. Supreme Court ruled in *Goss v. Lopez* that the Due Process Clause requires school officials give notice and a hearing to students facing suspension. The case arose after nine students at several high schools and junior high schools in Columbus, Ohio, were suspended for 10 days for disruptive conduct during February and March 1971.

Under Ohio law, school officials could suspend students without giving them a hearing to contest the charges. Under the law, school officials only had to notify the student's parents within 24 hours and state the reasons for the discipline. The student could appeal the decision to the board of education and could speak at the next board meeting. The law provided that the board could reinstate the suspended student.

The students challenged the law in federal court. They argued that the failure to grant them a hearing either before the hearing or immediately after the suspension violated their rights to procedural due process. The students argued that they had a liberty interest in their reputations and a property interest in their right to a public education.

The school officials conceded that the Due Process Clause protects students who suffer a "severe loss." The state argued, however, that a 10-day suspension is not a severe enough punishment to involve the Due Process Clause. The school officials also argued that the schools must have some flexibility in imposing discipline to ensure a safe learning environment.

The Supreme Court ruled for the students. The court determined that a 10-day suspension "is a serious event" for the suspended student. The court concluded that "at the very minimum," students facing suspension "must be given some kind of notice and afforded some kind of hearing."

The Supreme Court recognized that schools face a challenging task in imposing discipline. The Court also recognized that school officials must sometimes impose immediate punishment in order to effectively run the school. However, the Court said that fundamental fairness requires that a student receive notice and a hearing:

> The prospect of imposing elaborate hearing requirements in every suspension case is viewed with great concern, and many school authorities may well prefer the untrammeled power to act unilaterally, unhampered by rules about notice and hearing. But it would be a strange disciplinary system in an educational institution if no communication was sought by the disciplinarian with the student in an effort to inform him of his dereliction and to let him tell his side of the story in order to make sure that an injustice is not done.

The Court also noted that its decision dealt with suspensions for less than 10 days. "Longer suspensions, or expulsions for the remainder of the school term, or permanently, may require more formal procedures."

These issues are vitally important to public school students today. Now, many public schools, in an effort to combat juvenile violence and drug use, have adopted so-called zero-tolerance policies. Under these policies, schools can impose long-term suspensions and even expulsions for first-time student offenders. If students accused of violating a provision under a zero-tolerance policy are not given notice and a proper hearing, the potential for injustice could be great.

# Substantive Due Process

In addition to ensuring fair procedures, the Due Process Clause also protects individual liberty against arbitrary and unreasonable laws. In other words, the Due Process Clause also contains a "substantive" component or part. This is known as substantive due process.

Substantive due process means that the government may not pass laws that have an unreasonable substance or purpose. For example, the government would violate substantive due process if it tried to regulate certain aspects of citizens' private lives, such as the right to use birth control, the right to pursue a certain job, or the right to marry a person of the same sex.

In the early twentieth century, the court used a theory of substantive due process to strike down laws that regulated the economy. For example, in *Lochner v. New York*, the Court ruled that a New York law limiting the number of hours a baker could work every week violated due process. The 1897 law limited the number of hours a baker could work to 60 hours a week or 10 hours a day. Union representatives had successfully petitioned the state legislature to pass the law to protect the health of workers.

The New York legislature passed the law to protect workers from potentially dangerous and unsafe working conditions, but the Supreme Court majority reasoned by a narrow 5–4 vote that the law unreasonably interfered with the freedom of an employer to contract with its employees. In other words, the employer's freedom to contract received more constitutional protection than the employee's right to a safe working environment.

The majority of the Court believed they had a duty and the constitutional power to review laws that interfered with our free enterprise system and our laissez-faire economy. Four justices, including Justice John Marshall Harlan I and Justice Oliver Wendell Holmes Jr. (1841–1935), dissented. Harlan believed that the Court should exercise judicial restraint and not strike down a law enacted as a health measure. Holmes wrote a more colorful dissent. He believed that the Fourteenth Amendment did not allow the Court to substitute its own judgment as to what is the best economic policy.

## Parents Rights of Educating Children

When discussing substantive due process, the key is whether a law or policy directly impacts a fundamental right. If a law or policy does directly impact a fundamental right, there is a good chance that the reviewing court might strike down the law.

As we saw with the *Lockner* decision, during the early part of the twentieth century, the Supreme Court was not bashful and often struck down laws that regulated the economic and social lives of Americans.

The Court also examined legislation that affected the fundamental rights of parents to rear their children as they saw fit. For example, in its 1923 decision *Meyer v. Nebráska*, the Supreme Court struck down a Nebraska state law that prohibited the teaching of any foreign languages. The Court determined that the law was arbitrary and unreasonable, noting that it is "well known that proficiency in a foreign language seldom comes to one not instructed at an early age."

The Court also recognized the fundamental rights of parents in *Pierce v. Society of the Sisters of the Holy Names of Jesus and Mary* (1925), striking down an Oregon law

The Court has repeatedly asserted the rights of parents to have a role in the education of their own children. Parents can home school their kids or send them to a private school if they choose.

that prohibited parents from sending their children to private schools. Writing that "the child is not the mere creature of the State," the Court concluded that the law interfered with the liberty of parents to control the upbringing of their children in matters of education.

These cases represented the type of cases that the Court would examine under due process. After 1937, the Supreme Court began to shift its focus "from property rights to human rights." In a footnote, the Court indicated that it would more closely examine laws that directly impacted fundamental rights or negatively impacted "discrete and insular" minorities. This footnote signaled a sea change in modern constitutional law. Now, the Court applied greater scrutiny to laws that impacted fundamental individual rights than to those protecting property and contract rights.

It was in subsequent decades that the Court expanded the reach of substantive due process and closely examined laws that impacted the right to marry, the right to have children, the right to marital privacy, the right to use birth control devices, and the right to have an abortion.

## Right to Marital Privacy

In a famous due process case, the Court struck down an unusual Connecticut law that prohibited the sale of contraceptives even to married couples. The law said that any person who uses or aids another in using "any drug, medicinal article or instrument for the purpose of preventing conception" could be fined and subject to a 60-day jail term.

Estelle T. Griswold (1900–1981), the executive director of the Planned Parenthood League of Connecticut, and others gave information to married couples on the use of contraceptives. After they were fined $100, Griswold and others claimed that the laws violated the Fourteenth Amendment liberty interest in marital privacy.

The Supreme Court agreed in *Griswold v. Connecticut* that the laws invaded a fundamental right protected by the Fourteenth Amendment. In his main opinion for the Court, Justice William O. Douglas ruled that although the right to privacy was not specifically mentioned in the Constitution, several provisions in the Bill of Rights contained "penumbras" or "zones of privacy."

"Would we allow the police to search the sacred precincts of marital bedrooms for telltale

An odd Connecticut law said that even married couples were not allowed to purchase birth control pills, a law that the Supreme Court struck down as a blatant violation of personal privacy rights.

signs of the use of contraceptives?" Douglas asked. "The very idea is repulsive to the notions of privacy surrounding the marriage relationship."

## Right to an Abortion

The *Griswold* decision and its protection of bedroom privacy paved the way for an even more momentous decision, one that still harbors controversy and creates dissension in society—*Roe v. Wade* (1973). The Court determined that Jane Roe, real name Norma McCorvey (1947–2017), had a constitutional right to choose to have an abortion.

At that time, Texas had a law on the books that criminalized abortions unless such a procedure was necessary to save the life of the childbearing woman. Writing for a seven-member majority, Justice Harry Blackmun (1908–1999) asserted that the "right of privacy … is broad enough to encompass a woman's decision whether or not to terminate her pregnancy." Blackmun divided the pregnancy period into three periods called trimesters, with women having an unqualified right to seek an abortion during the first trimester and the state having much stronger interests to regulate such procedures during the third trimester.

Critics charged the Court with acting as a super-legislature and not protecting the right of the unborn. Judge Robert Bork (1927–2012) famously criticized the Court for acting with "judicial imperialism," injecting personal police preferences into constitutional law.

The precedent set by *Roe v. Wade* that women should be allowed to have abortions came under threat of an overturn by the Supreme Court in 2021 as it ruled on a Mississippi law that bans abortions for pregnancies that are more than 15 weeks along.

## Limits on Due Process

The Supreme Court has placed limitations on the use of the Due Process Clause to remedy wrongs. In 1989, the High Court found no due-process violation in *DeShaney v. Winnebago County Department of Social Services*—a case with profoundly disturbing facts. Joshua DeShaney, a young boy from Wisconsin, was beaten severely by his father and suffered permanent brain damage. The Winnebago County Department of Social Services (DSS) had learned from the police and neighbors that Joshua had suffered physical abuse at the hands of his father.

A local child protection team examined Joshua's case and determined there was insufficient evidence of child abuse. This unfortunate decision led to Joshua being placed back with his father, who beat him severely, causing permanent brain damage.

Joshua's mother sued the local government officials, arguing that they had a duty to protect a child that they knew had suffered from physical abuse at the hands of his father. However, the U.S. Supreme Court ruled that the Due Process Clause does not require local officials to "protect life, liberty and property of its citizens against invasion by private actors."

The decision caused Justice Blackmun to begin his dissenting opinion with the exclamation "Poor Joshua!" He termed the majority's decision a "sad commentary upon American life."

A similar tragedy occurred in *Town of Castle Rock v. Gonzales* (2005), a case in which an estranged father, who was the subject of a restraining order taken out by his wife, killed his three daughters. Jessica Gonzales had repeatedly contacted local police, asking for their help to intervene and enforce the restraining order. The police did nothing each time, and later that evening, the father killed the three girls. Jessica sued, alleging a violation of due process. The Supreme Court once again reasoned that the Constitution does not provide protection from privately inflicted harms, only governmentally inflicted harms.

Constitutional scholar Erwin Chemerinsky explains in his book *Constitutional Law: Polices and Principles* that these decisions reflect the principle that "only if the government literally creates the danger or a person is in government custody, is there any constitutional duty for the government to provide protection."

# Equal Protection

The Equal Protection Clause provides that no state shall "deny to any person equal protection under the laws." This part of Section I of the Fourteenth Amendment provides that the government should treat similarly situated individuals the same and not engage in arbitrary treatment of different classes or groups of people.

> *Normally, the government must show only that it has a rational basis for a law that treats people differently.*

Normally, the government must show only that it has a rational basis for a law that treats people differently. For example, if a law requires chiropractors to engage in certain conduct but not other professions, the question becomes whether the government has a legitimate reason for treating chiropractors differently. Furthermore, when the government must only meet this low-level rational basis standard, the burden is on the challengers, not the government.

However, if the law affects a suspect class, such as race, or involves a fundamental right, such as voting or education, then the government must show that its law satisfies the highest form of judicial review, known as strict scrutiny. When this high level of strict scrutiny applies, the government has the burden of justifying the law.

## Race and the Equal Protection Clause

Much of the Court's equal protection jurisprudence arose out of cases involving abject racial discrimination. The question of race has been a defining feature of the American experience. In the famous words of W. E. B. Du Bois (1868–1963), the problem of the twentieth century is the "problem of the color line."

In equal protection law, any law that draws racial classifications is inherently suspect. The same Radical Republicans of the Thirty-ninth Congress passed not only the Reconstruction Amendments but also a series of civil rights laws to provide protection to the recently emancipated African Americans.

For example, Congress passed the Civil Rights Bill of 1875, which provided that all persons are entitled to "equal enjoyment of the accommodations, advantages, facilities, and privileges of inns, public conveyances on land or water, theaters and other places of public amusement." Congress passed the bill because states and individuals throughout the country continued to discriminate against blacks, denying them admission to inns, theaters, railway companies, and other places of public accommodation.

However, the U.S. Supreme Court determined that Congress did not have the power to pass the Civil Rights Act of 1875 in a series of cases known collectively as the *Civil Rights Cases* (1883). The cases involved African Americans denied admission to either railways, hotels, or theaters in Kansas, Missouri, California, New York, and Tennessee. The cases provided the Supreme Court with the opportunity to affirm Congress's national policy to rid society of segregation.

A sign in an Ohio restaurant's window in 1938 clearly declares the racism of the owners of the establishment. For many decades, the Supreme Court supported and allowed such discrimination.

The key legal issue was whether Congress had the authority, under the Thirteenth and Fourteenth Amendments, to pass the 1875 civil rights law and outlaw racial discrimination in public accommodations. The Court ruled 8–1 that Congress did not have the authority under the Reconstruction Amendments to pass the civil rights bill. The High Court noted that the Fourteenth Amendment was concerned with actions by state officials, not private individuals. "It is state action of a particular character that is prohibited," the Court wrote. "Individual invasion of individual rights is not the subject matter of the amendment." The actions in these cases were simply "private wrongs," according to the majority, adding incredibly that at some point the black man "ceases to be the special favorite of the laws."

Justice John Marshall Harlan I was the lone dissenter. He warned that "the substance and spirit of the recent amendments of the constitution have been sacrificed by a subtle and ingenious verbal criticism." Harlan warned that the effect of the Court's decision would be to create different classes of citizenship.

The Court's decision unfortunately led to more segregation laws and policies inflicted upon African Americans. It also set back the civil rights cause for decades upon decades. The case also established the state action doctrine—that the Constitution only limits governmental actors, not private actors.

Fifteen years later, the U.S. Supreme Court further sanctioned discrimination against blacks by upholding a legal doctrine known as "separate but equal" in *Plessy v. Ferguson* (1896). The case involved a man named Homer Plessy (1862–1925), who was one-eighth African American. In the South, one drop of "black blood" consigned people to second-class citizenship.

Plessy challenged a Louisiana law that mandated for separate railway accommodations on the basis of race. Louisiana argued that the segregation law did not violate the Equal Protection Clause because both whites and blacks could access the railways—they just had to sit separately. Even though the laws were unfair and racist, legislators justified them by relying on the noxious "separate but equal" doctrine. Sadly, the facilities for blacks paled in comparison to those provided to whites. The reality was "separate and unequal."

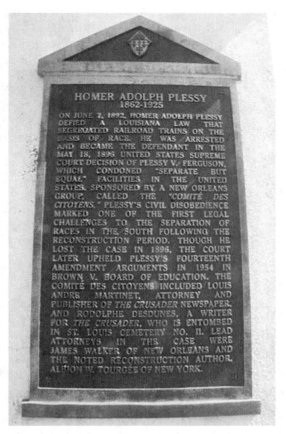

The U.S. Supreme Court deemed the Louisiana law constitutional, writing that laws requiring separation of the races "do not necessarily imply the inferiority of either race to the other." The Court majority noted that many states had established separate schools for blacks and whites. The Court majority also noted that the states had forbade blacks and whites to marry each other. The majority also infamously wrote: "If one race be inferior to the other socially, the constitution of the United States cannot put them upon the same plane."

Once again, Justice John Marshall Harlan I was the lone dissenter, earning his moniker "the Great Dissenter." He waxed eloquent, using language that has become constitutional lore:

But in view of the constitution, in the eye of the law, there is in this country no su-

Homer Plessy's tomb in New Orleans includes a large plaque about the *Plessy v. Ferguson* case and its later influence on *Brown v. Board of Education*.

perior, dominant ruling class of citizens. There is no caste here. Our constitution is color-blind and neither knows nor tolerates classes among citizens. In respect of civil rights, all citizens are equal before the law. The humblest is the peer of the most powerful.

Harlan even correctly predicted in his opinion that in the future society would regard the majority's decision "as pernicious as the decision" in the *Dred Scott* case.

# *Brown v. Board of Education*

In the *Plessy* case, the U.S. Supreme Court had justified the Louisiana Jim Crow law by relying on the fact that segregation was common in education. The Court majority cited examples of segregated public education from the city of Boston and the District of Columbia.

It would be delicious irony that the evil of segregation would be successfully attacked in an education case. This happened in the historic U.S. Supreme Court decision of *Brown v. Board of Education*.

*Brown* involved four cases from Kansas, South Carolina, Virginia, and Delaware. The lead case was *Brown v. Board of Education* in Topeka, Kansas. Oliver Brown (1918–1961) sued after his young daughter, Linda Brown (1943–2018), was not allowed to enroll at a nearby all-white school. At that time, as in many places across the country, public education remained rigidly segregated.

The National Association for the Advancement of Colored People (NAACP), a leading civil rights organization, had been challenging segregation policies in education for decades. Originally, the NAACP would challenge laws under the separate but equal doctrine, arguing (correctly) that local authorities provided many more resources and money for schools attended by Caucasian students than those schools reserved for African American students. The disparities were often gross and severe.

But, over time, the NAACP—led by Charles Hamilton Houston (1895–1950) and his protégé, Thurgood Marshall (1908–1993)—decided to challenge the *Plessy* precedent head-on, arguing that the "separate but equal" doctrine itself violated the Equal Protection Clause.

Initially, the NAACP achieved success, challenging segregation bans at law schools. The NAACP convinced the Supreme Court that the state of Texas had to admit African American Heman Sweatt (1912–1982) to the University of Texas law school instead of building a law school specifically for African Americans.

However, the real challenge was to desegregate the nation's public secondary schools. Resistance to integration from white America was fierce in many communities, but the NAACP pursued the legal challenges and ultimately prevailed in the historic *Brown v. Board* decision.

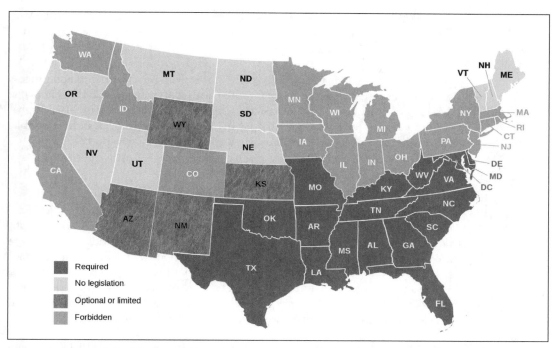

Required
No legislation
Optional or limited
Forbidden

Before *Brown v. Board of Education,* states decided whether or not schools were segregated. In some states, segregation was even mandatory.

The Court first heard oral arguments in the case in 1952. The Court initially seemed to want to decide the case under the rubric of separate but equal, but then Chief Justice Fred Vinson (1890–1953) suffered a fatal heart attack. President Dwight D. Eisenhower (1890–1969) appointed Earl Warren (1891–1974) as Vinson's replacement. Chief Justice Warren exhibited great leadership in marshalling the Court toward unanimity.

Warren wrote the opinion for the unanimous Court, reasoning that segregation in public schools violates the Equal Protection Clause. "We conclude that in the field of public education, the doctrine of 'separate but equal' has no place," Warren wrote. "Separate educational facilities are inherently unequal."

In footnote 11, Warren cited several psychological studies showing that segregated schools imposed a badge of inferiority among minority students. For example, the Court in a footnote cited a study by Kenneth B. Clark (1914–2005), a highly regarded African American social scientist. Clark had tested black children in Philadelphia, Boston, and other communities by showing them white and black dolls. The black children overwhelmingly preferred the white dolls and showed signs of self-rejection.

The decision in *Brown* was a landmark one, but it did not lead to the immediate integration of the public schools, particularly in the South. White resistance was fierce in certain communities. Some state governors, such as Alabama's George Wallace (1919–1998) and Arkansas's Orval Faubus (1910–1994), extolled segregation and defied federal authorities.

Furthermore, the Court in *Brown* did not explain how the integration process would occur. A year later, in *Brown II* (1955), the Court ordered that the schools be desegregated "with all deliberate speed." Unfortunately, many local officials emphasized the adjective "deliberate" instead of the noun "speed." Thus, many public schools in the South were not actually desegregated until the early 1970s.

## Interracial Marriage

Bans on interracial marriage, like segregated schools, also fell to the Equal Protection Clause jurisprudence of the Warren Court. For years, states had so-called antimiscegenation laws, rooted in the doctrine of white supremacy. Sadly, the laws were allowed to remain on the books and in some jurisdictions were enforced at least sporadically. By 1967, 16 states still had laws on the books banning interracial marriages. Virginia's law provided that if a white person intermarried with a "colored person," the white person would be guilty of a felony. A few states, such as Tennessee, had provisions in their state constitutions prohibiting interracial marriage.

Mildred Jeter (1939–2008), an African American woman, and Richard Loving (1933–1975), a white man, married in the District of Columbia in 1958. Shortly

The state of Virginia tried to argue that its law against interracial marriage was constitutional because it treated blacks and whites equally (neither could marry someone not of their own race). The Supreme Court wasn't buying it.

after they married, the couple moved back to their home state of Virginia. Richard Loving was arrested by the police for violating the so-called antimiscegenation law. A trial judge sentenced him to one year in jail but suspended the sentence as long as the Lovings left the state and didn't return for 25 years. The judge stated:

Almighty God created the races white, black, yellow, malay and red, and he placed them on separate continents. And but for the interference with his arrangement there would be no cause for such marriages. The fact that he separated the races shows that he did not intend for the races to mix.

The Virginia appellate courts affirmed the trial judge's ruling and upheld the ban on interracial marriage. The Lovings appealed to the U.S. Supreme Court. They argued that the interracial marriage ban violated their rights to equal protection and due process under the Fourteenth Amendment.

The state argued that its law did not violate the Equal Protection Clause because the law treated both blacks and whites equally. This was known as "the equal application" theory. In other words, the state argued that because the law punished both races, neither race was disadvantaged.

Attorneys for the state of Virginia also argued that statements by various representatives in the Thirty-ninth Congress show that the framers of the Fourteenth Amendment did not intend for the amendment to allow interracial marriages. The state also argued that the Court's 1883 decision in *Pace v. Alabama* supported its reasoning. In *Pace*, the high court upheld an Alabama law that imposed greater penalties on those who committed adultery with a member of another race.

The U.S. Supreme Court rejected all of the state's arguments. The Court ruled that the law had an "invidious" purpose—the advancement of white supremacy. "There can be no doubt that restricting the freedom to marry solely because of racial classifications violates the central meaning of the Equal Protection Clause," Chief Justice Warren wrote for a unanimous Court.

The Supreme Court also determined that the Virginia law violated the Due Process Clause. The High Court reasoned that "the freedom to marry has long been recognized as one of the vital personal rights essential to the orderly pursuit of happiness by free men."

|| *The Loving decision was also important because it later served as the key precedent that guided the Court in striking down a ban on same-sex marriage in* Obergefell v. Hodges *(2015).* ||

The *Loving* decision is important not only because it struck down flagrantly discriminatory interracial bans but also because the decision showed that oftentimes a law can violate both the Due Process and Equal Protection Clauses of the Fourteenth Amendment. The *Loving* decision also was important because it later served as the key precedent that guided the Court in striking down a ban on same-sex marriage in *Obergefell v. Hodges* (2015).

## Discrimination in Jury Selection

Another significant area of equal protection impact was jury selection. In 1986, the U.S. Supreme Court ruled in *Batson v. Kentucky* that the Equal Protection Clause requires that a prosecutor in a criminal case not exclude potential jurors based on race. In court, a group of citizens is called into a courtroom to serve as potential jurors. The process of selecting jury members is known as *voir dire*.

Each side or litigant is allowed to strike certain people from serving as juror members. There are two types of challenges: "for cause" challenges—challenging someone because they reflect a bias that would not allow them to judge the case impartially—and peremptory challenges—challenging someone for any reason at all. Each legal side in a case has a certain number of peremptory challenges. Attorneys in death penalty cases have the greatest number of peremptory challenges.

However, the Supreme Court placed constitutional limits on peremptory challenges in the *Batson* case. James Batson, an African American man, was charged with burglary and receipt of stolen property. In the case, the prosecutor used his peremptory challenges to strike all African Americans from the jury panel. On appeal, Batson's lawyers argued that using peremptory challenges to strike people of a certain race violates the Equal Protection Clause. The High Court agreed that Batson was denied equal protection of the law.

The Court reasoned that both jurors and litigants have a right to be free from group stereotypes rooted in historical prejudices. The Court later extended this principle to civil cases and ruled that the Equal Protection Clause limits defense attorneys' racially discriminatory use of peremptories and that the same principle applies in civil cases.

# Affirmative Action

One of the more divisive equal protection issues in modern America concerns affirmative action, policies that are designed to promote diversity. Proponents insist

President John F. Kennedy signed Executive Order 10925 on March 6, 1961, which states that job applicants and employees must be treated "without regard to their race, creed, color, or national origin."

that affirmative action policies are necessary to remedy the past effects of rampant societal discrimination and to add much-needed diversity to a workforce or student body. In a famous 1965 speech at Howard University, President Lyndon B. Johnson (1908–1973) said, "You do not take a man who for years has been hobbled by chains, liberate him, bring him to the starting line of race, saying 'you are free to compete with all the others,' and still justly believe you have been completely fair."

Opponents counter that at least some affirmative action policies devolve into racial discrimination themselves. Some critics accuse the policies of constituting a form of reverse discrimination and turning the Equal Protection Clause on its head.

The U.S. Supreme Court first waded into these troubled waters in its 1978 decision *Regents of the University of California v. Bakke*. Allan Bakke, a white male, sued after he was denied admission to the medical school at the University of California at Davis. Bakke claimed that the school violated his right to equal protection because it admitted several minority candidates whose qualifications were beneath his.

The university had a special admissions policy under which 16 of 100 slots were reserved for minority applicants. The Court emphasized that the Equal Protection Clause protects all persons, regardless of race or sex. "The guarantee of equal protection cannot mean one thing when applied to one individual and something else when applied to a person of another color," the Court wrote. "If both are not accorded the same protection, then it is not equal."

The High Court reasoned that any racial classification is "inherently suspect." The university argued that its special admissions program was necessary to benefit those who had suffered general "societal discrimination" and to create a diverse student body.

The Supreme Court ruled in favor of Allan Bakke and ordered the school to admit him. The Court ruled that the "fatal flaw" in the school's admission policy was "its disregard of individual rights." The Court, however, did not say that the school could not consider race as a factor in the admissions policy. The Court ruled that under a more "flexible" policy, a university can use race as one of many factors in its admission decisions.

Twenty-five years later, the Court returned to the subject of affirmative action policies in higher education with a pair of decisions involving affirmative action policies at the undergraduate and law school levels at the University of Michigan. The undergraduate policy added a certain number of points to an applicant's admission score if they belonged to an underrepresented racial group, while the law school policy was more nuanced and considered race as one of many other factors.

The Court split the difference in its decisions, striking down the undergraduate policy as an impermissible quota but upholding the law school policy as a permissible way to increase diversity. In the law school case, *Grutter v. Bollinger* (2003), Justice Sandra Day O'Connor (1930–) wrote, "We expect that 25 years from now, the use of racial preferences will no longer be necessary to further the interest approved today."

# Gender Discrimination

Racial discrimination is not the only blot on our nation's history, as it also has suffered from severe gender discrimination. Consider that women did not even receive the right to vote until the passage of the Nineteenth Amendment in 1920. When the Founding Fathers wrote the words "We the People" in the Constitution, they were referring to white males—not females of any race.

In the nineteenth and much of the twentieth century, the U.S. Supreme Court did not offer much relief to women seeking justice and equal protection

Despite being qualified, Myra Bradwell was denied the right to practice law in Illinois, a decision that the Supreme Court upheld in 1873. She went on to be the publisher of *Chicago Legal News* and was inducted into the National Women's Hall of Fame in 1994.

under the Fourteenth Amendment. For most of the twentieth century, women were denied admission to graduate schools and not allowed to serve as jurors.

In 1872, the U.S. Supreme Court ruled that a woman did not have a Fourteenth Amendment right to earn a living as a lawyer. Myra Bradwell (1831–1894), a resident of Chicago, had petitioned the state of Illinois for a license to practice law. She previously had practiced law in Vermont without incident, but the state of Illinois denied her a law license solely because she was female. After she was rejected, she filed a lawsuit. She argued that the Fourteenth Amendment Privileges and Immunities Clause protected her basic liberty right to earn a living as a lawyer. The courts rejected her claim, based upon its narrow reading of the Privileges and Immunities Clause.

Another example of a state law that discriminated on the basis of gender was a Michigan law that prohibited females from working as bartenders in cities of 50,000 or more unless their "father or husband" owned the bar. In 1948, Valentine Goesaert and her daughter challenged the law as a violation of their equal protection rights. After all, Valentine was the owner of the bar, but the Supreme Court ruled the law constitutional. The Court reasoned that the presence of women bartenders in larger cities could present moral and societal problems.

In the 1970s, a female law professor named Ruth Bader Ginsburg (1933–2020)—decades before her ascendancy to the Supreme Court and "RBG" cultural icon status—led the fight against laws that discriminated on the basis of gender. Of the six gender cases she argued before the Supreme Court, she won five. In the 1970s, the Supreme Court began to apply the Equal Protection Clause more strongly to gender cases. In 1971, the Court for the first time ruled in favor of a woman who alleged that her equal protection rights had been violated by a gender discriminatory law. The high court invalidated an Idaho law that preferred males over females for administrators of certain estates. In 1973, the Supreme Court ruled that female military members should be entitled to claim their male spouse as a dependent for increased medical benefits.

Several of Ginsburg's clients were male. She was able to successfully challenge laws that discriminated against males based on their sex. After all, the Equal Protection Clause protects all persons regardless of race or gender. Even though the clause has traditionally been used to protect the rights of African Americans and women, the Constitution provides protection to all people.

> *Ginsburg was never able to convince five justices of the Court that gender discriminatory bans should be subject to the same high level of scrutiny as racial classifications.*

However, Ginsburg was never able to convince five justices of the Court that gender discriminatory bans should be subject to the same high level of scrutiny as racial classifications. While racially discriminatory laws are subject to strict scrutiny, gender classifications are subject to intermediate or mid-level scrutiny. Under this middle level of scrutiny, the government still needs a substantial or important governmental interest.

The Court decided a landmark equal protection case in 1982 when it ruled that the Mississippi University for Women violated the equal protection rights of Joe Hogan when it denied his application to nursing school. The Mississippi University for Women argued that its females-only admissions policy was to compensate for past discrimination against women. The school argued that its policy was a form of educational affirmative action.

However, Justice Sandra Day O'Connor, the first woman appointed to the U.S. Supreme Court, wrote for the Court that the policy constituted gender discrimination in violation of the Equal Protection Clause. She also wrote that a state must have an "exceedingly persuasive justification" for a policy that classifies people based on their gender.

Similarly, in 1994, the Supreme Court ruled that a prosecutor violated the Equal Protection Clause by striking male jurors in a paternity and child support case. Thus, the Court extended its *Batson* ruling to cover the gender discriminatory use of peremptory challenges. An Alabama prosecutor had used 9 of its 10 peremptory challenges to remove male jurors. As a result, a male defendant in a child support case was tried and convicted by an all-female jury. The prosecution argued that male jurors would be more sympathetic to the male defendant in a paternity and child support case. However, the Court reasoned that this line of reasoning represented "the very stereotype the law condemns."

The Supreme Court wrote that jury selection, like voting, is an important way for the average citizen to participate in our democratic system of government. "When persons are excluded from participation in our democratic processes solely because of race or gender, this promise of equality dims, and the integrity of our judicial system is jeopardized," the Court wrote.

A few years later, the Court decided another important gender discrimination case—*United States v. Virginia* (1996), a case involving the admission policies of the all-male military college, Virginia Military Institute. History provided a fitting scenario in this case, as Justice Ruth Bader Ginsburg, only the second woman justice on the U.S. Supreme Court, wrote the Court's majority opinion that traced the nation's long history of sex discrimination in the country. Recall that it was Justice Ginsburg who as an advocate had won many of the early sex discrimination cases before the Court.

*Classifications based on sex, ruled Justice Ginsburg, can no longer be used to "create or perpetuate the legal, social, and economic inferiority of women."*

Classifications based on sex, ruled Justice Ginsburg, can no longer be used to "create or perpetuate the legal, social, and economic inferiority of women." The state of Virginia argued that single-sex education offers legitimate educational benefits to students. The state also argued that mixing sexes would negatively affect three important aspects of the VMI program: physical training, the absence of privacy, and the adversarial approach. The state hired expert witnesses who testified that men tend to prefer a competitive, adversarial environment, while women tended to prefer a more cooperative environment.

Finally, the state argued that it would create another single-sex school just for women called the Virginia Women's Institute for Leadership (VWIL). The state described this proposal as a "parallel program" that would give women equal opportunities. Justice Ginsburg dismissed the state's arguments. She noted that similar objections were made when women began applying to law schools, medical schools, and federal military institutes. She concluded that the state's reasons were based on improper sweeping stereotypes.

Ginsburg compared the state's offer to create a separate school for woman to a situation in Texas more than 50 years earlier when an African American applied to the Texas Law School. Because the state did not want to admit African Americans to the main law school, the state set up a separate law school for African American students. In *Sweatt v. Painter*, the U.S. Supreme Court ruled that the state of Texas had failed to show that the schools would be substantially equal.

Ginsburg concluded that the plan offered by the state of Virginia with respect to VMI was the same as that offered by the state of Texas with respect to the Texas Law School. The Court determined that the state must admit qualified women to VMI to fulfill its constitutional obligation of "genuinely equal protection."

## Sexual Orientation and Same-Sex Marriage

A defining aspect of modern equal protection jurisprudence has been the application of equal protection principles to the LGBTQ community—a process that took far too long. Back in 1986, the Supreme Court rejected an equal protection challenge to a Georgia same-sex sodomy law in *Bowers v. Hardwick* (1986). The Court majority cavalierly declared that "[n]o connection between family, marriage, or procreation on the one hand and homosexual activity on the other has been demonstrated." Justice Byron White (1917–2002) in his majority opinion wrote that there was no fundamental right to engage in homosexual activity.

It took the Supreme Court 17 years to overrule *Bowers* in its 2003 decision in *Lawrence v. Texas* (2003), emphasizing that there is constitutional protection for all persons in intimate sexual privacy. "To say that the issue in *Bowers* was simply the right to engage in certain sexual conduct demeans the claim the individual put forward, just as it would demean a married couple were it to be said marriage is simply about the right to have sexual intercourse." The Court invalidated the Texas same-sex sodomy law that demeaned gay and lesbians' ability to engage in sexual relationships.

The *Lawrence* decision was a significant ruling on the path to the Court's ultimate decision in *Obergefell v. Hodges*, striking down same-sex marriage bans as violative of both equal protection and due process. Once again Justice Anthony Kennedy (1936–) wrote the Court's majority opinion, and he emphasized the connectivity between the Due Process and Equal Protection Clauses, writing: "The Due Process Clause and the Equal Protection Clause are connected in a profound way, though they set forth different principles."

Justice Anthony Kennedy, who sat on the Supreme Court bench from 1988 to 2018, wrote majority opinions on four major cases involving gay rights: *Romer v. Evans* (1996), *Lawrence v. Texas* (2003), *United States v. Windsor* (2013), and *Obergefell v. Hodges* (2015).

Kennedy waxed eloquent, asserting that "in interpreting the Equal Protection Clause, the Court has recognized that new insights and society understandings can reveal unjustified inequality within our most fundamental institutions that once passed unnoticed and unchallenged." Kennedy explained that the Equal Protection Clause has been used as a primary vehicle through which the judicial branch—and particularly the Supreme Court—has often recognized new inequalities through the passage of time.

The Court's decision in *Obergefell* is a pristine example of how the Equal Protection Clause is applied in many different circumstances. It serves to ensure that people are treated fairly and not subject to discrimination. Simply stated, "the equal protection guarantee has become the single most important concept in the Constitution for the protection of individual rights."

# Conclusion

The Fourteenth Amendment revolutionized American constitutional law. It represents the true meaning of the spirit of equality found in the Declaration of Independence. When the Constitution was drafted, African Americans and women were treated as second-class citizens or as slaves. The Fourteenth Amendment sought to ensure that African Americans could participate as citizens in a free society.

While our country still has problems with discrimination, the Fourteenth Amendment has provided the constitutional means to achieve social progress. It contains arguably the two most important phrases in American constitutional law: due process and equal protection. Take a look at today's newspaper headlines and the hot-button issues in our nation. Some of them involve social justice and interaction with the police, racial profiling, abortion rights, the right to die, affirmative action, and grandparent visitation rights. Many of these issues have been fought out in the courts with legal arguments about the Fourteenth Amendment.

# Miscellaneous Amendments

There have been 27 amendments to the U.S. Constitution in the nation's history. We already have examined the Bill of Rights—the first 10 amendments to the U.S. Constitution, which were added a mere four years after the ratification of the Constitution—and the Fourteenth Amendment.

In this chapter, we examine several more significant amendments to the Constitution.

## Thirteenth Amendment

### Section 1

Neither slavery nor involuntary servitude, except as a punishment for crime whereof the party shall have been duly convicted, shall exist within the United States, or any place subject to their jurisdiction.

### Section 2

Congress shall have power to enforce this article by appropriate legislation.

The U.S. Constitution was a magnificent accomplishment. The fact that it has existed for more than 200 years with so very few changes confirms this. However, the Constitution did have an original sin—its acceptance of slavery. While the word "slavery" is not mentioned in the Constitution, it did contain the Three-Fifths Clause and the Fugitive Slave Clause. The Three-Fifths clause provided that slaves would be counted as three-fifths of a person for population purposes. The Fugitive Slave Clause allowed a mechanism by which fugitives from slavery could be returned to their slaveowners.

Fortunately, the Radical Republicans of the Thirty-ninth Congress sought to breathe a spirit and reality of equality and end the peculiar institution. They did so with the so-called Reconstruction Amendments. The first of the three was the Thirteenth Amendment. It outlawed slavery and involuntary servitude.

# Fifteenth Amendment

Section 1

The right of citizens of the United States to vote shall not be denied or abridged by the United States or by any State on account of race, color, or previous condition of servitude.

Section 2

The Congress shall have the power to enforce this article by appropriate legislation.

The third of the three Reconstruction Amendments is the Fifteenth Amendment. It prohibits restricting voting on the basis of race. For a brief period, African Americans were elected to Congress, including Senator Hiram Revels (1827–1901) of Mississippi and U.S. representative Joseph Rainey (1832–1887) of South Carolina. For this short period of time, the Radical Republicans ensured that the country was committed to truly freeing those previously enslaved.

Sadly, the Compromise of 1877 led to President Rutherford B. Hayes (1822–1893) not enforcing federal civil rights law and allowing the former Confederate states to govern as they saw fit. These states reverted in a significant sense, some passing so-called Black Codes and later Jim Crow laws. They enacted and enforced segregation laws and at times unleashed race-based violence and terror to maintain their hegemony.

Unfortunately, the Fifteenth Amendment was circumvented for nearly 100 years. States came up with various tests to deny African Americans the vote, including literacy tests, poll taxes, and bizarre qualification tests. In some jurisdictions, prospective white voters would have to pass the easiest test imaginable, but prospective black voters would be asked a bevy of the most arcane and difficult questions about the Constitution.

One of the crowning achievements of the Civil Rights Movement of the 1950s and 1960s was the Voting Rights Act of 1965. The previous year, the U.S. Supreme Court had invalidated the poll tax.

# Eighteenth and Twenty-first Amendments

## Eighteenth Amendment

### Section 1

After one year from the ratification of this article the manufacture, sale, or transportation of intoxicating liquors within, the importation thereof into, or the exportation thereof from the United States and all territory subject to the jurisdiction thereof for beverage purposes is hereby prohibited.

### Section 2

The Congress and the several States shall have concurrent power to enforce this article by appropriate legislation.

### Section 3

This article shall be inoperative unless it shall have been ratified as an amendment to the Constitution by the legislatures of the several States, as provided in the Constitution, within seven years from the date of the submission hereof to the States by the Congress.

## Twenty-first Amendment

### Section 1

The eighteenth article of amendment to the Constitution of the United States is hereby repealed.

### Section 2

The transportation or importation into any State, Territory, or Possession of the United States for delivery or use therein of intoxicating liquors, in violation of the laws thereof, is hereby prohibited.

This article shall be inoperative unless it shall have been ratified as an amendment to the Constitution by conventions in the several States, as provided in the Constitution, within seven years from the date of the submission hereof to the States by the Congress.

The Eighteenth and Twenty-first Amendments to the U.S. Constitution are unique in that they contain an amendment and then a later amendment that repealed the previous one. In other words, the Twenty-first Amendment is the only amendment to the U.S. Constitution that repeals another amendment in its entirety. The Eighteenth Amendment, of course, was the Prohibition Amendment.

Supporters of the Temperance Movement had pushed for Prohibition for decades, believing that alcoholism was a crippling problem that led to health problems, poverty, joblessness, and crime. They believed that it was a cause worth fighting for across the country. Beginning in the early part of the twentieth century, groups such as the Anti-Saloon League and the Woman's Christian Temperance Union stepped up efforts at the state level pushing for prohibition. Many states responded by banning saloons and even the production of alcohol.

Federal agents destroy illegal alcohol in this 1922 photo from Washington, D.C. The Eighteenth Amendment put Prohibition in place in 1919, and the Twenty-first Amendment repealed it in 1933.

Congress approved of the Prohibition Amendment, and it was quickly ratified in the states, as many states already had taken measures against alcohol consumption. Two states, however—Connecticut and Rhode Island—rejected the Prohibition Amendment.

Congress then responded in 1919 by passing enabling legislation called the Volstead Act, named after Representative Andrew Volstead (1859–1947) of Minnesota, who was head of the House Judiciary Committee.

There were many efforts to bypass Prohibition with rum-running and bootlegging. Prohibition created many opportunities for organized crime. It also led to an increase in crime. The Great Depression only increased opposition to Prohibition.

This led to the Twenty-first Amendment. Franklin Delano Roosevelt (1882–1945) had called for the repeal of Prohibition. This was the only amendment ever ratified at state ratifying conventions instead of by the state legislators. The thinking was that the temperance lobby would still be an active force at the state legislatures.

History reveals that Prohibition was a failed experiment, but at least the country moved past it after little more than a decade.

# Nineteenth Amendment

The right of citizens of the United States to vote shall not be denied or abridged by the United States or by any State on account of sex.

Congress shall have power to enforce this article by appropriate legislation.

The right to vote was limited to white males for quite some time. After the passage of the Fifteenth Amendment, many African American males were able to vote at least until various devious forms of racism would close the doors in some parts of the country, but women were not allowed to vote.

In the middle of the nineteenth century, at Seneca Falls, New York, the first women's rights convention was held. Chief on the agenda was pushing for women's suffrage. This conference included the Declaration of Sentiments, which included the famous provision that "all men and women are created equal." Famous suffragists such as Elizabeth Cady Stanton (1815–1902) and Lucretia Mott (1793–1880) spoke at the convention. Suffragists pushed the envelope by taking to the streets and marching for women's rights. Carrie Chapman Catt (1859–1947), a leading suffragist at the time, pushed hard for the passage of the Nineteenth Amendment, which was finally approved in 1919 and ratified in 1920. She later founded the League of Women Voters in 1920.

# Resolutions and the Declaration of Sentiments

## Resolutions

Whereas, the great precept of nature is conceded to be, "that man shall pursue his own true and substantial happiness," Blackstone, in his Commentaries, remarks, that this law of Nature being coeval with mankind, and dictated by God himself, is of course superior in obligation to any other.

It is binding over all the globe, in all countries, and at all times; no human laws are of any validity if contrary to this, and such of them as are valid, derive all their force, and all their validity, and all their authority, mediately and immediately, from this original; Therefore,

Resolved, That such laws as conflict, in any way, with the true and substantial happiness of woman, are contrary to the great precept of nature, and of no validity; for this is "superior in obligation to any other."

Resolved, That all laws which prevent woman from occupying such a station in society as her conscience shall dictate, or which place her in a position inferior to that of man, are contrary to the great precept of nature, and therefore of no force or authority.

Resolved, That woman is man's equal—was intended to be so by the Creator, and the highest good of the race demands that she should be recognized as such.

Resolved, That the women of this country ought to be enlightened in regard to the laws under which they live, that they may no longer publish their degradation, by declaring themselves satisfied with their present position, nor their ignorance, by asserting that they have all the rights they want.

Resolved, That inasmuch as man, while claiming for himself intellectual superiority, does accord to woman moral superiority, it is pre-eminently his duty to encourage her to speak, and teach, as she has an opportunity, in all religious assemblies.

Resolved, That the same amount of virtue, delicacy, and refinement of behavior, that is required of woman in the social state, should also be required of man, and the same transgressions should be visited with equal severity on both man and woman.

Resolved, That the objection of indelicacy and impropriety, which is so often brought against woman when she addresses a public audience,

Suffragists are shown here protesting in San Franisco in 1915, five years before they finally won the right to vote.

comes with a very ill grace from those who encourage, by their attendance, her appearance on the stage, in the concert, or in the feats of the circus.

Resolved, That woman has too long rested satisfied in the circumscribed limits which corrupt customs and a perverted application of the Scriptures have marked out for her, and that it is time she should move in the enlarged sphere which her great Creator has assigned her.

Resolved, That it is the duty of the women of this country to secure to themselves their sacred right to the elective franchise.

Resolved, That the equality of human rights results necessarily from the fact of the identity of the race in capabilities and responsibilities.

Resolved, therefore, That, being invested by the Creator with the same capabilities, and the same consciousness of responsibility for their exercise, it is demonstrably the right and duty of woman, equally with man, to promote every righteous cause, by every righteous means; and especially in regard to the great subjects of morals and religion, it is self-evidently her right to participate with her brother in teaching them, both in private and in public, by writing and by speaking, by any instrumentalities proper to be used, and in any assemblies proper to be held; and this being a self evident truth, growing out of the divinely implanted principles of human nature, any custom or authority adverse to it, whether modern or wearing the hoary sanction of antiquity, is to be regarded as self-evident falsehood, and at war with the interests of mankind.

## Declaration of Sentiments

When, in the course of human events, it becomes necessary for one portion of the family of man to assume among the people of the earth a position different from that which they have hitherto occupied, but one to which the laws of nature and of nature's God entitle them, a decent respect to the opinions of mankind requires that they should declare the causes that impel them to such a course.

We hold these truths to be self-evident; that all men and women are created equal; that they are endowed by their Creator with certain inalienable rights; that among these are life, liberty, and the pursuit of happiness; that to secure these rights governments are instituted, deriving their just powers from the consent of the governed. Whenever any form of government becomes destructive of these ends, it is the right of those who suffer from it to refuse allegiance to it, and to insist upon the institution of a new government, laying its foundation on such principles, and organizing its powers in such form, as to them shall seem most likely to effect their safety and happiness. Prudence, indeed, will dictate that governments long established should not be changed for light and transient causes; and, accordingly, all experience hath shown that mankind are more disposed to suffer, while evils are sufferable, than to right themselves by abolishing the forms to which they were accustomed. But when a long train of abuses and usurpations, pursuing invariably the same object, evinces a design to reduce them under absolute despotism, it is their duty to throw off such government, and to provide new guards for their future security. Such has been the patient sufferance of the women under this government, and such is now the necessity which constrains them to demand the equal station to which they are entitled.

The history of mankind is a history of repeated injuries and usurpations on the part of man toward woman, having in direct object the establishment of an absolute tyranny over her. To prove this, let facts be submitted to a candid world.

He has never permitted her to exercise her inalienable right to the elective franchise.

He has compelled her to submit to laws, in the formation of which she had no voice.

He has withheld from her rights which are given to the most ignorant and degraded men—both natives and foreigners.

Having deprived her of this first right as a citizen, the elective franchise, thereby leaving her without representation in the halls of legislation, he has oppressed her on all sides.

He has made her, if married, in the eye of the law, civilly dead.

He has taken from her all right in property, even to the wages she earns.

He has made her morally, an irresponsible being, as she can commit many crimes with impunity, provided they be done in the presence of her husband. In the covenant of marriage, she is compelled to promise obedience to her husband, he becoming, to all intents and purposes, her master—the law giving him power to deprive her of her liberty, and to administer chastisement.

He has so framed the laws of divorce, as to what shall be the proper causes of divorce, in case of separation, to whom the guardianship of the children shall be given; as to be wholly regardless of the happiness of the women—the law, in all cases, going upon a false supposition of the supremacy of man, and giving all power into his hands.

After depriving her of all rights as a married woman, if single and the owner of property, he has taxed her to support a government which recognizes her only when her property can be made profitable to it.

He has monopolized nearly all the profitable employments, and from those she is permitted to follow, she receives but a scanty remuneration.

He closes against her all the avenues to wealth and distinction, which he considers most honorable to himself. As a teacher of theology, medicine, or law, she is not known.

He has denied her the facilities for obtaining a thorough education—all colleges being closed against her.

He allows her in church, as well as State, but a subordinate position, claiming Apostolic authority for her exclusion from the ministry, and, with some exceptions, from any public participation in the affairs of the Church.

He has created a false public sentiment by giving to the world a different code of morals for men and women, by which moral delinquencies which exclude women from society, are not only tolerated but deemed of little account in man.

He has usurped the prerogative of Jehovah himself, claiming it as his right to assign for her a sphere of action, when that belongs to her conscience and her God.

He has endeavored, in every way that he could to destroy her confidence in her own powers, to lessen her self-respect, and to make her willing to lead a dependent and abject life.

Now, in view of this entire disfranchisement of one-half the people of this country, their social and religious degradation, in view of the unjust laws above mentioned, and because women do feel themselves aggrieved, oppressed, and fraudulently deprived of their most sacred rights, we insist that they have immediate admission to all the rights and privileges which belong to them as citizens of these United States.

In entering upon the great work before us, we anticipate no small amount of misconception, misrepresentation, and ridicule; but we shall use every instrumentality within our power to effect our object. We shall employ agents, circulate tracts, petition the State and national Legislatures, and endeavor to enlist the pulpit and the press in our behalf. We hope this Convention will be followed by a series of Conventions, embracing every part of the country.

Firmly relying upon the final triumph of the Right and the True, we do this day affix our signatures to this declaration.

The youngest man to serve as a Tennessee state senator when he was elected to office at the age of 22, Harry T. Burn is best remembered for changing his mind at the last minute and voting in favor of women's suffrage.

A constitutional amendment had been proposed in 1878, but it got rejected. However, in 1919, Congress passed the measure and sent it to the states. The last necessary state for ratification (the 36th state) was Tennessee, a key battleground state for ratification of the amendment.

The approval of the Nineteenth Amendment was not a foregone conclusion in the state of Tennessee. A deciding vote was cast by state legislator Harry Burn (1895–1977) from McMinn County. He knew that most of his constituents did not approve of women's suffrage. He had earlier indicated that he would vote against the measure. As he waited to cast his vote, he read a letter from his mother that said, "Don't forget to be a good boy and help out Mrs. Catt." Burn read the letter and gained resolve. After his vote for ratification, he had to jump out a window from the legislative building to avoid physical attacks from some of his colleagues.

He later stated: "I appreciate the fact that an opportunity seldom comes to a mortal man to free seventeen million women from political slavery … and I knew that a mother's advice is always safest for a boy to follow, and my mother wanted me to vote for ratification."

The Nineteenth Amendment should have happened sooner, but it was the crowning achievement of many brave and committed suffragists from Susan B. Anthony (1820–1906) to Alice Paul (1885–1977).

# Twenty-second Amendment

### Section 1

No person shall be elected to the office of the President more than twice, and no person who has held the office of President, or acted as President, for more than two years of a term to which some other person was elected President shall be elected to the office of President more than once. But this Article shall not apply to any person holding the office of President when this Article was proposed by Congress, and shall not prevent any person who may be holding the office of President, or acting as President, during the term within which this Article becomes operative from holding the office of President or acting as President during the remainder of such term.

### Section 2

This article shall be inoperative unless it shall have been ratified as an amendment to the Constitution by the legislatures of three-fourths of the several States within seven years from the date of its submission to the States by the Congress.

The Twenty-second Amendment was largely passed in response to one dominant political figure in American history—Franklin Delano Roosevelt. Though crippled by polio, Roosevelt was beloved by millions of Americans. Many believed that his economic New Deal policies had lifted the country out of the Great Depression, and they supported him at the polls.

Some previous presidents had contemplated running for a third term, but all two-term presidents had followed the lead of George Washington (1732–1799), who could easily have won a third term. However, FDR was different; he actually won four presidential elections.

FDR was a Democrat, so the bulk of the support for a constitutional amendment limiting the terms of the president came from Republicans. For example, the measure passed the House 285–121. Of the 285 votes, more than 240 votes came from Republicans.

Through the years, prominent members of Congress have introduced measures calling for the repeal of the Twenty-second Amendment.

# Twenty-fourth Amendment

## Section 1

The right of citizens of the United States to vote in any primary or other election for President or Vice President, for electors for President or Vice President, or for Senator or Representative in Congress, shall not be denied or abridged by the United States or any State by reason of failure to pay poll tax or other tax.

## Section 2

The Congress shall have power to enforce this article by appropriate legislation.

One of the more insidious ways to keep African Americans from voting was through the use of poll taxes. It also was used to keep some poor whites from voting. The U.S. Supreme Court had rejected a constitutional challenge to poll taxes in the case *Breedlove v. Suttles* (1937).

The Twenty-fourth Amendment, which was ratified in January 1964, ended poll taxes for federal political races. Later that year, the U.S. Supreme Court ruled in *Harper v. Virginia Board of Elections* (1964) that poll taxes for any political race violate the Equal Protection Clause of the Fourteenth Amendment.

## Section 1

The right of citizens of the United States, who are eighteen years of age or older, to vote shall not be denied or abridged by the United States or by any State on account of age.

## Section 2

The Congress shall have power to enforce this article by appropriate legislation.

# Twenty-sixth Amendment

Section 2 of the Fourteenth Amendment—a provision passed to deal in the wake of the Civil War—protected the right to vote for the "male inhabitants of [each] state, being twenty-one years of age, and citizens of the United States." Thus, the standard voting rights age for persons nationally was 21 years of age.

Though the years, various states had lowered the voting age to 18. A prevailing sentiment was that if a person was old enough to go overseas and die for his country at age 18, he or she ought to have the right to vote. The Voting Rights Act Amendment of 1970 enabled states to lower the voting age to 18 in both national and state elections.

One of the most popular presidents in American history, Franklin D. Roosevelt won the presidency four times, passing away during his fourth term. It is because of him that we now have an amendment that limits politicians to no more than two terms as U.S. president.

However, the U.S. Supreme Court ruled in Oregon v. Mitchell (1970) that Congress had the power to change the voting age for national elections (elections for federal office) but did not have the power to change the voting age for local or state elections—that power resided in the states under Article I, Section 4 of the Constitution. The Supreme Court was very sharply divided on this question. Four justices ruled that Congress could limit the voting age in both federal and state elections. Four justices ruled that Congress could not limit the voting age in either federal or state elections. Justice Hugo Black's (1886–1971) sole opinion, then, became the deciding vote for the Court. Black reasoned that Congress did have the power to lower the voting age in national elections but not in state or local elections.

|| *A prevailing sentiment was that if a person was old enough to go overseas and die for his country at age 18, he or she ought to have the right to vote.* ||

The decision in *Oregon v. Mitchell* was quite unpopular and was met with swift reaction in the form of the Twenty-sixth Amendment.

# Twenty-seventh Amendment

No law varying the compensation for the services of the Senators and Representatives, shall take effect, until an election of Representatives shall have intervened.

The Twenty-seventh Amendment has the strangest history of any constitutional amendment. Ratified in 1992, it also is the most recent amendment. James Madison (1751–1836) originally had included this provision limiting congressional pay raises before the voters had a chance to vote on them in his original submissions. The measure was one of the 12 amendments sent to the U.S. Senate for approval.

However, for some reason, this provision never made it out of the Senate. We don't know why because the Senate did not keep notes of the proceedings. It lay dormant and out of existence.

Along came college student Gregory Watson, then a college sophomore at the University of Texas. "I'll never forget this as long as I live," Watson told National Public Radio (NPR) in 2017. "I pull out a book that has within it a chapter of amendments that Congress has sent to the state legislatures, but which not enough state legislatures approved in order to become part of the Constitution. And this one just jumped right out at me." Watson wrote in a paper for class that since there was no time limit on Madison's original amendment, it could still be submitted to the states for ratification. Watson received a "C" grade for the paper.

However, that paper and his research inspired Watson to do something dramatic—for 10 years, he advocated for what became the Twenty-seventh Amendment. As NPR wrote in a 2017 story on Watson and his amendment, "it's a heartening reminder of the power of individuals to make real change."

And, yes, years later, Watson's professor says that he should have received an "A" grade. His former professor, Shannon Waite, said: "Goodness, he certainly proved he knew how to work the Constitution and what it meant and how to be politically active. So, yes, I think he deserves an A after that effort—A-plus!"

# Continuing Constitutional Controversies

The U.S. Constitution remains the longest-standing constitution in the world and a document that has helped take a fledging motley crew of a country into the world's premier superpower. This may be due in no small measure to the genius of the Founding Fathers and their design of a government rooted in the principles of federalism, separation of powers, and checks and balances—those key structural protections for liberty—but also it is the Constitution's jealous protection of individual rights that has stood the test of time.

The Constitution continues to be sorely tested in modern society, as different emergency-like circumstances arise. A recent example was the pandemic known as COVID-19 that spread across the globe, killing millions upon millions of people.

The pandemic caused by the pervasive spread of COVID-19, a disease caused by a type of coronavirus, placed significant pressures on government officials to act quickly to try to save lives or slow the spread of the virus. Many officials responded with significant restrictions in the form of emergency stay-at-home orders, executive orders closing all but "essential" businesses, and bans on public gatherings—often of more than 10 people.

Such measures received pushback from church parishioners who wanted to worship together, business owners who wanted to reopen to avoid economic collapse, and persons who wanted to be able to assemble together either for communal, protesting, or other purposes. Chatter on Facebook and other forms of social media subsequently degenerated into a veritable hodgepodge of the political blame game, inspired debates over federalism and the proper allocation of power between federal and state governments, and presented people with a dizzying array of quite different medical information and numbers.

|| *The question arises whether the exigencies of the COVID-19 pandemic justify direct restrictions on fundamental rights.* ||

The question arises whether the exigencies of the COVID-19 pandemic justify direct restrictions on fundamental rights. As Justice Robert Jackson (1892–1954) famously warned in *Terminiello v. Chicago* (1949)—albeit in dissent—"There is danger that, if the Court does not temper its doctrinaire logic with a little practical wisdom, it will convert the constitutional Bill of Rights into a suicide pact."

More to the point on health measures, the U.S. Supreme Court had rejected a challenge to a state vaccination law by a pastor named Peter Henning Jacobson more than 100 years ago. "There are manifold restraints to which every person is necessarily subject for the common good," wrote Justice John Marshall Harlan I (1877–1911), the so-called "Great Dissenter," in *Jacobson v. Massachusetts* (1905). In this case, the police powers of Massachusetts trumped the pastor's individual right for an exemption. However, that case was decided back in 1905, long before many important provisions in the Bill of Rights were given significant attention by the Court.

Ultimately, many of these disputes have ended in the current U.S. Supreme Court—a Court whose composition changed with the replacement of the liberal icon Justice Ruth Bader Ginsburg (1933–2020) with Justice Amy Coney Barrett (1972–). The Court invalidated certain restrictions on religious gatherings as violative of the Free Exercise Clause of the First Amendment. In the memorable words of Justice Neil Gorsuch (1967–), a wordsmith in the tradition of the great Justice Robert Jackson, "Even if the Constitution has taken a holiday during this pandemic, it cannot become a sabbatical."

Reasonable minds can differ on the Supreme Court when it comes to carefully calibrating the balance between public order and safety on the one hand and individual liberties on the other.

Consider the approaches of Justices Neil Gorsuch and Elena Kagan (1960–)—both Harvard-trained lawyers with impeccable legal credentials.

Justice Gorsuch:

No doubt, California will argue on remand, as it has before, that its prohibitions are merely temporary because vaccinations are underway. But the State's "temporary" ban on indoor worship has been in place since

August 2020, and applied routinely since March. California no longer asks its movie studios, malls, and manicurists to wait. And one could be forgiven for doubting its asserted timeline. Government actors have been moving the goalposts on pandemic-related sacrifices for months, adopting new benchmarks that always seem to put restoration of liberty just around the corner. As this crisis enters its second year—and hovers over a second Lent, a second Passover, and a second Ramadan—it is too late for the State to defend extreme measures with claims of temporary exigency, if it ever could. Drafting narrowly tailored regulations can be difficult. But if Hollywood may host a studio audience or film a singing competition while not a single soul may enter California's churches, synagogues, and mosques, something has gone seriously awry.

Justice Kagan:

Justices of this Court are not scientists. Nor do we know much about public health policy. Yet today the Court displaces the judgments of experts about how to respond to a raging pandemic. The Court orders California to weaken its restrictions on public gatherings by making a special exception for worship services. The majority does so even

Millions of Americans felt that the restrictions on attending public and private gatherings imposed by state and local governments because of the COVID-19 pandemic violated their constitutional rights to freedom of assembly.

though the State's policies treat worship just as favorably as secular activities (including political assemblies) that, according to medical evidence, pose the same risk of COVID transmission. Under the Court's injunction, the State must instead treat worship services like secular activities that pose a much lesser danger. That mandate defies our caselaw, exceeds our judicial role, and risks worsening the pandemic.

The differing approaches over how to deal with COVID-19 are but one of many constitutional controversies lying ahead. In the near future, the U.S. Supreme Court must consider a Mississippi law that imposes additional restrictions on the right to abortion, the validity of new federal and state gun legislation and whether it survives various Second Amendment challenges; the validity of university measures designed to increase diversity with the use of race as a key factor, the power of local governments vis-à-vis state governments; additional challenges to whether the lethal injection mode of execution comports with the Constitution; whether Fourth Amendment jurisprudence should continue with the third-party doctrine; and the proper division of authority between Congress and the president over how to deal with national security threats that might call for a declaration of war.

New constitutional crises will emerge. It is inevitable in a world beset with conflict, religious wars, differing viewpoints and perspectives, and uncertain times. But the U.S. Constitution has stood as a steady bulwark that still exists in times of stability and fragility.

Yes, the Constitution was conceived in original sin, as the Founding Fathers did not have the political strength or absolute moral certitude to end slavery. However, they did create a process that has led to significant changes, with the Thirteenth Amendment ending slavery, the Nineteenth Amendment giving women the right to vote, and the Twenty-fourth Amendment ending noxious poll taxes that limited African American voting power.

Congress passed the Civil Rights Act of 1964, the Voting Rights Act of 1965, and the Fair Housing Act of 1968—major policy objectives of the Civil Rights Movement. The U.S. Supreme Court invalidated bans on interracial marriage in 1967 and gay marriage in 2015. Presidents have ended slavery and segregation in the armed forces with executive orders. There is also a chance that the leaders of the country will remember and revere the words of the Preamble to the Constitution and "establish Justice, insure domestic Tranquility, provide for the common defence, promote the general Welfare, and secure the Blessings of Liberty to ourselves and our Posterity."

*It is the Constitution and our societal application of it that distinguish the United States most from other countries around the globe, but we must appreciate it and revere it.*

The late, great Al Knight once wrote of the Constitution and the legal system it established: "When all that we have known and done are buried beneath the debris of time, what may be remembered most about us is our legal system. Nothing like it has ever been seen before on this planet so far as we know. It is distinguished above all else, by its breathtaking generosity to the individual."

It is the Constitution and our societal application of it that distinguish the United States most from other countries around the globe, but we must appreciate it and revere it. Another late, great writer on the Constitution, Nat Hentoff (1925–2017), once wrote that "unless more Americans know the Constitution and live the Bill of Rights, the future of the nation as a strongly functioning constitutional democracy will be at risk."

Challenges will arise, emergencies will surface again, and, as John P. Frank (1917–2002) warned back in 1958, "the passions of any given moment are such that danger is always present and always seems clear."

However, the U.S. Constitution provides us with a solid foundation. It provides the American experiment with the moorings to move forward as that shining city on the hill, as the beacon of light in an often very dark world.

# THE CONSTITUTION
## of the United States

We the People of the United States, in Order to form a more perfect Union, establish Justice, insure domestic Tranquility, provide for the common defence, promote the general Welfare, and secure the Blessings of Liberty to ourselves and our Posterity, do ordain and establish this Constitution for the United States of America.

## Article. I.

### SECTION. 1.

All legislative Powers herein granted shall be vested in a Congress of the United States, which shall consist of a Senate and House of Representatives.

### SECTION. 2.

The House of Representatives shall be composed of Members chosen every second Year by the People of the several States, and the Electors in each State shall have the Qualifications requisite for Electors of the most numerous Branch of the State Legislature.

No Person shall be a Representative who shall not have attained to the Age of twenty five Years, and been seven Years a Citizen of the United States, and who shall not, when elected, be an Inhabitant of that State in which he shall be chosen.

[Representatives and direct Taxes shall be apportioned among the several States which may be included within this Union, according to their respective Numbers, which shall be determined by adding to the whole Number of free Persons, including those bound to Service for a Term of Years, and excluding Indians not taxed, three fifths of all other Persons.]* The actual Enumeration shall be made within three Years after the first Meeting of the Congress of the United States, and within every subsequent Term of ten Years, in such Manner as they shall by Law direct. The Number of Representatives shall not exceed one for every thirty Thousand, but each State shall have at Least one Representative; and until such enumeration shall be made, the State of New Hampshire shall be entitled to chuse three, Massachusetts eight, Rhode-Island and Providence Plantations one, Connecticut five, New-York six, New Jersey four, Pennsylvania eight, Delaware one, Maryland six, Virginia ten, North Carolina five, South Carolina five, and Georgia three.

When vacancies happen in the Representation from any State, the Executive Authority thereof shall issue Writs of Election to fill such Vacancies.

The House of Representatives shall chuse their Speaker and other Officers; and shall have the sole Power of Impeachment.

### SECTION. 3.

The Senate of the United States shall be composed of two Senators from each State, [chosen by the Legislature thereof,]* for six Years; and each Senator shall have one Vote.

Immediately after they shall be assembled in Consequence of the first Election, they shall be divided as equally as may be into three Classes. The Seats of the Senators of the first Class shall be vacated at the Expiration of the second Year, of the second Class at the Expiration of the fourth Year, and of the third Class at the Expiration of the sixth Year, so that one third may be chosen every second Year; [and if Vacancies happen by Resignation, or otherwise, during the Recess of the Legislature of any State, the Executive thereof may make temporary Appointments until the next Meeting of the Legislature, which shall then fill such Vacancies.]*

No Person shall be a Senator who shall not have attained to the Age of thirty Years, and been nine Years a Citizen of the United States, and who shall not, when elected, be an Inhabitant of that State for which he shall be chosen.

The Vice President of the United States shall be President of the Senate, but shall have no Vote, unless they be equally divided.

The Senate shall chuse their other Officers, and also a President pro tempore, in the Absence of the Vice President, or when he shall exercise the Office of President of the United States.

The Senate shall have the sole Power to try all Impeachments. When sitting for that Purpose, they shall be on Oath or Affirmation. When the President of the United States is tried, the Chief Justice shall preside: And no Person shall be convicted without the Concurrence of two thirds of the Members present.

Judgment in Cases of Impeachment shall not extend further than to removal from Office, and disqualification to hold and enjoy any Office of honor, Trust or Profit under the United States: but the Party convicted shall nevertheless be liable and subject to Indictment, Trial, Judgment and Punishment, according to Law.

## SECTION. 4.

The Times, Places and Manner of holding Elections for Senators and Representatives, shall be prescribed in each State by the Legislature thereof; but the Congress may at any time by Law make or alter such Regulations, except as to the Places of chusing Senators.

The Congress shall assemble at least once in every Year, and such Meeting shall be [on the first Monday in December,]* unless they shall by Law appoint a different Day.

## SECTION. 5.

Each House shall be the Judge of the Elections, Returns and Qualifications of its own Members, and a Majority of each shall constitute a Quorum to do Business; but a smaller Number may adjourn from day to day, and may be authorized to compel the Attendance of absent Members, in such Manner, and under such Penalties as each House may provide.

Each House may determine the Rules of its Proceedings, punish its Members for disorderly Behaviour, and, with the Concurrence of two thirds, expel a Member.

Each House shall keep a Journal of its Proceedings, and from time to time publish the same, excepting such Parts as may in their Judgment require Secrecy; and the Yeas and Nays of the Members of either House on any question shall, at the Desire of one fifth of those Present, be entered on the Journal.

Neither House, during the Session of Congress, shall, without the Consent of the other, adjourn for more than three days, nor to any other Place than that in which the two Houses shall be sitting.

## SECTION. 6.

The Senators and Representatives shall receive a Compensation for their Services, to be ascertained by Law, and paid out of the Treasury of the United States. They shall in all Cases, except Treason, Felony and Breach of the Peace, be privileged from Arrest during their Attendance at the Session of their respective Houses, and in going to and returning from the same; and for any Speech or Debate in either House, they shall not be questioned in any other Place.

No Senator or Representative shall, during the Time for which he was elected, be appointed to any civil Office under the Authority of the United States, which shall have been created, or the Emoluments whereof shall have been encreased during such time; and no Person holding any Office under the United States, shall be a Member of either House during his Continuance in Office.

## SECTION. 7.

All Bills for raising Revenue shall originate in the House of Representatives; but the Senate may propose or concur with Amendments as on other Bills.

Every Bill which shall have passed the House of Representatives and the Senate, shall, before it become a Law, be presented to the President of the United States; If he approve he shall sign it, but if not he shall return it, with his Objections to that House in which it shall have originated, who shall enter the Objections at large on their Journal, and proceed to reconsider it. If after such Reconsideration two thirds of that House shall agree to pass the Bill, it shall be sent, together with the Objections, to the other House, by which it shall likewise be reconsidered, and if approved by two thirds of that House, it shall become a Law. But in all such Cases the Votes of both Houses shall be determined by Yeas and Nays, and the Names of the Persons voting for and against the Bill shall be entered on the Journal of each House respectively, If any Bill shall not be returned by the President within ten Days (Sundays excepted) after it shall have been presented to him, the Same shall be a Law, in like Manner as if he had signed it, unless the Congress by their Adjournament prevent its Return, in which Case it shall not be a Law.

Every Order, Resolution, or Vote to which the Concurrence of the Senate and House of Representatives may be necessary (except on a question of Adjournment) shall be presented to the President of the United States; and before the Same shall take Effect, shall be approved by him, or being disapproved by him, shall be repassed by two thirds of the Senate and House of Representatives, according to the Rules and Limitations prescribed in the Case of a Bill.

## SECTION. 8.

The Congress shall have Power To lay and collect Taxes, Duties, Imposts and Excises, to pay the Debts and provide for the common Defence and general Welfare of the United States; but all Duties, Imposts and Excises shall be uniform throughout the United States;

To borrow Money on the credit of the United States;

To regulate Commerce with foreign Nations, and among the several States, and with the Indian Tribes;

To establish an uniform Rule of Naturalization, and uniform Laws on the subject of Bankruptcies throughout the United States;

To coin Money, regulate the Value thereof, and of foreign Coin, and fix the Standard of Weights and Measures;

To provide for the Punishment of counterfeiting the Securities and current Coin of the United States;

To establish Post Offices and post Roads;
To promote the Progress of Science and useful Arts, by securing for limited Times to Authors and Inventors the exclusive Right to their respective Writings and Discoveries;

To constitute Tribunals inferior to the supreme Court;

To define and punish Piracies and Felonies committed on the high Seas, and Offenses against the Law of Nations;

To declare War, grant Letters of Marque and Reprisal, and make Rules concerning Captures on Land and Water;

To raise and support Armies, but no Appropriation of Money to that Use shall be for a longer Term than two Years;

To provide and maintain a Navy;

To make Rules for the Government and Regulation of the land and naval Forces;

To provide for calling forth the Militia to execute the Laws of the Union, suppress Insurrections and repel Invasions;

To provide for organizing, arming, and disciplining, the Militia, and for governing such Part of them as may be employed in the Service of the United States, reserving to the States respectively, the Appointment of the Officers, and the Authority of training the Militia according to the discipline prescribed by Congress;

To exercise exclusive Legislation in all Cases whatsoever, over such District (not exceeding ten Miles square) as may, by Cession of particular States, and the Acceptance of Congress, become the Seat of the Government of the United States, and to exercise like Authority over all Places purchased by the Consent of the Legislature of the State in which the Same shall be, for the Erection of Forts, Magazines, Arsenals, dock-Yards and other needful Buildings; -And

To make all Laws which shall be necessary and proper for carrying into Execution the foregoing Powers, and all other Powers vested by this Constitution in the Government of the United States, or in any Department or Officer thereof.

## SECTION. 9.

The Migration or Importation of such Persons as any of the States now existing shall think proper to admit, shall not be prohibited by the Congress prior to the Year one thousand eight hundred and eight, but a Tax or duty may be imposed on such Importation, not exceeding ten dollars for each Person.

The Privilege of the Writ of Habeas Corpus shall not be suspended, unless when in Cases of Rebellion or Invasion the public Safety may require it.

No Bill of Attainder or ex post facto Law shall be passed.

[No Capitation, or other direct, Tax shall be laid, unless in Proportion to the Census or Enumeration herein before directed to be taken.]*

No Tax or Duty shall be laid on Articles exported from any State.

No Preference shall be given by any Regulation of Commerce or Revenue to the Ports of one State over those of another: nor shall Vessels bound to, or from, one State, be obliged to enter, clear, or pay Duties in another.

No Money shall be drawn from the Treasury, but in Consequence of Appropriations made by Law; and a regular Statement and Account of the Receipts and Expenditures of all public Money shall be published from time to time.

No Title of Nobility shall be granted by the United States: And no Person holding any Office of Profit or Trust under them, shall, without the Consent of the Congress, accept of any present, Emolument, Office, or Title, of any kind whatever, from any King, Prince, or foreign State.

## SECTION. 10.

No State shall enter into any Treaty, Alliance, or Confederation; grant Letters of Marque and Reprisal; coin Money; emit Bills of Credit; make any Thing but gold and silver Coin a Tender in Payment of Debts; pass any Bill of Attainder, ex post facto Law, or Law impairing the Obligation of Contracts, or grant any Title of Nobility.

No State shall, without the Consent of the Congress, lay any Imposts or Duties on Imports or Exports, except what may be absolutely necessary for executing it's inspection Laws: and the net Produce of all Duties and Imposts, laid by any State on Imports or Exports, shall be for the Use of the Treasury of the United States; and all such Laws shall be subject to the Revision and Controul of the Congress.

No State shall, without the Consent of Congress, lay any Duty of Tonnage, keep Troops, or Ships of War in time of Peace, enter into any Agreement or Compact with another State, or with a foreign Power, or engage in War, unless actually invaded, or in such imminent Danger as will not admit of delay.

# Article. II.

## SECTION. 1.

The executive Power shall be vested in a President of the United States of America. He shall hold his Office during the Term of four Years, and, together with the Vice President, chosen for the same Term, be elected, as follows:

Each State shall appoint, in such Manner as the Legislature thereof may direct, a Number of Electors, equal to the whole Number of Senators and Representatives to which the State may be entitled in the Congress: but no Senator or Representative, or Person holding an Office of Trust or Profit under the United States, shall be appointed an Elector.

[The Electors shall meet in their respective States, and vote by Ballot for two Persons, of whom one at least shall not be an Inhabitant of the same State with themselves. And they shall make a List of all the Persons voted for, and of the Number of Votes for each; which List they shall sign and certify, and transmit sealed to the Seat of the Government of the United States, directed to the President of the Senate. The President of the Senate shall, in the Presence of the Senate and House of Representatives, open all the Certificates, and the Votes shall then be counted. The Person having the greatest Number of Votes shall be the President, if such Number be a Majority of the whole Number of Electors appointed; and if there be more than one who have such Majority, and have an equal Number of Votes, then the House of Representatives shall immediately chuse by Ballot one of them for President; and if no Person have a Majority, then from the five highest on the List the said House shall in like Manner chuse the President. But in chusing the President, the Votes shall be taken by States, the Representation from each State having one Vote; A quorum for this Purpose shall consist of a Member or Members from two thirds of the States, and a Majority of all the States shall be necessary to a Choice. In every Case, after the Choice of the President, the Person having the greatest Number of Votes of the Electors shall be the Vice President. But if there should remain two or more who have equal Votes, the Senate shall chuse from them by Ballot the Vice President.]*

The Congress may determine the Time of chusing the Electors, and the Day on which they shall give their Votes; which Day shall be the same throughout the United States.

No Person except a natural born Citizen, or a Citizen of the United States, at the time of the Adoption of this Constitution, shall be eligible to the Office of President; neither shall any person be eligible to that Office who shall not have attained to the Age of thirty five Years, and been fourteen Years a Resident within the United States.

[In Case of the Removal of the President from Office, or of his Death, Resignation, or Inability to discharge the Powers and Duties of the said Office, the Same shall devolve on the Vice President, and the Congress may by Law provide for the Case of Removal, Death, Resignation or Inability, both of the President and Vice President, declaring what Officer shall then act as President, and such Officer shall act accordingly, until the Disability be removed, or a President shall be elected.]*

The President shall, at stated Times, receive for his Services, a Compensation, which shall neither be increased nor diminished during the Period for which he shall have been elected, and he shall not receive within that Period any other Emolument from the United States, or any of them.

Before he enter on the Execution of his Office, he shall take the following Oath or Affirmation:- "I do solemnly swear (or affirm) that I will faithfully execute the Office of President of the United States, and will to the best of my Ability, preserve, protect and defend the Constitution of the United States."

## SECTION. 2.

The President shall be Commander in Chief of the Army and Navy of the United States, and of the Militia of the several States, when called into the actual Service of the United States; he may require the Opinion, in writing, of the principal Officer in each of the executive Departments, upon any Subject relating to the Duties of their respective Offices, and he shall have Power to grant Reprieves and Pardons for Offenses against the United States, except in Cases of Impeachment.

He shall have Power, by and with the Advice and Consent of the Senate, to make Treaties, provided two thirds of the Senators present concur; and he shall nominate, and by and with the Advice and Consent of the Senate, shall appoint Ambassadors, other public Ministers and Consuls, Judges of the supreme Court, and all other Officers of the United States, whose Appointments are not herein otherwise provided for, and which shall be established by Law: but the Congress may by Law vest the Appointment of such inferior Officers, as they think proper, in the President alone, in the Courts of Law, or in the Heads of Departments.

The President shall have Power to fill up all Vacancies that may happen during the Recess of the Senate, by granting Commissions which shall expire at the End of their next Session.

## SECTION. 3.

He shall from time to time give to the Congress Information of the State of the Union, and recommend to their Consideration such Measures as he shall judge necessary and expedient; he may, on extraordinary Occasions, convene both Houses, or either of them, and in Case of Disagreement between them, with Respect to the Time of Adjournment, he may adjourn them to such Time as he shall think proper; he shall receive Ambassadors and other public Ministers; he shall take Care that the Laws be faithfully executed, and shall Commission all the Officers of the United States.

## SECTION. 4.

The President, Vice President and all civil Officers of the United States, shall be removed from Office on Impeachment for, and Conviction of, Treason, Bribery, or other high Crimes and Misdemeanors.

## Article. III.

### SECTION. 1.

The judicial Power of the United States, shall be vested in one supreme Court, and in such inferior Courts as the Congress may from time to time ordain and establish. The Judges, both of the supreme and inferior Courts, shall hold their Offices during good Behaviour, and shall at stated Times, receive for their Services, a Compensation, which shall not be diminished during their Continuance in Office.

### SECTION. 2.

The judicial Power shall extend to all Cases, in Law and Equity, arising under this Constitution, the Laws of the United States, and Treaties made, or which shall be made, under their Authority; - to all Cases affecting Ambassadors, other public Ministers and Consuls; - to all Cases of admiralty and maritime Jurisdiction; - to Controversies to which the United States shall be a Party; - to Controversies between two or more States; - [between a State and Citizens of another State;-]* between Citizens of different States, - between Citizens of the same State claiming Lands under Grants of different States, [and between a State, or the Citizens thereof;- and foreign States, Citizens or Subjects.]*

In all Cases affecting Ambassadors, other public Ministers and Consuls, and those in which a State shall be Party, the supreme Court shall have original Jurisdiction. In all the other Cases before mentioned, the supreme Court shall have appellate Jurisdiction, both as to Law and Fact, with such Exceptions, and under such Regulations as the Congress shall make.

The Trial of all Crimes, except in Cases of Impeachment; shall be by Jury; and such Trial shall be held in the State where the said Crimes shall have been committed; but when not committed within any State, the Trial shall be at such Place or Places as the Congress may by Law have directed.

### SECTION. 3.

Treason against the United States, shall consist only in levying War against them, or in adhering to their Enemies, giving them Aid and Comfort. No Person shall be convicted of Treason unless on the Testimony of two Witnesses to the same overt Act, or on Confession in open Court.

The Congress shall have Power to declare the Punishment of Treason, but no Attainder of Treason shall work Corruption of Blood, or Forfeiture except during the Life of the Person attainted.

# Article. IV.

## SECTION. 1.

Full Faith and Credit shall be given in each State to the public Acts, Records, and judicial Proceedings of every other State. And the Congress may by general Laws prescribe the Manner in which such Acts, Records and Proceedings shall be proved, and the Effect thereof.

## SECTION. 2.

The Citizens of each State shall be entitled to all Privileges and Immunities of Citizens in the several States.

A Person charged in any State with Treason, Felony, or other Crime, who shall flee from Justice, and be found in another State, shall on Demand of the executive Authority of the State from which he fled, be delivered up, to be removed to the State having Jurisdiction of the Crime.

[No Person held to Service or Labour in one State, under the Laws thereof, escaping into another, shall, in Consequence of any Law or Regulation therein, be discharged from such Service or Labour, but shall be delivered up on Claim of the Party to whom such Service or Labour may be due.]*

## SECTION. 3.

New States may be admitted by the Congress into this Union; but no new State shall be formed or erected within the Jurisdiction of any other State; nor any State be formed by the Junction of two or more States, or Parts of States, without the Consent of the Legislatures of the States concerned as well as of the Congress.

The Congress shall have Power to dispose of and make all needful Rules and Regulations respecting the Territory or other Property belonging to the United States; and nothing in this Constitution shall be so construed as to Prejudice any Claims of the United States, or of any particular State.

## SECTION. 4.

The United States shall guarantee to every State in this Union a Republican Form of Government, and shall protect each of them against Invasion; and on Application of the Legislature, or of the Executive (when the Legislature cannot be convened) against domestic Violence.

# Article. V.

The Congress, whenever two thirds of both Houses shall deem it necessary, shall propose Amendments to this Constitution, or, on the Application of the Legislatures of two thirds of the several States, shall call a Convention for proposing Amendments, which in either Case, shall be valid to all Intents and Purposes, as Part of this Constitution, when ratified by the Legislatures of three-fourths of the several States, or by Conventions in three fourths thereof, as the one or the other Mode of Ratification may be proposed by the Congress; Provided that no Amendment which may be made prior to the Year One thousand eight hundred and eight shall in any Manner affect the first and fourth Clauses in the Ninth Section of the first Article; and that no State, without its Consent, shall be deprived of its equal Suffrage in the Senate.

# Article. VI.

All Debts contracted and Engagements entered into, before the Adoption of this Constitution, shall be as valid against the United States under this Constitution, as under the Confederation.

This Constitution, and the Laws of the United States which shall be made in Pursuance thereof; and all Treaties made, or which shall be made, under the Authority of the United States, shall be the supreme Law of the Land; and the Judges in every State shall be bound thereby, any Thing in the Constitution or Laws of any State to the Contrary notwithstanding.

The Senators and Representatives before mentioned, and the Members of the several State Legislatures, and all executive and judicial Officers, both of the United States and of the several States, shall be bound by Oath or Affirmation, to support this Constitution; but no religious Test shall ever be required as a Qualification to any Office or public Trust under the United States.

# Article. VII.

The Ratification of the Conventions of nine States, shall be sufficient for the Establishment of this Constitution between the States so ratifying the Same.

Done in Convention by the Unanimous Consent of the States present the Seventeenth Day of September in the Year of our Lord one thousand seven hundred and Eighty seven and of the Independence of the United States of America the Twelfth In Witness whereof We have hereunto subscribed our Names,

Go. Washington--Presidt:
and deputy from Virginia

## NEW HAMPSHIRE

John Langdon
Nicholas Gilman

## MASSACHUSETTS

Nathaniel Gorham
Rufus King

## CONNECTICUT

Wm. Saml. Johnson
Roger Sherman

## NEW YORK

Alexander Hamilton

## NEW JERSEY

Wil: Livingston
David Brearley
Wm. Paterson
Jona: Dayton

## PENNSYLVANIA

B Franklin
Thomas Mifflin
Robt Morris
Geo. Clymer
Thos. FitzSimons
Jared Ingersoll
James Wilson
Gouv Morris

## DELAWARE

Geo: Read
Gunning Bedford jun
John Dickinson
Richard Bassett
Jaco: Broom

## MARYLAND

James McHenry
Dan of St. Thos. Jenifer
Danl Carroll

## VIRGINIA

John Blair-
James Madison Jr.

## NORTH CAROLINA

Wm. Blount
Richd. Dobbs Spaight
Hu Williamson

## SOUTH CAROLINA

J. Rutledge
Charles Cotesworth Pinckney
Charles Pinckney
Pierce Butler

## GEORGIA

William Few
Abr Baldwin

Attest William Jackson Secretary

In Convention Monday
September 17th, 1787.
Present
The States of
New Hampshire, Massachusetts, Connecticut, Mr. Hamilton from New York, New Jersey, Pennsylvania, Delaware, Maryland, Virginia, North Carolina, South Carolina and Georgia.

Resolved,
That the preceeding Constitution be laid before the United States in Congress assembled, and that it is the Opinion of this Convention, that it should afterwards be submitted to a Convention of Delegates, chosen in each State by the People thereof, under the Recommendation of its Legislature, for their Assent and Ratification; and that each Convention assenting to, and ratifying the Same, should give Notice thereof to the United States in Congress assembled. Resolved, That it is the Opinion of this Convention, that as soon as the Conventions of nine States shall have ratified this Constitution, the United States in Congress assembled should fix a Day on which Electors should be appointed by the States which shall have ratified the same, and a Day on which the Electors should assemble to vote for the President, and the Time and Place for commencing Proceedings under this Constitution.

That after such Publication the Electors should be appointed, and the Senators and Representatives elected: That the Electors should meet on the Day fixed for the Election of the President, and should transmit their Votes certified, signed, sealed and directed, as the Constitution requires, to the Secretary of the United States in Congress assembled, that the Senators and Representatives should convene at the Time and Place assigned; that the Senators should appoint a President of the Senate, for the sole Purpose of receiving, opening and counting the Votes for President; and, that after he shall be chosen, the Congress, together with the President, should, without Delay, proceed to execute this Constitution.

By the unanimous Order of the Convention

Go. Washington-Presidt:
W. JACKSON Secretary.

* Language in brackets has been changed by amendment.

# THE AMENDMENTS TO THE CONSTITUTION OF THE UNITED STATES AS RATIFIED BY THE STATES

## Preamble to the Bill of Rights

CONGRESS OF THE UNITED STATES
BEGUN AND HELD AT THE CITY OF NEW-YORK, ON
WEDNESDAY THE FOURTH OF MARCH,
ONE THOUSAND SEVEN HUNDRED AND EIGHTY NINE

THE Conventions of a number of the States, having at the time of their adopting the Constitution, expressed a desire, in order to prevent misconstruction or abuse of its powers, that further declaratory and restrictive clauses should be added: And as extending the ground of public confidence in the Government, will best ensure the beneficent ends of its institution.

RESOLVED by the Senate and House of Representatives of the United States of America, in Congress assembled, two thirds of both Houses concurring, that the following Articles be proposed to the Legislatures of the several States, as amendments to the Constitution of the United States, all, or any of which Articles, when ratified by three fourths of the said Legislatures, to be valid to all intents and purposes, as part of the said Constitution; viz.

ARTICLES in addition to, and Amendment of the Constitution of the United States of America, proposed by Congress, and ratified by the Legislatures of the several States, pursuant to the fifth Article of the original Constitution.

*(Note: The first 10 amendments to the Constitution were ratified December 15, 1791, and form what is known as the "Bill of Rights.")*

## Amendment I.

Congress shall make no law respecting an establishment of religion, or prohibiting the free exercise thereof; or abridging the freedom of speech, or of the press, or the right of the people peaceably to assemble, and to petition the Government for a redress of grievances.

## Amendment II.

A well regulated Militia, being necessary to the security of a free State, the right of the people to keep and bear Arms, shall not be infringed.

## Amendment III.

No Soldier shall, in time of peace be quartered in any house, without the consent of the Owner, nor in time of war, but in a manner to be prescribed by law.

## Amendment IV.

The right of the people to be secure in their persons, houses, papers, and effects, against unreasonable searches and seizures, shall not be violated, and no Warrants shall issue, but upon probable cause, supported by Oath or affirmation, and particularly describing the place to be searched, and the persons or things to be seized.

## Amendment V.

No person shall be held to answer for a capital, or otherwise infamous crime, unless on a presentment or indictment of a Grand Jury, except in cases arising in the land or naval forces, or in the Militia, when in actual service in time of War or public danger; nor shall any person be subject for the same offence to be twice put in jeopardy of life or limb; nor shall be compelled in any criminal case to be a witness against himself, nor be deprived of life, liberty, or property, without due process of law; nor shall private property be taken for public use, without just compensation.

# Amendment VI.

In all criminal prosecutions, the accused shall enjoy the right to a speedy and public trial, by an impartial jury of the State and district wherein the crime shall have been committed, which district shall have been previously ascertained by law, and to be informed of the nature and cause of the accusation; to be confronted with the witnesses against him; to have compulsory process for obtaining witnesses in his favor, and to have the Assistance of Counsel for his defence.

# Amendment VII.

In suits at common law, where the value in controversy shall exceed twenty dollars, the right of trial by jury shall be preserved, and no fact tried by a jury shall be otherwise re-examined in any Court of the United States, than according to the rules of the common law.

# Amendment VIII.

Excessive bail shall not be required, nor excessive fines imposed, nor cruel and unusual punishments inflicted.

# Amendment IX.

The enumeration in the Constitution, of certain rights, shall not be construed to deny or disparage others retained by the people.

# Amendment X.

The powers not delegated to the United States by the Constitution, nor prohibited by it to the States, are reserved to the States respectively, or to the people.

## AMENDMENTS 11-27

# Amendment XI.

Passed by Congress March 4, 1794. Ratified February 7, 1795.

*(Note: A portion of Article III, Section 2 of the Constitution was modified by the 11th Amendment.)*

The Judicial power of the United States shall not be construed to extend to any suit in law or equity, commenced or prosecuted against one of the United States by Citizens of another State, or by Citizens or Subjects of any Foreign State.

# Amendment XII.

Passed by Congress December 9, 1803. Ratified June 15, 1804.

*(Note: A portion of Article II, Section 1 of the Constitution was changed by the 12th Amendment.)*

The Electors shall meet in their respective states, and vote by ballot for President and Vice-President, one of whom, at least, shall not be an inhabitant of the same state with themselves; they shall name in their ballots the person voted for as President, and in distinct ballots the person voted for as Vice-President, and they shall make distinct lists of all persons voted for as President, and of all persons voted for as Vice-President, and of the number of votes for each, which lists they shall sign and certify, and transmit sealed to the seat of the government of the United States, directed to the President of the Senate;-the President of the Senate shall, in the presence of the Senate and House of Representatives, open all the certificates and the votes shall then be counted;-The person having the greatest number of votes for President, shall be the President, if such number be a majority of the whole number of Electors appointed; and if no person have such majority, then from the persons having the highest numbers not exceeding three on the list of those voted for as President, the House of Representatives shall choose immediately, by ballot, the President. But in choosing the President, the votes shall be taken by states, the representation from each state having one vote; a quorum for this purpose shall consist of a member or members from two-thirds of the states, and a majority of all the states shall be necessary to a choice. [And if the House of Representatives shall not choose a President whenever the right of choice shall devolve upon them, before the fourth day of March next following, then the Vice-President shall act as President, as in case of the death or other constitutional disability of the President.-]* The person having the greatest number of votes as Vice-President, shall be the Vice-President, if such number be a majority of the whole number of Electors appointed, and if no person have a majority, then from the two highest numbers on the list, the Senate shall choose the Vice-President; a quorum for the purpose shall consist of two-thirds of the whole number of Senators, and a majority of the whole number shall be necessary to a choice. But no person constitutionally ineligible to the office of President shall be eligible to that of Vice-President of the United States.

*Superseded by Section 3 of the 20th Amendment.

# *Amendment XIII.*

Passed by Congress January 31, 1865. Ratified December 6, 1865.

*(Note: A portion of Article IV, Section 2 of the Constitution was changed by the 13th Amendment.)*

## SECTION 1.

Neither slavery nor involuntary servitude, except as a punishment for crime whereof the party shall have been duly convicted, shall exist within the United States, or any place subject to their jurisdiction.

## SECTION 2.

Congress shall have power to enforce this article by appropriate legislation.

# *Amendment XIV.*

Passed by Congress June 13, 1866. Ratified July 9, 1868.

*(Note: Article I, Section 2 of the Constitution was modified by Section 2 of the 14th Amendment.)*

## SECTION 1.

All persons born or naturalized in the United States and subject to the jurisdiction thereof, are citizens of the United States and of the State wherein they reside. No State shall make or enforce any law which shall abridge the privileges or immunities of citizens of the United States; nor shall any State deprive any person of life, liberty, or property, without due process of law; nor deny to any person within its jurisdiction the equal protection of the laws.

## SECTION 2.

Representatives shall be apportioned among the several States according to their respective numbers, counting the whole number of persons in each State, excluding Indians not taxed. But when the right to vote at any election for the choice of electors for President and Vice President of the United States, Representatives in Congress, the Executive and Judicial officers of a State, or the members of the Legislature thereof, is denied to any of the male inhabitants of such State, [being twenty-one years of age,]* and citizens of the United States, or in any way abridged, except for participation in rebellion, or other crime, the basis of representation therein shall be reduced in the proportion which the number of such male citizens shall bear to the whole number of male citizens twenty-one years of age in such State.

## SECTION 3.

No person shall be a Senator or Representative in Congress, or elector of President and Vice President, or hold any office, civil or military, under the United States, or under any State, who, having previously taken an oath, as a member of Congress, or as an officer of the United States, or as a member of any State legislature, or as an executive or judicial officer of any State, to support the Constitution of the United States, shall have engaged in insurrection or rebellion against the same, or given aid or comfort to the enemies thereof. But Congress may by a vote of two-thirds of each House, remove such disability.

## SECTION 4.

The validity of the public debt of the United States, authorized by law, including debts incurred for payment of pensions and bounties for services in suppressing insurrection or rebellion, shall not be questioned. But neither the United States nor any State shall assume or pay any debt or obligation incurred in aid of insurrection or rebellion against the United States, or any claim for the loss or emancipation of any slave; but all such debts, obligations and claims shall be held illegal and void.

## SECTION 5.

The Congress shall have the power to enforce, by appropriate legislation, the provisions of this article.

*Changed by Section 1 of the 26th Amendment.

## Amendment XV.

Passed by Congress February 26, 1869. Ratified February 3, 1870.

### SECTION 1.

The right of citizens of the United States to vote shall not be denied or abridged by the United States or by any State on account of race, color, or previous condition of servitude.

### SECTION 2.

The Congress shall have the power to enforce this article by appropriate legislation.

## Amendment XVI.

Passed by Congress July 2, 1909. Ratified February 3, 1913.

*(Note: Article I, Section 9 of the Constitution was modified by the 16th Amendment.)*

The Congress shall have power to lay and collect taxes on incomes, from whatever source derived, without apportionment among the several States, and without regard to any census or enumeration.

## Amendment XVII.

Passed by Congress May 13, 1912. Ratified April 8, 1913.

*(Note: Article I, Section 3 of the Constitution was modified by the 17th Amendment.)*

The Senate of the United States shall be composed of two Senators from each State, elected by the people thereof, for six years; and each Senator shall have one vote. The electors in each State shall have the qualifications requisite for electors of the most numerous branch of the State legislatures.

When vacancies happen in the representation of any State in the Senate, the executive authority of such State shall issue writs of election to fill such vacancies: Provided, That the legislature of any State may empower the executive thereof to make temporary appointments until the people fill the vacancies by election as the legislature may direct.

This amendment shall not be so construed as to affect the election or term of any Senator chosen before it becomes valid as part of the Constitution.

## Amendment XVIII.

Passed by Congress December 18, 1917. Ratified January 16, 1919. Repealed by the 21st Amendment, December 5, 1933.

### SECTION 1.

After one year from the ratification of this article the manufacture, sale, or transportation of intoxicating liquors within, the importation thereof into, or the exportation thereof from the United States and all territory subject to the jurisdiction thereof for beverage purposes is hereby prohibited.

### SECTION 2.

The Congress and the several States shall have concurrent power to enforce this article by appropriate legislation.

### SECTION 3.

This article shall be inoperative unless it shall have been ratified as an amendment to the Constitution by the legislatures of the several States, as provided in the Constitution, within seven years from the date of the submission hereof to the States by the Congress.

## Amendment XIX.

Passed by Congress June 4, 1919. Ratified August 18, 1920.

The right of citizens of the United States to vote shall not be denied or abridged by the United States or by any State on account of sex.

Congress shall have power to enforce this article by appropriate legislation.

# Amendment XX.

Passed by Congress March 2, 1932. Ratified January 23, 1933.

*(Note: Article I, Section 4 of the Constitution was modified by Section 2 of this Amendment. In addition, a portion of the 12th Amendment was superseded by Section 3.)*

## SECTION 1.

The terms of the President and the Vice President shall end at noon on the 20th day of January, and the terms of Senators and Representatives at noon on the 3d day of January, of the years in which such terms would have ended if this article had not been ratified; and the terms of their successors shall then begin.

## SECTION 2.

The Congress shall assemble at least once in every year, and such meeting shall begin at noon on the 3d day of January, unless they shall by law appoint a different day.

## SECTION 3.

If, at the time fixed for the beginning of the term of the President, the President elect shall have died, the Vice President elect shall become President. If a President shall not have been chosen before the time fixed for the beginning of his term, or if the President elect shall have failed to qualify, then the Vice President elect shall act as President until a President shall have qualified; and the Congress may by law provide for the case wherein neither a President elect nor a Vice President shall have qualified, declaring who shall then act as President, or the manner in which one who is to act shall be selected, and such person shall act accordingly until a President or Vice President shall have qualified.

## SECTION 4.

The Congress may by law provide for the case of the death of any of the persons from whom the House of Representatives may choose a President whenever the right of choice shall have devolved upon them, and for the case of the death of any of the persons from whom the Senate may choose a Vice President whenever the right of choice shall have devolved upon them.

## SECTION 5.

Sections 1 and 2 shall take effect on the 15th day of October following the ratification of this article.

## SECTION 6.

This article shall be inoperative unless it shall have been ratified as an amendment to the Constitution by the legislatures of three-fourths of the several States within seven years from the date of its submission.

# Amendment XXI.

Passed by Congress February 20, 1933. Ratified December 5, 1933.

## SECTION 1.

The eighteenth article of amendment to the Constitution of the United States is hereby repealed.

## SECTION 2.

The transportation or importation into any State, Territory, or possession of the United States for delivery or use therein of intoxicating liquors, in violation of the laws thereof, is hereby prohibited.

## SECTION 3.

This article shall be inoperative unless it shall have been ratified as an amendment to the Constitution by conventions in the several States, as provided in the Constitution, within seven years from the date of the submission hereof to the States by the Congress.

# Amendment XXII.

Passed by Congress March 21, 1947. Ratified February 27, 1951.

## SECTION 1.

No person shall be elected to the office of the President more than twice, and no person who has held the office of President, or acted as President, for more than two years of a term to which some other person was elected President shall be elected to the office of President more than once. But this Article shall not apply to any person holding the office of President when this Article was proposed by Congress, and shall not prevent any person who may be holding the office of President, or acting as President, during the term within which this Article becomes operative from holding the office of President or acting as President during the remainder of such term.

## SECTION 2.

This article shall be inoperative unless it shall have been ratified as an amendment to the Constitution by the legislatures of three-fourths of the several States within seven years from the date of its submission to the States by the Congress.

# Amendment XXIII.

Passed by Congress June 16, 1960. Ratified March 29, 1961.

## SECTION 1.

The District constituting the seat of Government of the United States shall appoint in such manner as Congress may direct:

A number of electors of President and Vice President equal to the whole number of Senators and Representatives in Congress to which the District would be entitled if it were a State, but in no event more than the least populous State; they shall be in addition to those appointed by the States, but they shall be considered, for the purposes of the election of President and Vice President, to be electors appointed by a State; and they shall meet in the District and perform such duties as provided by the twelfth article of amendment.

## SECTION 2.

The Congress shall have power to enforce this article by appropriate legislation.

# Amendment XXIV.

Passed by Congress August 27, 1962. Ratified January 23, 1964.

## SECTION 1.

The right of citizens of the United States to vote in any primary or other election for President or Vice President, for electors for President or Vice President, or for Senator or Representative in Congress, shall not be denied or abridged by the United States or any State by reason of failure to pay poll tax or other tax.

## SECTION 2.

The Congress shall have power to enforce this article by appropriate legislation.

# Amendment XXV.

Passed by Congress July 6, 1965. Ratified February 10, 1967.
*(Note: Article II, Section 1 of the Constitution was modified by the 25th Amendment.)*

## SECTION 1.

In case of the removal of the President from office or of his death or resignation, the Vice President shall become President.

## SECTION 2.

Whenever there is a vacancy in the office of the Vice President, the President shall nominate a Vice President who shall take office upon confirmation by a majority vote of both Houses of Congress.

## SECTION 3.

Whenever the President transmits to the President pro tempore of the Senate and the Speaker of the House of Representatives his written declaration that he is unable to discharge the powers and duties of his office, and until he transmits to them a written declaration to the contrary, such powers and duties shall be discharged by the Vice President as Acting President.

## SECTION 4.

Whenever the Vice President and a majority of either the principal officers of the executive departments or of such other body as Congress may by law provide, transmit to the President pro tempore of the Senate and the Speaker of the House of Representatives their written declaration that the President is unable to discharge the powers and duties of his office, the Vice President shall immediately assume the powers and duties of the office as Acting President.

Thereafter, when the President transmits to the President pro tempore of the Senate and the Speaker of the House of Representatives his written declaration that no inability exists, he shall resume the powers and duties of his office unless the Vice President and a majority of either the principal officers of the executive department or of such other body as Congress may by law provide, transmit within four days to the President pro tempore of the Senate and the Speaker of the House of Representatives their written declaration that the President is unable to discharge the powers and duties of his office. Thereupon Congress shall decide the issue, assembling within forty-eight hours for that purpose if not in session. If the Congress, within twenty-one days after receipt of the latter written declaration, or, if Congress is not in session, within twenty-one days after Congress is required to assemble, determines by two-thirds vote of both Houses that the President is unable to discharge the powers and duties of his office, the Vice President shall continue to discharge the same as Acting President; otherwise, the President shall resume the powers and duties of his office.

# Amendment XXVI.

Passed by Congress March 23, 1971. Ratified July 1, 1971.

*(Note: Amendment 14, Section 2 of the Constitution was modified by Section 1 of the 26th Amendment.)*

## SECTION 1.

The right of citizens of the United States, who are eighteen years of age or older, to vote shall not be denied or abridged by the United States or by any State on account of age.

## SECTION 2.

The Congress shall have power to enforce this article by appropriate legislation.

# Amendment XXVII.

Originally proposed Sept. 25, 1789. Ratified May 7, 1992.

No law, varying the compensation for the services of the Senators and Representatives, shall take effect, until an election of representatives shall have intervened.

# FURTHER READING

Adams. Les. *The Second Amendment Primer*. New York: Skyhorse Publishing, 1996.

Alderman, Ellen, and Caroline Kennedy. *The Right to Privacy*. New York: Alfred A. Knopf, 1995.

Amar, Akhil Reed. *The Words That Made Us: American's Constitutional Conversation, 1760–1840*. Basic Books, New York, 2021.

Banner, Stuart. *The Death Penalty: An American History*. Cambridge: Harvard University Press, 2002.

Bass, Jack. *Unlikely Heroes*. Tuscaloosa: University of Alabama Press, 1990.

Bauer, Bob, and Jack Goldsmith. *After Trump: Reconstructing the Presidency*. Washington, D.C.: LawFare Press, 2020.

Berger, Raoul. *Government by Judiciary: The Transformation of the Fourteenth Amendment*. Boston: Harvard University Press, 1977.

Black, Charles L. "The Unfinished Business of the Warren Court", 46 *Washington Law Review*, 3 (1970).

Bork, Robert. *Neutral Principles and Some First Amendment Problems*. 47 *Indiana Law Journal*, 1 (1971).

Bowen, Catherine Drinker. *Miracle at Philadelphia*. Boston: Little, Brown, 1966.

Brest, Paul. *The Fundamental Rights Controversy: The Essential Contradictions of Normative Constitutional Scholarship*. 90 *Yale Law Journal*, 1063 (1981).

Burns, James MacGregor. *Packing the Courts: The Rise of Judicial Power and the Coming Crisis of the Supreme Court*. New York: Penguin Publishing Group, 2009.

Carter, Robert, and Thurgood Marshall. "The Meaning and Significance of the Supreme Court Decree," 24 *Journal of Negro Education* 397 (Summer 1955).

Chemerinsky, Erwin. *Constitutional Law: Principles and Policies,* 6th edition. New York: Wolters Kluwer, 2019.

———. *We the People: A Progressive Reading of the Constitution*. New York: MacMillan, 2018.

Clark, Ramsey. *Crime in America: Observations on Its Nature, Causes, Prevention and Control*. New York: PocketBooks, 1971.

Cole, David. *Engines of Liberty: How Citizen Movements Succeed*. New York: Basic Books, 2016.

Collier, Christopher, and James Lincoln Collier. *Decision in Philadelphia: The Constitutional Convention of 1787*. New York: Ballantine Books, 1986.

Curtis, Michael Kent. *Free Speech, the People's Darling: Struggles for Freedom of Expression in American History*. Durham, NC: Duke University Press, 2000.

Douglas, William O. *Court Years 1939–1975: The Autobiography of William O. Douglas*. New York: Random House, 1980.

Driver, Justin. *The Schoolhouse Gate: Public Education, the Supreme Court, and the American Mind*. New York: Pantheon Books, 2018.

Ellis, Joseph J. *Founding Brothers: The Revolutionary Generation*. New York: Vintage Books, 2000.

Faber, Doris, and Harold Faber. *We the People: The Story of the United States Constitution since 1787*. New York: Charles Scribner's Sons, 1987.

Fisher, Louis. *Defending Congress & the Constitution*. Lawrence, KS: University Press of Kansas, 2011.

———. *Supreme Court Expansion of Presidential Power*. Lawrence, KS: University Press of Kansas, 2017.

Foner, Eric. *The Story of American Freedom*. New York: W. W. Norton, 1988.

Frank, John P. *Historical Bases of the Federal Judicial System*, 13 *Law & Contemporary Problems*, 3 (1948).

———. *Marble Palace: The Supreme Court in American Life*. New York: Alfred A. Knopf, 1958.

Friendly, Fred, and Martha J. H. Elliott. *The Constitution: That Delicate Balance*. New York: Random House, 1984.

Goldwin, Robert A. *From Parchment to Power: How James Madison Used the Bill of Rights to Save the Constitution*. Washington, DC: The AEI Press, 1997.

Halbrook, Stephen P. *The Founders' Second Amendment: Origins of the Right to Bear Arms*. Chicago: Ivar R. Dee, 2012.

Hentoff, Nat. *Free Speech for Me—But Not for Thee: How the American Left and Right Relentlessly Censor Each Other*. New York: HarperCollins, 1992.

———. *Living the Bill of Rights: How to Be an Authentic American*. Sacramento: University of California Press, 1999.

Hudson, David L., Jr. *The Bill of Rights: The First Ten Amendments of the Constitution*. Berkeley Heights, NJ: Enslow Publishers, 2002.

———. *Let the Students Speak!: A History of the Fight for Freedom of Expression in American Schools*. Boston: Beacon Press, 2011.

Irons, Peter. *The Courage of Their Convictions: Sixteen Americans Who Fought Their Way to the Supreme Court*. New York: Free Press, 1988.

———. *A People's History of the Supreme Court*. New York: Viking, 1999.

Kaminski, John P. *Restoring the Grand Security: The Debate Over a Federal Bill of Rights*. 33 *Santa Clara Law Review*, 887 (1993).

Kaplan, Fred. *John Quincy Adams: American Visionary*. New York: HarperCollins, 2014.

Kluger, Richard. *Simple Justice: The History of Brown v. Board of Education and Black America's Struggle for Equality*. New York: Alfred A. Knopf, 1975.

Knight, Alfred H. *The Life of the Law*. New York: Crown Publishers, 1996.

Lessig, Lawrence. *Fidelity & Constraint: How the Supreme Court Has Read the American Constitution*. London: Oxford University Press, 2019.

Levy, Leonard. *Origins of the Bill of Rights*. New Haven: Yale University Press, 1999.

Lewis, Anthony. *Gideon's Trumpet*. New York: Random House, 1964.

———. *Make No Law: The Sullivan Case and the First Amendment*. New York: Random House, 1991.

Karlan, Pamela S. *A Constitution for All Times*. Cambridge, MA: The MIT Press, 2013.

McCloskey, Robert. *The American Supreme Court*. Chicago: Chicago University Press, 2000.

McCullough, David. *John Adams*. New York: Simon & Schuster, 2001.

Meese, Edwin III. *The Law of the Constitution*, 61 *Tulane Law Review*, 979 (1987).

Monk, Linda R. *The Words We Live By: Your Annotated Guide to the Constitution*. New York: Hatchette Books, 2015.

Neuborne, Burt. *Madison's Music: On Reading the First Amendment*. New York: The New Press, 2015.

Norris, Clarence, and Sybil D. Washington. *The Last of the Scottsboro Boys*. New York: G.P. Putnam's Sons, 1979.

Peltason, J.W. *Fifty-Eight Lonely Men: Southern Federal Judges and School Desegregation*. Champaign: University of Illinois Press, 1971.

Powell, H. Jefferson. *The Original Understanding of Original Intent*. 98 *Harvard Law Review*, 885 (1985).

Rakove, Jack N. *Original Meanings: Politics and Ideas in the Making of the Constitution*. New York: Alfred A. Knopf, 1996.

Raphael, Ray. *The U.S. Constitution: Explained—Clause by Clause—For Every American Today*. New York: Vintage Books, 2016.

Saphire, Richard B. *Judicial Review in the Name of the Constitution*, 8 *University of Dayton Law Review*, 745 (1983).

Scalia, Antonin. *A Matter of Interpretation: Federal Courts and the Law*. Princeton, NJ: Princeton University Press, 1997.

Schwartz, Bernard. *The Great Rights of Mankind: A History of the American Bill of Rights*. New York: Oxford University Press, 1977.

———. *Super Chief: Earl Warren and His Supreme Court*. New York: New York University Press, 1983.

Smith, Jean Edward. *John Marshall: Definer of a Nation*. New York: Henry Holt, 1996.

Stevens, Justice John Paul. *The Making of a Justice*. New York: Little, Brown, 2018.

Story, Joseph. *Commentaries on the Constitution of the United States*. Boston: Gray & Co., 1833.

Tribe, Laurence. *God Save This Honorable Court*. New York: Random House, 1985.

Veit, Helen E., et al., eds. *Creating the Bill of Rights: The Documentary Record from the First Federal Congress*. Baltimore: John Hopkins University Press, 1991.

Waldman, Michael. *The Second Amendment: A Biography*. New York: Simon & Schuster, 2014.

Warren, Earl. *The Memoirs of Earl Warren*. New York: Doubleday, 1977.

Wehle, Kim. *How to Read the Constitution and Why*. New York: HarperCollins, 2019.

Weiss, Elaine. *The Woman's Hour: The Great Fight to Win the Vote*. New York: Penguin Books, 2019.

West, Thomas G. *Vindicating the Founders: Race, Sex, Class and Justice in the Origins of America*. Lanham, MD; Rowman & Littlefield, 2001.

Williams, Juan. *Thurgood Marshall: An American Revolutionary*. New York: Crown, 2000.

Yoo, John. *The Powers of War and Peace*. Chicago: University of Chicago Press, 2005.

# INDEX